Birds of Lane County, Oregon

Birds of Lane County, Oregon

EDITED BY ALAN CONTRERAS

Illustrated by Barbara B. C. Gleason

Maps by Kit Larsen

Site Guides by

Vjera Arnold, Dave Brown, Barbara Combs, Don DeWitt, Daniel
Farrar, Steve Gordon, Hydie Lown, Steve McDonald, Tom Mickel,
Diane Pettey, Paul Sherrell and Bill Stotz

Oregon State University Press
Corvallis

The paper in this book meets the guidelines for permanence and
durability of the Committee on Production Guidelines for Book
Longevity of the Council on Library Resources and the minimum
requirements of the American National Standard for Permanence of
Paper for Printed Library Materials Z39.48-1984.

Library of Congress Cataloging-in-Publication Data
Birds of Lane County, Oregon / edited by Alan Contreras ; illustrated by
Barbara B. C. Gleason ; maps by Kit Larsen ; site guides by Vjera Arnold ...
[et al.].
   p. cm.
   Includes bibliographical references and index.
   ISBN-13: 978-0-87071-180-0 (alk. paper)
   ISBN-10: 0-87071-180-6 (alk. paper)
1. Birds—Oregon—Lane County. 2. Bird watching—Oregon—Lane
County—Guidebooks. 3. Birding sites—Oregon—Lane County—
Guidebooks. 4. Lane County (Or.)—Guidebooks. I. Contreras, Alan,
1956-
   QL684.O6B555 2006
   598.09795'31--dc22
   2006010283

First published in 2006 by Oregon State University Press
Printed in the United States of America

Oregon State University Press
500 Kerr Administration
Corvallis OR 97331-2122
541-737-3166 • fax 541-737-3170
http://oregonstate.edu/dept/press

To the memory of Clarice Watson,
whose contributions to knowledge of Lane County birds
were always thorough and reliable,
and whose friendship was my privilege for 35 years.

Contents

Introduction

Lane County has the greatest variety of habitat and therefore the greatest variety of birds of any Oregon county. It has also been studied by ornithologists and birders for a long time by Oregon standards. It has had an active birding community for decades (well over a century if you consider the early field ornithologists), and was the cradle of Oregon Field Ornithologists, which grew from the Southern Willamette Ornithological Club, established in 1974 by George "Chip" Jobanek, Aaron Skirvin, Herb Wisner, Larry McQueen, and others.

I first came to Lane County in 1966, and this is where I began birding in 1967, at age eleven, when Sayre Greenfield, my fellow fifth grader at Condon Elementary School, asked me if I would like to go look at birds. Condon (now Agate Hall, where Vaux's Swifts gather) is where I saw my first Bald Eagle, which turned out to be a crow carrying a white dixie cup. Nearby Washburn city park is where I first dared go birding by myself. That day I remember seeing a Red-shafted Flicker, a Red-breasted Sapsucker, and a flock of Plain Titmice, which would be the only county record had they not sounded so much like Cedar Waxwings.

I also found a White-breasted Nuthatch nest in an ancient willow tree, of all things, and later took a picture of it with my Kodak Instamatic. That turned out to be an interesting record, since that species was rare in east Eugene even then, and rarely used willow trees for anything, let alone breeding. This was my earliest introduction to the fact that birds do not always do what the books say they do.

I have been birding in Lane County ever since, except for the three years I lived in Missouri. It is a wonderful place to be outdoors and this book is my way of thanking all of the birding companions who have made my own experiences so much more enjoyable.

Acknowledgements

Special thanks are due to many individuals and institutions for their assistance in providing and evaluating the data used in preparing this book, especially the species accounts. Hendrik Herlyn did most of the work in downloading Christmas Bird Count (CBC) data and making it user-friendly not only for me as

I prepared species accounts, but to count leaders, who have now been provided with the best single databases ever available for the ongoing Eugene and Florence CBCs. Kathy Klimkiewicz from the Bird Banding Laboratory provided a download of Lane County records that provided considerable information on movements of certain species. Thanks to Barbara Combs and Hendrik Herlyn for converting and evaluating that data.

Some of the information used in this book was originally sifted from field notes as we prepared a Lane County checklist in 2002. Principal sifters and reviewers in that project were Dennis Arendt, Vjera Arnold, Dave Brown, Barbara Combs, Don DeWitt, Daniel Farrar, the late LeRoy Fish, David Fix, Dan Gleason, Steve Heinl, Matt Hunter, Dave Irons, Larry McQueen, Tom Mickel, Mark Nikas, Alan Reid, and Roger Robb.

Additional data contributed for this book came from Dennis Arendt, Dave Brown of Alvadore, dean of Lane County observers, whose experience with the county's birds goes back to the mid-20th century, Don DeWitt, Daniel Farrar, the late LeRoy Fish, Greg Gillson (pelagic trip data), Dan and Barbara Gleason, Sayre Greenfield, Steve Heinl, Matt Hunter, Larry McQueen, Diane Pettey, Al Prigge, Joe Russin, Paul Sherrell, Bill and Zanah Stotz, Noah Strycker, the late Clare Watson, and Herb Wisner. As always, the immense historical record so clearly presented by George Jobanek in his *Bibliography of Oregon Ornithology* provided the baseline, along with the solid work of Alfred Cooper Shelton (1917) and Gordon Gullion (1951).

The joy of birding Lane Co.: Paul Janzen, Don DeWitt, Dennis Arendt, and Paul Sherrell checking a high-tide shorebird roost at the Port of Siuslaw, 2005. Photo by Alan Contreras.

Pete Peterson of Harrisburg provided insight into raptor movements on the valley floor. Tim Lee checked Long-eared Owl records at the Cascades Raptor Center. Randy Moore provided recent information on the distribution of Horned Larks.

Special thanks from writer Barbara Combs to Sylvia Maulding for help in tracking mileages and for lists of birds seen at Deception Creek and Elijah Bristow State Park. Also many thanks to Robin Gage for her bird lists from Leaburg, Gate Creek, and McKenzie Bridge and her help with tallying mileages between sites. Thanks for information useful in the preparation of site guides to Greg Koester, Willamette National Forest; Kari E. O'Connell and Jason Schilling, H. J. Andrews Experimental Forest; Gordon Crismon, Hoodoo Recreation Services; Ruby Seitz and Stacey Smith, McKenzie River Ranger District; Dan and Anne Heyerly; Deborah L. Quintana, Middle Fork Ranger District, Willamette National Forest; Alan Reid, George Jobanek, and Ruth Padgett. Deborah Quintana was especially helpful in providing detailed information about both the Middle Fork as a geographic region and also the ranges of certain bird species within the region.

Special thanks to Wayne Morrow of the Oregon Department of Fish and Wildlife (Fern Ridge) for permission to use ODFW maps of the Fern Ridge area as the basis for those in this book. Thanks to Rick Maulding for assisting in the preparation of maps. Cress Bates from the Lane County staff provided the recent precise survey data for the north and south boundaries of the county on the outer coast (useful for pelagic trips). When I was a "kid birder," Eva Schultz and Al Prigge took me birding more often than I deserved, and I thank them.

It is inevitable that a book of this nature, containing so much detail, will have some errors and omissions. If you have corrections or recommended changes, please send them to the Lane County Audubon Society (see contact information on page 347).

Good birding !

Alan Contreras
Eugene, November 2005

Physical Geography of Lane County

PACIFIC OCEAN

The ocean off Lane County is relatively shallow far offshore compared to most of coastal Oregon. This is because of the Perpetua Bank and Heceta Bank complex, which lies roughly 25-40 miles offshore, primarily from off Waldport, Lincoln Co., to just south of Florence. For this reason, the edge of the continental shelf (generally considered the 100-fathom line), which lies about 25 miles west of Coos Bay or Newport, lies about 50 miles west of Florence (Loy, 1976).

For observers at sea who want to keep track of whether birds seen on pelagic trips are in Lane County waters, precise data have been hard to come by. The southern county boundary where it meets the ocean lies at 124° 9′ 24.66″ W and 43° 51′ 49.40″ N. The northern county boundary where it meets the ocean is 124° 6′ 55.32″ W and 44° 16′ 34.26″ N.

In summer, the nearshore northward flow of warmer waters is usually below 200 meters, and thus mainly below the shelf line; in winter this warmer flow is at the surface, which moderates the coastal climate. Surface waters generally move southward in summer and northward in winter. Changes in this pattern, e.g., El Niño Southern Oscillation conditions, can have significant effects on the nesting success or even survival of seabirds.

Owing to the small size of the port of Florence, pelagic trips do not leave directly from Florence, and thus knowledge of the birds offshore is less detailed than such knowledge off Coos Bay or Newport. However, pelagic trips run out of Newport and Winchester Bay often enter Lane County, precisely because the birds over Heceta Bank are often concentrated and varied. Much of the data about seabirds in this book is based on a combination of Lane County observations and those from adjacent counties for which far more information is available.

Siuslaw River mouth, looking southeast from the north jetty toward the base of the south jetty. Photo by Noah K. Strycker.

OUTER COAST

The outer coast, as used in this book, consists of the beaches, headlands, and immediately adjacent lower estuaries, deflation plains, and wooded shoreline, generally within a couple of miles of the ocean.

This area is characterized in the north by a mix of low rocky headlands and flat beaches, in the center by extremely steep (often vertical) cliff faces (e.g., the 300-foot-high cliff at Sea Lion Caves and the face of Heceta Head), and from Lily Lake southward, the flat sweep of beach and dune that characterizes the south-central Oregon coast.

Heceta Head. Photo by Noah K. Strycker.

COAST RANGE

These relatively low, heavily dissected mountains occupy much of the western quarter of the county, from the coastal headlands of Cape Perpetua and Cape Mountain east to the edge of the Willamette Valley. The western part of this range is dominated by the Siuslaw River valley (including the Lake Creek valley east of Swisshome) and the valley of the North Fork of the Siuslaw. This relatively moist, heavily wooded region is sometimes referred to in this book as part of the "coastal slope," which also includes the outer coast. Unlike the eastern edge of the Coast Range, the coastal slope has few if any oaks, which results in a slightly different avifauna than that at the edge of the Willamette Valley.

The eastern edge of the Coast Range consists of hills and small valleys that drop gently to the Willamette Valley floor, more steeply south of Eugene.

This edge region harbors certain species, e.g., Nashville Warbler, White-breasted Nuthatch, and Western Kingbird, that are generally absent to the west. Triangle Lake is the only significant body of water in the Coast Range region.

The western edge of the Coast Range supports a dense mix of trees, shrubs, and forbs. The mix of Douglas-fir and oak, as shown here, is a favorite of Hutton's Vireo. Photo by Alan Contreras.

WILLAMETTE VALLEY FLOOR

The terms "Willamette Valley floor" and "valley floor" are used more or less interchangeably in the book, and refer to the generally flat region between the Coast Range and the Western Cascades, with an elevation of between 400 and 500 feet. The region is dominated by agricultural and grazing land in the north and south and by the Eugene-Springfield urbanized area in the center.

Although the avifauna is similar throughout the region, the presence of Fern Ridge Reservoir and its ancillary wildlife areas in the northwest part of the region has a substantial effect. This includes very large numbers of waterfowl in surrounding fields, substantial movements of shorebirds at certain seasons, and a large raptor population. The valley of the Coast Fork of the Willamette is smaller and has much the look and feel of the Coast Range valleys, while the flatlands of the lower McKenzie and lower Middle Fork Willamette contain a mix of small farms, suburban homes, and pastureland.

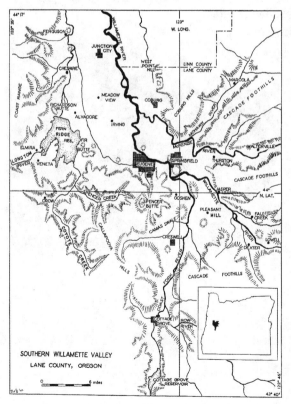

Map from Gordon Gullion's Birds of the Southern Willamette Valley *(1951) provides an idea of the human geography of Lane Co. at mid-20th-century. Note that Thurston, now essentially part of Springfield, was entirely rural. Fern Ridge Reservoir (1941) was quite new, as was Cottage Grove Reservoir (1942). Reprinted from* Condor *with permission.*

Mt. Pisgah.
Photo by
Noah K.
Strycker.

Within the valley region are several small hill complexes that have a slightly different mix of birds, the most distinctive of which is Mt. Pisgah, south of Springfield, which has a much drier aspect on its south face than most Lane County features, with significant open grassy areas and stands of Ceanothus. Such species as Blue-gray Gnatcatcher, Ash-throated Flycatcher, Say's Phoebe, Lewis's Woodpecker, and Horned Lark have occurred here.

Spencer Butte on the southern edge of Eugene is something of a geographic anomaly, in many ways part of the Coast Range but with an open, rocky top that has attracted some birds normally associated with the High Cascades or even eastern Oregon, such as nesting Rock Wrens, visiting Clark's Nutcrackers, and Common Poorwills.

In addition to Fern Ridge Reservoir, the valley has many small ponds on its floor and is fringed with flood-control and power-generating reservoirs that lie generally just above the valley floor. These are Cottage Grove, Dorena, and Dexter reservoirs. Above Dexter Reservoir lies Lookout Point Reservoir, which extends far into the Western Cascades.

WESTERN CASCADES

The bulk of eastern Lane County comprises the Western Cascades, a vast region dominated by Douglas-fir/mountain hemlock forests, extending from the eastern edges of the Willamette Valley to an elevation of about 3500 feet, above which lie the lava fields and volcanic peaks of the High Cascades. The northwest "corner" of this region reaches the Coburg Hills, which tower over the valley, rising almost vertically to 2500 feet north of Springfield and 3115 feet at nearby Buck Mountain, above the northern Mohawk River valley. The central part of the region is heavily dissected by the McKenzie and Middle Fork Willamette systems, which begin as small, fast mountain streams and eventually reach the valley floor.

The southwestern flank of the region joins the east-west ridge complex known as the Calapooya Divide south of Cottage Grove. This ridgeline averages about 1700 feet in elevation and separates the Willamette and Umpqua river drainages. A small area of south-central Lane County 30 miles southeast of Cottage Grove Reservoir is in the Umpqua drainage.

Reservoirs and lakes within the region are about the only place where waterbirds can be found. The principal water features are Cougar and Blue River reservoirs above the upper McKenzie valley, the Carmen-Trail Bridge Reservoir complex just inside Linn County on the upper McKenzie, Lookout Point along the Middle Fork of the Willamette, and Hills Creek Reservoir southeast of Oakridge.

Horsepasture Mtn., just west of the Three Sisters, shows typical broken evergreen forest habitat of the higher peaks of the Western Cascades. Photo by Brooke DeWitt.

HIGH CASCADES

Lane County is bounded on the east by the crest of the Cascade Range. The High Cascades of the crest area have been built by more recent vulcanism than the Western Cascades. Extensive lava flows, pumice, ash, and other extrusive materials characterize the area from the Linn County boundary southward to the vicinity of the South Sister. The lava flows are of geologically recent origin. A few stunted trees occur, but the lava flows are essentially devoid of vegetation. Parts of the area underlain by volcanic ash and other extrusives are covered by lodgepole pine, Douglas-fir, true firs, and hemlock. The Three Sisters peaks, each over 10,000 feet in elevation, dominate the area.

Farther south, a series of lower igneous peaks covered with lodgepole pine, true fir, hemlock, and spruce extends along the relatively flat summit region, with many small lakes and large Waldo Lake, the headwaters of the northern arm of the Middle Fork of the Willamette River at 5,414 feet. Near Waldo is Gold Lake, a smaller lake at 4,813 feet, with an extensive bog where Solitary Sandpiper has undoubtedly nested. Willamette Pass, at 5,128 feet the highest major highway pass kept open through the Cascades in winter, lies between these lakes and the Diamond Peak Wilderness at the southern edge of the county. The Emigrant Pass region just south of Diamond Peak is just within Lane County, and in some years has supported such species as Brewer's Sparrow and Green-tailed Towhee, otherwise difficult to find in the county. Summit Lake, just over the line in Klamath County, has occasionally harbored summering and possibly breeding Red-necked Grebes.

North and Middle Sister. Photo by Luke Bloch.

WATER

Lane County is generally a rather moist place except from July to mid-September, when it can be very warm and dry, especially in the interior valleys. Major rivers are the upper Willamette system, most of the McKenzie drainage, and the great bulk of the Siuslaw drainage. Smaller rivers such as the Mohawk, Row (pronounced like "cow"), and Long Tom flow into the Willamette or the lower McKenzie. The county contains several large natural lakes, including Waldo (6,298 acres), Siltcoos (3,164 acres), a portion of which is in Douglas Co., Woahink (820 acres), Mercer (359 acres), Triangle (279

Marshes in the Fisher Unit at Fern Ridge Reservoir (Gibson Island on the horizon left of center). Photo by Alan Contreras.

Looking north across the east end of Dorena Reservoir. Marsh areas here receive insufficient coverage from observers. Photo by Don Lown.

acres), Munsel (110 acres), Sutton (107 acres) and Gold (96 acres). All of these except Triangle, Waldo, and Gold are in the coastal plain.

The county contains many large reservoirs, all of which, especially Fern Ridge, get significant use by birds. The major reservoirs are Fern Ridge on the Long Tom River and Coyote Creek (9,360 acres), Dorena on the Row River (1,840 acres), Cottage Grove on the Coast Fork of the Willamette (1,139 acres), Dexter (1,025 acres), Lookout Point (4,360 acres), and Hills Creek (2,735 acres) on the Middle Fork of the Willamette, Fall Creek on the creek of that name (1,860 acres), Cougar on the south McKenzie (1,280 acres), and Blue River on the river of that name (935 acres).

The Carmen-Trail Bridge Reservoir complex on the upper McKenzie lies just inside Linn County and is commonly visited by birders using the Clear Lake cutoff (Hwy. 126) between Hwy. 242 and Hwy. 20.

Salt Creek Falls between Oakridge and Willamette Pass. Photo by Noah K. Strycker.

Birding Opportunities in Lane County

Starting to Watch Birds from Central Lane County

Don DeWitt

If you are a visitor to the west coast, a university student, or other newly arrived resident of the area (or perhaps a fledgling birder), here is a brief orientation to the geography and bird life starting at the core of Lane Co.

Lane is a large county, some 4,600 square miles, which includes a section of the Oregon coast and the western half of part of the Cascade Mountain range. Map A-1 shows the county in context of the surrounding counties, highlighting the major population centers and highways. The I-5 corridor bisects the county north to south, and runs through the Eugene-Springfield metropolitan area, home to over 95 percent of the county's population.

Map A-2 shows the geographic area covered by each of the major regions in the site guides that follow. Some regions also have more detailed local maps. The guides begin with a basic discussion of the county's core, then proceed from west to east in detail.

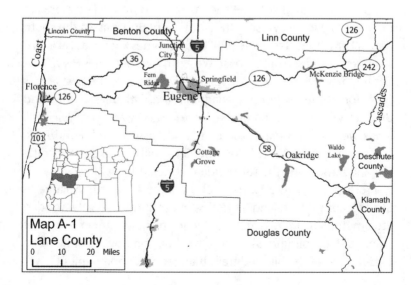

Map A-1
Lane County
0   10   20   Miles

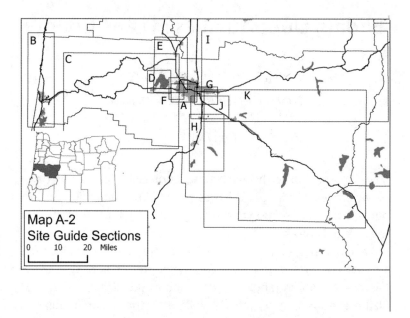

Map A-2
Site Guide Sections
0   10   20   Miles

Over 300 bird species may be found in Lane Co. during part or all of the year. At least 200 of these species are available within or very close to the Eugene/Springfield area. This means that many of the specialty Northwest bird species and a large portion of Lane Co.'s other avifauna are available with little or no use of automobiles. A good bus system, networks of bike and hiking trails, and bird-friendly urban habitats make birding productive in central Lane Co.

This map (A-3) of central Lane Co. radiates from a few blocks of downtown Eugene. West 11th Ave., westbound, passes the south end of Fern Ridge Reservoir (FRR) and becomes known as Hwy. 126 to Florence and the outer coast. West 6th Ave. becomes Hwy. 99. A left turn from 99 onto Royal Ave. takes you west to the best access point for FRR and adjacent wetland birding, with miles of trails and dikes to walk on. A little farther north on Hwy 99, Clear Lake Rd. leads west, to FRR parks, the dam, and adjacent Kirk Pond/Park. A turn north from Clear Lake onto Greenhill Rd. takes you to the Eugene Airport and the surrounding agricultural fields.

From downtown Eugene, a short drive south on Willamette Street leads to the hiking trails of Spencer Butte (a mostly wooded little mountain). Immediately to the north of downtown is another staple of local birding, Skinner Butte. You can drive or walk up to bird the top of the hill, and trails (flagged for "improvement" over

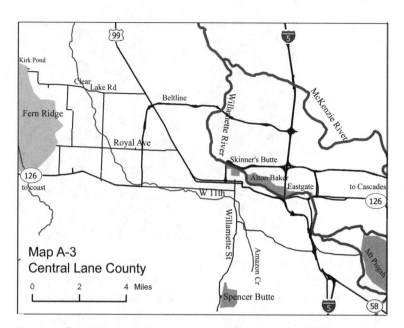

Map A-3
Central Lane County

0   2   4   Miles

the next few years) lead down into the lower part of Skinner Butte Park and to bikepaths along the Willamette River on the south side of the river. More bikepaths are on the north side of the river, conveniently accessed by crossing the DeFazio footbridge just upstream from the Ferry Street automobile bridge.

Bike paths along the Willamette near downtown make possible 12 miles and more of travel along both sides of the river through Eugene and into Springfield to the east. The paths lead also to Delta Ponds to the west (near Valley River Center mall). Five pedestrian/bike footbridges cross the river: Owosso Street; Valley River Center; near Ferry Street Bridge; north of the University of Oregon; and a mile east of the University, the Knickerbocker footbridge near the main I-5 bridge. These paths and bridges provide varied routes and easy access to the eastern part of Alton Baker Park and to Island Park further east in Springfield (or the western parks for Springfield birders heading west). Eugene's core parks and paths connect a variety of birding habitats. Casual walking and biking through all this area, over a period of just a day or throughout the year, will yield lots of birding interest.

From downtown headed east, 7th Ave. becomes East Broadway, which passes between the Willamette River and the University of Oregon and acquires yet another new name as Franklin Blvd. on its way to Springfield and beyond. Known as Hwy. 126 eastbound, this

Even outside the urban area, bike paths are often available. The north side of Dorena Lake boasts this excellent path. Photo by Don Lown.

route leads on along the McKenzie River, to reservoirs, to Cascade Mountain hiking, and on into Linn and Deschutes counties to the north and east. Yet another driving route east can be taken from downtown Eugene. Pearl St. south to Amazon Parkway (name changes at 19th Street) is one route to 30th Ave. 30th Ave. going east takes you past the Lane Community College area and to an intersection with Interstate 5. Cross I-5 to the Seavey Loop area and access to the west side of Mt. Pisgah.

Or take the I-5 entrance southbound, go a mile or so and get off at the Goshen Exit (188A) to enter Hwy. 58, eastbound. Hwy 58 leads to Pleasant Hill (access to the east side of Mt. Pisgah) and on past Jasper Park, Bristow Park, Dexter Reservoir, to Oakridge, Gold and Waldo Lakes, and roads and hiking trails into the high Cascades. Across Willamette Pass lie Deschutes and Klamath Co., the Cascade lake district, Bend, Central Oregon, and beyond.

Regional specialty species available in our urban core area or the nearby sites listed above include Chestnut-backed Chickadee, Western Scrub-Jay, Red-breasted Sapsucker, Lesser Goldfinch, Northern Pygmy-Owl, Bullock's Oriole, Hutton's and Cassin's Vireo, Black-throated Gray, Hermit, Townsend's and MacGillivray's Warblers, and Lazuli Bunting.

Go to the coast for Black Oystercatcher, Pelagic and Brandt's Cormorant, Snowy Plover, and others. Mountain sites of eastern Lane Co. offer such birds as Black-backed and American Three-Toed Woodpeckers, Gray Jay, Northern Goshawk, Clark's Nutcracker, Mountain Bluebird, grouse species, and others. (Mountain Quail are where you find them.)

Good luck in your birding of Lane Co. Some very good birding opportunities exist close to the city center, and biking, jogging, walking, or meandering along the paths and trails available here may yield some of the best birding of all.

Best 100 Birding Sites in Lane County

Spring: ****   *Summer: ***   *Fall: *** Winter: **

The seasonal star codes as shown above are intended to indicate the best seasons to visit a specific area. Codes are provided only for the major birding sites within each region; most nearby sites show similar characteristics.

****   Excellent. Exceptional variety of species present, with many easy to observe, and/or a good chance of finding something unusual. Fern Ridge Reservoir at peak spring migration or the Siuslaw estuary in fall and winter are examples.

***   Good. A good variety of species can be found, with some chance of unusual numbers or species. The Eugene airport area in winter or Springfield's Island Park in fall are good examples.

**   Fair. Species variety or numbers are likely to be limited, with some extra effort required to find what is there. Montane areas in late fall and the valley floor in midsummer are examples.

*   Poor. Few species can be found and observational conditions may be difficult. There are always some birds around, of course, but Salt Creek Falls in winter provides an experience more esthetic than ornithological—unless you are looking for Dippers or montane finches.

Sites that offer the best birding from a wheelchair are introduced with this standard symbol. This is intended as general guidance, not a definitive statement of access, and local conditions can change.

The Coast

Bill Stotz

THE IMPORTANCE OF THE TIDE

Nothing is more important to an enjoyable birding trip in coastal Oregon than an awareness of the tides. A tide table is essential birding equipment. Siuslaw tides are published in *The Register-Guard* in the weather section, and pocket tide tables are available from sporting goods stores and many coastal businesses. These site guides contain recommended tide stage information.

In general, coastal sites offer better birding opportunities at lower or falling tides because more mud or sand is available, freshly stocked with edibles for shorebirds, gulls, and passerines such as pipits that often feed on mud. However, some roost sites are better at higher tides.

Tide Status Codes

↑   best at HIGH or rising tide

→← best at MID tides, rising or falling

↓   best at LOW or falling tide

∅   visit at any tide; tide is not a major factor

For orientation, all route mileages will start from the intersection of Hwys. 126 and 101 in Florence. These routes provide numerous birding opportunities with stops at the ocean edge and access to the mountains.

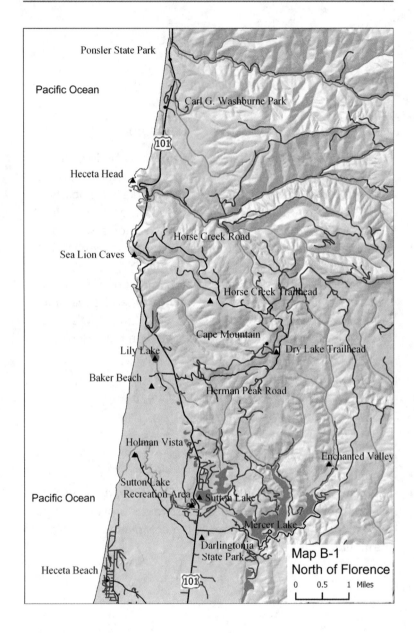

Ponsler State Park

Pacific Ocean

Carl G. Washburne Park

101

Heceta Head

Horse Creek Road

Sea Lion Caves

Horse Creek Trailhead

Cape Mountain

Lily Lake

Dry Lake Trailhead

Baker Beach

Herman Peak Road

Holman Vista

Enchanted Valley

Sutton Lake Recreation Area

Pacific Ocean

Sutton Lake

Mercer Lake

Darlingtonia State Park

Map B-1
North of Florence

0   0.5   1   Miles

Heceta Beach

101

North from Florence on Highway 101

Sutton Creek Recreation Area/Holman Vista

TIDE ∅

At mile 4.9 is a road leading into the Sutton Creek Recreation Area. The campground is a good place to try for owls. Great Horned, Northern Saw-whet, Western Screech-Owl, and Northern Pygmy-owls have all been seen. During breeding season warblers, vireos, flycatchers, Band-tailed Pigeons, and grosbeaks join the year-round residents. Winter residents include chickadees, finches, sparrows, and often Townsend's Warblers. Wrentits are easily heard if not seen in the dense low vegetation.

Continue west on the access road to Holman Vista at the end; a short boardwalk leads to the overlook. To the north is a winter pond that is good for waterfowl (including Tundra Swans in some years) and shorebirds in migration. Raptors patrol the area.

Mercer Lake Road/Enchanted Valley

TIDE ∅

At mile 5.1 Mercer Lake Rd. leads east to Enchanted Valley, an extensive meadow being developed by the U.S. Forest Service. Spring is the most active time, with yellowthroats, Marsh Wrens, sparrows, and swallows dominating. An old gravel road currently serves as the start of the trail which crosses a small creek at several locations and eventually leads into the forest providing a different habitat.

Darlingtonia Wayside

One place of interest just off Hwy. 101 on this road is the Darlingtonia Wayside. The short boardwalk leads through a marsh where these insect-eating plants can be found blooming in the spring.

Sutton Lake

Continue north on 101 to mile 5.6 for access to the Sutton Lake boat ramp from which wintering ducks and grebes can be seen (Common Goldeneye and Ruddy Duck are possible). Wood Ducks breed here.

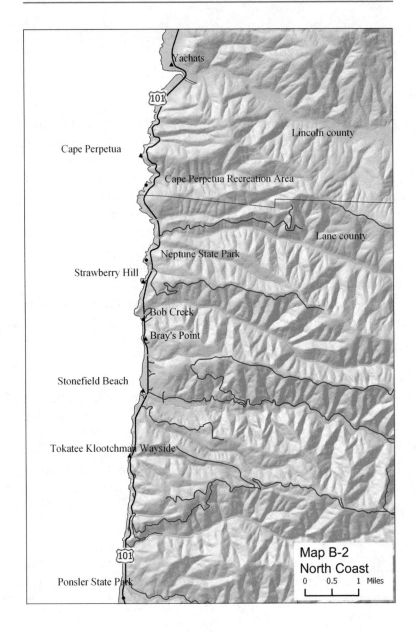

Yachats

101

Lincoln county

Cape Perpetua

Cape Perpetua Recreation Area

Lane county

Neptune State Park

Strawberry Hill

Bob Creek

Bray's Point

Stonefield Beach

Tokatee Klootchman Wayside

101

Map B-2
North Coast
0   0.5   1 Miles

Ponsler State Park

Herman Peak/Cape Mountain
contributed by Diane Pettey

Spring: ***   *Summer: ****   *Fall: ***   *Winter: ***

Herman Cape Rd. (a hybrid name offering a loop around Cape Mtn. and access to the Herman Peak spur) is a loop road 8.5 miles long that passes Horse Creek Trail Campground and Dry Lake Trailhead Campground and begins and ends on Hwy. 101 (separate entrances). Dry Lake Trailhead Campground (3 miles up Herman Cape Rd. from the north entrance) has a primitive campsite with a picnic table, a pit toilet, two horse corrals, and a spring-fed (non-potable) watering trough. Horse Creek Trailhead Campground (2.5 miles beyond Dry Lake) has several campsites with picnic tables, a pit toilet, and several horse corrals.

Wheelchair access is fair to poor: parking areas at campgrounds are dirt/gravel, relatively flat. The trails at all locations are too narrow and/or steep with logs, ruts, and uneven surfaces.

About 8.1 miles north of the Hwy. 101/126 intersection in Florence, turn right on Herman Cape Rd. (look for larger "Oregon Coast Horse Trail" sign across Hwy. 101). The road is paved for about one mile at each end of the loop and beyond that, gravel. Except under unusual conditions it is easily passable for passenger cars.

Herman Cape Rd. has a few pullouts/wide spots to park and bird near your car. The first mile has rural residents; respect for private property is recommended, but a smile and wave generally are greeted likewise. After 4.6 miles, take the left fork to continue on Herman Cape Rd. Horse Creek Trailhead Campground is 1.3 miles beyond the fork.

The habitat consists of mixed woods—red alder, Oregon ash, Douglas-fir, and Sitka spruce—with salmonberry, red elderberry, currant, and thimbleberry. In spring and summer, Band-tailed Pigeons are frequently seen in the tree tops; Great Horned, Northern Pygmy, and Saw-whet, Barred (recently), and Western Screech-Owls have been heard or observed year round. Warblers include Hermit, Black-throated Gray, and MacGillivray's as well as wintering Townsend's and Yellow-rumped. Also look for Red Crossbills, Western Tanagers, Black-headed and Evening Grosbeaks, Warbling and Hutton's Vireos, Wrentits, and flycatcher species (Hammond's, Pacific-slope and Olive-sided) as well as Black-capped and Chestnut-backed Chickadees. Brown Creepers and kinglet species can also be seen and heard.

A Red-tailed Hawk is sometimes seen perched near the road and Hairy, Downy, and Pileated Woodpeckers, Northern Flickers, and Red-breasted Sapsuckers are present. Anna's Hummingbirds are found year round at the lower elevations and Rufous hummers are present in spring and summer. Swainson's, Hermit, and Varied Thrushes are found singing on territory in spring and early summer. Varied Thrushes are present year round and can also be found at lower elevations in winter.

In 2003, an Ovenbird was heard and a singing Northern Parula was observed while it flitted through the trees at the bottom of Herman Cape Rd., near Hwy. 101.

Hooded Mergansers are sometimes found in the very small "lake" at Dry Lake Campground. Gray Jays can occasionally be seen at the top of Cape Mountain trail (out of Dry Lake Campground).

Baker Beach and Lily Lake

*Spring: ***   Summer: **   Fall: *** Winter: ****

TIDE ⊘ Avoid extreme high tides

Further north a tenth of a mile is Baker Beach Rd., a gravel road heading west from 101. In the marsh area along the road Virginia Rails are found year round. Wood Ducks breed here, as do swallows, Marsh Wrens, Song Sparrows, and other songbirds. Look for woodpeckers, including Pileated, and Red-shouldered Hawks in fall and winter. Black Phoebe, Swamp Sparrow, and Northern Waterthrush are among the more unusual species that have been found here.

At the end of Baker Beach Road (less than a mile from 101) is a horse campground and parking for a trail to the beach (roughly 400 yards) through and over the dunes. Baker Beach has Snowy Plovers year round. Often the winter flock of a dozen or so birds is near where the trail reaches the beach. In breeding season (March 15 to Sept. 15) the area near the foredune is roped off to protect the plover nests.

Although Lily Lake does not get much use by waterfowl, a loop trail is worth walking (*Note*: it gets some horse traffic). One end of the loop starts at the parking lot and follows the west edge of the bluff. Peregrine Falcon and Bald Eagle can sometimes be found at the northern end of this loop. The creek along the northern end of the trail sometimes has ducks or even shorebirds. This area is deserving of more coverage by birders. The trail crosses a low sand ridge east to the marsh by Lily Lake, returning south through an open forest and emerging by the "No Parking" sign at the highest point on Baker Beach Rd. The complete loop is about a mile and a quarter long; the western leg can be slow going on sand or hummocks; the eastern leg is flat and easy.

Note: a good walking map of this small, lovely area can be found in William Sullivan's *100 Hikes/Travel Guide to the Oregon Coast & Coast Range* (Navillus Press, second edition, 2002, 2004).

Sea Lion Caves

TIDE ∅

The next spot of interest is Sea Lion Cave at mile 11.1, the "largest sea cave in the world" and home to breeding sea lions and Rhinoceros Auklets. Tours of the cave are available at the gift shop (*fee*). From here north are several pullouts from which to check the ocean for alcids, gulls, loons, grebes, cormorants, and pelicans in the proper seasons. The pullout immediately north of the cave house is often a good place from which to observe Rhinoceros Auklets without paying the fee to enter the cave. Some years Black Oystercatchers can be found nesting on the rocks below.

Heceta Head

TIDE ∅ *Avoid extreme high tides or storm surge*

After passing through the tunnel, the road to Heceta Head Lighthouse State Park (*fee*) is just north of the bridge at mile 12.1. Entrance is on a dangerous curve. From the parking area rest rooms are available. The protected beach has tide pools on the northwest edge. The trail of 500 yards to the lighthouse takes off from the north end of the lot. From the lighthouse, check the large rocks to the south and north for nesting cormorants (particularly the Brandt's with its bright blue throat patch), gulls, murres, and a few guillemots. In past years Tufted Puffins have bred on the first rock to the south. Check the ocean from here for pelagic species. Watch for Peregrine Falcons and Bald Eagles. The peregrines like the north rock in fall and winter for perching. To the southeast of the parking lot is a gravel road under the highway bridge that leads to a small bridge (100 yds) where Dippers have nested for several years.

Washburne State Park

Washburne State Park (14.3 miles) has rest rooms and beach access to the west and a campground to the east where Gray Jays can be found on occasion.

COAST WAYSIDES

Spring: ***   *Summer: ***   *Fall: *** Winter: ****

North of here are numerous overlooks or parking areas to access the beach. Check waters around rock outcroppings for Harlequin Ducks and scoters year round. In the winter look for all three scoters on the ocean and Surfbirds and Black Turnstones on the rocks. Oystercatchers are here year round. Wandering Tattlers can be seen in the fall more easily than spring. Check the ocean and sky for pelagic birds.

At mile 17.8 is a small parking lot (named *Tokatee Klootchman*) that overlooks rocks that uncover at lower tides and where Harlequin Ducks often can be found in the water or on the rocks.

TIDE ∅

Long-tailed Duck and Black Scoter have been regular here in recent years. This is probably the best general sea-watching location in Lane Co. other than the Siuslaw jetties. It is especially good very early in the morning. There are two parking areas, one higher up

Jeff Hayes checks the surf at Bob Creek, one of the better birding pullouts along the northern Lane Co. coast. Photo by Alan Contreras.

the hill on Hwy. 101, so that if surf mist is a problem, an observer can simply switch sites. *Stonefield Beach* (mile 18.9) is good for rock shorebirds, Harlequin Ducks and a good variety of gulls.

TIDE ∅ *Avoid extreme high tide or storm surge*

A Snow Bunting was found here once. It is sometimes closed in winter owing to high water, but the parking area on the north side of *Tenmile Creek* also provides access to the mouth (and good passerine birding).

Brays Point (mile 20.1) gives an ocean view from its elevated site.

 At mile 20.5 is a parking area at *Bob Creek* that overlooks excellent rocky habitat.

TIDE ∅

Harlequin Ducks, Surf Scoters, and oystercatchers usually show up here. This is also a good place to study gulls, as several species can be found here from October through April. It is one of the most regular sites on the coast for Thayer's Gull. *Strawberry Hill* overlook has a harbor seal colony and provides exposed rocks and ocean viewing.

TIDE ∅

Neptune State Wayside (mile 21.1) has a rest room, beach access, and tide pools. The county line with Lincoln Co. is Mile 22.9.

Cape Perpetua Visitor Center

Cape Perpetua Visitor Center at mile 23.2 has rest rooms and is the starting point for a variety of trails. This U.S. Forest Service facility has a great deal of information available, exhibits, movies and guided tours. The center is closed during much of the winter.

Yachats

TIDE ∅ *Steeply sloped creek estuary has gull roost even at higher tides.*

The town of Yachats in south Lincoln County provides a good birding spot and turnaround place for Lane Co. birders. In addition to rock shorebirds off the small park on the north side of the estuary, this is an excellent place for gulls at all seasons.

NORTH JETTY AND HECETA BEACH

Spring: ****   *Summer: ****   *Fall: *****   *Winter: *****

Harbor Vista County Park

From the intersection of 101 and 126 in Florence go west on the extension of 126 now called Ninth Street. In 0.9 miles the street dead-ends into Rhododendron Drive. Turn right and go 3.0 miles to North Jetty Rd. to the left. This road goes past the entrance to Harbor Vista Co. Park, which has rest rooms, camping facilities, and a chance to see local songbirds.

North Jetty tidal flats

Continue on North Jetty Rd. to the foot of the hill where there is a tidal mud flat. At lower tides this can be a good place for migrating shorebirds. Such unusual species as Curlew Sandpiper and Semipalmated Sandpiper have been seen here. Gulls are year round and some ducks use the area in migration and winter.

TIDE →←

Check the river beyond the rocks for loons, grebes, alcids, gulls, Red-breasted Mergansers, Surf Scoters, and other rarer pelagic birds depending on the season. Common Murres often can be seen and heard in large numbers during the summer, feeding with young. The contrasting low- and high-pitched calls of the adults and young can be almost deafening.

Siuslaw jetties. Both jetties are easy to walk on for the first few hundred yards, then become very rough. Photo by Diane Pettey.

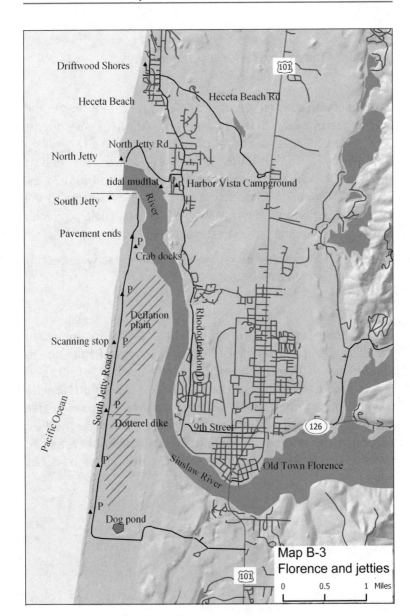

Driftwood Shores

Heceta Beach

Heceta Beach Rd

101

North Jetty Rd

North Jetty

tidal mudflat

Harbor Vista Campground

South Jetty

Pavement ends

P

Crab docks

P

Deflation plain

Rhododendron Dr

Scanning stop P

South Jetty Road

P

Dotterel dike

9th Street

126

P

Siuslaw River

Old Town Florence

Pacific Ocean

P

Dog pond

Map B-3
Florence and jetties

0   0.5   1 Miles

101

North Jetty

Continue to the parking lot for access to the jetty.

TIDE ∅

In summer and early fall, Ospreys and Brown Pelicans feed in the river or nearby ocean. In late summer and early fall, family groups of Rhinoceros Auklets can be found with some regularity here.

The jetty becomes more difficult to walk as the end is approached. However, further out it is easier to find turnstones, Surfbirds, Wandering Tattlers, and Rock Sandpipers (rare) on the rocks in migration and winter. It is also easier to find pelagic species in the ocean from the outer stretches of the jetty.

Note: Watch for sneaker waves when out on the jetty, especially during storms or at high tide.

Heceta Beach

Heceta Beach to the north should be checked for migrating shorebirds and winter flocks of Sanderlings. Returning to Rhododendron Drive, the beach can also be reached at Driftwood Shores Resort. At the intersection with Heceta Beach Rd. (1.2 miles from the north jetty turnoff) turn left, then right to a parking area just south of the resort. This spot allows the beach to be checked, particularly for migrating shorebirds. From here either return to town via Rhododendron or go to 101 using Heceta Beach Rd. (2.1 miles).

East of Florence on Highway 126

Siuslaw Estuary mudflats

Spring: ***   *Summer: ***   *Fall: ****   *Winter: ****

TIDE ↓

The busy highway stays close to the north side of the river all the way to Mapleton. There is a large area of tidal mudflats just outside Florence, but safe turnouts are few until the north fork bridge (1.0 miles). Just east of the bridge is an open gravel parking area that once was used for scaling trucks. Long-time birders often refer to this empty space as "the scaling station" despite the manifest absence of any such station, which can be confusing.

Note: there are some rough areas in the lot, left over from its former use, that can blow a tire if you enter too fast.

During fall migration and a few times in the winter shorebirds use this area as the tide lowers. Dowitchers, peeps, and plovers often appear in large numbers along with a few Greater Yellowlegs. The

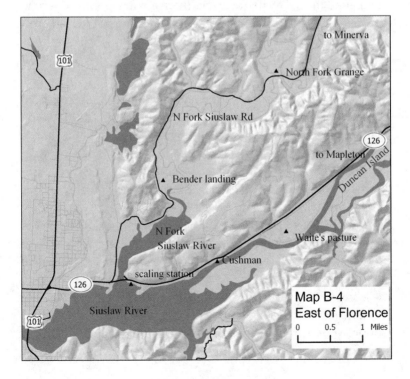

Map B-4
East of Florence
0   0.5   1 Miles

mudflats to the west have also supported such unusual species as Snowy Egret, American Avocet, Buff-breasted Sandpiper, and Willet.

North Fork of the Siuslaw

Spring: *** _Summer: **_ _Fall: **_ _Winter: ***_

TIDE: ↑ _or_ ∅ _Shorebird use increases at high tide in winter, waterfowl not affected._

Just west of the bridge, North Fork Rd. turns off to the left. In the winter the narrow valley's pastures flood and provide habitat for dabbling ducks and other waterfowl. There are few places to get off the road; rest rooms and river access are available at the Bender boat landing 2.9 miles up from Hwy. 101. One or two Eurasian Wigeon often can be found with more common ducks in a pond on the north side just beyond the North Fork Grange (5.6 miles). There is a safe pulloff at this point. Most of the road has no shoulder or pullouts except for mailboxes, so use extreme care. Look for raptors including White-tailed Kites and Red-shouldered Hawks in the fall and winter. Western Bluebirds turn up occasionally. After the grange the valley narrows and there are few ponds. The road leads eventually into the mountains connecting with U.S. Forest Service roads in some 20 to 25 miles.

Minerva cutoff

One option is to take the narrow, mostly gravel connector from Minerva junction east over the ridge to Hwy 36, and then to Mapleton or Junction City. This road is usually in fairly good condition and is easily passable for passenger cars, but the upper part of it (crossing the ridge) is mainly tight switchbacks and requires care. After storms the road may be blocked by downed trees or branches. This route is a good place to find Northern Pygmy-Owl.

If you continue up the Siuslaw valley, at mile 19 a side road leads to the PAWN trail, which provides a short walk through an old-growth area. (PAWN is an acronym for the four families who were instrumental in establishing a post office on the upper portion of the North Fork Siuslaw River above Minerva in the early 1900s. The four families were the Pooles, Akerleys, Worthingtons, and Nolands. Marion Woosley ran the post office so the "W" eventually came to stand for Woosley.) Back in the 1990s Spotted Owls nested over the ridge here and might be heard calling during the day. The last few miles before the trail is mostly forested and produces Black-headed Grosbeaks, Western Tanagers, warblers, and vireos from the roadside.

Cushman to Mapleton

If you return to Hwy. 126, continue east 2 miles to the small town of Cushman. From here check the docks and bridge structure for shorebirds (mainly at high tide), nesting Purple Martins, wintering gulls (Glaucous Gull used the bridge pilings to roost one winter) waterfowl, cormorants, and raptors. Osprey nest on power poles all along the river.

At mile 5.4 the river swings away from the highway exposing a long stretch of pasture (usually called Waite's pasture) that has much winter waterfowl activity. The problem is that there are no decent pullouts and the paved shoulder is barely wide enough to get off the road. This area has turned up Eurasian Wigeon, Cattle Egret, Trumpeter Swan, and Ross's, Emperor, and White-fronted geese in the winter. Bald Eagles can be found particularly the last few miles before Mapleton.

Old Town Florence

*Spring: ***   *Summer: **   *Fall: ***   *Winter: ****

TIDE ∅

This is the commercial area east of Hwy. 101 bordering on the river. Bay Street runs under the 101 bridge and leads to access to the river shore at a small park with rest rooms. Check the river edge for shorebirds anywhere along the river edge. This is one of the only regular places for Spotted Sandpiper in winter in western Lane Co. Further east begin the commercial docks, which should be checked for herons and sandpipers in season.

This area includes a parking lot with a boardwalk along the dock area. Additional parking for the boat ramp area is along more docks that should be checked, especially during winter storms, for flocks of Black Turnstones and Least Sandpipers plus other shorebirds. This stretch of docks also is used in the spring/summer as a fishing spot for Green Herons, which nest across the river. Also across the river is a colony of Double-crested Cormorants.

Old Town Florence, looking northeast from the Hwy. 101 bridge. Birding can be good along the waterfront and in clumps of trees. Photo by Noah K. Strycker.

Common Goldeneye are seen some years off of Old Town, and Yellow-billed Loon has occurred (see photo in species accounts). Just west of the boat ramp are Purple Martin houses that are quite active from April on into the early summer. Beyond the docks is a part of the city campground and storage area for commercial fishermen. This should be checked for passerines. Palm Warblers can be found here in some winters. Also check the mudflats to the east for shorebirds in season.

Urban Florence has had some exciting birds over the years, mainly in winter, including Clay-colored Sparrow, Tennessee Warbler, Chestnut-sided Warbler, Northern Parula, Lawrence's Goldfinch, Baltimore Oriole, Yellow-bellied Sapsucker, and American Tree Sparrow. No one location or feeder is the best place, but the town is always full of birds and worth checking. For several years Western Scrub-jays have appeared to nest west of Kingwood on Eighth Street.

South on Highway 101

South Jetty Road

Spring: ****   *Summer:* **   *Fall:* ****   *Winter:* ****

Shortly after crossing the bridge, the Oregon Dunes National Recreation Area begins and continues some 45 miles to Coos Bay. At mile 1.4 the northern access to this area, South Jetty Rd., heads west. This is a *fee* area but provides the best birding.

The Dog Pond

TIDE ∅

After 1.8 miles is a small parking lot with a pond (known as the Dog Pond). By late summer the pond nearly dries up. This is the first stop to look for shorebirds in summer and fall. Ruff and Sharp-tailed Sandpipers have been seen here along with regulars. Waterfowl are also here regularly. American Bittern should be looked for from March through at least November (some years they may overwinter). A Tropical Kingbird was here for several fall days.

A rough trail leads east along the southern side of the Dog Pond, then turns and runs about 75 yards north through dense pines to emerge by a second pond usually called the "back pond." During low-water periods in late summer and early fall, it can have shorebirds such as Pectoral Sandpipers, dowitchers, and yellowlegs. This trail can become overgrown.

Note: approach both of these ponds *slowly*. Shorebirds are often on the southern side of each, hidden in grass, and can be flushed by a loud or fast approach. The best shorebird area is usually the eastern lobe of the Dog Pond, which is quite shallow or, in late summer, sometimes dry.

South Jetty Rd. heads north just west of the pullout at the Dog Pond and parallels the ocean behind the foredune. On the left are a series of parking lots that provide access to the beach. On the right is the deflation plain which is slowly filling with vegetation. It is possible to work through this vegetation from any spot, but probably isn't worth the effort. The cover is extremely dense and interspersed with sinkholes. Quicksand is possible in less densely vegetated spots.

Once the fall rains begin small pools of water appear that can have birds like Red Phalarope after big storms. Anywhere along the road Northern Harriers can be found year round and Northern Shrikes in the winter. Particularly in migration or after big storms almost anything can turn up. At the second parking lot (2.8 miles) is a rough dike heading east with several ponds. It is tough walking but Pectoral and Buff-breasted Sandpipers have been found at the eastern end. Unfortunately the grasses, etc., are ruining the habitat.

The Dotterel Dike and the deflation plain

Spring: **	*Summer:* **	*Fall:* ****	*Winter:* ***

TIDE ↑

At the third parking lot (3.5 miles) is a dike that impounds water on the south side. Many birders think of it as the Dotterel Dike because Oregon's only record of Eurasian Dotterel was found there in September 2000. Again vegetation is taking over, but the low water in late summer and fall still attracts shorebirds. Both the ponds on the walk out and the flat plain to the north (the deflation plain) attract shorebirds when wet—and sometimes when dry.

Park at lot (immediately to the north) and walk out the sand trail, which meanders along the top of the dike between clumps of willow, occasional pines, and tall, sharp-pointed beach grass. The grass can be wet. Early in the morning the ponds often contain an American Bittern, and many kinds of waterfowl and shorebirds have been found here. Palm Warbler and Northern Mockingbird have been found in the trees.

At the east end of the dike, walk north and look for migrating shorebirds. Oregon's first record of Eurasian Dotterel was found in September 2000 a quarter-mile north. The deflation plain and ponds along the dike have yielded Pacific and American Golden Plovers, Ruff, Buff-breasted Sandpiper, Stilt Sandpiper, and Hudsonian Godwit plus the usual migrant shorebirds. In addition, such uncommon land birds as Burrowing Owl, Lapland Longspur, and Horned Lark have occurred.

In winter the deflation plain develops a large area of water that Tundra Swans use. Some waterfowl also use it, including such uncommon species as Common Goldeneye. The northern end of the area (see below) sometimes has a significant gull roost in late fall and winter. In years of Snowy Owl incursions, check the area around the dike or from the road nearby. Short-eared Owls appear some falls, as do Rough-legged Hawks and Northern Shrikes anywhere along the road. Northern Harriers are year-round residents.

Scanning stop
TIDE ↑

At the fourth parking lot (4.4 miles), climb up the dune with your spotting scope if the deflation plain is flooded in late fall or winter. Find a comfortable place to stand or sit and turn your scope

Dotterel Dike, looking west toward South Jetty Road from the end of the trail. Water levels vary, but it is worth walking at any season. Photo by Alan Contreras.

The deflation plain, looking north from the east end of Dotterel Dike. The low flat area often has standing water, with shorebirds in summer and fall and waterfowl in winter. Photo by Alan Contreras.

eastward. You can see over the pine and willow stands and locate Tundra Swans (November-March) and often large gull roosts, especially after storms.

Crab Dock and Cove

Spring: ***   *Summer:* **   *Fall:* ****   *Winter:* ***

TIDE →←

North of the fourth parking area (at about 5.5 miles) is a small, rough pullout on the right side of the road, overlooking a cove, beyond which can be seen a public fishing pier usually called the "Crab Dock." Here is a tidal mudflat that should be checked for migrant shorebirds. The bird mix here changes constantly, and should be checked except during the peak of high tide, when most birds are gone. Hudsonian and Bar-tailed Godwits have both occurred here, and Least Tern was found once. Check shrubs and grasses too. The paved portion of the road ends just beyond the parking lot on the river (5.7 miles) where the fishing pier is located.

Rest rooms are available at the Crab Dock lot and at the large lot where the paved road ends, as well as at several other parking areas. The pier itself provides a great view of the lower estuary. Sabine's Gull, Common and Elegant Tern, King Eider, Horned Puffin, Yellow-billed Loon, and many commoner species have been seen in the lower estuary.

Crab Dock Cove, with the main parking area and pier in background, looking northeast from near the gravel pullout. Photo by Alan Contreras.

The gravel pans and "longspur grass"

The open gravelly area has standing water after storms and should be checked for shorebirds (at high tide) as well as Horned Larks and American Pipits. In some winters, Lapland Longspurs or Snow Buntings are found. Both American and Pacific Golden-plovers have been found here, standing quietly at the edge of the shorter grass in the gravel pans. Tropical Kingbird has been seen in the scrub pines here.

Note: Although the gravel pans are too rough for easy wheelchair use (they are usable with care), the north end of the parking area provides a superb view of the lower estuary from a vehicle.

Also check the low hummock west of the road and the flat grassy area between the hummock and the foredune. This area has had Lapland Longspur and often contains Western Meadowlark. In migration it sometimes has hundreds of Savannah Sparrows and small flocks of American Pipits.

South Jetty walk

TIDE ∅

The road gives out at the foredune. From here it is possible to walk along the river and out the South Jetty. As with the North Jetty, pelagic species are the main attractions. Higher tides may be better for seeing some of the offshore species, but visibility is usually better at lower tides (less spray and easier to see "down" over the wave crests), so the jetty is worth walking at any tide.

The South Jetty has a higher "hump" as you walk out; this is a good place from which to watch the ocean. There is often a gull roost just beyond the hump. Use a spotting scope and keep an eye on what is going by off the ends of both jetties. Black-legged Kittiwake is regular here from late fall through winter, and Northern Fulmar can sometimes be seen, especially in October and November. Sooty Shearwater is regular in small numbers from midsummer through October (can be seen any time), although they often appear as a brief view of stiff wings gliding through the wave troughs, not looping upward as much as do the fulmars.

This is also a good location for grebes of several species, loons, scoters, and, especially in late summer, alcids. Horned Puffin, Yellow-billed Loon, and King Eider have all been seen here. Winter rock birds move in flocks between the two jetties. Gulls tend to collect on the jetty or beach to the south. Check for Herring, Mew, California, and Thayer's Gulls and Black-legged Kittiwakes among the Western and Glaucous-winged Gulls.

Retrace the road back to 101.

CANARY ROAD AND THE BACK OF SILTCOOS LAKE

Honeyman and Woahink state parks

Spring: ***   *Summer: ***   *Fall: ***   *Winter: ****

At mile 3.3 on 101 is Canary Rd. to the left and Honeyman State Park (*fee* and rest rooms) to the right. The park is worth checking for winter ducks on Cleawox Lake (Redheads have occurred a couple of years). The woods around the lake are good for passerines year round. After turning onto Canary Road is the entrance to Woahink State Park (mile 0.4) with rest rooms. Woahink Lake has had Common Goldeneye some winters as well as the usual ducks, geese, Common Loons and grebes. Palm Warblers are possible.

South Slough Road

TIDE ↓

Continue on Canary Rd. to South Slough Rd. (mile 2.9), a narrow road with a few wide shoulders passing through private land. Some maps call it South Inlet Rd. Stay on the road to bird the winter water for ducks and shorebirds, including yellowlegs, Wilson's Snipe, and sometimes Eurasian Wigeon. Spring brings swallows and breeding Wood Ducks. Turn around where the road crosses the dike at the head of the tidal slough. Check the slough before returning to Canary Rd.

At mile 5.1 Canary Rd. turns south and passes through a couple of miles of pasture land that floods in the winter and early spring.

TIDE: ∅

These ponds attract Green-winged Teal and Ring-necked Ducks, Mallards, Pintail, Gadwall, Northern Shovelers, Hooded Mergansers (sometimes dozens), American Wigeon, and in some years a Eurasian Wigeon. Raptors, egrets, herons, kingfishers, goldfinches, swallows, and Western Bluebirds (some years) are readily found, depending on the season.

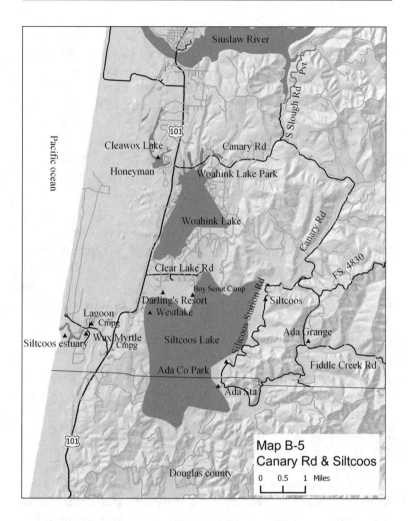

Map B-5
Canary Rd & Siltcoos

0   0.5   1   Miles

Ada-Siltcoos loop

TIDE: ∅

Siltcoos Station Rd. intersects at mile 7.8. This begins an 11-mile loop. This guide assumes that you will stay on Canary Rd. and do the loop "left to right." Continue on Canary Rd. to the top of the hill (mile 8.7) where Forest Service road 4830 leads into the mountains. This road is paved for 3 or 4 miles and is especially active in the spring with warblers (Hermit and Wilson's), Hutton's, Warbling, and Cassin's Vireo, waxwings, woodpeckers, Winter Wren, Band-tailed Pigeon, and maybe Mountain Quail or Ruffed Grouse. Turn around when the pavement gives out and return to Canary Rd.

At mile 9.9 is an intersection with Fiddle Creek Rd. The small buildings here constitute the Ada Grange, where nesting Cliff Swallows can be seen. The road to the left passes through more pastureland that floods in the winter. Of special interest are Black Phoebes, that have bred here since 2002. A farm at mile 1 has active phoebes year round, the only regular site in Lane Co. At mile 1.8 are two bridges where breeding phoebes have been verified. Other past sightings on this road include Western Kingbird, Sora, Cattle Egret, Solitary Sandpiper, and one year a singing Willow Flycatcher.

Back at the Ada Grange the loop section to the west passes along Fiddle Creek slough out to the main body of Siltcoos Lake, entering Douglas Co. for a couple of miles. The road narrows to one lane and has few turnouts. Winter ducks vary as the water deepens. As many as fifty Great Blue Herons have been seen in the fall. At the turnoff for the Ada Resort stay to the right and re-enter Lane Co. where the road widens into gravel. At Lane Co.'s Ada Park is a boat ramp and a railroad trestle from which the lake can be viewed. In the winter check the lake for large numbers of Ruddy Ducks, Canvasbacks (some years), scaup, and Western Grebes.

Lane Community College owns a small retreat center which is shown on maps as Siltcoos Station. Just north of the buildings is a pullout, and the wet sump along the lake can be checked for passerines. Anna's Hummingbird is regular here, as is Hutton's Vireo.

Continuing on towards the intersection with Canary Rd., the paved section comes down a long hill then passes a year-round pond on the left (0.3 miles from Canary Rd.) This pond should be checked for breeding wood ducks and marsh wrens along with year-round Virginia Rails. On this flat stretch of road can be found spring birds including waxwings, Black-headed Grosbeaks, Western Tanagers, Warbling Vireos, and Pacific-slope and Olive-sided Flycatchers. Return to 101.

Darling's Resort

Spring: ***   *Summer:* **   *Fall:* **   *Winter:* ****

TIDE: ∅

Clear Lake Rd. (to North Beach and Boy Scout Camp Baker) leaves 101 to the east at 5.7. About one-tenth mile along this road, take the right-hand spur toward Darling's Resort.

[♿] This is an excellent place in winter to observe the exceptional numbers of ducks gathered on Siltcoos Lake. Large rafts of Canvasback, Ruddy Duck, scaup, Ring-necked Duck, and others can be found here. Lane Co.'s first record of Tufted Duck came from this area.

Note: Ask for permission at the store before walking onto the pier. The owners are friendly and interested in wildlife. Shopping there will help ensure that birders are welcome.

West Lake

TIDE: ∅

West Lake Rd. is at mile 6.5 south of Florence on 101. A short street (0.3 miles) leads to the boat ramp.

[♿] From here scan the lake for ducks, coots, grebes, and cormorants. There are nesting Red-winged Blackbirds and Purple Martins here. The house on the north side of the ramp often has active feeders. The trees to the north and along the lake edge have produced Yellow Warblers and Western Tanagers. The exposed lake edge in the late summer has had Sora, Virginia Rail, and Green Heron. Pied-billed Grebe breeds in marshes here. Return to 101.

SILTCOOS RIVER AND ESTUARY

Spring: ***   Summer: **   Fall: ***   Winter: ***

TIDE →←

The last stop on 101 is the Siltcoos River access road and campground complex (mile 7.7), which has rest rooms and a *fee*. The road paralleling the river passes two campgrounds, Lagoon on the right (0.9 miles) and Waxmyrtle just beyond on the left across the river. The road continues to a parking area behind the foredune.

Northern beach and river access

The beach over the dune is Snowy Plover territory. From March 15 to September 15 the upper beach is roped off to protect the nesting birds. However, feeding plovers can often be found near the high-tide line. In the winter a flock of twenty to thirty plovers is often found less than a mile to the north near a large ATV dune

This means you. Access to the backwaters of the Siltcoos is closed to the public during breeding season. After Sep. 15 this is an excellent place to seek shorebirds. Photo by Alan Contreras.

crossing. They generally roost in ATV tracks or footprints near the dune, but feed closer to the ocean.

To the south the large expanse of open sand at the mouth of the river should be checked for migrating shorebirds. Between September 15 and March 15, the narrow slough just east of the main parking area provides a good route to the river and beach. Stilt Sandpiper, Red-necked Stint (both of Lane Co.'s records), Willet, and Oregon's first record of Smith's Longspur have been seen here, as have Baird's Sandpiper and other more common species. A small gravel pullout is just across the road from this access point.

Lagoon Campground
TIDE: ∅

The Lagoon Campground is bordered by water on three sides in the winter, but is changing to a meadow-like environment in the spring and summer on the east and north sides. Several pairs of American Bittern used to nest here regularly, but the deteriorating habitat seems to have driven them elsewhere. Occasionally one can be seen, as can a Green Heron. In the spring along the water's edge Virginia Rail (seldom), Marsh Wrens, Song Sparrows, and Common Yellowthroat can be found. Olive-sided Flycatchers sing from the tops of trees ringing the lagoon. Bald Eagles (mainly in fall) perch in the trees to the west. Bushtits, thrushes, chickadees,

Siltcoos R. mouth from the end of the Waxmyrtle river trail, breeding and wintering ground for Snowy Plovers. The area is open during the nonbreeding season and has harbored many unusual species. Photo by Noah K. Strycker.

Wrentits, Song and White-crowned Sparrows are common. In the winter bird activity continues to be high. Hooded Mergansers use the lagoon then.

Waxmyrtle Campground, southern beach and river access

The Waxmyrtle Campground is more open and the roads allow easy walking to bird in the winter. Just over the bridge is the start of the Waxmyrtle trail to the ocean. During Snowy Plover nesting season a portion of the river trail is closed, but the detour reconnects to the trail. The mudflats along the river can be great for migrating shorebirds, but access is limited by the roped-off area. After September 15 the area is open and can still have excellent shorebirds. The plovers do not seem to winter on this side. Near the mouth of the river, goldeneyes and Long-tailed Ducks turn up some winters along with the normal Buffleheads, mergansers, and scoters. Always check the ocean from atop the foredune or from the beach for pelagic species.

The small ponds and backwaters on the south side of the mouth of the Siltcoos are always shifting, and have supported such rarities as Curlew Sandpiper, Wilson's Phalarope, Ruff, and Stilt Sandpiper.

The Coast Range

Tom Mickel

There are hundreds of miles of mostly gravel roads in the Coast Range with very few signs, making it very easy to get lost. If you're planning to do much driving on these roads, stop at the BLM office on Chad Drive in Eugene before your trip and buy one of their "blue line" maps for the Coast Range (1 inch to the mile). These are about the most up-to-date maps you can find but don't be surprised to find new roads that aren't on the map and new gates that block some roads.

Other tips for driving in the Coast Range include: have a full tank of gas before you start; drive slowly and keep to the right, especially around corners; if the road looks heavily used, watch out for log trucks; most of this area *does not* have cell phone coverage, so if you have a problem you'll most likely have to walk out to the nearest highway to get help!

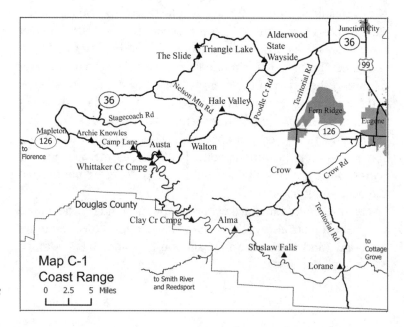

Map C-1
Coast Range
0   2.5   5   Miles

Highway 36 Sites

Alderwood State Wayside

Spring: ***   *Summer:* ***   *Fall:* **   *Winter:* *

Wheelchair Access: The parking areas and the trails to the bridges are paved but the trail along the river between the bridges isn't. The wayside is 77 acres of large second-growth Douglas-fir with limited hardwoods along the Long Tom River next to Hwy. 36. Because of this uniformity in habitat, there aren't a lot of species in the park but it's a good place to look for species of the Douglas-fir forest (i.e., Hammond's and Pacific-slope Flycatchers, Chestnut-backed Chickadee, Golden-crowned Kinglet, Hermit Warbler, and Western Tanager).

The wayside is 13.7 miles west of Junction City on Hwy. 36. There are two parking areas, one at each end of the park—the first is a gravel lot with a few tables, the second has tables and a rest room. The two parking areas are connected by a quarter-mile trail across the Long Tom River from the highway. Walking the trail will get you into the forest but the noise from the highway makes it difficult to hear birds. Mid-way along the trail between the two bridges is a "way" trail that heads straight up the hill to a pump house. This trail is quite steep but it gets you away from the highway noise. There's a small gravel road up to the pump house but it quickly crosses on to private property and so shouldn't be used for birding outside the park.

Triangle Lake

Spring: **   *Summer:* **   *Fall:* **   *Winter:* **

Paved parking area and trail to dock. A small county park on the west side of Triangle Lake (the only natural lake in the Coast Range of Lane County) offers the opportunity to scope the lake for waterfowl during the winter and Osprey, swallows, etc., during the summer. The lake is heavily used in the summer, so this isn't the place to stop on a warm summer day, unless you're looking for ski boats!

The park is located 25.4 miles west of Junction City on Hwy. 36 and has a boat ramp, dock, tables, and rest rooms. The park is mostly parking lot but does have a little grass and a few alder trees along the lake edge. To view the lake, a scope is needed and can be set up on the dock or shore, depending on the waves. Triangle Lake is ringed by summer homes, so getting a view of the lake is next to impossible except from the county park.

The Slide

Wheelchair access: There is no wheelchair access except for the parking lot.

The Slide is a rocky cascade/falls on Lake Creek where it flows out of Triangle Lake. The habitat is a mix of Douglas-fir and hardwood forests on the steep hillsides. Normal species include: Band-tailed Pigeon, Red-breasted Sapsucker, Olive-sided Flycatcher, empidonax flycatchers (Hammond's and Pacific-slope), vireos (Hutton's and Warbling), jays (Gray and Steller's), Chestnut-backed Chickadee, Winter Wren, warblers (Orange-crowned, Black-throated Gray, Hermit, and Wilson's), Western Tanager, Black-headed Grosbeak, Red Crossbill, and the possibility of American Dipper in the creek.

The parking area for the Slide is 1.2 miles west of Triangle Lake Co. Park or 26.6 miles west of Junction City on Hwy. 36. The area around the parking lot is a hardwood forest and can offer good birding away from the highway and creek noise. There are a couple of "way" trails from the parking area that could be walked in search of birds. The trail to the Slide crosses the highway from the parking area and proceeds along the highway about a quarter mile before dropping steeply to the creek.

Once at the creek you can walk up or down the creek on rocks but watch your footing because the rocks are normally quite slick. The trail along the highway is quite noisy from the creek and traffic, making it hard to hear bird sounds, and the area at the Slide is also quite noisy because of the creek. The Slide is a traditional swimming area on hot summer days, so isn't the place to try and bird on warm summer afternoons!

Continuing west on Hwy. 36 past the Slide, it is about 26 miles to Mapleton and Hwy. 126. There are a few boat ramps along Lake Creek west of the town of Deadwood that provide parking to bird along the creek.

Connecting routes between Highways 36 and 126

There are a couple of county roads that go between Hwy. 36 and 126, providing opportunities for additional birding. The first is Nelson Mountain county road, which is about 8.5 miles past the Slide parking area and has a covered bridge over Lake Creek that's visible from the highway. Just south of the bridge is a good place to stop; there are local feeders in addition to native habitat. Nelson Mountain county road intersects Hwy. 126 just west of Walton (a café, post office, and sometime store which is about 14 miles from the Veneta light) and is 11 miles from highway to highway.

Nelson Mountain county road is partially paved and partially gravel and the only intersection that could be confusing is at the end of the pavement (2.9 miles) coming from the Hwy. 36 side. The county road turns right up the hill while a dead-end BLM road continues up Nelson Creek, straight ahead. The gravel portion of the road goes up and over the ridge (Nelson Divide) and back down into the Chickahominy Creek drainage. This portion of the road is a good place to look for typical forest species as is the dead-end BLM road up Nelson Creek.

Stagecoach county road is the other county road and turns off of Hwy. 36 at Swisshome (17.5 miles west of the Slide) and crosses over Lake Creek on a large concrete bridge before following the Siuslaw River upstream to Hwy. 126 at Richardson (about 23 miles west of the Veneta light). The road is 11.5 miles of mostly gravel road that parallels the Siuslaw River and railroad tracks upstream with numerous places to park for birding the habitats along the river.

Highway 126 Sites

Hale Valley

Wheelchair access: Mostly gravel roads and off-trail walking with a very limited amount of paved road.

This area is typical Coast Range habitat with a succession of recent clear-cuts to older second-growth forests and their associated bird species. Normal species include Ruffed Grouse, Mountain Quail, Band-tailed Pigeon, Northern Pygmy-Owl, Red-breasted Sapsucker, Olive-sided Flycatcher, Empidonax flycatchers (Willow, Hammond's, and Pacific-slope), vireos (Hutton's and Warbling), jays (Gray and Steller's), Chestnut-backed Chickadee, wrens (Bewick's, House, and Winter), warblers (Orange-crowned, Black-throated Gray, Hermit, MacGillivray's, and Wilson's), Western Tanager, Black-headed Grosbeak, and Red Crossbill.

To get to the Hale Valley site proceed west on Hwy. 126 from the light at Veneta, 8.9 miles to a paved road on your right signed "IP Deeded Road." Turn right on IP Deeded Rd. and proceed up the hill, just past the end of the pavement (0.5 miles) to a gravel circle and parkmiles. The land along this road is a combination of private and public (USDI Bureau of Land Management), so birding from the road is best. From this location you can walk any of the paved/gravel roads to find the above species. By proceeding up the main road you can get into more forested habitats to find those species; a good area with larger trees is up the road about a mile (0.9 miles). This area is posted private property, so please bird from the road. In this general area a Magnolia Warbler was found on 4 June 1981.

> **Directions to a reliable Northern Pygmy-Owl site:** From the gravel circle described above, proceed 4.7 miles to a dirt road on your right. Park in the wide spot just before the road and walk down the road about a quarter mile to where the road enters an old partial cut and is on top of the ridge. Calling from this point will normally get a response and as often as not the bird will fly in. If you don't get any response, walk further down the dirt road and try again. The road continues for about a half mile before coming to a dead end. Northern Pygmy-Owls have been found in this area for at least the last ten years.

Austa

Spring: ***	Summer: ***	Fall: **	Winter: *

Wheelchair access: Mostly gravel roads and off trail walking with a very limited amount of paved road.

This area is mostly the riparian forest along the Siuslaw River, Wildcat Creek, and the old Austa log pond, plus the lower edge of the Austa Fire that burned in September 1999. Normal species include Ruffed Grouse, Mountain Quail, Band-tailed Pigeon, Belted Kingfisher, Red-breasted Sapsucker, Olive-sided Flycatcher, empidonax flycatchers (Willow, Hammond's, and Pacific-slope), vireos (Hutton's and Warbling), Steller's Jay, swallows (Violet-green and Northern Rough-winged), Chestnut-backed Chickadee, wrens (Bewick's, House, and Winter), warblers (Orange-crowned, Black-throated Gray, Hermit, MacGillivray's, and Wilson's), Western Tanager, and Black-headed Grosbeak.

To get to the Austa site proceed 20.4 miles west on Hwy. 126 from the light at Veneta, to the sign for Whittaker Creek and Clay Creek recreation areas and make a left turn just before the bridge over the Siuslaw River. Proceed less than 0.1 miles to Siuslaw River Rd. and turn right under the Hwy. 126 bridge and the railroad bridge over the Siuslaw River, which is signed for Austa county Boat Ramp.

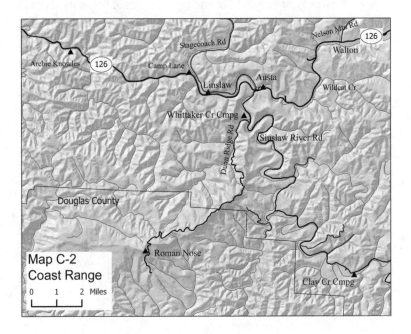

Map C-2
Coast Range
0   1   2 Miles

Immediately on the other side of the bridges is a gravel road to the right and straight ahead is a covered bridge over Wildcat Creek. On the other side of Wildcat Creek is the Austa Co. boat ramp and parking.

You can park anywhere in this area. The gravel road to the right with the large yellow gate goes into the old Austa mill site and log pond. The pond is located straight ahead of you as you walk along the railroad tracks and can best be viewed from under the powerline after the road makes a right-angled corner away from the railroad. Approach the edge of the pond *slowly* and scan any portion of the pond as it becomes visible; birds on the pond will normally swim back into the vegetation upon seeing or hearing you. Hooded Merganser with downy young have been found here in the past and it is also a good place to look for the Belted Kingfishers that have nested in the banks of Wildcat Creek and the Siuslaw River in the area of the boat ramp; the kingfisher likes to sit on the wires over the pond. These same dirt banks provide nesting habitat for the Northern Rough-winged Swallows.

At the Austa county boat ramp the road splits and one fork goes up Wildcat Creek and rejoins Hwy. 126 in 2.0 miles. The other fork goes down the Siuslaw River and also rejoins Hwy. 126 at Richardson (about 23 miles from the Veneta light)—a large concrete bridge just upstream from Camp Lane Co. Park. *Note*: Both of these roads have gates that are closed in the winter because of hazardous driving conditions.

Near this junction is where the Austa Fire started and even though most of the area has been replanted, numerous snags still provide habitat for Olive-sided Flycatchers and woodpeckers (Red-breasted Sapsucker, Hairy, and Flicker).

Linslaw County Park

Continuing west on Hwy. 126 past Austa, it is about 12 miles to Mapleton and Hwy. 36. About 2 miles west of the Austa turnoff is Linslaw Co. Park (22.4 miles from the Veneta light), along the Siuslaw River, with a paved parking area and handicapped-access bathrooms. The riparian habitat in the park is a good place to look for Pacific-slope Flycatcher, Warbling Vireo, Steller's Jay, Chestnut-backed Chickadee, Winter Wren, Black-throated Gray and Wilson's Warbler, Black-headed Grosbeak, etc.

Archie Knowles Campground

Another place to stop and bird is Archie Knowles Campground, a USDA Forest Service *fee* site, which is about 29 miles from the Veneta light and about 3 miles from Mapleton. It is located along Knowles Creek, with a mix of hardwood and conifer habitats, and is open for camping only during the summer season. If you're staying the night, be sure and listen at first light for Marbled Murrelets flying between their nesting areas and the ocean.

Whittaker Creek Campground and Trail

Spring: ***	*Summer: ****	*Fall: ***	*Winter: **

Wheelchair access: Paved roads in the campground but trails are dirt.

This area is mostly the riparian forest along the Siuslaw River and Whittaker Creek. Normal species include Ruffed Grouse, Mountain Quail, Band-tailed Pigeon, Belted Kingfisher, Red-breasted Sapsucker, Olive-sided Flycatcher, empidonax flycatchers (Hammond's and Pacific-slope), vireos (Hutton's and Warbling), Steller's Jay, Violet-green Swallow, Chestnut-backed Chickadee, wrens (Bewick's, House, and Winter), warblers (Orange-crowned, Black-throated Gray, Hermit, MacGillivray's, and Wilson's), Western Tanager, and Black-headed Grosbeak.

To get to the Whittaker Creek Campground, follow the directions to the Austa site and at the Siuslaw River Rd. turn left instead of right and proceed 1.5 miles to the signed junction for the campground and trail. The road to the campground crosses over the Siuslaw River on a concrete bridge, allowing views of the river. The campground is a U.S. *fee* site and has both camping and picnic sites. Normal riparian species can be found in the campground.

The Old-growth Ridge Trail starts across the road from between campsites 23 and 24, which is across Whittaker Creek. It's best to park in the area to the right after entering the campground and walk across the bridge to the trail. The trail switchbacks up a ridge through a second-growth stand of mixed conifer and hardwoods with a few scattered remnant old-growth Douglas-fir.

Other habitats can be found by following the paved Whittaker Creek Rd. past the campground. At 1.5 miles from the Siuslaw River bridge the paved Dunn Ridge Rd. turns to the right and proceeds to Roman Nose mountain and the Kentucky Falls trail, both in Douglas Co.

The Whittaker Creek Rd. continues for about 3 miles from the Siuslaw River bridge and dead-ends in an old-growth stand. The far end of the road is a good area to look for Ruffed Grouse on the road because of the limited traffic. The older conifer habitats are good places to look for Hammond's Flycatcher (they like to sing from the dead limbs at the base of the live crown) and Gray Jays; and try calling for Northern Pygmy-Owl. The Siuslaw River Rd. passes through a couple of these older habitats between Austa and Whittaker Creek as well as in the area at the end of the Whittaker Creek Rd.

Clay Creek Campground and Trail
With contributions from Dave Brown

Spring: ***   *Summer:* ***   *Fall:* **   *Winter:* *

Wheelchair access: Paved roads in the campground but the trail is dirt.

This area is mostly the riparian forest along the Siuslaw River and Clay Creek. Normal species include Ruffed Grouse, Mountain Quail, Band-tailed Pigeon, Red-breasted Sapsucker, Empidonax flycatchers (Willow, Hammond's, and Pacific-slope), vireos (Hutton's and Warbling), Steller's Jay, Violet-green Swallow, Chestnut-backed Chickadee, wrens (Bewick's, House, and Winter), warblers (Orange-crowned, Black-throated Gray, Hermit, MacGillivray's, and Wilson's), Western Tanager, and Black-headed Grosbeak.

To get to the Clay Creek Campground, follow the directions to Whittaker Creek Campground and continue 14.7 miles from the junction for Whittaker Creek Campground to the signed junction for the Clay Creek campground and trail. The campground is a U.S. *fee* site and has both camping and picnic sites. Normal riparian species can be found in the campground. The trailhead is a short way up the Clay Creek Rd. from the bridge over the Siuslaw River. The trail crosses over Clay Creek on a wooden bridge and continues switchbacking toward the top of the ridge through an old-growth stand with numerous singing Hammond's Flycatchers and Hermit Warblers.

From Clay Creek you can continue up the Siuslaw River on the Siuslaw River Rd. to Lorane or Crow. From the turnoff into the campground, it's 9.3 miles to the Alma junction. If you turn right, the road takes you over the Oxbow Divide and down the Smith

River to Hwy. 101 (50.5 miles) between Reedsport (to the south) and Gardiner (to the north). It's 3.4 miles to the Lane /Douglas county line along this route.

If you turn left you can continue to Territorial Hwy. at Crow or Lorane. Continue left for 1.7 miles to the junction with Wolf Creek Rd., after passing the Alma Forest Work Camp on your right. To get to Crow, turn left on Wolf Creek Rd. and continue 11.4 miles to Territorial Hwy. and then turn left again for 1.2 miles.

Siuslaw River falls

To get to Lorane, continue on Siuslaw River Rd. for 17.1 miles. The Siuslaw River falls is located 8.4 miles from the Wolf Creek Rd. junction toward Lorane. There are no facilities at the falls, just a dirt trail down to the "falls"—more of a cascade. This area is a mixture of private forestland and USDI Bureau of Land Management lands with recent clear-cuts to old-growth forests. By stopping in the appropriate habitat you can find a number of different species. In clear-cuts and new forests: Willow Flycatcher, Bewick's and House Wren, Orange-crowned and MacGillivray's Warblers, Spotted Towhee, etc. In conifer forests: Hammond's Flycatcher, Hutton's Vireo, Gray and Steller's Jays, Chestnut-backed Chickadee, Winter Wren, Hermit Warbler, Western Tanager, etc. in hardwood and mixed forests: Pacific-slope Flycatcher, Warbling Vireo, Steller's Jay, Chestnut-backed Chickadee, Winter Wren, Black-throated Gray and Wilson's Warbler, Western Tanager, Black-headed Grosbeak, etc.

From Crow you can take Territorial Hwy. north to Hwy. 126 at Veneta or take Crow Rd. (1.0 miles south on Territorial Hwy. or 0.2 miles north on Territorial Hwy. from the Wolf Creek road junction) northeast to Hwy. 126 at the Greenhill Rd. intersection a few miles west of Eugene.

From Lorane you can take Territorial Hwy. north to Hwy. 126 at Veneta or take the Cottage Grove-Lorane road to Cottage Grove and I-5. If traveling north on Territorial Hwy., you can take Lorane Hwy. into southeast Eugene and south Willamette Street. The junction of Territorial and Lorane highways (Gillespie Corners) is 3.4 miles north of Lorane.

The area around Lorane, Crow, and northeast toward Eugene is primarily private pasture land with very few places to stop along the main roads. During the summer it is a good area to find Western Kingbirds sitting on the fences and power lines. South of Lorane was the location of one of the first breeding records of White-tailed Kite in the late 1970s and the area from Crow to Eugene and the southern end of Fern Ridge Reservoir is now breeding habitat for Red-shouldered Hawks.

In winter the area can be good for White-tailed Kites, Rough-legged Hawks, and the occasional Northern Shrike. A Ferruginous Hawk was found in the area during fall migration in 1992 and large flocks of swallows line the power lines before heading south every fall.

South-central Lane County

Dave Brown

The routes described below are best in spring and summer, though they can be covered at any time of year. Birds are typical of the eastern Coast Range, with opportunities to come across species such as Mountain Quail, Western Bluebird and Ruffed Grouse, among others.

Oak Hill/Greenhill/Willow Creek Loop

From the K. R. Neilson Rd. and Cantrell Rd. intersection (see also the Fern Ridge Reservoir guide, Map D-1), head east on Cantrell Rd. Go east 1.3 miles until you come to the intersection with Cherry Ridge Rd. This location has had a summering Ash-throated Flycatcher and wintering Turkey Vultures. Vesper Sparrow can sometimes be found along the roadside in this area. After another 1.6 miles east, Cantrell Rd. intersects with Oak Hill Drive. Go north on Oak Hill Drive, then east to Crow Rd and Greenhill Rd., then north to Hwy. 126 (West 11th) or south on Green Hill.

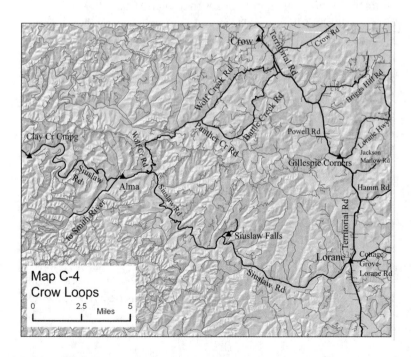

Map C-4
Crow Loops

0   2.5   5
         Miles

From here to the top of the hill on Green Hill Rd. heading south is 1.5 miles. At the top of the hill the road becomes Willow Creek Rd. Follow this road east, then north with a jog left (west) on West 18th Ave., then in 2.7 miles turn north on Willow Creek Rd. to return to Hwy 126. To head back to Greenhill Rd. go west (left). The Willow Creek/Greenhill Loop is 4.2 miles. The Green Hill – Willow Creek loop is especially good in spring migration for warblers, vireos, and grassland species. See also the West Eugene Wetlands guide (Map F-1) for links.

Crow Loops and south Lane access

Take Wolf Creek Rd. from Territorial Rd. (Hwy.) just south of downtown Crow. It is 2.0 miles to Battle Creek Rd., then 1.7 miles to Coyote Rd. and 0.2 back out to Territorial Rd. farther southwest of Crow. To go southwest and west to Willow Creek Farm is 1.4 miles. Another 1.7 miles brings you to the intersection of Donner Rd. It is then 1.5 miles more to the intersection with Powell Rd.

If you want to continue on Territorial Rd., it is 0.9 miles to Gillespie Corner Junction. You can return to Eugene from this junction by turning left (east) on Lorane Hwy. and going into Eugene on Lorane or Fox Hollow Rd. (See Spencer Butte guide). These routes do not have much parking or access to public land, but provide access to routes into the Coast Range or southern Lane Co.

If you continue down Territorial, in 1 mile you will reach the Jackson Marlow Rd. and about a mile later, Iris Hill Lane. In a further 0.5 miles you will reach Hamm Rd. (this leads to Creswell via Camas Swale Rd.) and 3.3 miles later, you will reach downtown Lorane. At this point you need to decide which way to go, which may depend on how much time you have. The main choices are as follows:

Head for the coast

Head south 0.3 miles until Territorial turns into Siuslaw Rd. heading southwest. There is a gravel and dirt road on the left after 1.9 miles. The sign calls it a Fire Road. Another 7.2 miles beyond on Siuslaw Rd. is the intersection with Siuslaw Falls Rd. on the right. On down Siuslaw Rd. 23.4 miles there is a small pond on the left in the wooded area.

This area has a lot of woods with small meadows and some farm areas and logging areas. Another 5.6 miles down Siuslaw Rd.

you come to the first of two intersections with signs to Clay Creek Rd. (see also the Clay Creek guide), Wolf Creek Rd., Cottage Grove, Gardiner, and Eugene.

Continue on Siuslaw Rd. 1.5 miles on to the Lane Co. Sheriff's Work Camp. In 0.3 miles there is another intersection signed for Hwy. 38, Hwy. 126, and Gardiner.

Ahead to the left are Smith River and Oxbow Rd., which can be taken into the old Oxbow Burn area that is now grown up. It is 23.3 miles down to the Smith River Falls, in Douglas Co. It is another 11.2 miles to the town and community of Smith River. It is another 16.0 miles to Hwy. 101 between Reedsport (to the south) and Gardiner (to the north).

Return to the valley via Cottage Grove

Turn left (east) onto Cottage Grove-Lorane Rd. from Lorane, or go 3 miles south of Lorane and take Gowdyville Rd. east. Both lead to west Main Street in Cottage Grove (about a dozen miles on Gowdyville, slightly longer the other way) through a mix of wooded and rural residential areas. Gowdyville Rd. can provide excellent birding in spring migration.

Return to the Eugene area

Go back north on Territorial Rd. to Gillespie Corners.

Continue south to reach I-5 southbound

Stay on Territorial Rd. southbound out of Lorane until you reach the freeway entrance about 10 miles south at Curtin.

Fern Ridge Reservoir

Daniel Farrar

Spring: **** Summer: **** Fall: **** Winter: ****

Many sites at Fern Ridge are easily navigated by wheelchair. Specific information regarding wheelchair/limited mobility access is provided in the notes on individual sites.

Fern Ridge Reservoir, the finest all-round birding site in the Willamette Valley, is located at the heart of Lane Co.; it lies nestled between Eugene to the east and the Coast Range to the west. Known as "Malheur West" in the summer and "Klamath Marsh" in the winter, Fern Ridge is home to a diverse array of wildlife in all seasons. Its muddy waters boast huge wintering populations of waterfowl and in summer breeding marsh birds are abundant. Fern Ridge is a breeding area for a large group of birds that generally nest east of the Cascade divide, such as Redhead, Black-necked Stilt, Wilson's Phalarope, Yellow-headed Blackbird, and Black Tern. Attracted here by the warm, shallow waters and marshes, birds stay all summer, including a small population of American White Pelicans (not breeding—yet).

With habitat ranging from oak woodlands and native wet prairies to year-round marsh and streamside riparian, there is always something to see at Fern Ridge. During migration passerines can be exceptionally abundant and shorebirding is a must. Rarities such as Ruff, Stilt Sandpiper, and Sharp-tailed Sandpiper have been found on the mudflats in the fall as the water is drawn down. During the spring influx landbirds are funneled up the peninsulas before crossing the reservoir. No matter when you visit Fern Ridge, expect to have an enjoyable day of birding at this unique reservoir in the southern Willamette Valley.

To adequately cover the Fern Ridge area, a vehicle is a must. The area is simply too large to cover on foot. A car loop around the lake is up to 30 miles depending on how adventurous you are. Many areas also require a substantial amount of walking to be properly covered.

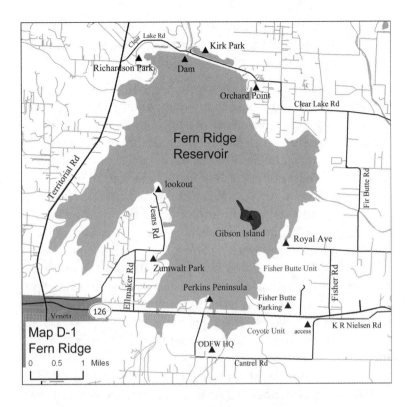

Royal Avenue Lake Access Point/Fisher Butte Unit

Spring: *** Summer: **** Fall: **** Winter: ***

This site is wheelchair accessible in the summer. During fall and winter the dikes become very soggy and slippery from the wet clay. Please use caution. Rest rooms are available in the parking area.

Our tour of Fern Ridge begins at Meadowlark Prairie (please see the Eugene (West Eugene Wetlands) section of the book [page 90] for information on this site). Begin by driving north on Greenhill Rd. until you reach Royal Ave. (0.4 miles). Turn west (left) on Royal and follow it until you reach the end of the road near the red pipe gate (2.4 miles). Caution! Do not run into the pipe gate! It has happened many times and will cause serious damage to your vehicle and you. Once you reach the end of the road, turn right into the small lot to the north. There are plans for a permanent rest room at this location. Be sure to lock your car and valuables at this location.

Note: Beware of hunting in progress especially during fall and winter. Hunting times and closures are posted. This is also a popular area for dog training.

Royal Ave. is surrounded by sensitive native habitats. There is native wet upland prairie to the north and south. Most of the ponds and marshes are being managed to combat non-native grasses, so please use caution not to spread grass seeds, which can stick to clothing and shoes. The Royal Ave. parking area is the main access to the east portion of Fern Ridge Reservoir. To the north is a Research Natural Area (RNA), which has old oak groves, native grasslands, and a variety of forests including fir and old orchards.

In spring and summer this is a great area to see Western Meadowlark and Savannah Sparrow, as well as many native wildflowers. The upland area is very rough terrain and extremely difficult to walk in. Look for the plowed fire line and stick to it when exploring the areas north of Royal Ave. Call the Reservoir Headquarters at 541-687-1431 for more info on RNAs. During winter keep an eye open for the winter flock of Tundra Swans to the west near Gibson Island.

To the south is a vast system of dikes and marshes. The dike system is large, but goes in a circle, so it is hard to get totally lost. A lookout platform south of Royal and west of the parking area provides one of the best places to see summer breeders. The rushes and reeds provide nesting habitat for Black Terns, American Bittern, grebes, ducks, and rails. Black-crowned Night Herons are usually seen by August and are suspected of secretly breeding. Early morning is the best time to visit. Summer afternoons can be quiet and warm. This area is also excellent for shorebirds, especially in fall, as the ponds are drawn down, creating a shorebird mecca.

Special Note: On your way out of Royal there is a large grove of oak trees just before Fisher Rd. This is one of the most reliable spots in the county for Acorn Woodpecker. They live here all year round, from nesting in spring to storing acorns in late summer to survive the winter. This is also a good area for White-breasted Nuthatch. In fall and sometimes winter Lewis's Woodpeckers are found; while this is not an annual bird here, over the years this location has proven worthy of checking.

Fisher Butte Unit

Anytime you visit Fern Ridge, the Fisher Butte Unit is a must stop. If you do not take the goose loop below, after leaving Royal Ave. heading east, turn right onto Fisher Rd. and follow it to Hwy. 126. Turn right onto Hwy. 126. About 1 mile west is another parking area for the Royal Ave. area; this is the Fisher Butte parking area. This gravel lot with an old road leading north can be excellent for sparrows in winter (some unusual winter species such as Vesper and Grasshopper Sparrow have been seen here, and Swamp Sparrow can be found in some winters). The adjacent planted corn field attracts large numbers of winterers by providing an easy food source. At other seasons the parking area provides a southern access

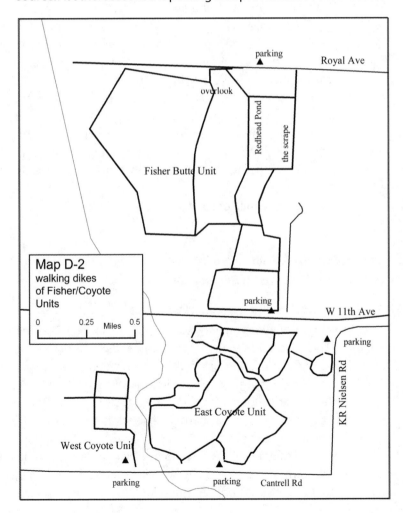

Map D-2
walking dikes
of Fisher/Coyote
Units

0   0.25   Miles   0.5

A birding group walks in to the southern access road in the Fisher Unit. Photo by Lydia Cruz.

(via the Fisher Unit) into the huge diked marshes. It is possible to walk all the way to Royal Ave. from the Fisher Butte parking area. By doing so one could expect to see many of the breeders in the marsh, which include Blue-winged Teal and Wilson's Phalarope.

The lot also provides access to the south sections of marsh (Coyote Units). Cross Hwy. 126 (*Note*: traffic can be extremely fast and heavy here) and walk into the East Coyote Unit marsh complex by going around the gate, across the tracks and walking in on the low dike. Don't worry, there is also easy access to the Coyote Units from Cantrell Rd. on the optional goose loop if the busy highway scares you.

Continue west for a mile or so on Hwy. 126 to Perkins Peninsula Park.

Optional Cantrell Road Goose Car-loop/East Coyote Unit Access OR Cantrell/K. R. Nielson Road Loop

Spring: **   *Summer:* **   *Fall:* ***   *Winter:* ****

After leaving Royal Ave., you may want to do the optional Cantrell Rd. loop. This road takes you through farmlands that often host huge flocks of Canada and Cackling Geese in winter. From Royal Ave. heading east, turn right on Fisher Rd. Take Fisher to Hwy. 126, then turn left toward Eugene. Take Hwy. 126 to K. R. Nielson Rd. and turn right; be careful—this is a sharp reverse-angle turn. Take K. R. Nielson until it turns to gravel.

In summer the power substation and nearby fenceline is a good place for Western Kingbird and the woodland edges sometimes have breeding Lazuli Buntings. In winter look for rare visitors such as Prairie Falcon, Rough-legged Hawk, or Golden Eagle on the power poles.

Stay on the road and look in the large fields for flocks. Just as you are forced to turn a sharp left there is a small lot for access to the southeastern section of marsh habitat (East Coyote Unit), which hosts similar birds to the Fisher Unit north of Hwy. 126. To continue the goose loop keep going south on K. R. Nielson Rd.

Turn right onto Cantrell as K. R. Nielson comes to an end. Less than a mile from this corner is a small lot to the north, which provides southern access to the Coyote Unit and its marsh birds. After Cantrell turns back to pavement, check for the Oregon Department of Fish and Wildlife headquarters on the right, stop in and grab a checklist; you may need it later and you will already have a lot of birds to check off. Red-shouldered Hawks often nest in this area and Band-tailed Pigeons can be heard cooing away in summer behind the office. Take Cantrell to Perkins Rd., then turn right and head to Hwy. 126. Across the highway is Perkins Peninsula Park.

Perkins Peninsula Park

 Spring: ******** *Summer:* ******   *Fall:* *******   *Winter:* *******

This site is wheelchair accessible with rest rooms. This is a *fee* site. Perkins Peninsula juts into the lake from the south. This creates a "funnel" effect and causes spring migration to be concentrated into the trees and bushes on the north side of the park. Check for early migrants such as Orange-crowned Warbler and Warbling Vireo by early April and expect many more through late May. In the large trees warbler flocks vary, but can include Yellow-rumped, Townsend's, and Black-throated Gray. Chipping Sparrow breeds in the more open southern section of the park.

The bushes in the north and east corners are worth checking anytime for an assortment of sparrows. Variety peaks in late winter and usually includes a White-throated Sparrow or two. Unusual species such as Lark Sparrow have been seen here in spring. The large oak trees at the north end of the park sometimes contain White-breasted Nuthatches or Acorn Woodpeckers, but both have declined around Eugene in the past 20 years and can be hard to find.

Near the west end of the park, south of the parking and swimming area, is a nature trail that includes a boardwalk over the marsh. In summer and late spring, the willows here are reliable for nesting Yellow Warblers and Willow Flycatchers. In summer, breeding Western and sometimes Clark's Grebes can be seen west of the swimming area if you use a scope. Look and especially listen for Swamp Sparrows in the reeds in winter.

This park is easily birded in an hour or two. It is an easy loop in either direction. Watch out for tourists in summer.

Zumwalt Park Area

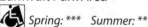 *Spring: *** Summer: ** Fall: *** Winter: ****

Wheelchair accessible. Portable rest rooms near parking area.

From Perkins Park, turn right and take Hwy. 126 west 1 to 2 miles to a right turn (just before the Dari-Mart) on Ellmaker Rd. Take this road north for 1 mile until it ends at a T intersection with Jeans Rd. Turn right onto Jeans Rd and follow it east for less than a mile to Zumwalt parking area and interpretive display. The parking area is not well marked; it is on the right in a dense stand of Douglas-fir just before Jeans Rd. makes a 90-degree turn left (north) at the edge of the reservoir. You will see a pipe gate blocking traffic from driving into the lake at this turn.

From this lot you can walk the paved trail into Zumwalt Park. There is marsh and riparian habitat on the way out to the park. Look for a curious Hutton's Vireo or a Black-capped Chickadee in the forest. The walk in is among the best areas for Wrentit in the Eugene area. The marshy area is good for Common Yellowthroat and Marsh Wren and you can't miss the Red-winged Blackbirds. There are many old trees in the park and warbler flocks mix with vireos and flycatchers in spring. Scan the lake for gulls, terns, and the occasional jaeger in fall.

From the parking area you can either take Jeans Rd. to its end, where you can access the Jeans Unit at Fern Ridge, or you can head to the dam. If you choose Jeans Rd., it is a great place to look for migrants; the funnel effect occurs here just as it does at Perkins. There are usually Bald Eagles near by and you can observe Purple Martin nesting on the nearby Osprey poles (which have boxes attached). Access is limited to a small, muddy parking area at the dead-end (be sure to lock your vehicle), but this area is worth a quick stop in spring through fall. In winter, walking to the end of the trail provides a superb look across the open mudflats and distant waters of Fern Ridge Reservoir. A scope is needed.

Dam Area, Richardson and Orchard Point Parks

*Spring: ****   Summer: ***   Fall: *****   Winter: *****

Easy wheelchair access to most areas (almost entirely paved, with exception of the dike portion of dam, which is gravel and flat on top). Rest rooms are available at parks.

From Zumwalt Park (or the end of Jeans Rd.) take Jeans Rd. west to its beginning in Veneta where it intersects with Territorial Hwy. This is a good time to stop for lunch if you are spending the whole day traveling around Fern Ridge, as there is a good variety of food choices at the market near the intersection and even more choices if you enter the town of Veneta by heading left (south) onto Territorial. Otherwise, take a right (north) on Territorial and head through the small town of Elmira on your way to the dam and north end of the reservoir.

It is about 5 miles to the dam turnoff, which is poorly marked (but does have a blinking yellow, traffic caution light). Turn right (east) onto Clear Lake Rd. and drive a quarter mile to the Richardson Park area (*note*: this is a *fee* area and is used heavily for recreation). The many small forested areas around the park can be good for migrants. There are also a lot of brushy areas to the north which create habitat for wintering birds such as sparrows. This site has even hosted Harris' Sparrow in the past, the most difficult to come by *Zonotrichia* sparrow in Lane Co. Scan the lake from the dock area as many gulls roost in the mud of the drawdown in winter; a recent unusual sighting was a Franklin's Gull.

From the park continue north, then east, on Clear Lake Rd., looking for Lesser Goldfinch on the fence posts of the surrounding houses. Just before the dam is the office of the Army Corps of Engineers. The Corps maintains the dam and most of the lake and they are a great source of information about birds, butterflies, flowers, and other wildlife. Stop in and grab a copy of the Fern Ridge Bird Checklist, updated by Noah Strycker in 2003. After visiting the Corps, head to the dam, which is just a few hundred yards past the headquarters. This is one of the best places to scan the lake. Look for odd gulls, loons, ducks, etc.

If you're lucky, you will visit after a large storm, as many oddities are often blown in. Some notable reports from this location include Leach's Storm-Petrel, Yellow-billed Loon, Parasitic and Pomarine Jaeger, Whimbrel, White-winged Scoter, Sabine's Gull, Black-legged

Kittiwake, and Oregon's only Lesser Black-backed Gull. If you walk the length of the dam, you will end up at Orchard Point Park which is quite similar to Richardson. A Great-tailed Grackle in the early 2000s made this park famous to bird enthusiasts in Lane Co. After you have finished scoping from the dam, head down to Kirk Park and Pond just below the dam.

Kirk Park and Pond

Spring: ****   Summer: ***   Fall: **   Winter: ***

Mostly wheelchair accessible. Some trails in the forest and around the pond are not. Rest rooms are available in the parking area.

Not long ago Kirk Pond (a borrow pit pond that has acquired its informal name from the adjacent park) earned a reputation for wintering waterfowl when it hosted Oregon's first Falcated Duck. It also hosted a dozen Eurasian Wigeon in one flock, a record for Lane Co. To bird this area start in the parking area near the dam, looking for Cliff Swallows nesting on the dam and listening for chats downriver. As you walk through the park soak in the ethereal song of the Swainson's Thrush. White-breasted Nuthatches can be found in the oaks, as can other breeders like Western Wood-Pewee, Western Scrub Jay, and Brown Creeper. Towards the east end of the park is Kirk forest, a large stand of fairly old riparian trees. The east end of the pond is where Greater Scaup are usually found.

There are trails leading through the forest to the east end of Kirk Pond. This forest hosts a large variety of western breeders but can be difficult to access. Egrets often congregate in large flocks during winter, when Western Bluebirds are usually around in small flocks. Osprey always nest in the top of one of the old snags in summer. Look for rails around the marshy areas in the same season.

From Kirk Park you can continue north on Clear Lake Rd. You can either go back into Eugene or you can loop back to Royal Ave. and do it all over again. Don't let this book limit your explorations of Fern Ridge. There are many trails and areas of limited access that host an abundance of wildlife. Check in with the Corps or Oregon Department of Fish and Wildlife and get more information. There is vast opportunity for wildlife discovery around every corner; don't miss out.

Junction City Area

Barbara Combs

With contributions from Dave Brown

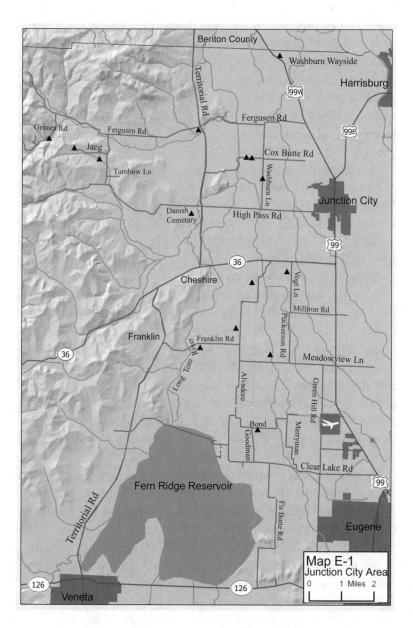

Spring: ***   *Summer:* **   *Fall:* **   *Winter:* ***

The rural roads northwest of Eugene and south of Junction City are popular from late fall to early spring for birders seeking out overwintering waterfowl and possible rarities.

Wheelchair access to specific sites in this region is generally poor, but most of the area can be covered only by car anyway. Availability of accessible rest rooms is limited. Washburne State Wayside, at the north end of the area on the Lane/Benton Co. line, is one place to stop. Some businesses and public areas in Junction City have accessible rest rooms. For the price of short-term parking, it is possible to go inside the Eugene airport on Greenhill Rd. and use the accessible rest rooms near the baggage claim area on the left side of the building. Parks at Fern Ridge Reservoir offer accessible rest room facilities, but many of these are closed from fall through spring.

This is one of the best areas in the county to find sizeable flocks of Tundra Swans, as well as several raptor species. Trumpeter Swan, Rough-legged Hawk, Bald Eagle, Golden Eagle, Merlin, Prairie Falcon, Peregrine Falcon, Short-eared Owl, and Burrowing Owl are all possibilities in the winter, in addition to the more common species, Red-tailed Hawk and American Kestrel. Snowy Owl has been found in some years at the airport.

Look for Bald Eagle especially in lambing season (January/ February), patrolling the fields for afterbirth. Milliron Rd. (not listed below) has been a productive location for Bald Eagle as well as Rough-legged Hawk. A group of three Swainson's Hawks spent several days in this area in September 2004. Harris's (rare) and White-throated Sparrows are possible in brushy thickets anywhere. Flocks of Horned Larks use the fields at times, although their numbers seem to have fallen over the last 30 years. Other locally rare species to be looked for include Cattle Egret, Mountain Plover (two records just to the north in Benton County), Black-bellied Plover, American Golden-Plover, Mountain Bluebird, Snow Bunting, and longspurs.

The arrival and abundance of migrants and wintering species are dependent upon a number of factors, including the status of prey and habitat further north (water frozen over or open) and the availability of prey and habitat in this area. A normal amount of rainfall in the season ensures that there will be much suitable habitat for shorebirds and waterfowl. A healthy vole population means there will be good birding for raptors. Some sites are also good places to enjoy local birds during the breeding season.

The area extends from Hwy. 99 north of Eugene to the Benton Co. border, and west to the towns of Alvadore, Franklin, and Cheshire. Some of these roads are heavily traveled, so it is important to be especially cautious when stopping along the road to bird. Be sure to find a safe pullout completely out of the traffic lanes when birding this area. Places along the road that have been paved or graveled to be used as tractor entrances to farm fields can work well as pullout spots. Don't leave your car blocking a farm road or field access. Some small bridges have extra wide paved areas before and/or after their guard rails that can be used as pullouts. Road shoulders may be very soft so it is important to be cautious when pulling off to the side to get out of the way of traffic.

While the directions below show how to get to some specific sites in the area, the strategy employed by most birders will simply be to drive around on all of the roads, stopping where something draws their attention. Tundra Swans, in particular, tend to move around in the area so the field in which they were found on one day may be devoid of any waterfowl on the next. Swans also use other areas, some to the east of Hwy. 99 and some along Hwy. 99E toward or beyond Harrisburg (Linn Co.), so it is worth checking these locations if swans are known to be present but cannot be located in the area mapped here. Some places that have been favored by swans include the intersection of Meadowview Rd. and Purkerson Rd. and the field west of Vogt Rd. at its intersection with State Hwy. 36.

Wherever there is a flock of geese, unusual species such as Greater White-fronted Goose, Brant, Emperor Goose, Snow Goose, or Ross's Goose may be in the flock, so check each flock carefully. Side-by-side comparisons of Cackling and Canada Geese are possible in this area. From fall to spring, clouds of hundreds of Dunlin may rise from the wet fields, delighting passing birders with their synchronized flight. Killdeer nest in the area and tend to feed in large groups in wet fields during the winter. Scan for unusual species such as Mountain Plover wherever a large flock of Killdeer is feeding.

The following list is a sample of nice birding spots in this area with places to pull off the road safely. Directions are given from Hwy. 99 for each, but many of them can be reached more quickly by using side roads shown on the map instead of going back to Hwy. 99.

Washburne Wayside

Travel to Junction City on Hwy. 99. Take the left fork (Hwy. 99W) at the traffic signal where Hwy. 99W and Hwy. 99E split near the Safeway at the north end of town. Travel about 4.25 miles north and turn right into the parking lot for the highway rest area on the east side of the road. This small woodsy oasis can provide good birding for passerines, especially during spring migration and breeding season. A Hooded Warbler was found here in July 1974.

Pond at Ferguson Rd. and Territorial Highway

Travel to Junction City and take the left fork (Hwy. 99W) at the traffic signal where Hwy. 99W and Hwy. 99E split near the Safeway at the north end of town. Drive about 1.9 miles and turn left (west) on Ferguson Rd. Drive west on Ferguson Rd. about 3.4 miles to the blinking light where it intersects with Territorial Hwy. The pond is at the southwest corner of this intersection. There are good places to pull off the road at this corner. A variety of ducks, geese, and grebes take refuge on this pond; take care not to spook them when you exit your vehicle. Pied-billed Grebe, Wood Duck, Hooded Merganser, American Wigeon, and Ring-necked Duck are all possible. Canada Goose and American Coot (and possibly other waterfowl) breed here. Check the adjacent habitat for passerines, as well.

Danish Cemetery

Travel to Junction City and turn west off of Hwy. 99 at the traffic light near the southern end of town amid a mass of recreational vehicle and car dealership lots where a sign says "To High Pass Road." Follow this road for about 4.2 miles to Territorial Hwy. Cross Territorial Hwy. and continue another 0.3 miles to the cemetery's driveway. Turn left (south) up the driveway. Flooded fields near the cemetery provide waterfowl habitat during the wet season. The cemetery itself has nice habitat for passerines. Dark-eyed Junco has nested here.

Washburn Lane/Cox Butte Road

Note: signage spells the name both Washburn and Washburne.

Travel to Junction City and turn west off of Hwy. 99 at the traffic light near the southern end of town amid a mass of recreational vehicle and car dealership lots where a sign says "To High Pass Road." Drive about 2.3 miles and turn north (right) on Washburn Lane, a gravel road. After about 0.9 miles, extensive areas on both sides of the road have been developed into waterfowl habitat by private interests. In winter, it is possible to stop and scope out a wide variety of waterfowl from this road, but please do not trespass on the private property.

From the initial stop on Washburn Lane, drive 0.6 miles north to Cox Butte Rd., turn left and drive 0.3 miles to find a small pullout on the north side of the road. Park here and view the wildlife area to the south of the road. Bald Eagles sometimes sit in the trees along this portion of the road. Golden Eagle and Peregrine Falcon may also be present in the area, mostly outside of the breeding season. A wetland area about 0.2 miles further west down Cox Butte Rd. can be productive for birding in any season.

Fern Ridge Hunt Club/East of Franklin

Travel north from Eugene on Hwy. 99 about 2.7 miles past its intersection with Airport Rd. Turn west (left) onto Meadowview Rd. and drive about 2 miles to the Fern Ridge Hunt Club, where there is a group of ponds on the north side of the road. There are several places to pull off the road nearby. Please do not trespass on this private property. Waterfowl sometimes find ponds like these when they are looking for a place to land at night and they see light reflected off the water. These birds often remain only until human disturbance begins in the morning hours. These ponds and others like them may be most productive when it is just getting to be light enough to see.

From the hunt club, continue about another 1.0 miles west on Meadowview Rd. to the T intersection with Alvadore Rd. Turn north (right) on Alvadore Rd. After a little less than 0.5 miles, turn left (west) on Franklin Rd. Within a mile you will arrive at an area with habitat that hosts waterfowl during the wet season. Pullouts are available in several places along the road. Some non-waterfowl species that may be seen in this area during the winter months include Great Egret, Short-eared Owl, American Pipit, and Lapland Longspur.

Vogt Lane/State Highway 36

From the traffic signal on Hwy. 99 for Airport Rd., drive about 5.7 miles north on Hwy. 99 to the traffic signal for State Hwy. 36. Turn left at this traffic signal. Drive about 1.3 miles to the intersection with Vogt Lane and turn left (south). It is possible to pull off the road at the side of the substation driveway on Vogt Rd. just south of this intersection; however, the view of the field behind the substation is partially blocked from this location.

Just south of the substation, there are two suitable pullout spots that are used as tractor entrances to the field. Both of these have unobstructed views. Tundra Swans sometimes use the large field at the southwest corner of this intersection. Trumpeter or even Whooper Swan (not yet recorded in Lane Co. but found in Klamath and Polk Co.) may be present in large swan flocks so such flocks should be scoped out with care.

Hunting Area along Alvadore Rd. South of Highway 36

From the traffic signal on Hwy. 99 for Airport Rd., drive about 5.7 miles north on Hwy. 99 to the traffic signal for State Hwy. 36. Turn left at the traffic signal. Drive about 1.9 miles to the intersection of State Hwy. 36 with Alvadore Rd. Turn left (south) and drive about 0.8 miles. There is a pullout for a private hunting area on the west side of the road. Watch for the silhouette of a quail on the gate and amusing signage posted nearby. Birders face almost directly west at this location so it is best surveyed early in the day except when there is much cloud cover. It is usually a good place to find waterfowl from fall to spring. Rough-legged Hawk, Cooper's Hawk, Peregrine Falcon, and Short-eared Owl have all been seen at this location.

Jaeg Road

Travel north from Eugene on Hwy. 99 to Junction City. At the first traffic signal at the south end of town (amid a mass of car and recreational vehicle dealership lots), turn left (west). There is a sign on the right side of the road indicating that this turn will lead to High Pass Rd. Travel about 7.7 miles west on this road from Junction City. Turn right on Turnbow Lane. After about 0.9 miles, turn left on Jaeg Rd., a short road that dead-ends at a winery (Pfeiffer Vineyards).

The winery and April's Acres Alpacas, at the corner of Jaeg Rd. and Turnbow Lane, are both open on weekends as part of the Long

Tom Country Trail. Obtain a brochure for the trail by calling 1-877-276-8636 or visiting the website at OregonCountryTrails.com. The trail includes a wide variety of places to visit in the area covered here, many with birding opportunities and rest-room facilities, so that a non-birder on the trip can have an enjoyable time while the birder is offered access to private areas not otherwise open to the public.

A female Wild Turkey with its brood of small young, as well as a persistently singing House Wren, were present at April's Acres in July 2005. White-tailed Kites may be seen along Jaeg Rd. A juvenile was found here during the fieldwork period for the Oregon Breeding Bird Atlas project. At about 0.7 miles down Jaeg Rd. there is a small pond with a duck-sized nest box visible on the south side of the road. Hooded Merganser has been seen here. Bullock's Oriole and Warbling Vireo are among the species present during the breeding season.

At the end of the road, about 0.2 miles past this pond, Pfeiffer Vineyards offers wine tastings and other hospitality services. On the grounds is a large pond that harbors a variety of ducks, especially in the winter. Vaux's Swift is abundant here during the breeding season. Watch for them especially in the evening in summer as they gather to perform mosquito control over the ponds. The lovely pond at Pfeiffer Vineyards is not visible from the public road.

Bond Road

Travel north from Eugene on Hwy. 99 about 0.5 miles past the Beltline overpass to Clear Lake Rd. Turn left (west) and drive 3.9 miles to Goodman Rd. Turn right (north) and drive about 1.1 miles to Bond Rd. Turn right onto this gravel road. When there has been a lot of rain, a portion of this road (about 0.4-0.5 miles to the east of the turnoff) may be flooded, so watch out for road conditions in times of wet weather.

The fields to the south of this road can be full of waterfowl and shorebirds when conditions are suitable. Birders along this road are infrequently disturbed by passing traffic. Bird along the road as it curves around to the left and then to the right. A Blue Grosbeak was found one winter near the spot where the road bends to the right; it seems possible to find almost any species here if the roadside is carefully scrutinized.

At the T intersection, turn right on Merryman Rd. and follow it as it curves around the back side of the Eugene airport. At the south end of the road, a left turn onto Kokkeler Rd., where there is a dead end to the right and a right turn almost immediately afterward where the road ahead is closed, will lead to an intersection with Clear Lake Rd. A left turn on to Clear Lake Rd. will take you back to Hwy. 99. A right turn will take you to the dam at Fern Ridge Reservoir.

Grimes Road

Travel north from Eugene through Junction City. Take the left fork (Hwy. 99W) at the traffic signal where Hwy. 99W and Hwy. 99E split near the Safeway at the north end of town. Drive about 1.9 miles and turn left (west) on Ferguson Rd. Drive about 8 miles to Grimes Rd. and turn left (south).

The highlight of the road is a marsh that is centered about 1.1 miles south of Ferguson Rd.; Common Yellowthroat, Willow Flycatcher, and Virginia Rail are all attracted to this marsh. Extensive riparian habitat along this road precedes the marsh area. Many local passerine species such as House Wren, Song Sparrow, Cedar Waxwing, American Goldfinch, and Olive-sided Flycatcher inhabit the drier areas nearby. Very little traffic passes on this road, making the birding experience here especially enjoyable. During wet periods, a flooded road at the marsh may prevent further travel.

From the marsh, birders may go back to Ferguson Rd. or continue on up Grimes Rd. to take advantage of birding opportunities in the Coast Range. The road is paved for at least 2.7 miles from Ferguson Rd. and offers birding both in deep woods and in clear-cut areas.

Eugene and Adjacent Wetlands

Steve Gordon

The City of Eugene and the metropolitan region have a marvelous park system, enhanced by past cooperation among the City, Lane Co., State Parks, Bureau of Land Management, The Nature Conservancy, and McKenzie River Trust. The Corps facility at Fern Ridge serves as an important resource to Lane Co. birders.

With 2,902 acres of parks and 30 miles of off-street paths, Eugene is renowned as a great place to enjoy the outdoors and nature

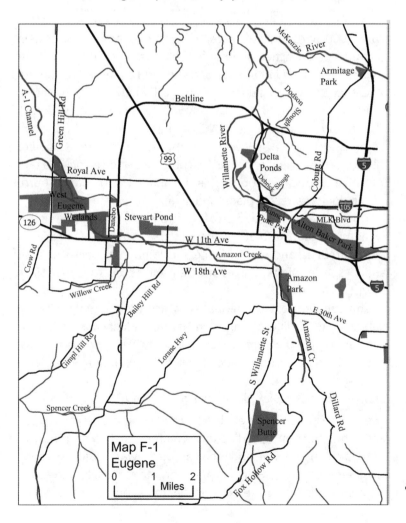

Map F-1
Eugene
0   1   2
|___|___| Miles

within a city. Alton Baker Park, Skinner Butte Park, and Delta Ponds are linked along the Willamette River Greenway Park system by 12.5 miles of paths and five footbridges over the Willamette. Few American cities can rival our Greenway for river access; we get to enjoy America's thirteenth-largest river (by volume), an American Heritage River, the Willamette.

The paved Fern Ridge Path parallels Amazon Creek from the Fairgrounds to Meadowlark Prairie for a distance of 6 miles. The entire length offers wheelchair access and many opportunities to observe birds, wildflowers, native prairie, and other wildlife.

WEST EUGENE WETLANDS

Spring ****	Summer **	Fall ***	Winter ****

With 3,000 acres of open space, the west Eugene wetland system is a growing attraction among local birders. Since 1992, the *West Eugene Wetland Plan* has provided the public policy direction for a partnership that includes the City of Eugene (City), Bureau of Land Management (BLM), U.S. Army Corps of Engineers (Corps), The Nature Conservancy (TNC), Oregon Youth Conservation Commission, McKenzie River Trust, and the Willamette Resources and Educational Network (WREN), to purchase land, restore habitats, inform and educate the public, and manage this natural resource system for its variety of plants and animals.

This area was created to preserve rare wetlands and a rare plant community, the Willamette Valley wet prairie; a suite of rare plants; rare butterflies; and other wildlife, including 204 species of birds and 39 species of dragonflies and damselflies recorded here since 1974.

This section treats three places, which have slightly different habitats and birdlife: 1) Bertelsen Nature Park, including Stewart and Sandpiper Ponds and Bertelsen Slough; 2) Meadowlark Prairie; and 3) The Nature Conservancy's Willow Creek Natural Area.

Stewart Pond Complex (Bertelsen Nature Park)

The first stop is the Bertelsen Nature Park with Stewart, Grimes, and Sandpiper ponds, and Bertelsen Slough. From West 11th Ave., turn north on Bertelsen and then east on Stewart Rd. just after you cross Amazon Creek. Pull over and scan the seasonal pond across from Euphoria Chocolate Co. This is a good spot to find dabbling

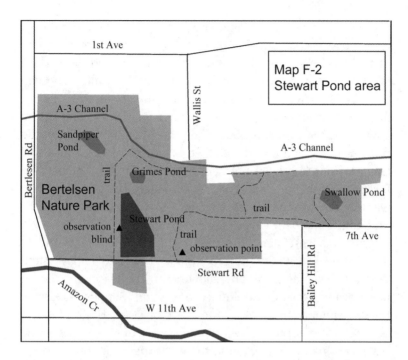

ducks, gulls, and shorebirds, and a good spot to find Eurasian Wigeon in winter. Continue up the road and park in the lot near the barricade.

Take time to scan Stewart Pond and the habitat around the parking lot. The nearby trees are a good place to find some forest species, like Red-breasted Nuthatch. Lazuli Bunting in spring and summer and wintering sparrow flocks can be found in the brushy areas along the fence rows and the path. Stewart Pond is becoming overgrown and has not been as productive for waterbirds as it was 10 years ago, but was cleared in 2005 to improve waterbird habitat. Rare birds found at Stewart Pond have included Ruff, American Avocet, Eurasian Green-winged Teal, and Black Tern. This spot can be great for shorebird migration with two species of Phalaropes (Wilson's and Red-necked), Semipalmated Plover, and Solitary Sandpiper, as well as migrating Virginia Rails and Sora. Five species of Swallows have been seen perched near Stewart Pond at one time. Green Heron frequently visit Stewart Pond.

Follow the path to the base of Stewart Knoll and the Malik trail. The ash-oak forests are good for songbirds, Black-capped Chickadees, Downy Woodpecker, Black-headed Grosbeak, and Bewick's Wren. Follow the boardwalk through the ash-oak forest wetlands to the A-3 Channel and 5th Ave. Continue westward to the overlook at Teal Slough and Grimes Pond. Three species of teal (Green-winged, Cinnamon, and Blue-winged) have been seen here at one time. Overhead in peak spring migration you can often find five swallow species and Vaux's Swift. Once a Black Swift was observed here. Scope Grimes Pond for diving ducks; sometimes Ring-necked Duck is the most common duck on the pond, but Hooded Merganser, Pied-billed Grebe, Great Blue and Green Herons, Ruddy Duck, American Coot, Spotted Sandpiper, and Belted Kingfisher are frequently encountered. This pond is best in wet months. In summer, it is a hot spot for over a dozen species of dragonflies and damselflies.

Continue west along the dike on the south side of the A-3 Channel. The woods here are good places to find Western Wood-Pewee and Common Yellowthroat. The teasel in adjacent fields attract American Goldfinch and Lazuli Bunting. Also look for Red-shouldered Hawk in these ash-oak woods. Continue to the south and approach Sandpiper Pond to the west. This is one place with permanent water in the wetlands. Its shores are great places for shorebirds, many kinds of ducks winter here (similar to those found in Grimes Pond), and swallows glide over the water in large numbers. Semipalmated Sandpiper has been seen here in fall migration and Palm Warbler has wintered here. Continue south along the hedgerow toward Stewart Rd. Watch for Western Kingbird, Savannah and "Crowned" Sparrows, and warblers along the way. You can return to the parking lot from here, but watch the wetlands south of the road and the trees on the south edge of Stewart Pond. Sometimes in spring migration, warblers flit across the road and drip from these short trees at nearly eye level. These trees are sometimes teeming with Yellow-rumped Warblers (Myrtle and Audubon's), which can number close to one hundred here.

Meadowlark Prairie

The second stop is Meadowlark Prairie on Greenhill Rd. just south of Royal Ave. A parking area, picnic tables, interpretive signs, and portable toilets make this a convenient stop. Previously, this area was called "Amazon Flats" or the "Lower Amazon Project." It is the site of a $6 million City, Corps, and BLM restoration project that covers 400 acres. The levees along Amazon Creek and the Diversion, "A," and A-3 Channels were removed. Amazon Creek's floodplain

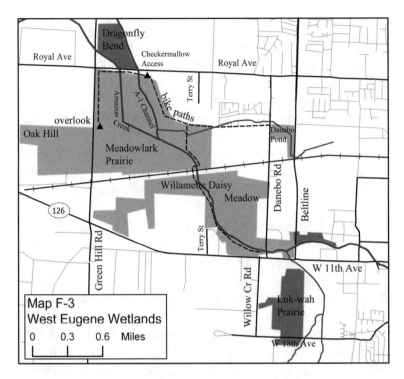

Map F-3
West Eugene Wetlands
0   0.3   0.6   Miles

spreads onto restored wetlands. From the paved viewing area, you get a bird's view of a current birding "hot spot." You can find ducks, shorebirds, swallows, and birds of prey.

Among exciting observations here in the past few years are: Eurasian Wigeon, Black-necked Stilt, Wilson's and Red-necked Phalaropes, Solitary Sandpiper, Blue-winged Teal, Bald Eagle, Peregrine Falcon, Rough-legged Hawk, White-tailed Kite, Northern Harrier, and five species of swallows (Tree, Violet-green, Northern Rough-winged, Barn, and Cliff). Numerous nesting and wintering Western Meadowlarks are one of the real treats here.

A new paved path allows you to walk for 3 miles atop a berm at the edge of the floodplain to observe this wonderful site from its periphery. Take the time to view the Cascades (you can see the Three Sisters at times). You will also have excellent views of the Coast Range, Coburg Hills, and Eugene's South Hills. Signs and a self-guided tour, complete with informational bronze plaques imbedded in the path, aid interpretation of this prairie habitat. In winter watch for Short-eared Owls hunting over the fields (seven were counted on a recent Christmas Bird Count). Future plans call for extending this path westward to Fern Ridge.

Willow Creek Natural Area

The last wetland spot is the Willow Creek Natural Area owned by The Nature Conservancy. Drive south on Greenhill Rd. to West 11th Ave. Travel east to Bertelsen Rd. and turn south. At its intersection with West 18th Ave., turn west to reach the Willow Creek site. Park at the westernmost parking pull-out on the north side of West 18th Ave. Cross 18th to the east side of the west branch of Willow Creek. Here an old fire break road leads south along the creek. Watch for beaver dams and dragonflies. Stay on the fire break path to avoid trampling any rare plants and stay between flags that warn you of sensitive plant locations.

This road loops eastward near a grove of fir trees, a good spot for finding Hutton's Vireo. Then the trail loops back toward 18th Ave. along the west side of the east branch of Willow Creek. Willow Creek is a good place to find Red-shouldered Hawk, Willow Flycatcher, Yellow-breasted Chat, Wrentit, Black-headed Grosbeak, Lazuli Bunting, and other songbirds. Ash-throated Flycatcher (October) and White-throated Sparrow (December) have been found here. Long-eared Owls have been seen and heard here more than from any other location in Eugene. The highlight occurs in April, May, or June when the camas and other wildflowers are in full bloom. This site is a jewel in the wetlands and the best remaining prairie in any Oregon city.

As you visit these sites, take a moment to appreciate these unique wetlands and the agencies that, with great public support from many sides, set them aside for the plants, birds, and your pleasure. Come visit them in all seasons; just be sure to wear your boots in winter. While focused on protection of rare plants, the collective of land managers are now studying ways to make better habitat improvements for wildlife. Bird viewing at these sites can be expected to improve over time.

Skinner Butte

Spring ****   *Summer* **   *Fall* ***   *Winter* ***

The loop trail atop the Butte and the path along the Willamette River are both paved. The loop trail follows an old asphalt road that is now closed to traffic. In places it is beginning to deteriorate, and needs patch work to maintain its accessibility.

The 110–acre Skinner Butte Park includes the forested butte and adjacent riverfront park and trail extending from the Ferry Street Bridge and DeFazio bike bridge west to the Jefferson-Washington Street Bridge across from Valley River Center. The Butte provides excellent views of the surrounding cities, the Willamette River, the Cascades, and Spencer Butte, and is of historical significance to Eugeneans. Over 140 species of birds have been recorded in the park. It is a premier place to watch the spring landbird migration.

Marie Winn's *Red-Tails in Love* was not only a story about Central Park in New York and hawks, but also about the gathering of bird watchers who enjoyed birding Central Park. Skinner Butte serves that purpose in Eugene. At the peak of spring migration, you can not only find ten species of warblers and three species of vireos, but you can find twenty local birding acquaintances and a college class or nature club touring the Butte. You see friends you haven't seen in a year. This is especially true on weekend mornings, but can occur during the week among retirees and those who benefit from the Eugene life-style; that is, those fortunate people who don't work 8:00 to 5:00 for five days a week.

The Butte was the 1846 home of Eugene Skinner, the founder and first mayor of Eugene in 1852. Eugeneans began protection of the Butte in 1908, and continue that process through today. The City recently developed a master plan for the Park that includes native habitat restoration and thinning of some non-native trees that are crowding out the views from the south side of the Butte.

To reach the Butte from the intersection of 11th Ave. and Willamette Street, turn north on Olive one block past Willamette, and continue north to 5th Ave. Turn east on 5th and go to the stop sign at Pearl Street. Turn north again onto Pearl and cross the railroad tracks, continuing north to 3rd Ave. Turn west (left) on 3rd and enter the Park. Soon you will come to an intersection; turn sharply right up the hill and climb to the parking lot on top. Drive carefully here; the road is narrow and cars, pedestrians, joggers, and bicyclists share the narrow lanes. Another option is to park near the bottom of the Butte and walk to the top through the cedar forest on the south side of the Butte. This is a good way to find Chestnut-backed Chickadee and Hutton's Vireo. Cooper's Hawks have nested among these cedars for the past few years.

The Butte is a migrant trap located just north of downtown. Sitting high above the city and the river, it attracts birds migrating at night to land on the south side of the Butte and begin feeding. They work their way toward the top as the morning progresses. If you are on top by 7:00 or 8:00 a.m., you should see the peak of the movement as migrants fly across the opening on the Butte and feed among the oaks, cherries, firs, and cedars along the edge.

The north side of the Butte is heavily forested with Douglas-fir and grand fir with big leaf maples straining for sunlight under the taller conifers. This part of the loop trail is good year round for forest species like Brown Creeper, Winter Wren, Golden-crowned Kinglet, and Chestnut-backed Chickadee. In winter, Varied Thrush feed along the trail. In spring both Hermit and Swainson's Thrushes pass through the Park. During peak spring migration in late April, you can watch dozens of Western Tanagers along the loop. Osprey have nested on a nesting platform provided by the local Rotary Club. Great Horned Owls also have nested among the conifers on the north slope. One winter a Red-naped Sapsucker showed up here on the Christmas Bird Count. Another winter treat in an invasion year was Mountain Chickadees mixed among the Black-cappeds and Chestnut-sideds. A maze of dirt trails crisscrosses the north side and can be followed to the base of the Butte on the river side; in early spring and winter this option can be muddy and slippery.

As you work around the loop, listen for mixed flocks of birds. The northwest corner of the loop trail is often a hot spot. At this corner and near the parking lot are two good locations for Lesser Goldfinch. There is a clearing on the east side of the Butte that is worth checking. In spring it is a good place to find sparrows, Calliope Hummingbird, and numerous flycatchers. You can follow dirt paths around the Butte onto the north side, or return to the parking area from the clearing.

The parking lot offers great views of Eugene, the McKenzie River gap, and the Eugene South Hills, and is worth checking for Anna's Hummingbirds, which often perch atop small trees. Just below the parking lot is a water reservoir. Check out this area—it once hosted a Gray Flycatcher. In mid-morning in early May, scan the Vaux's Swift masses for Black Swift. Twice they have been seen mixed with the Vaux's. Other unusual spring birds discovered on the Butte are Ash-throated Flycatcher on the north slope, Sandhill Crane flocks overhead, and once a flock of White-faced Ibis overhead. After tree clearing on the south slope in 2004, a flock of Western Bluebirds showed up—bird number 141 on the Butte list.

The paved path along the Willamette River below the Butte is good for riparian species and waterbirds. Lesser and Greater Scaup are found in rafts on the river. Six species of gulls have been identified flying up and down the river. In winter, American Dipper has been found on occasion working among the rootlets on the Willamette's banks. A Black-and-white Warbler worked among the cottonwoods one winter. In late spring Willow Flycatchers and Yellow Warblers can be found among the willows along the Willamette.

You can continue on the Willamette River path in either direction from Skinner Butte Park. You can continue downstream to the Maurie Jacobs landing and study gulls in winter. Or you can continue downstream and cross the Valley River footbridge to bird Delta Ponds. Upstream from Skinner Butte, you can cross the DeFazio footbridge and bird Alton Baker Park. Or you can visit the 5th Street Market on a cold winter morning for a pastry and hot coffee or chocolate after a successful birding trip to Skinner Butte.

Delta Ponds and the East Bank Bike Path

Spring ****	Summer **	Fall **	Winter ****

Portions of this site are currently accessible from the Valley River Center parking lot on the paved path along the East Bank Willamette River. Future plans for paths at Delta Ponds will provide more wheelchair access in the future.

The East Bank path is part of Eugene's Willamette Greenway park and trail system, and the East Bank path passes through and connects to Delta Ponds. The 125-acre Delta Ponds City Park was once an old sand and gravel extraction site. The river and ponds attract water and riparian birds, with 116 species on the checklist. It is an excellent place for close observation of winter waterfowl. In the breeding season, it is a good place to find Green Heron, Wood Duck, and Willow Flycatcher. Delta Ponds is scheduled for a $5 million restoration and trail expansion project by the City and U.S.

Army Corps of Engineers beginning in 2005. This park is within the Willamette River Greenway and floodplain.

From downtown Eugene at the intersection of Willamette Street and 11th Ave., drive west 0.4 miles and turn north onto Washington Street. At West 6th Ave., continue north onto the on-ramp northward over the Washington-Jefferson Street Bridge and across the Willamette River. As you cross the river, stay in the right lane and take the Delta Hwy./Valley River exit that loops under I-105 and leads north on Delta Hwy. Merge into one of the two right-hand lanes and turn east at the first exit to Valley River Center. Stay in one of the two right-hand lanes and loop over Delta Hwy. heading west on Valley River Drive. At its intersection with Goodpasture Island Rd. (on the northwest end of the Valley River Shopping Center by Marie Callendar's restaurant), turn north and continue to Wimbleton Drive. While there are two small gravel parking places along Goodpasture Island Rd. (a new parking lot is planned in this location), it is safer to park along Wimbleton.

The Delta Ponds are located on Goodpasture Island along old meanders and sloughs that were once part of the Willamette River. In 1979, the City purchased 85 acres as part of its Willamette River Greenway park system with funds from a 1976 parks bond passed by Eugene voters. The Delta Ponds are wonderful remnants of an old gravel mining operation. The gravel pits are now filled with water and the dikes between the ponds provide good walking access to the area.

Habitats include the open water and surrounding shallow shores that contain emergent vegetation, such as cattails. The riparian boundaries include willow, black cottonwood, and red alder, typical of Willamette River shoreline habitats. Water movement through the ponds is slow in summer and as water temperatures rise, the ponds are clogged by thick mats of algae.

Wildlife at Delta Ponds includes active beavers, nutria, and 116 species of birds, including herons, Bald Eagle, Osprey, swallows, and many species of songbirds. Sometimes river otters visit the ponds from the nearby Willamette River. These mammals always provide an exciting show with their active behaviors. During the winter, the ponds host a variety of waterbirds represented by Pied-billed Grebe, Double-crested Cormorant, Canada Goose, Mallard, Gadwall, American Wigeon, Ring-necked Duck, and American Coot. The "rattling" call of Belted Kingfisher can be heard as they fly over the ponds hunting for small fish. From the willows and alders, Red-winged Blackbirds begin singing their familiar song as the males stake out nesting territories in early spring. In fall, Cedar Waxwings sally forth from willow and cottonwood branches to catch small flying insects. The ponds are an excellent place to visit on an early spring day. The Canada Geese are matched in mating pairs. Early-arriving Tree Swallows flit above the ponds snatching flying insects. Scan the fallen logs at the ponds' edges for western pond turtles basking in the sun. Among the willows you may spot an early Mourning Cloak butterfly which has come out of its winter hibernation. In the Eugene area, this large dark butterfly with a broad yellow border on its wings is usually the first butterfly to be seen in the spring.

From Wimbleton, cross Goodpasture Island Rd. and walk 100 yards north along the sidewalk. Scan the northwestern pond for waterbirds. Similarly, from the sidewalk, scan the open ponds south of Wimbleton. A new parking lot along Goodpasture Island Rd. is located at the north end of the ponds and will connect to a new path along the north end.

About 300 yards south of Wimbleton, look for a "Stream Team" sign on the east side of the road, indicating the Delta Ponds trailhead. The Friends of Delta Ponds have assisted in improving the trails into the ponds. Scan the south pond from the trail. The Delta Ponds are one of the best places in Eugene to view Gadwall. This duck with subtle coloring has a dark bill and a broad black area under its tail. Scan the cottonwoods east of Delta Hwy. and you will see a Great Blue Heron heronry (with seven active nests in 2005). In February, when the herons return to the heronry, you can watch their mating displays and nest building before the cottonwoods leaf out.

Follow the trail as it turns northward. It passes many side trails that offer views of ponds on both sides of the trail. In the blackberries, Song Sparrows and Spotted (formerly Rufous-sided) Towhees are common. In spring, watch for tiny gray Bushtits building their pendulous nests just above eye level in the maples, alders, and cottonwoods. In spring, check the cottonwoods for migrants; in winter and early spring, large flocks of Yellow-rumped Warblers frequent these trees. Look for signs of beavers where small trees and branches have been gnawed with chisel-sharp incisors.

At the ponds' shallow edges, stop to explore pond life. Water boatmen, water beetles, pollywogs, and nymphs swim among the submerged plants and water striders take advantage of water tension to skip along the pond surface. Dragonflies and damselflies zing over the ponds and land on emergent plants.

As you retrace your steps and leave the trail system, cross Goodpasture Island Rd. and walk north along the sidewalk back to Wimbleton. Scan the ponds on the west side of the Rd. for more waterfowl and songbirds among the cottonwoods.

To explore the East Bank Path, return south on Goodpasture Island Rd. to the Valley River Center parking lot. Drive west and park near the paved path. This new extension to the Greenway path system leads north and crosses Delta Ponds near the connection to the Willamette River. Be careful of bicycles zooming along the path. This path leads north 3 miles to the Owosso bike bridge and passes through good riparian habitat. This trail is excellent for Black-headed Grosbeak, Western Wood-Pewee, warblers, and typical riparian birds like chickadees, creepers, nuthatches, and various sparrows. Scan the river for Common Merganser and both Lesser and Greater Scaup in winter. The East Bank trail passes some of the Delta Ponds, so look for many of the same species mentioned in the pond description above. At the Owosso bridge, you can turn around to return to Valley River Center, or cross the Willamette and take the West Bank loop path south to the Valley River bridge. Cross this bridge and you return to the parking lot. This stretch of the river is a good place to find an occasional Bald Eagle or Peregrine Falcon in winter and Osprey in late spring and summer. In the fall, hundreds of Cedar Waxwings make wide sallies over the river flycatching for insects. In the winter, at least 200 Double-crested Cormorants roost at night along this segment of the Willamette River.

This site will become easier to access in the near future and new trails and bike path connections will make it even better for birding observation. Extensive pond modifications and replanting of native plants will enhance birding here in the near future. This park is a gem in the rough.

Hendricks Park

Spring ****	*Summer* **	*Fall* ***	*Winter* **

Wheelchair Access: Limited

Hendricks Park is Eugene's oldest park, started with a 10-acre donation to the city. Located along the Judkins Point ridge, this 78-acre park contains the Rhododendron Garden and extensive old-growth conifer forest. Trails weave throughout the forest, providing ample birding opportunities.

To reach Hendricks Park from downtown Eugene, travel east on Broadway Street and continue east on Franklin Boulevard past the University of Oregon. Turn south on Walnut Street and continue to Fairmount Boulevard. After traveling about two blocks, turn east onto Summit and go up into the park. Parking spaces for about 40 cars can be found near the Rhododendron Garden. From there you can bird along the paved road (watch for vehicles) or hike the trails among 200-year old Douglas-firs.

This park and the Rhododendron Garden are wonderful in spring, when the oaks in the garden may teem with warblers, vireos, and other neotropical migrants. Hendricks Park is another spot in Eugene to find Pileated Woodpecker, which is fairly regular in the park. Forest birds similar to those found at Spencer Butte may be found here, as well. Listen for Evening Grosbeaks high in the firs. You may also hear Band-tailed Pigeon and their deep "hoos." This park can be very busy when the azaleas and rhododendrons are in bloom. Mother's Day is the peak visitation day, right at the peak of spring migration. Sometimes the best spring migration birding is on the edges of the park in residential neighborhoods, especially at the northwest corner of the park.

Spencer Butte

Spring ****	*Summer* **	*Fall* **	*Winter* ***

Wheelchair access: none.

This 393-acre park is a crown on Eugene's South Hills Park system. At 2,068 feet in elevation, Spencer Butte is the highest point on the Eugene landscape. The Butte is forested with old-growth Douglas-fir forest and was purchased with voter-approved bonds for $40.5 million by Eugeneans in 1938 to prevent the Butte from being logged. This is the best place to find forest birds around Eugene.

To reach Spencer Butte from downtown Eugene, drive south on Willamette Street from 11th Ave. for 4.9 miles and look for the subtle park signs east of the road. A paved parking lot has signs directing park users to the trail system leading to the Butte's crest. The trails at Spencer Butte connect to a 7.5-mile ridgeline system along Eugene's South Hills. You will hike through old-growth firs and cedars on your way to the top and should find: Winter Wren,

Red-breasted Nuthatch, Golden-crowned Kinglet, Varied Thrush, Chestnut-backed Chickadee, Steller's Jay, Brown Creeper, Cassin's Vireo, Townsend's Warbler, and other forest birds in the proper season. This is the most reliable place around the city to find Pileated Woodpecker and Northern Pygmy-Owl, and occasionally, Mountain Quail.

At the top of the Butte, the forest opens to a rocky outcrop. Watch out for poison oak and rattlesnakes here. Unusual birds recorded from this location include Rock Wren, White-throated Swift, Sooty Grouse, and Common Poorwill. There is a historic record for Northern Spotted Owl from Spencer Butte. Vaux's Swifts and Turkey Vultures often pass directly overhead at the top. You get excellent views in all directions from this vantage point. Even if you aren't birding, the hike up the Butte for the view and exercise is worth the effort.

Boardwalk portion of the trail up Spencer Butte. Photo by Noah K. Strycker.

Armitage County Park
contributed by Vjera Arnold

Spring: ***   *Summer: ***   *Fall: ***   *Winter: ***

 Wheelchair accessible, with a paved path along the river and wheelchair parking.

Armitage is a 57-acre park with grass surrounded by mixed forest, just north of Eugene city limits, on the south bank of the McKenzie River. Head north on Coburg Rd. The park entrance is on the left half a mile past the intersection with North Game Farm Rd.. Park hours are from dawn to dusk. There is a *fee* for a day use permit, which is required from May through September.

There are parking and picnic tables spread throughout the park. Other facilities include rest rooms, group picnic areas, a boat ramp, and fishing access. A paved path starts at the boat ramp and goes along the river for almost half a mile. There are other paths in the park, allowing access to the mixed forest, with large maples and other trees. A good area for spring migration, Armitage was heavily birded in the 1960s-1970s as a spring migration site; it is rarely visited by birders today but is a very enjoyable site. It is also a good area to combine family activities and birding.

North of Armitage lies the town of Coburg, with access beyond to the open agricultural lands of the southern Willamette valley, where the best birding is in winter, when raptors and waterfowl can be found in good numbers.

Springfield Area

Vjera Arnold

Island Park

Spring: ****   *Summer: ***   *Fall: ****   *Winter: ****

The paths through the park are paved and wheelchair accessible. Except for one older path they are all smooth. The dirt trails are narrow and can be muddy in the rainy season. The majority of the park is grassy and fairly level.

Island Park is a 14-acre park next to the Willamette River, designed for family use as well as providing access to natural areas. A bike path meanders through an open grassy area bordered by two small creeks, riparian habitat, and the Willamette River. It has a large winter roosting site for Double-crested Cormorants and is a good area for spring migration. Island Park is connected by bike path to Alton Baker through the West D Street Greenway path.

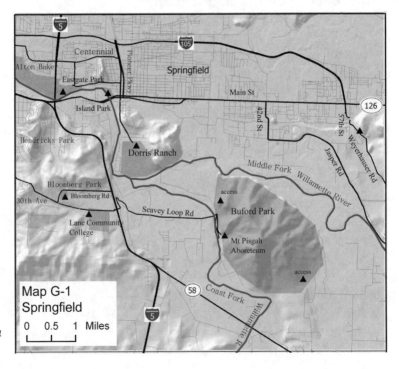

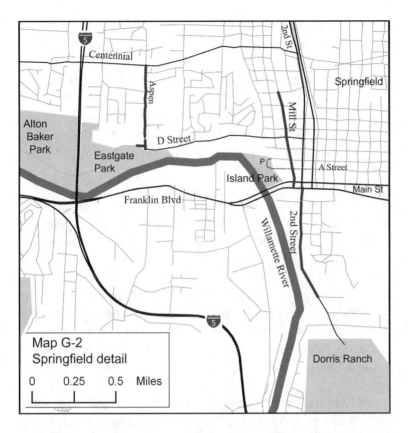

If one is birding by car, the parking lot can be found by heading south on Mill Street in Springfield. After crossing South A Street, the road takes a forced turn to the right, down to the parking lot. From here the park can be easily walked from end to end. It is open from 6 a.m. to 10 p.m., and the facilities include rest rooms (closed during the winter), playground, picnic tables, shelters, fishing, and a boat landing.

At the entrance to the parking lot there is a boat ramp. A path goes a short distance (50 feet) up the creek that enters the Willamette just upriver from the boat ramp. It is worth checking in the spring and summer for herons or Common Merganser with young; it is also a historical location for American Dipper. This path is not paved, has some rocks, and may be muddy in the fall and winter. An Osprey nest on top of the railroad bridge should be visible downriver from the boat ramp. Cliff Swallows usually nest on the bridge that crosses above the parking lot.

Go back through the parking lot and walk along the paved path that parallels the river. In the winter, gulls gather for roosting on the rocks in the middle of the river, Lesser Scaup (with an occasional Greater) will usually be feeding just downriver, and American Wigeon will be mixed in with the resident Mallards and Canada Geese. Spotted Sandpipers often flush off the edge of the bank during the winter and Bald Eagles can be seen overhead sometimes. During the spring migrants can be found working the trees and brush bordering the river.

Follow the paved path down an eighth of a mile to the west end of the park. Behind the stage are dirt trails that allow exploration of the natural habitat along the river's edge. These trails are narrow, in some places overgrown, and muddy after rain. They are also subject to flooding if the river is high. This area is more secluded than the rest of the park due to the abundance of undergrowth, therefore caution and awareness of surroundings is necessary in this area. Continue to walk along the river, past the stage, into the trees. The Double-crested Cormorant roost is here, at the west end of the park. There can be as many as 350 birds roosting here, mainly from early fall through late spring. Nesting has not been confirmed yet.

The river and a creek border the park; once you get to the water you will have to turn around and work your way back. The dirt trails crisscross each other and there is more than one way to walk back. The creek that runs through the north edge of the park can be followed back to the parking lot. If you wish to continue on the bike path to Alton Baker Park, from the stage follow the path over the bridge (north) and turn west onto D Street. It is about half a mile to the entrance to Alton Baker.

The whole loop in Island Park is not more than a quarter of a mile in distance. There have been at least 85 species recorded here.

Eastgate Woodlands or Alton Baker Park east access (Whilamut Natural Area)

Spring ****   *Summer* **   *Fall* ***   *Winter* ***

 The parking lot has one wheelchair parking spot on hard packed gravel, no curbs. Paths are paved.

A network of bicycle paths, walking paths, and jogging trails go through a wooded area and open field, bordered by the

Willamette river, a canal, and a pond. The woods are very good for migrants and are home to a small Great Blue Heron heronry. The field has grasses, cottonwoods, and blackberries on top of an old landfill, and is good for wintering sparrows and Western Meadowlarks, breeding birds such as Lazuli Buntings, and less common migrants such as Say's Phoebe, Ash-throated Flycatcher, and Western Kingbird. The pond, canal, and river have a wintering population of Pied-billed Grebes, gulls, and ducks. Over 130 species have been recorded here.

The parking area for the Eastgate Woodlands is directly south of the intersection of Aspen and West D Street in Springfield. Directly east is the West D Greenway Path, which connects Alton Baker Park and Island Park. The park is open from 6 a.m. to 10 p.m. Alton Baker can be explored by bicycling, canoeing, boating, walking, or jogging. East Alton Baker Park is also officially known as the Whilamut Natural Area. The entire park stretches about 3 miles along the Willamette River (as far as the Ferry Street Bridge in Eugene) and is about 400 acres. The Whilamut Natural Area, named to honor the Kalapuya people, is 237 acres and is less developed than West Alton Baker Park, although it has an extensive trail and bicycle path system. Eleven "Talking Stones" are placed along the paths, inscribed with a Kalapuya word and the English meaning.

Adjacent to the parking lot is a boat launch for the Willamette River and a canoe launch for the canal, with 2.25 miles of canal available for canoeing. Three of the paths also start here. Heading west the paths go into Alton Baker; heading east they become the West D Greenway Path. Directly paralleling the river is the Riverside Trail, for foot traffic only. It proceeds for a quarter of a mile along the river through mixed woodlands before it joins with the Northbank Trail right before I-5 crosses over the Willamette and the park. The Northbank Trail starts at the parking lot, and follows the canal until it splits into the Northbank Trail and Canoe Canal Trail. The Northbank Trail parallels the Willamette through Alton Baker and past it, with several miles of riverside bicycling paths and walking paths. The Canoe Canal Trail parallels the canal for a mile until it reaches the pond. Also paralleling the canal is Pre's Trail, a sawdust and gravel running path.

The Great Blue Heron heronry can be observed from two locations in the park. It is on the north side of the canal, about an eighth of a mile from the parking lot. Follow Pre's Trail or the

Northbank Trail west along the canal and watch for a bench pointed toward a large tree, which should have one to five nests visible in it. Continue along the canal until you reach a bridge that crosses it to the north. From that bridge, look directly upstream (east) and slightly north and you will be able to see the tree from that angle as well. Best time to see birds visible here is starting as early as January and continuing into April and May.

This bridge leads to North Walnut Rd., where there is additional parking and access to the park. The section of woods here can be excellent for both migrants and winter foraging flocks. If you head south from the bridge you will join up with the Northbank Trail and the Riverside Trail. They merge together and continue east toward Knickerbocker Bridge, which crosses the Willamette River to another bicycle path on the south side of the Willamette. The area underneath the I-5 bridge can have Spotted Sandpipers in the winter and occasionally an American Dipper. From Knickerbocker the river can be checked for mergansers, ducks, and roosting gulls in the winter, and swallows and Osprey in the summer. One or two Osprey have wintered here the last several winters as well.

After Knickerbocker Bridge, the Northbank Trail follows the Willamette River. It continues in Alton Baker Park for 1 to 2 miles. The next footbridge is the Autzen Bridge. Most of the park along this trail is wooded and is good for spring and fall migrants, and wintering foraging flocks. It is the best path to follow for birding the trees bordering the river and for checking the river. It is paved and has a lot of bicycle traffic.

From Knickerbocker Bridge, Walnut Rd. splits from the Northbank Trail and heads east through an open field. It used to be open to road traffic but now only to bicycle and pedestrian traffic. Also, a jogging trail heads through the field between Northbank Trail and Walnut Rd. In the winter this field has Western Meadowlarks, Wilson's Snipe, and sparrow flocks. In the summer Lazuli Buntings and Common Yellowthroats breed in the field. Unusual birds that have been seen in this field include a couple of records of Ash-throated Flycatcher, Brewer's Sparrow, Say's Phoebe, Western Kingbird, and a Black Phoebe. A handful of dirt trails wander through the field north of Walnut Rd. and south of the canal and the Canoe Canal Trail.

Both Walnut Rd. and the Canoe Canal Trail meet up at the pond, known informally as the "Radio Tower Pond" because there are two large radio towers nearby. Pied-billed Grebes return to the Radio

Tower Pond in August, followed by several species of ducks that spend the winter on it. Eurasian Wigeon has been recorded a couple of times in Alton Baker Park. The bridge over the canal right before the pond leads to another parking area near Autzen Stadium. The woods on the path north of this bridge can be good in migration. If bicycling, you can follow the path on the south edge of Autzen Stadium past the Science Factory and to the main parking area of Alton Baker, by the DeFazio Bridge and Ferry Street Bridge.

From the Radio Tower Pond, Pre's Trail and walking and bicycling paths continue east another mile or two to the main entrance to Alton Baker. There is a dog park and an open-air amphitheater, Cuthbert Amphitheater, before you get to the main entrance. The main entrance, which is off Martin Luther King Boulevard, has extensive parking, a couple of picnic shelters, rest rooms, and more duck ponds. A Northern Mockingbird wintered once in the east-central end of the park. Historically this was also an area that was very good for unusual winter sparrows, including Clay-colored Sparrow, Grasshopper Sparrow, an Indigo Bunting, and even a Dickcissel. As the park has been cleaned up and bike paths and the dog park were added, the sparrow potential in this area of the park has diminished.

Lane Community College Area

Spring ***   *Summer***   *Fall ****   *Winter ****

Poor wheelchair access: no curb cuts or viewing area for ponds; trails difficult. Bloomberg Park has a gravel road behind a closed gate.

Three sewage ponds are located by a forested hill and creek, next to an open scrub area. The ponds are a good place for wintering ducks, often hosting an uncommon duck. The scrub area is very reliable for Wrentits and Yellow-breasted Chat, while forest breeders can be found in the forest. In nearby Bloomberg Park, a gravel road goes through an old landfill covered with blackberries and grasses and surrounded by forest.

The Lane Community College (LCC) sewage ponds are at the west end of LCC. There is no parking directly next to the ponds except for a pullout that holds one car as you drive past the first pond on the way in, but there is plenty of parking at the college and the ponds are a short walk away. From I-5, take the LCC exit (#189).

Sewage ponds are often good birding sites. Middle pond, Lane Community College. Photo by Alan Contreras.

Head west on 30th, past the first LCC entrance (Eldon Schafer Drive) at the light. Take the exit for LCC. Follow the entrance road around, past the ponds on your left. The road dead-ends into the parking lot (open to the public from 6 a.m. to 11 p.m.).

After parking, walk back down the road to check the ponds. Be careful of traffic, as the limit on this road is an astonishingly high 40 mph, and the corner by the ponds is somewhat blind. All three ponds should be checked. The ponds are a reliable spot for Ruddy Ducks, both species of scaup, along with other waterfowl species. Ruddy Ducks have been known to breed here in the past. Unusual records here include an occasional Barrow's Goldeneye and Eared Grebe, as well as the rarer Sharp-tailed Sandpiper, American Avocet and Red Phalarope.

The forested area on the opposite side of the road is a good area to check for migrants and local breeding birds. A trail starts on the east end, just south of the curve in the road. This dirt path goes through the coniferous forest, then along the edge of it through blackberries and other dense low bushes. At some places you may have to step over a log. In less than half a mile it comes out into the open scrub area behind LCC. The trail ends at a gravel road. The gates on this road currently have "No Trespassing" signs on them, so turn around and follow the trail back. First, listen in the open scrub for Yellow-breasted Chats, Dusky Flycatchers, and Wrentits. Unusual records here include Gray Flycatcher, Ash-throated Flycatcher, and Townsend's Solitaire.

Bloomberg Park

Bloomberg Park is a short drive away. Exit LCC and head east on 30th Ave. Turn left on the frontage road, following the I-5 north sign. Turn left again onto Bloomberg Rd. and go all the way to the end. Park in front of the gate and walk down the gravel road into the site. The park is open 6 a.m. to 11 p.m. You can walk a loop that is three-fourths of a mile on this gravel road through the blackberries, grasses, shrubs, and small trees. Possible birds include Western Kingbird, Wrentit, both Goldfinches, Lazuli Bunting, and the occasional Yellow-breasted Chat. It is worth checking for migrants in the spring and sparrows in the fall and winter. An Indigo Bunting spent two summers in a row here (1994 and 1995).

Old Weyerhaeuser Road

(Information provided by Steve McDonald)

Spring ***	*Summer ***	*Fall ****	*Winter **

Wheelchair access: The first (paved) section of the logging road could be wheelchair accessible from the end of Mt. Vernon Rd. An enterprising person in a wheelchair could bypass some of the other gates, but it would require going through some rough areas around the sides.

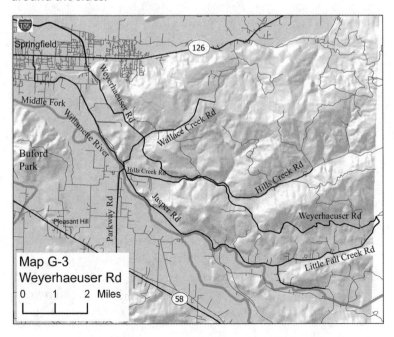

Map G-3
Weyerhaeuser Rd

0   1   2 Miles

*The Old
Weyerhaeuser
Rd. near
Springfield.
Photo by Steve
McDonald.*

This is a 22-mile old logging road that goes through mixed sections of forest, young tree plantations, grasslands, and clear-cuts southeast of Springfield. It is a good bicycling route for possible quail and grouse, woodpeckers, clear-cut breeders including Common Nighthawks, and migrants.

The start of the road is accessed from the end of the new extension of I-105 in Springfield. To access by car head south on Jasper Extension Rd. At the stop sign, turn right onto South 57th Street. Then turn left onto Mt. Vernon Rd. Mt. Vernon dead ends at Weyerhaeuser Rd. Park nearby. The first gate is about half a mile north. By bicycle, stay on the east sidewalk on Jasper Extension Rd. At the stop sign you will see a barricaded road directly ahead of you. This is the old Weyerhaeuser Rd. The first gate is just ahead.

This lower section of the road is frequented by walkers and bicycle riders and continues southeast. The entire road is off-limits to motor vehicles. The 22 miles of road loops into the end of Little Fall Creek Rd. The five separate sections of the road have locked gates, but bicycles can easily go around or under them. The bicycling can be a bit slippery during the wet season, if you stray over to the sides where there's slippery moss. It is possible to see black-tailed deer, elk, American black bear, coyote, cougar, or bobcat along the route. However, it is likely that you will only see deer.

The slopes and ridge to the east of the logging road between South 57th Street and Wallace Creek Rd. have numerous woodpeckers of all local species. Many Ruffed Grouse are on these slopes and also a few Sooty Grouse and Mountain Quail. On the ridge just before Wallace Creek, a pair of Goshawks with a young one has been seen in past summers. A Great Gray Owl was seen in this area once. Mourning Doves are common, and in the fall, Band-tailed Pigeons can be found feeding on elderberries.

The long section of the logging road that starts where it crosses Hills Creek Rd. is the most remote. This section is unpaved, but is smooth enough for easy riding, especially with a mountain bicycle. In the summer, Common Nighthawks can be found at dusk, skimming over the logged-over areas several miles up from Hills Creek. Western Screech Owls can be heard calling at night all through here. The road continues through similar habitat until it connects up with Little Fall Creek Rd., which can be followed to Jasper Rd. to make the route a loop.

Dorris Ranch

This site contains the oldest filbert (hazelnut) orchard in Oregon, with trails going through orchards and forest along a branch of the Willamette River.

Dorris Ranch is located by following Pioneer Parkway West in Springfield south until it turns into 2nd Street. Follow 2nd Street over the hill to the stop sign at Dorris Street, and Dorris Ranch will be straight ahead. The parking lot is open 6 a.m. to 10 p.m. The ranch is open to the public from 6 a.m. to dusk. A mile and a half of trails wander through the ranch property. The trails are dirt and bark and can be muddy after rain. The majority of the trails are shaded as they wind through the orchards and forest. This would be a nice cool place to explore on a sunny summer day. The information kiosk by the parking area has a property map and trail guide.

Creswell-Cottage Grove Areas

Hydie Lown

CRESWELL AREA

Creswell lies 8 miles south of Eugene along I-5. The principal birding site is Camas Swale, a grassy area of several hundred acres most recently used to pasture sheep. The swale is west of I-5, north of Creswell, and south of Dillard Rd. Birding is best here in winter and spring when the ground is wet, and since the swale is in private hands, most birding is done from public roads. Birds can be observed from Ricketts Rd., 2.4 miles north of Oregon St. in Creswell off route 99, or from Sher Khan Rd., 2.8 miles west of I-5 exit 182 off Camas Swale Rd.

Wintering birds include Bald Eagle, Peregrine Falcon, and other raptors; also Tundra Swan, Great Blue Heron, numerous ravens, and depending on the amount of rain, sometimes common shorebirds and waterfowl. An unidentified female goldeneye was seen in Camas Swale Creek in 1996. In late winter large flocks of Sandhill Cranes stop in the swale to rest. Spring birds include Vesper Sparrow and MacGillivray's Warbler.

The Creswell sewage ponds, to the south of Camas Swale, accessible in the past, are not open to any public access.

COTTAGE GROVE AREA

The small city of Cottage Grove lies at the head of the Willamette Valley in south Lane Co. about 20 miles south of Eugene. The surrounding area offers a variety of habitats for birding. The best, most easily accessed, birding habitats are found in East Regional Park, along the Row River Trail by the north shore of Dorena Reservoir, and at Cottage Grove Lake. Nearby Bureau of Land Management (BLM) land and the Umpqua National Forest offer additional wildlife viewing opportunities.

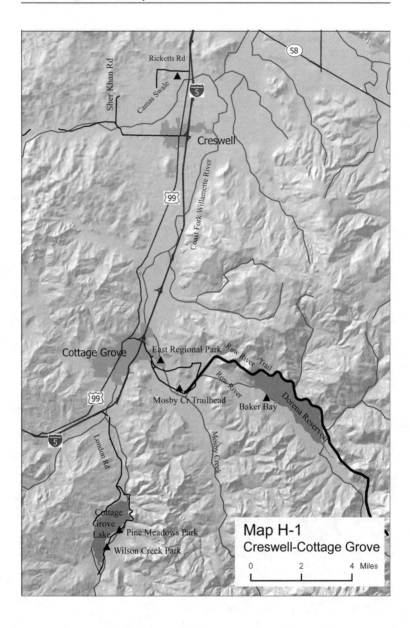

East Regional Park

Spring ***   *Summer***   *Fall ***   *Winter ****

Wheelchair accessibility is good along a blacktopped path leading from the weigh station north through the southwest section of the park. Some of the ponds and part of a creek are visible from this paved path.

This little-known, mostly undeveloped, and underused 56-acre city park is situated 1.1 mile east of I-5 exit 174 along Row River Rd. Parking is available on the road shoulder east of the weigh station or in an unpaved lot next to the BMX track. The only facilities consist of portable toilets behind the weigh station and at the BMX parking lot.

The park, a former gravel quarry, is bordered on the northeast side by the Row (pronounced like "cow") River and consists of several small ponds, grassy areas, deciduous trees, and invasive plants such as Himalayan blackberry and yellow iris. Dirt or wood-chipped trails meander through the park past the ponds and down to the river. The park is used mostly by anglers and dog-walkers, and is home to a large number of endangered western pond turtles.

The park boasts a fairly extensive bird list. Rarities include Black Phoebe, found in two consecutive winters. Green Herons winter here. The ponds host a variety of water birds and ducks including Pied-billed Grebe, Virginia Rail, Double-crested Cormorant, Wood Duck, Hooded Merganser, Bufflehead, Ring-necked Duck, Mallard, and American and Eurasian Wigeon. Ospreys and Bald Eagles can be found, as well as many passerines such as kinglets, Bushtits, flycatchers, sparrows and warblers. On April days, the trees may be full of migrating Yellow-rumped Warblers. Pileated Woodpeckers and Red-breasted Sapsuckers are often present, as well as Anna's and Rufous Hummingbirds and Yellow-breasted Chat.

Note: loudspeakers on the nearby water treatment building play predator calls to frighten starlings.

Row River Trail and Dorena Lake

Spring ***   Summer**   Fall ***   Winter ***

The 15.6 mile Row River Trail has been developed since 1994 as part of the Rails to Trails program. The trail begins in downtown Cottage Grove and passes through residential, forested, and agricultural habitats. The trail runs along the north side of Dorena Lake and ends in tiny, rural Culp Creek, formerly a mining and logging community. The trail is open to hikers, bikers, and horses, but not motor vehicles. Most of the trail is blacktopped.

Birders would likely want to skip the urban trailhead and proceed to the Mosby Creek trailhead on Layng Rd. at the corner of Mosby Creek Rd., or to one of the parking areas along the north shore of Dorena Lake. Amenities include ample RV and trailer parking, handicapped parking, rest rooms, and water. The Mosby Creek trailhead has, at times, resident hosts living in an RV, offering a measure of security to those leaving their vehicles behind during a hike or bike ride. The trailhead closes at dusk.

To reach the Mosby Creek trailhead from I-5 exit 174, proceed 1.1 mile east on Row River Rd., turn right on the Row River Connector, and drive a few hundred feet to Mosby Creek Rd. Turn right on Mosby Creek and proceed 1.7 miles to Layng Creek.

During nesting season one could expect to find Violet-green Swallow, MacGillivray's Warbler, Western Scrub-jay, Spotted Towhee, Lazuli Bunting, and Bewick's Wren along the first 5 or 6 miles of the

Dorena Dam and Cerro Gordo Mtn., looking north. Photo by Don Lown.

trail. Once at the lake, however, the habitat and birding become more varied. The first trailhead at Dorena Lake is located 5.5 miles east of I-5 exit 174 on Row River Rd. From this trailhead one can walk to the Dorena Dam to look for wintering waterfowl. Additional trailheads, some with rest rooms, are located 6 miles, 7.5 miles, and 11.5 miles from I-5 along the same road. One spot of particular interest is the Smith Creek wetland area, about 9.5 miles from I-5. Only a small highway pullout is available for car parking, but much of the wetland is visible from the Row River Trail. Sandhill Crane, Forster's Tern, Blue-winged Teal, and Redhead have been seen here.

The south side of Dorena Lake has only a few pullouts for viewing the lake, and one developed park, Baker Bay, that charges a day *fee* during the summer months. American Dipper can sometimes be found at the dam spillway.

Note: as this book was going to the publisher, the Forest Service opened a new paved connector road from Dorena Reservoir to Hills Creek Reservoir above Oakridge. To use this route, take Brice Creek Rd. (FS 22) where it begins east of Dorena Reservoir, follow it east until it merges with FS 5850 near Grass Mountain (5, 164 ft.) and then north to FS 2102, which leads to Hwy. 58 near Oakridge. No gas is available along this 76-mile (freeway to Hwy. 58) route once you leave Cottage Grove. The road is relatively narrow and may contain bike or motorcycle traffic. The eastern end may be closed by snow in winter.

Cottage Grove Reservoir

Spring ***	Summer**	Fall **	Winter ***

This is another little-birded area with opportunities to see uncommon and hard-to-find birds. The best birding is found on the east side of the lake, as the west side has limited public access and is bordered by a private industrial logging road.

From I-5 exit 172, travel 5 miles south on London Rd. Turn left on Cottage Grove Reservoir Rd. Several parks and campgrounds are located within the next 4 miles, all developed by the U.S. Army Corp of Engineers. All have rest rooms. The northeast corner of the reservoir is bordered by hillsides that have supported a population of Wrentit since at least the early 1970s.

Pine Meadows Park and Wilson Creek Park

Pine Meadows Park, located about 2.6 miles along the road, affords good viewing of wintering waterfowl; Eurasian Wigeon has been seen here. Purple Martins and Green Herons are among the summer birds that have been seen at Wilson Creek Park, about one mile farther. These parks are apt to be gated shut during the winter months; however, there is room for a small number of cars to park off the road. Such unusual birds as Red-necked Grebe and Sandhill Crane have been seen here. Both parks have paved parking and boat ramp areas, allowing some wheelchair access in the summer.

Bureau of Land Management (BLM) and Umpqua National Forest

The heavily logged rural forestland of south Lane Co. is a checkerboard of private and BLM land. Many BLM parcels are open to the public for recreational purposes. The northernmost section of Umpqua National Forest can be accessed to the east of Dorena Lake. The adventuresome birder who is willing to consult maps and seek out public forestland may be rewarded with views of such species as Mountain Quail, Sooty Grouse, Band-tailed Pigeon, Hermit Warbler, Hutton's Vireo, Gray Jay, or even Spotted Owl. Maps and information are available at the Umpqua N.F. Ranger Station 1.7 miles east of I-5 exit 174 on the corner of Row River Rd. and Cedar Park.

Fairview Peak and Bohemia Mountain sometimes have species associated with more easterly sites, including Calliope and Black-chinned (rare) Hummingbird and Mountain Chickadee.

Highway 126:

The McKenzie Valley and Cascade Mountains

Barbara Combs

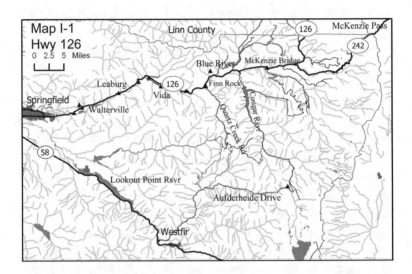

This area begins in the populated Willamette Valley and ends at relatively high-elevation areas in the Cascade Range. Away from population centers, sightings of birds that have relatively large home ranges, such as Peregrine Falcon and Spotted Owl, are more likely. Peregrine Falcon populations have increased due to hacking (release) activity and the ban on DDT in the U. S., while Spotted Owl populations are on the decline, due partly to habitat loss and partly to competition from the Barred Owl, a species that has recently become quite numerous in Lane Co. after entering Oregon in the early 1970s. In order to avoid disturbance of one area by many people, no specific sites will be listed for these two species. Birders who learn about the habitat preferences of the species they seek and use that knowledge will be more successful in finding them.

Rest room facilities are available at a number of campgrounds, boat ramps, and parks during the summer season. Many of these (especially campgrounds) are closed from fall to spring.

Accessible rest-room facilities are at the following sites along Hwy.

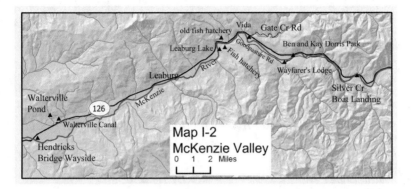

Map I-2
McKenzie Valley
0 1 2 Miles

126 in addition to those listed in the text descriptions below. Note that accessible here generally means large enough in which to maneuver a wheelchair. Some of these rest rooms may not meet all of the Americans with Disabilities Act requirements, particularly the requirement related to grab bars. As older rest rooms fall into disrepair, they are generally being replaced with ones that more closely comply with the requirements of the Act.

• The McKenzie River Fish Hatchery about 1.9 miles west of Leaburg Dam
• The Vida market in the town of Vida
• Helfrich Co. Park, about 3 miles east of the Goodpasture covered bridge and 0.5 miles west of Ben and Kay Dorris State Park
• McKenzie Bridge Campground, about 15.1 miles east of Silver Creek Boat Landing and 1.6 miles west of the McKenzie Bridge store (this stop also has an accessible picnic table)
• The McKenzie River Ranger Station about 2 miles east of McKenzie Bridge and 1.3 miles west of Paradise Campground
• Paradise Campground, about 1.3 miles east of the McKenzie River Ranger Station and 0.8 miles west of the intersection with Hwy. 242

Note: The last gas station along the highway before going through the pass area is about 2.1 miles east of the turnoff for Aufderheide Drive (Forest Service Rd. 19). The next available gas is in Sisters, about 50 miles away.

Some of the sites listed in the Cascades Birding Trail brochure are described here. They are: Delta Old-Growth Trail, McKenzie River Viewpoint (Hwy. 126 along the McKenzie River north of its junction with Hwy. 242), Cougar Reservoir, Box Canyon and Skookum

Meadows, Wayfarer Resort, Horsepasture Mountain, Dee Wright Observatory, and Scott Lake and Hand Lake.

The Cascades Birding Trail brochure is a good source for more information on sites beyond Lane Co. that are mentioned below, including lakes near the Santiam Pass, Indian Ford Campground, and Calliope Crossing. The brochure is available via download from the Internet at: <http://www.oregonbirdingtrails.org/cascades. htm>.

Walterville Pond

Start at the intersection of Hwy. 126 and I-105 in east Springfield. Drive east on Hwy. 126 toward the small town of Walterville. After about 5.3 miles, cross the bridge over the McKenzie River just before the Hendricks Bridge Wayside. Drive through Walterville to a small bridge over Walterville Canal—about 1.5 miles past the bridge over the McKenzie River. Immediately (about 5 feet) after the bridge over the canal, turn left (north) onto Page Rd. This gravel road with tattered rubber speed bumps at the beginning quickly turns westward to parallel the canal. Drive about 0.15 miles to a wide parking area where the road ends. Coming from the east along Hwy. 126, the turnoff for the pond is about 6.9 miles west of Leaburg.

Park and walk through the break in the fence at the end of the road and up the well-worn path. It is less than 0.1 miles to the bank of the reservoir. The break in the fence is about 40 inches wide and easily negotiated by a wheelchair. Most of the path is not very steep and has a reasonably smooth surface of small gravel and dirt, but the rise just before the reservoir is steeper and the path has larger gravel in many places (some that can be circumvented), making wheelchair travel a bit difficult.

Around the reservoir, the path is wide and fairly flat. In wet weather, mud could become a barrier for wheelchair travel. There is a non-accessible portable toilet at the parking lot. Hendricks Bridge Wayside, about 1.5 miles toward Springfield along Hwy. 126, should have accessible rest room facilities by the time this book is published.

Walterville Pond is a 65-acre body of water owned by the Eugene Water and Electric Board. Its greatest depth is 9 ft. The pond is a popular spot for fishing and dog walking, so the area is often so disturbed that waterfowl either leave or cluster toward the center of the pond. There are some shallow areas near the north shore that are most likely to host waterfowl when they are present and relatively undisturbed. The habitat surrounding the pond consists of some fairly dense brush and grassy open areas attractive to many species of passerines.

Great Blue Heron, Pied-billed Grebe, Mallard, Ring-necked Duck, Lesser Scaup, Bufflehead, Hooded and Common Merganser, and American Coot are among the water birds that use the pond regularly, particularly during the late fall to early spring. Canvasback and American Wigeon are present at times. Osprey is usually present during the breeding season. In winter, birders sometimes see Bald Eagle perched in the trees on the opposite side of Hwy. 126 from the southwest corner of the pond. Regular passerine species include Western Wood Pewee and House Wren (both in breeding season only), Black-capped Chickadee, American Goldfinch, Spotted Towhee, and Song Sparrow. Swallows of all species found in the state have been seen here, although Violet-green, Tree, Barn, and Cliff Swallows are the most likely to be seen, during the breeding season. Forster's Tern, Pacific Loon, and an unidentified jaeger have appeared at this location. Local birders visit this site less frequently than sites on the west side of the Willamette Valley, so the status of bird life here is less well known.

Leaburg Lake/Fish Hatchery/Waterboard Park/Leashore Drive

At the intersection of Hwy. 126 and I-105 in east Springfield, turn east and drive on Hwy. 126 about 15 miles to the town of Leaburg. Leaburg Lake is about 4 miles past town. Watch for the dam and the narrow paved road that crosses it on the south side of the road. Turn right and cross the dam. The road across the dam is one-way, so check for oncoming vehicles that may already be on the bridge before attempting to cross it. Coming from the east, turn left to cross the dam about 1.7 miles past the Goodpasture covered bridge.

Birding options in this area include the fish hatchery on the right, the shore of the lake, the park about 0.1 miles down the road on the left, and the residential area past the park.

The fish hatchery and the park both have accessible rest-room facilities. At the fish hatchery, drive straight through past the holding tanks and turn left where signage indicates that the road ahead leads to an area restricted to employees. Park on the right side of the road. The accessible rest-room facilities are on the east side of the administration building, at the middle of the structure. Enter them directly from the outside by going south on the paved road between buildings. Look for the entrance on the right. These facilities are usually open, even outside of regular business hours. At the park, accessible rest-room facilities are reachable from the pullout for picnic areas 2 and 4 on the north side of Leashore Drive. There is a good gravel path to the rest-room building, which is visible from the road. The park closes at sundown. Its rest-room facilities may be closed during the winter months.

Resident Mallards and exotic geese can usually be found on the lake, but other species visit as well. Canada Goose, Hooded Merganser, and Double-crested Cormorant may be on the lake at any season. American Wigeon and Barrow's Goldeneye may appear from fall through spring. Cliff Swallows entertain visitors early in the breeding season by gathering mud for their nests on the shore of the lake to the left just past the dam. Belted Kingfisher can usually be found looking for an easy meal in the hatchery tanks. Hammond's Flycatcher nests in the canopy at the park. The elusive MacGillivray's Warbler nests in thick brushy areas around the playing fields on the west side of the road through the park.

During the breeding season, flowering plants in the residential area past the park attract Rufous Hummingbird. Warbling Vireo and Winter Wren sing along the roadside. Pileated Woodpecker inhabits the taller trees, particularly on the west side of the road. The road through the residential area is only 0.5 miles long. Birders who would like to visit it would do best to walk down and back rather than drive to the end and use the turnaround before driving back out.

Visitor Information Center/Old McKenzie Fish Hatchery

About 0.5 miles to the east of Leaburg Dam on the north side of the road lies the Old McKenzie Fish Hatchery. The visitor information center there has information about recreation throughout the state.

Accessible rest rooms are available here during business hours. There is an accessible fish-feeding platform beside a pond along the path from the parking lot to the visitor center. A wheelchair can easily navigate the path along the pond in the vicinity of the observation platform, but the path becomes narrower with dropoffs as it crosses a bridge to the east to circle around the pond.

The pond may host species such as Green Heron, Mallard, and Wood Duck. MacGillivray's Warbler uses the brushy areas around the pond.

Goodpasture Road

At the intersection of Hwy. 126 and I-105, turn east on Hwy. 126 and drive about 19.5 miles. Turn right (south) and cross the Goodpasture covered bridge. From the east, travel about 0.7 miles west of Vida and turn left over the bridge. The road over the bridge is narrow, so it may be necessary to wait for oncoming traffic to pass through the bridge, depending on the size of the vehicle.

Goodpasture Rd. has some nice low-elevation birding sites away from the main highway. When the current construction project is complete, travelers will be able to drive about 8 miles along this road before reaching a dead end at Deer Creek. When pulling off the road to stop and bird, be sure that you are not blocking any portion of the traffic lane, since there is some traffic from local residents and people visiting the fishing areas along the road. Many of the spots to pull out off the road can be productive. Just a few are described below.

American Goldfinch nests in the area near the covered bridge. The residential road to the right less than 0.1 mile past the bridge can be quite birdy. It is worth checking out before moving on. Red-eyed Vireo has been found singing in tall deciduous trees along Goodpasture Rd. during more than one breeding season, but no nest has ever been found.

At about 3.6 miles, turn left (north) into the Wayfarer Resort. This is an 11-acre privately owned site with rental cabins. Birders are welcome on the grounds but must check in at the office first. Here, extensive gardens ensure sightings of Rufous Hummingbird at any time of the day during spring and summer, although the highest level of activity occurs in the evening hours before dark. Wood Duck may often be found in the pond at the resort, or in the small wet area just past the entrance along the main road.

From the riverbank, Common Merganser can sometimes be seen lounging on the rocks in the river. Canada Goose and Mallard nest here. Violet-green, Tree, and Barn Swallows, Warbling Vireo, Pacific-slope Flycatcher, Swainson's Thrush, and Western Tanager are present during the breeding season. Evening Grosbeak is sometimes in the area. Red-breasted Sapsucker, Downy Woodpecker, Mourning Dove,

Hutton's Vireo, Western Scrub-Jay, Steller's Jay, and Purple Finch are possible here year round. The gardens attract a large number of butterflies, particularly swallowtails.

Continue past the resort and find a safe place to pull off the road in about 0.7 mile. Scan the habitat on the right (south) side of the road for Western Bluebird. Local residents on this portion of the road have installed nest boxes attractive to this species. Continue along the road to the dead end, using pullouts to bird wherever they are available.

Gate Creek Road

In the town of Vida (2.5 miles east of Leaburg dam; about 2.7 miles w of Ben and Kay Dorris State Park) turn north on the paved road on the west side of the Vida Café. The first mile or so passes through a largely residential area. After about 2.5 miles, further passage along this road is blocked by gates preventing access to private property. The creek at this location is a pleasant stop and a good place to dangle hot feet in cool water. The birding along Gate Creek Rd. is all at elevations lower than 1000 ft. Band-tailed Pigeon, Pileated Woodpecker, Belted Kingfisher, and American Dipper are among the species that may be seen in this area.

Silver Creek Boat Landing/Watchable Wildlife area

The Silver Creek Boat Landing is about 4.5 miles east of Ben and Kay Dorris State Park and 4.2 miles west of Finn Rock. Osprey may be seen here, as well as other species that use the river as a flight corridor.

Silver Creek Boat Landing has an accessible rest-room facility. A short wheelchair-navigable path from the east side of the parking lot leads to an accessible observation deck that allows expansive views of the river.

FOREST SERVICE ROADS

Many Forest Service roads that intersect with Hwy. 126 provide enjoyable birding experiences. The predominant tree species in forested lower-elevation areas are Douglas-fir, western hemlock, and western red cedar. From 3500 to 4500 ft, Pacific fir and noble fir predominate. Few of these roads will reach higher-elevation habitats where subalpine fir, mountain hemlock, and lodgepole pine are the predominant tree species.

Along these roads, Rufous Hummingbird, Willow Flycatcher, Olive-sided Flycatcher, Warbling Vireo, MacGillivray's Warbler, Orange-crowned Warbler, Lazuli Bunting, and White-crowned Sparrow may be found in or around open areas (usually clear-cuts where shrubby plants have grown large enough to provide good

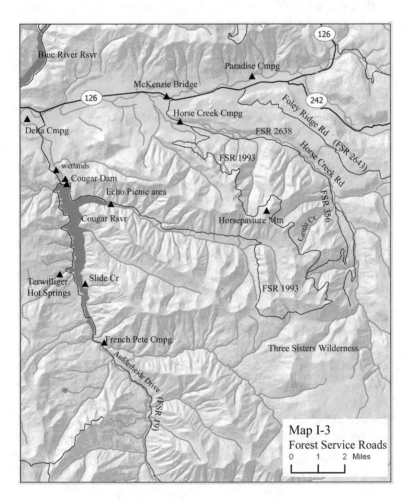

Map I-3
Forest Service Roads
0   1   2 Miles

cover) during the breeding season. From June through August, just before it gets dark, Common Nighthawk may be seen and heard while foraging overhead.

Swainson's Thrush, Varied Thrush, Hammond's and Pacific-slope Flycatchers, Western Wood-Pewee, Cassin's Vireo, House Wren, Hermit Warbler, Black-throated Gray Warbler, Wilson's Warbler, Cedar Waxwing, Western Tanager, Chipping Sparrow, and Black-headed Grosbeak breed here. The lengthy and beautiful song of the Winter Wren is almost ubiquitous in the forested areas in spring and early summer. Northern Saw-whet Owl inhabit primarily low- to mid-elevation coniferous and mixed forests. Their incessant call is most often heard at night during April and May at these elevations, but it is possible to find one at most times of the year either by searching near a mobbing flock of passerines during the daytime or going out at night and imitating its call.

Along fast-moving streams, watch for American Dipper. Whitewash on rocks in the stream is an indication that a dipper may have stopped there. On slower portions of streams and rivers with pebbled beaches, look for Spotted Sandpiper. Streams in this area may also host Harlequin Duck in the breeding season. Watch for them negotiating the current, loafing on rocks in streams and rivers, or resting on downed logs near the edge of the stream. Information on sites where Harlequin Duck has been found is available at the following web site: <http://members.aol.com/owlhooter/HQPAGE1.html>.

Blue and Ruffed Grouse, Mountain Quail, Pileated and Hairy Woodpecker, Northern Flicker, Red-breasted Sapsucker, Steller's Jay, Common Raven, Hutton's Vireo, Winter Wren, Red-breasted Nuthatch, Golden-crowned Kinglet, Spotted Towhee, Dark-eyed Junco, and Song Sparrow are present year round. Band-tailed Pigeon may be found in all but the coldest months, usually in areas with Douglas-fir forest.

At mid- to higher elevations, detections of Gray Jay, Townsend's Solitaire (breeding season), and Hermit Thrush (breeding season) become more possible. At times, Great Gray Owl can be present in higher-elevation areas. In spring and early summer, hearing Sooty Grouse booming along a trailside is a memorable birding experience. Some Blue Grouse protect their territories even against human intrusion, which can result in an even more memorable experience.

Birding on Forest Service roads usually consists of finding wide pullouts with good visibility from the road ahead and behind, pulling off the road, and spending time identifying the species present near that location. For the most part, Forest Service roads have spur roads that birders can walk or drive along to improve their chances of finding species they would like to see. Some even have trailheads for hiking trails. These roads, and others mentioned below that reach higher elevations, may become blocked by snow in the fall. Some may not open until late spring or early summer. Roads may become blocked by debris from falling trees at any season. If there is any question about the condition of a particular road, contact the nearest ranger station for information.

Travelers should obtain a Willamette National Forest (or Ranger District) map before going too far on spur roads. Maps can be purchased at ranger stations, the Willamette National Forest office in downtown Eugene (expected to move to Springfield in 2008), and many retail outlets. Ranger District maps may also be useful, especially if they are more up-to-date than the map covering the entire forest.

It is easy to find oneself far away from civilization in the middle of a maze of logging roads, some of which dead-end after many miles. Every journey into the forest in a vehicle should begin with a full tank of gas.

During fire season, requirements for carrying tools for fighting fires (e.g., water, shovel, axe, bucket, fire extinguisher) when traveling away from paved routes may be in effect. Travel on some roads may be prohibited or restricted. Check with the local ranger station to find out whether any such requirements are in effect for the roads you plan to travel. Open gates can be deceptive. If you go through a gate that is unlocked, you may find that it is closed and locked when you try to get back out. If a gate that is open appears to have been opened recently, don't drive through it and on up the road unless you are certain that the gate will still be open when you want to leave the area, or you know that another exit is ungated. Gates that are open but overgrown with weeds and brush can be considered safe to pass through.

It is always a good idea to watch and listen for log truck traffic on Forest Service roads.

One of the most rewarding experiences in birding can be finding a special bird at a place not specifically listed in a guide book like this. Those who venture along these roads and roads like them in other areas may enjoy their own special encounter.

Here is a selection of forest roads that birders have found to be productive birding areas.

Quartz Creek Road (Forest Service Road 2618)

Just west of Finn Rock, about 4 miles west of Ben and Kay Dorris State Park, turn east. Coming from the east, note the Finn Rock store/restaurant. Finn Rock (a monolith on the east side of the road with a wide parking area near it) is just past the store, and the turn eastward is directly after Finn Rock. Quartz Creek Rd. passes through private land for a number of miles before it enters Forest Service land, so log truck traffic is more frequent on this road than on some others. Be especially alert at blind curves and use pullouts on narrow stretches of road to let approaching log trucks pass safely by. Never stop along the road in a way that might block passage of a truck.

Harlequin Duck has been found in the creek along this road. This road, as it twists and turns along the creek, offers mainly lower-elevation birding. After about 13-14 miles, the elevation of the road reaches 3500 ft. Driving a long distance up Quartz Creek Rd., it is possible to link up with other roads to make a loop through several other destinations, including Cougar Reservoir, the South Fork of the McKenzie River at Aufderheide Drive, Oakridge, and Fall Creek Reservoir. Fill up the tank and consult a map before you go. Inquire at a ranger station if there is any question about road conditions.

Horse Creek Road (Forest Service Road 2638)

About 0.8 mile east of McKenzie Bridge Campground (about 0.1 mile west of Jennie B. Harris Wayside), turn south on the paved road, which winds through a resort area and changes to a gravel road. Horse Creek Rd. provides lower-elevation birding and access to some higher-elevation birding on the road to Horsepasture Mountain. After passing the Horse Creek Campground, continue straight on Horse Creek Rd. to bird along the creek. For spectacular views and some higher-elevation birding, turn right on FS Rd. 1993 about 0.1 mile past the entrance to the campground. FS Rd. 1993 eventually (after about 32 miles) leads to Echo Day Use area at Cougar Reservoir and can be used for a loop tour. A right turn just

*View looking southeast from Horsepasture Mountain. On a clear day the
Three Sisters are more visible. Photo by Brooke DeWitt.*

past Castle Creek on FS Rd. 356, about 9 miles up Horse Creek Rd.,
will also link up with FS Rd. 1993.

A left turn at the junction of FS Rd. 356 with FS Rd. 1993 will
bypass the higher-elevation birding areas and lead to Cougar
Reservoir. A right turn at this junction will lead to the spectacular
views at Horsepasture Mountain. At Horsepasture Mountain, a 1.5-
mile trail about 8.4 miles from the first turnoff from Horse Creek
Rd. leads to the 5660 ft summit. Continuing on the road toward the
north will lead back to Horse Creek Rd. A left turn at the intersection
will take you back to Hwy. 126.

Foley Ridge Road (Forest Service Road 2643)

About half a mile east of the McKenzie River Ranger Station (0.8
mile west of Paradise Campground on Hwy 126), turn south onto
this gravel road. All of the branches of this road lead to dead ends.
It does not achieve elevations over 4500 ft. Trails strike out into the
Three Sisters Wilderness from some of the dead ends. Trail #3511
begins at the end of FS Rd. 485, which branches off to the right of
FS Rd. 2643 about 9.4 miles from its beginning. It goes through the
forest to Substitute Point, at an elevation of 6344 ft, and beyond.
The hike to Substitute Point is a 9-10-mile round trip. The hike
beyond it leads to other trails, passes lake basins, and approaches
South Sister.

Forest Service Road 2649

About 2.5 miles north of the intersection of Hwys. 126 and 242 (4.5 miles south of Olallie Campground), turn east on the gravel road. FS Rd. 2649 travels up to some higher elevations and loops around to go back down to Hwy. 126. A good portion of the loop area is above 4000 ft; nearly all of it is above 3500 ft. At 4660 ft, Irish Camp Lake provides a nice stop near the portion of the loop furthest from the highway. About 1.5 miles south of Irish Camp Lake, the road achieves its highest elevation of about 4940 ft. FS Rd. 686, an unimproved road about 1.2 miles south of Irish Camp Lake, goes up above 5000 ft. There are many branch roads to explore in the area. Roads 2643, 2647, 2654, and 2657 will lead back to Hwy. 126. Roads with 3-digit labels are either unimproved, primitive roads or gravel roads not maintained for cars. A large percentage of these lead to dead ends. A ranger district map would be of great help in this area for those who want to explore its nooks and crannies.

Blue River Reservoir/H. J. Andrews Experimental Forest

Drive east about 14.3 miles on Hwy. 126 from Vida to Blue River. Turn left at the sign for the town of Blue River. Drive about 1.3 miles and turn north again on Blue River Rd. after passing the abandoned ranger station and just before reaching the town proper. Bear left

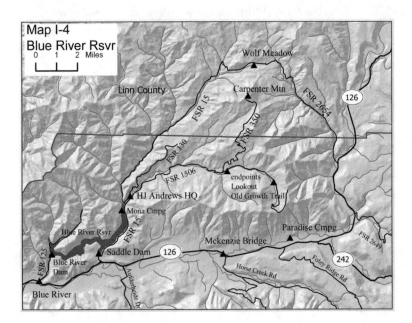

at the intersection with Marbrook Rd., traveling 1.5 miles from the turnoff in town to the dam viewpoint. There is a paved road over the dam that provides opportunities for those on foot to scope the reservoir with a clear view. The passageway between the gate across the road and a rock wall is too narrow for a wheelchair. The view at this site is breathtaking and away from the crowds in the principal recreation areas for the reservoir on the side by Saddle Dam. After viewing this site and perhaps exploring the gravel roads nearby, go back to Hwy. 126. The shortest way back to the highway is through town, so turn left at the intersection after coming down from the dam. Turn left (east) and travel about 3 miles to paved FS Rd. 15 to access the remainder of the reservoir. Turn left (northeast) here. The turn is not at a 90-degree angle, but bears gently to the left for drivers who turn onto it while driving east. Those who turn onto this road when approaching from the east will need to allow for making a wide turn at a sharp angle to go up to the reservoir. (From the east, FS Rd. 15 is about 1.5 miles west of the turnoff for Cougar Reservoir and Aufderheide Drive.)

Blue River Reservoir is 1420 acres in size at full pool. The reservoir's water level is lowered from fall through spring for flood control. Developed areas at the reservoir are currently *fee* areas that require a day use fee or a Northwest Forest Pass.

Accessible rest rooms are available at Saddle Dam, Lookout Day Use Area and Campground, Mona Campground (between campsites 6 and 7), and the H. J. Andrews Experimental Forest headquarters building (the latter during normal business hours only).

FS Rd. 15 rises quickly from Hwy. 126, and reaches Saddle Dam after about 0.9 mile. This is a place to stop and scope the reservoir. Travel across the dam and then about 0.6 mile across a point of land to reach a more secluded portion of the reservoir where birds may be less disturbed. The reservoir hosts some waterfowl species in all seasons, although usually they are not present in large numbers. Osprey nest here; some may spend the winter, as well. Western Grebe, Mallard, American Wigeon, Barrow's Goldeneye, Bufflehead (lower numbers now than in past years), and Common and Hooded Mergansers are among the species that may be found here from fall through winter. One or two swans (believed to be Trumpeter Swans) have been wintering on this reservoir and Trail Bridge Reservoir (further north on Hwy. 126 in Linn Co.) in recent times.

At about 3.6 miles from Hwy. 126 lies the principal gateway for exploring the H. J. Andrews Experimental Forest, FS Rd. 1506. Stop at the information kiosk to read about the forest. Many scientific studies are conducted in the H. J. Andrews Experimental Forest. For this reason, it is best to stay on the road and trails while birding there in order to avoid disturbing any data-collection activities that might be taking place nearby. If you believe that your hiking boots or car tires may be carrying seeds from invasive plant species, it would be a good idea to clean them off before entering the Experimental Forest. Seeds of the false-brome (an invasive non-native grass that is now found at many sites in Western Oregon) are of particular concern. Before you go, you may want to check the False-brome Working Group's web site: http://www.appliedeco. org/FBWG.htm. If in doubt, take the time to clean up your footwear and vehicle to avoid the possibility of carrying unwanted seeds. For more information while at the Experimental Forest, visit the headquarters building and look at the bulletin board there.

During normal business hours, if you would like to visit the headquarters building, continue past the kiosk and turnoff, driving a total of about 4.3 miles from Hwy. 126, and turn right (east) on FS Rd. 130. Travel about 0.4 mile to FS Rd. 132 and bear right. The headquarters building is about 0.2 mile down a paved driveway. Turn right upon entering the compound and park in the bricked area in front of the administration building. Hummingbirds feed actively at feeders by this building. Lookout Creek, which is along FS Rd. 130, is a good place to look for Harlequin Duck. The portion of the creek nearest to FS Rd. 15 has been one of the best places to search. Birds found here will be nesting and should be disturbed as little as possible. Return to FS Rd. 1506 for more birding.

Lookout Creek Old-Growth Trail, a moderate to difficult hiking trail, intersects with FS Rd. 1506 at about 7 miles and again at about 10 miles. The trail is roughly 3.5 miles long. For a shorter hike with a view, travel up FS Rd. 350, which intersects with FS Rd. 1506 about 0.2 mile before the first Old-Growth Trail access point. A 1-mile trail climbs to the Carpenter Mountain Lookout (in Linn Co.) where the views allow the visitor to appreciate the vastness and beauty of the forest. Exit the Experimental Forest the same way you came in.

About 0.2 mile beyond the Experimental Forest access point at the intersection for FS Rds. 15 and 1506, a the left turn over the bridge leads to Mona Campground. American Dipper often nests under bridges, so check for them here and at other bridges in the area. Here you may turn toward the campground and bird up the road that goes past it, or explore further up FS Rd. 15. It is possible to make a loop by birding up FS Rd. 15 past Wolf Rock and Wolf Meadow, turning right then left to go onto FS Rd. 2656, then turning right onto FS Rd. 2654 (Deer Creek Rd.) to connect back to Hwy. 126 about 5.5 miles north of its intersection with Hwy. 242. For destinations further north, continue on FS Rd. 15 until it reaches U. S. Hwy. 20. Near Wolf Rock, ephemeral ponds in spring attract a large variety of birds, including waterfowl. Wolf Meadow, just past Wolf Rock along the south side of the road, now has water year round due to a beaver dam. A 400-ft dirt road at the west end of the meadow leads to a primitive camping area, from which two trails provide access to the meadow. Wood Duck and Tree Swallow nest in nest boxes placed here. Mallard, Bufflehead, and Ring-necked Duck may be found on the flooded meadow, but an extensive growth of lily pads makes viewing ducks somewhat difficult. Sooty Grouse nest in the area and may be seen near the road. In winter, the road may be blocked by snow.

Note: U. S. Forest Service *Fee* Areas change from time to time as a result of legislation and administrative decisions. It is best to check in advance if there is any question about fees. The Northwest Forest Pass covers National Forest Fee areas except for Terwilliger Hot Springs, which requires a separate fee. Currently at some locations, a fee is required for day use but not for camping. A separate fee is required at some state parks. Use of some county parks is subject to another, separate fee.

AUFDERHEIDE DRIVE

From Eugene/Springfield, drive east on Hwy. 126 about 40 miles to Blue River and continue past the turnoff to the town. About 1.5 miles past the turnoff for Blue River Reservoir, turn right (south) on Aufderheide Drive (FS Rd. 19). From the east, turn left (south) about 9.6 miles past the intersection of Hwys. 126 and 242.

Aufderheide Drive runs from Cougar Reservoir off Hwy. 126 to Hwy. 58 near the towns of Oakridge and Westfir. Visitors may start at either end. Audio tapes and CDs describing points of interest along the drive are available during office hours (open on weekends in summer) at the McKenzie River Ranger Station just east of McKenzie Bridge and at the Middle Fork Ranger Station outside of Westfir. The McKenzie River Ranger Station is about 7.5 miles east of the turnoff

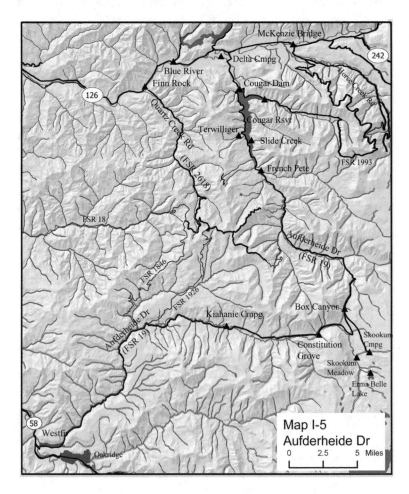

on Hwy. 126; the Middle Fork Ranger Station is straight ahead when exiting onto Hwy. 58. The tapes are free but should be returned; 24-hour return boxes are available at both stations.

Aufderheide is a popular drive during the fall when deciduous trees are displaying their red and yellow colors. It is not possible to travel the loop during the winter months because the road becomes blocked by snow. There are many birding opportunities along this approximately 60-mile drive. Advance signage for the many campgrounds, picnic areas, and trailheads along the drive often does not exist, so be alert and slow down a little when nearing a turn you plan to make. Be careful not to stop along Aufderheide Drive in a way that might block traffic, as the road can be very busy and some vehicles travel at high rates of speed.

Delta Old-growth Trail

Once on Aufderheide Drive, travel 0.2 mile and turn right (west) to go toward Delta Campground. Drive another 1.3 miles to the back of the campground and park at a wide parking area near the entrance to the trail.

Delta Old-growth Trail is an easy, flat wheel-chair accessible loop trail of about 0.5 miles. An accessible rest-room facility is available on the left side of the road just past the parking lot entrance. The amphitheater is also accessible.

Inquire at the Ranger Station concerning the schedule for programs that may be offered in the amphitheater, especially on summer weekends.

No fee payment is required at the current time. The trail passes through old-growth forest and riparian areas. Douglas-fir and western red cedar are the most common trees. Western hemlock, Pacific yew, grand fir, big leaf maple, western hazel, incense cedar, vine maple, and Oregon ash are also found along the trail. Many of the conifers are 200-500 years old. Hermit Warbler, House Wren, Western Bluebird, and Swainson's Thrush are likely during the breeding season. Pileated Woodpecker, Red-breasted Nuthatch, Hutton's Vireo, and Chestnut-backed Chickadee may be present at any season. One of the stops on the trail allows visitors to view a tree that a Pileated Woodpecker has drilled into.

Wetlands area

About a quarter mile past Delta Campground, Aufderheide Drive bears sharply to the right and the road to the powerhouse lies straight ahead. This road has pullouts that access the river and might be used for birding, but the noise of the rapids interferes with hearing bird sounds. Most visitors will want to continue another quarter mile on Aufderheide Drive to a gravel road that goes down toward the water on the left side of the drive. There is a small wetlands in this area and beyond, including a couple of ponds, of interest to birders.

Cougar Dam

About 3 miles past Delta Campground, turning the corner for a first view of Cougar Dam and Reservoir and the steep cliffs that surround them is a breathtaking experience. Turn left to cross the dam, and then left again after about 0.3 mile into a paved parking lot just before concrete guardrails line the road.

Here, the wheelchair-accessible paved path provides spectacular views of the area around and below the dam. Those not too distracted by the view may find Northern Rough-winged, Violet-green, and Cliff Swallows flying overhead from spring to fall. Cross back over the dam and stop at the overlook to read information about the area and enjoy the spectacular scenery and the swallows from this viewpoint.

Cougar Reservoir

The reservoir is 1,280 acres at full pool. It is drawn down for flood control during the winter months. Pull off the road at various points to look out over the reservoir and to check for birds that may be using the cliffs and dry areas nearby. At some places, the road passes high above a wide reservoir so use of a spotting scope for viewing waterfowl (mainly from fall through spring) can be a frustrating experience at times. The parking lot at Terwilliger Hot Springs is one of the better places to set up a spotting scope. It is on Aufderheide Drive about 4.4 miles past the dam. A climb up or down the small hill next to the parking lot is necessary, however. This parking lot and the hot springs are covered by a *fee* that is separate from the Northwest Forest Pass, specifically to maintain the hot springs area, but birders who park in the lot for a half hour or less are not expected to pay a fee. If the lot is crowded (usually on summer weekends), anyone staying more than a half hour may be asked to pay for parking or move to another location to allow others to use the limited space in the parking lot.

The hot springs, with its access trail on the opposite side of the road from the parking lot, is a popular clothing-optional destination. Birding with binoculars on this trail and at the hot springs is not recommended.

Wheelchair access: There are accessible rest-room facilities here, but reservoir birding is not very accessible. At some places in the parking lot it may be possible to find a place to slip a wheelchair between the large rocks, but going to the places closest to the reservoir means traveling a bit down hill at a place where there are no guardrails. These areas may be slippery and muddy from spring through fall when waterfowl viewing is best.

There are Osprey nests near the reservoir, and some birds may spend the winter in the area. Bald Eagle, Red-tailed Hawk, and Cooper's Hawk can be seen in the area. Common Loon, Canada Goose, Western Grebe, Mallard, American Wigeon, Hooded and Common Mergansers, Bufflehead (fewer now than in past years), Ruddy Duck, and both goldeneyes are among the species that may be seen here, mostly from fall through spring and not usually in large numbers. A Redhead with young was reported near the Slide Creek boat ramp in summer 2005.

Reach the end of the reservoir 2.2 miles south of the hot springs parking lot. Here, both the West Side boat ramp on the east side of the road and Cougar Crossing day use area on the west side have accessible rest-room facilities; the day use area facilities have slightly better access. Riparian area birding opportunities can be found in the vicinity of the boat ramp and day use area, and at Sunnyside Campground.

To find Sunnyside Campground, travel 0.2 mile along gravel FS Rd. 500 and turn left down a steep entrance road that leads to a flat camping area along the reservoir. About 1.2 miles further down the gravel road is Slide Creek Campground, which also offers a closer view of the water. Generally, the birdiest spot along the reservoir is along its banks within a mile or so of where the stream fans out into the reservoir proper. In spring and early summer, the area between Sunnyside Campground and Slide Creek is the most productive. In winter, Slide Creek Campground is near the end of the reservoir's pool so the area along the reservoir just to the north of Slide Creek should be visited. Pullouts along the road past Slide Creek along the east side of the reservoir can be used as birding stops. Vehicle access to the reservoir from this road used to be possible, but now the short roads that lead to the water are walking paths only.

Forested areas from the reservoir to Westfir

Birding along this part of the drive is similar to birding along other forest roads, with similar species expected. Habitat is largely mixed conifers with riparian areas. At campgrounds, watch for birds coming down near the ground to pick through ashes from campfires. Spur roads and trails to explore intersect Aufderheide Drive periodically throughout its entire length. There are some *fee* areas, especially at trailheads and campgrounds.

French Pete Creek. Harlequin Duck has been found in French Pete Creek, about 1.4 miles south of the West Side boat ramp. French Pete is a popular recreation area, though, so birders seeking solitude may want to avoid it. The campground has a rest-room facility between sites 12 and 13 large enough for a wheelchair to maneuver in, but the seat is only 17 inches high.

Box Canyon Campground. About 15.6 miles southeast of the West Side boat ramp, at the highest elevation on the drive, lies Box Canyon Campground (with facilities for horses). In this area, visit the Landis Cabin just north of the Campground and bird in the meadow below. Watch for Rufous Hummingbird here until mid- to late summer. The Forest Service has planned a prescribed fire project in the meadow due to the encroachment of small conifers. Read the material on the signs along the road beside Box Canyon Campground for information about the area's birds. Then, across the road and just past Box Canyon Campground, climb 4.1 miles up FS Rd. 1957, a narrow gravel road with steep dropoffs to the west.

Skookum Creek Campground. A nice-looking gravel road bears to the right less than a mile from the beginning of the road; bear left at this intersection to continue the steady climb to Skookum Creek Campground, at 4500 ft. This is a *fee* area. The huge parking lot makes a wide open area from which birds flying overhead between the tall conifers can be viewed easily. A trailhead with the starting point for trails to several lakes lies over the bridge at the back of the campground.

♿ There is an accessible rest room here as well as three accessible campsites. Lower Erma Bell Lake. The 1.75-mile trail to Lower Erma Bell Lake is wheelchair-accessible, although it is a difficult trail considered to be a "wilderness challenge" for those who have the skills to negotiate it in a wheelchair. For those on foot, the trail is known as one of the easier trails in the area to hike and enjoy some higher-elevation birding. Insect repellent is advisable due to the area's mosquitoes, which may carry the West Nile virus.

Shale Ridge Trail. About 2.1 miles south of Box Canyon Campground, on the south side of the road just past where the road curves to the northwest, is a trailhead for Shale Ridge Trail #3567. The trail wanders through a grove of huge western red cedar trees about 2 miles from the trailhead. Some of these trees are over 800 years old. Skookum Meadows, the wetland area where Northern Waterthrush was found singing in the early 1990s (see status section, page 299), is along this trail at the confluence of Skookum Creek and the North Fork of the Middle Fork of the Willamette River, a tricky river crossing about 2.5 miles up the trail. After birding at this location, many hikers will want to turn around and hike back to Aufderheide Drive.

Constitution Grove. The Constitution Grove trailhead is on the south side of Aufderheide Drive about 3.6 miles past Box Canyon Campground. From Hwy. 58 at the turnoff for Aufderheide Drive by the ranger station near Westfir, Constitution Grove is just past milepost 28. This trail provides access to a grove of 200-year-old Douglas-firs. Below 3000 feet in elevation, it is open most of the year. Continue west on Aufderheide Drive past Constitution Grove to complete the loop.

♿ *Kiahanie Campground.* About 12.5 miles from Box Canyon, Kiahanie Campground has accessible rest-room facilities opposite campsite #9. From here, it is about 17-18 miles back to the beginning of the drive, where there is an interpretive sign for the drive on the se side of the road.

The end of Aufderheide Drive (FS Rd. 19) near Westfir is described in the section on Hwy. 58. Those who have managed to miss seeing a dipper during the day can try for one at the green bridge, providing that there is still some daylight left.

HIGHWAY 126 TO SANTIAM PASS

Continuing northeast on Hwy. 126 past the Hwy. 242 junction takes an observer into what is commonly known as the "Clear Lake Cutoff," the southern access to the Santiam Pass.

McKenzie River Viewpoint

On the west side of Hwy. 126 about 4.7 miles north of its intersection with Hwy. 242, a short walk from the roadside parking lot at the McKenzie River Viewpoint leads to an observation deck overlooking the McKenzie River. The rest room at this location and the trail to the viewpoint are accessible.

Sightings of Harlequin Duck, American Dipper, and Belted Kingfisher are possible here. These species cannot be expected to be at the site on cue when birders arrive, but it is clear from the whitewash on the rocks in the river that American Dipper is frequently present.

Trail Bridge and Carmen Smith reservoirs,
Clear Lake, and Fish Lake

It is less than 2 miles north to the Lane Co. line from here. Birders can find good opportunities to enjoy their time in the field at Trail Bridge and Carmen Smith reservoirs, Clear Lake, and Fish Lake before Hwy. 126 and Hwy. 20 join on the way to the Santiam Pass. The stone bridge at the northern end of Trail Bridge Reservoir is very reliable for American Dipper and there are occasionally Harlequin Ducks upstream. Barrow's Goldeneye can almost always be found at Fish Lake, as long as there is open water.

Indian Ford Campground, Calliope Crossing

More lakes with good birding opportunities are along the remainder of the road to the pass area. Beyond the pass, many birders like to stop at Indian Ford Campground or take Indian Ford Rd. to Calliope Crossing (the birding community's name for the utterly rural Pine Street crossing of Indian Ford Creek north of Sisters) on their way to points further east. Consult the Cascades Birding Trail guide for more information.

In winter, birding here can be very slow. It is very birdy during the breeding season, attracting species that use ponderosa pine habitat. During migration, birds that are not often seen in the state are found here with some regularity.

McKenzie Pass Area

With contributions from Paul Sherrell

From Hwy. 126, turn south on Hwy. 242 5.2 miles east of the McKenzie Bridge Campground entrance road, or, if coming from the east, about 7 miles past Olallie Campground. Hwy. 242 is a narrow, winding paved road that goes from Hwy. 126 through the McKenzie Pass to the town of Sisters in Deschutes Co.

From Alder Springs Campground to 3 miles east of Windy Point on the east side of the pass, the vehicle length restriction on the road is 35 feet. Some overly wide or long vehicles may have difficulty traveling safely on this route. High lava walls can damage wide vehicles on turns. The road has steep dropoffs with no guardrails and severe switchbacks. Sharp curves limit travel to 15-20 mph, particularly on the middle portion of the road.

From Hwy. 126, Hwy. 242 climbs 22.3 miles through Douglas-fir forest to high-elevation conifer forest, then to the Dee Wright Observatory set in the vast lava field at the pass level just inside Linn Co. The higher-elevation birding sites are of most interest to birders taking this route. Accessible rest-room facilities are available at several sites, including the west side of the observatory.

Hwy. 242 closes in the fall after the first significant snowfall and often does not open until late spring or early summer, depending on when the road is clear of snow and debris that have accumulated

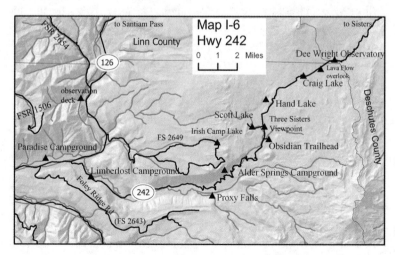

during its closure. The road is typically open from July through October. Lower-elevation portions of the road may be open earlier and later. An anxiously awaited announcement appears in the local press when the road opens for the season all the way through the pass.

Campgrounds on the way to the pass

Stops at campgrounds on the way up to the pass are likely to yield species such as Swainson's Thrush (during breeding season), Winter Wren, Golden-crowned Kinglet, and Chestnut-backed Chickadee. Limberlost Campground is only 1.6 miles from the beginning; Alder Springs Campground is about 8.2 miles further up the road. Proxy Falls, 8.9 miles from the junction of Hwys. 126 and 242, is a heavily visited site. It does not offer a special birding experience, but the hike in to the scenic falls is only about a half mile and is well worth the effort. Although the trail is not accessible, the rest rooms at the trailhead are.

The spur roads off Hwy. 242, all at elevations below 2300 ft, generally dead-end or rejoin the highway within about a mile. Most of the lower and middle portions of the road provide few pullouts that are away from the flow of traffic and suitable for birding.

Obsidian Trailhead/The Sisters Viewpoint/Scott Lake/Hand Lake

There is a turnoff onto a gravel road for the Obsidian Trailhead about 15.4 miles up the highway, on the east side. The Obsidian Trailhead (currently a *fee* area) is a launching site for hikes in the Three Sisters Wilderness. Hikers in these areas have encountered some of the rarer breeding species for the county, including American Pipit and Gray-crowned Rosy-Finch. They are most likely to be found above timberline. The edges of snowfields are favorite foraging spots for high-elevation passerines. Known Sandhill Crane areas are closer to trailheads in the Frissell Crossing area of Aufderheide Drive, but these areas cannot be comfortably reached by most birders on a day hike.

At 16.0 miles along Hwy. 242, a viewpoint on the east side of the road provides a place to stop and enjoy views of the Three Sisters (snow-covered mountain peaks more than 10,000 feet high). Species that have been found here include Northern Goshawk, Black-backed Woodpecker, Mountain Chickadee, and Red Crossbill. The entrance road for Scott Lake Campground is 0.1 mile up the highway from this viewpoint. Birders may want to stop at the beginning of this road for another chance at some high-elevation species. Coming from the north, the turn is 1.1 miles past the Hand Lake trailhead. It is the second turnoff from the highway in this area; the first is to a trailhead parking lot for Trail #3521, which begins across the highway from the road to the lake. The Scott Lake turnoff comes immediately after the trailhead parking lot. If you make a premature turn, you can drive through the parking lot and along a bumpy side road that comes out at the road to Scott Lake. American Three-toed Woodpecker has been found here.

Scott Lake, at an elevation of 4820 ft, is located in a mixed-conifer forest of true fir, mountain hemlock, and lodgepole pine. The camping area along the lake begins about 0.6 mile from the beginning of a rutted gravel access road. The small cove visible from the road near the beginning of the lake may harbor a few ducks. Breeding Mallard and Barrow's Goldeneye are most likely here. Non-campers should continue through the camping area and park in the parking lot just past the quarry, where the road dead-ends. There is currently no fee for camping, parking, or accessing trails at this location, but the policy concerning fees is subject to change.

Rock Wren nests at the quarry. Bufflehead nest here and may be seen at times on the lake. Other species to listen and watch for include Northern Goshawk, Sooty Grouse, Black-backed Woodpecker, American Three-toed Woodpecker, Gray Jay, Steller's Jay, Common Raven, Red-breasted Nuthatch, Golden-crowned Kinglet, Black-capped Chickadee, Townsend's, Hermit, Yellow-rumped, and Yellow Warblers, Pine Siskin, Evening Grosbeak, Dark-eyed Junco, Chipping Sparrow, and Red Crossbill. Look closely at crossbill flocks. A White-winged Crossbill was in the campground in August 1985.

Observers who hike quietly and stand in one spot for a while may be treated to a view of pine marten, which has been seen in the woods along Trail #3502 on the way to Scott Mountain and also at nearby Melakwa Lake. This trail passes Benson Lake and Tenas Lakes before reaching the peak. The habitat along the trail is similar to that of the campground and provides additional opportunities to see high-elevation species. Many hikers go as far as the lake area about 1.2-2.2 miles up the trail and return without climbing the rest of the way up the mountain. Short trails lead to the small lakes from the main trail. A GPS unit would be useful here as an aid to finding the lakes.

The first rest room along the campground road is accessible with a small climb. At the far end of the parking lot on the right side Hand Lake Trail #3513 begins. It is relatively flat and accessible for the less than 0.2 mile to a picnic table in a peaceful setting on the shore of the lake. An accessible rest room, with a flat approach easier than that to the first rest room, is about halfway between the table and the parking lot. Neither of these rest rooms had grab bars at the time of this writing, but they were large and well maintained.

From the picnic area, the shelter at Hand Lake is about 1.4 miles. An alternate, shorter approach to Hand Lake is available from Hwy. 242 about 1.1 miles up Hwy. 242 from the road to Scott Lake Campground. The trailhead is on the west side of the highway; paved trailhead parking is available along the east side. In the breeding season, Lincoln's Sparrow may be heard singing in the riparian area near the road at the beginning of the trail. Clark's Nutcracker rattles like a noisemaker from the treetops, contrasting with the ethereal music of the Hermit Thrush down below. Spotted Sandpiper and Tree Swallow breed at the lake.

Be very cautious along the trail as it nears the lake in 0.3 mile or less, especially if a nearby Spotted Sandpiper appears to be agitated. Its nest is in a cup on the ground, sometimes in the grass very near the trail. These nests are well concealed and easy to step on by those who unwisely venture off the trail. The lake is bounded in most places by grassy margins, and on one side by a lava flow. A Solitary Sandpiper was once found on the shore of the lake in summer, but it was most likely a post-breeding wanderer (Dan Gleason, p.c.). The lake is a fall stopover point for migrating shorebirds such as Western, Least, and Baird's Sandpiper and Semipalmated Plover. In summer, Common Nighthawk begins foraging in the sky around dusk. American Pipit, Barrow's Goldeneye, and Western Meadowlark are other species that may be present here.

Craig Lake

Campers Lake, shown on maps as being across Hwy. 242 from the entrance road to Scott Lake Campground, often has no water in it. For a small lake with water, travel about 4 miles further toward the McKenzie Pass on Hwy. 242 and turn onto a dirt road on the south side of the highway. Watch for the pullout with the monument to the pioneer mailman on the south side of the road and turn right after about 0.1 mile onto the next road. Drive forward to park. It is possible to continue forward on this road and exit the parking area from another access point a short distance away. The lake is somewhat visible for those approaching from the west, but easy to miss for those coming from the east. It is about 2.2 miles west of the Dee Wright Observatory. If you see the pioneer monument pullout when coming from the east, turn into it and go back 0.1 mile.

Craig Lake is located in a mixed forest of pine, fir, and mountain hemlock at an elevation of about 5100 ft. Across the road from the lake is an extensive lava field. Patches of trees among the lava (called lava islands) may be home to Mountain Bluebird during the breeding season. Rock Wren may also be found in the lava. Craig Lake in fall is a reliable spot in which to find Mountain Chickadee and Clark's Nutcracker. Townsend's and Hermit Warblers are present during the breeding season. Red Crossbill may be seen here. White-winged Crossbill was found at a fire pit in the parking areas during the week of September 23 1999; look over crossbill flocks carefully here as well as at other nearby sites.

From Craig Lake, walk east across a low ridge and find an old abandoned road that parallels Hwy. 242. Walk along this road as it turns south and parallels a lava flow. The road enters the forest and gains elevation on its approach to Huckleberry Lake, which is to the east just before the trail ends in a clearing. The hike is slightly less than a mile one way. No unique species are to be found on the hike, but it is a pleasant excursion from the paved road to search for high-elevation species in a more peaceful setting.

Lava Flows/Dee Wright Observatory

Northeast of Craig Lake, the amount of lava along the roadside increases. There are several pullouts to use as viewpoints for birds. A large one is about 0.7 mile past Craig Lake, 20.8 miles from Hwy. 126. Rock Wren and Mountain Bluebird may be observed from this location. In fall, Lewis' Woodpecker passes through the area on migration. Green-tailed Towhee was found near the Lane/Linn Co. line on 10 August 1999. Other species expected to be found on the east side of the Cascades, such as Pygmy Nuthatch, may eventually be found here as it is just a short distance away from their preferred habitat.

Only 0.9 mile past the county line into Deschutes Co., Dee Wright Observatory is worth the stop. It has accessible rest rooms.

Lava flows near Belknap Crater; Three Sisters in background. Photo by Alan Contreras.

The paved trail up to the first level of the observatory, while wide enough for a wheel chair, is a bit steep and is not on the National Forest's list of accessible sites. Reached by a set of steps, the top section of the observatory is a metal wheel showing the names of all the peaks that can be seen from the magnificent view at that location.

From here, birders may either go back down Hwy. 242 or drive to Sisters, near which there are birding opportunities for eastside species such as White-headed Woodpecker, Williamson's Sapsucker, Calliope Hummingbird, and Pygmy Nuthatch. The state park east of town and Calliope Crossing to the north are both excellent places to bird, as is Cold Springs Campground west of Sisters.

Highway 58: Valley Parks

Don DeWitt and Barbara Combs

This section contains guides for the cluster of large parks between Hwy. 58 and Springfield, and also sites along Hwy. 58 farther east to the summit of the Cascades. Dexter Lake, though only slightly above the valley floor, is included in the second part of this section devoted to the Cascade Mountains (see page 158), because it represents a transition place and is often visited by people heading into the Cascades, which the three "flatland" parks are not.

Mt. Pisgah (Buford Park), Elijah Bristow, and Jasper parks lie within a few miles of each other north of Hwy. 58 just southeast of Eugene and south of Springfield. All three offer good opportunities to see many of the commonly occurring passerine and resident species to be found in the upper Willamette Valley. A few species

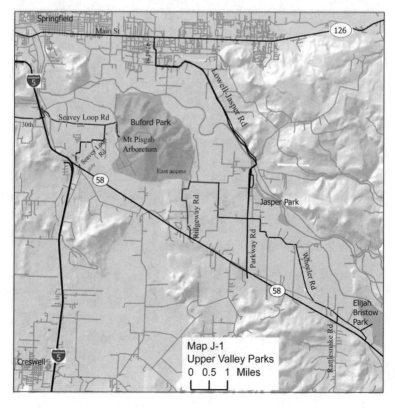

Map J-1
Upper Valley Parks
0   0.5   1   Miles

are generally more readily found at one or another of the parks, though.

The parks differ markedly in means of access—hiking with significant elevation gain (Pisgah); level trails for biking/horseback/walking (Bristow); or level paved roads and sidewalks offering best access to wheelchair users (Jasper).

Mt. Pisgah/Buford Park

Don DeWitt

Spring ***   *Summer****   *Fall ****   *Winter ***

Mt. Pisgah is a huge (2,200 acres) Lane Co. park. It offers some of the best hiking and birding close to the urban area, and some oak savannah and madrone/ceanothus habitat more commonly found in southwestern Oregon. A seasonal *fee* is required in spring and summer.

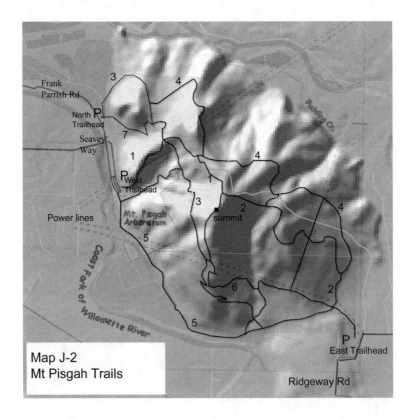

Map J-2
Mt Pisgah Trails

West Access:

(a) Heading east on Eugene's 30th Ave., pass Lane Community College (LCC), drive across I-5 to the frontage road, and turn north (left.) At the first right, just past the gas station, begin to follow the signs to Lane Co.'s largest park, usually referred to as Mt. Pisgah.

(b) Or drive onto I-5 southbound at LCC. Take the first exit, 188A, onto Hwy. 58, at about 0.9 mile. Watch for the turn left onto Seavey Loop Rd. (1.8 miles from I-5 entrance from LCC) and follow the county park signs. Using either approach, the signs will direct you east across the bridge over the Coast Fork of the Willamette River. Once across the bridge, turn right to the main parking area at the portion of the park known as "The Arboretum." (Along the access road pay the required daily *fee*. Seasonal passes are also available.) Walking gravel and dirt trails is required to bird Pisgah, and little of the park is really wheelchair accessible.

Where to bird here? Many local birders favor the mixed woods and grassy areas of the 200-acre Arboretum along with the networks of trails leading upslope onto the west side of the 1,000 foot-high mountain that dominates much of Buford Park. Hutton's Vireo, Black-throated Gray Warbler, Black-capped and Chestnut-backed Chickadee, Red-breasted Nuthatch, Pileated Woodpecker, and others breed here within an area that can be covered comfortably in a morning's birding walk. Many warbler, flycatcher, and other passerine species are present, especially during migration. The water garden area can be good, as can the trails leading off farther to the south, passing near the Coast Fork of the Willamette.

Hiking the rest of the park can take more time. Check the large map boards near the Arboretum and at trailheads to see the layout of the more than 20 miles of trail in Buford Park. The 1.5-mile trail called the #1 trail takes the most direct route to the grassy top of the hill. Another good hike from the west side is the #3 trail, accessible at the north trailhead (drive left immediately after crossing the Coast Fork bridge). You can also turn onto trail #3 where it crosses trail #1 at its 0.6 mile marker.

Hiking these trails and others gives you a more open view of raptors, woodpeckers, turkeys, and many other resident and passerine species. Small numbers of Western Bluebirds fly all over the mountain in fall and winter. The grassy area at the top of the hill sometimes, particularly in fall and winter, can have a few grassland species not commonly seen elsewhere in the area. These have included annual Horned Lark, and Western Meadowlark, and less often Lapland Longspur, American Pipit, and Snow Bunting. Northern Pygmy Owls are often heard and sometimes seen in the woods near the top and on down the slopes. Vesper Sparrows breed at Pisgah and can sometimes be seen and heard singing along several of the trails as well as at the top. In spring and in fall flocks of migrating birds such as White-fronted Geese and Sandhill Cranes move over Buford Park to the delight of birders hiking a thousand feet above the valley floor.

East Access:

Heading east along Hwy. 58, turn north onto Ridgeway Rd. at the Subway Sandwich/Gas Station in Pleasant Hill (about 5.2 miles from the LCC entrance to I-5) and drive 1.6 miles to a gravel parking lot. (Daily *fee* required at a self-pay station just inside the gate.) This access point, also used by people riding horses, is the quickest way to get to some of the unusual types of birding habitat available in parts of Buford Park.

The first stretch of the eastside trail passes a small wetland dominated by Douglas spirea and Oregon ash, habitat well worth a birder's time. Virginia Rail and Yellow-breasted Chat are usually here during summer as are abundant Common Yellowthroats. Some Marsh Wrens and Lincoln's Sparrows generally use this area in winter, and flocks of other wintering sparrows are always along here, too. Early summer rarities such as Ash-throated Flycatcher and even Eastern Kingbird have been seen a time or two.

Several trails take off from the trail junction 0.3 mile from the eastside gate. (There is a large map displayed here to help guide you.) Off to the far left is the low-lying trail along the grassy south slope of the hill. More often birders take either of two rough gravel roads, the grassy/shrubby #6 trail that follows the powerlines most of the way to the top, or the #2 trail to the right that heads off through mixed fir and oak woodland and connects to the #1 (westside) trail near the top.

There is yet another trail on this side of Pisgah, the steep and wooded #4 trail along the north side. Several cross trails, some of them unsigned, can also be explored. An ambitious hiker can select among several routes from eastside to westside and back for a total distance of 7 miles or much more.

Along the #6 trail birders find such species as Lazuli Bunting, Willow Flycatcher, California Quail, and Yellow-breasted Chat during summer, and large flocks of wintering sparrows, Juncos, and Yellow-rumped Warblers in winter. Western Kingbirds often nest in the metal power structures overhead and resident Wrentit use the thick habitat along the slopes. In September wandering Lewis's Woodpeckers often stop by Mt. Pisgah for a few days or weeks and this section of the park is a good place to watch for them. Except for breeding season, occasional Prairie Falcon and Golden Eagle sightings are reported along here, too. Rarities have included nearly annual Ash-throated Flycatchers and a few years Blue-gray Gnatcatchers were found around the ceanothus bushes, rare habitat this far north in Oregon, at the Buckbrush Creek crossing 1.1 mile up the trail.

Along the #2 trail there is good viewing of passerines, and sometimes a surprise such as Northern Pygmy Owl or other owl species, Ruffed Grouse, wintering Townsend's Solitaire, accipiter species, even rare sightings of a Goshawk. A horse trail up the grassy slope to the top branches off from this trail about a half mile below the summit, or you can just take the gravel road on to its intersection with the #1 trail and then turn left, upslope to the top of Mt. Pisgah.

From here there are good views of the Eugene/Springfield area all around and of the Coast Range and Cascade mountain ranges. (Note: if time allows after your hike back to the vehicle, a meandering route on some of the rural roads east of Mt. Pisgah might turn up an unusual species such as one of the nearly annual spring Say's Phoebes or something rarer such as a Sage Sparrow, Mountain Bluebird, or an uncommon raptor or flycatcher. Edenvale Rd. and the Jasper/Creswell road take you back south to Hwy. 58.

To access Jasper and Elijah Bristow parks, which are farther east on Hwy. 58, take I-5 southbound from any part of Eugene-Springfield. From the 30th Ave. exit in south Eugene travel approximately 0.8 mile south to exit (188A) for Hwy. 58 towards Oakridge and Klamath Falls. This exit is on the right at a place where the freeway itself curves to the left. Birding opportunities are abundant via long and short side trips from the highway.

The sites described below provide excellent birding opport-unities, but there are many other hidden trails and forest service roads that can provide similar opportunities. Start with these known sites, and do some exploration of your own as you become familiar with the area. Driving directions are based on travel up Hwy. 58 from the Willamette Valley, but they can be used in reverse by someone coming from the southeast over the Willamette Pass.

Jasper Park

Don DeWitt and Barbara Combs

Spring ***   *Summer****   *Fall ***   *Winter ** (closed to cars)*

Drive 5.5 miles southeast of Eugene on Hwy. 58. Turn north (left) on Parkway Rd. at the blinking traffic signal. Drive 2.1 mile. to Jasper Park Drive. Turn right (east) and travel 0.2 mile to the park gate.

Jasper Park is a *fee* park, with accessible rest rooms and developed picnic and recreation areas. A State Parks season pass is available. This 60-acre park is almost entirely circled by a paved road and has some sidewalks and other level trails, as well as improved rest rooms, two children's play areas, and group picnic areas. Often there is a park host in residence—sometimes that site has bird feeders. The park is small enough to park your vehicle only once and walk from there.

Note: As of this writing, the park is accessible by car only from May 1 to September 30, during which time the fee is required and there is no parking outside the gate. However, from October 1 through April 30, access by foot or bike is allowed and there is no fee, with limited parking outside the gate.

Jasper Park is one of the few sites in Lane Co. that has regularly hosted Red-eyed Vireo. They have bred here in most years since at least the mid-1970s. One year, a nest was found in the low branches of a small tree in the grassy island between the park road and the main parking lot. During early to mid-summer visits, look for these along the entrance road and in the undeveloped areas on the right as you enter the park. Another possible location for these birds is along the river bank.

The large cottonwoods and other trees all along the right side of the entrance road host many species including flycatchers, thrushes, warblers, and Hutton's, Cassin's, and Warbling vireos. Grassy areas along the road and parking areas of the park can be good for Chipping and other sparrow species, California Quail, and

Lesser Goldfinch. Jasper is one of the most reliable sites to find Red-breasted Sapsucker, with these birds often seen flying across the park between the river and their nests back in the trees along the access road.

The river edge with its cottonwoods, maples, and oaks is a good place to watch for the sapsuckers as well as Yellow Warbler, goldfinches, Western Tanagers, Black-headed Grosbeaks, and the annually nesting Bullock's Orioles which at this site recycle discarded monofilament fishing line into nest balls that they suspend near the ends of branches of riparian cottonwoods.

Green Heron have nested in the park. Keep a close eye on the river for fly-bys of species such as Bald Eagle and Band-tailed Pigeon. Spotted Sandpipers may be along the river edge and Northern Rough-winged Swallows may be among the many Violet-Greens and others overhead. The wilder areas along the fringes of the park are often very birdy. Lazuli Bunting may be heard singing in an adjacent field.

Elijah Bristow State Park

Don DeWitt and Barbara Combs

Spring ***   *Summer****   *Fall ****   *Winter ***

From the I-5 turnoff for Hwy. 58, travel about 8.5 miles southeast. Turn left (east) at the blinking traffic signal onto Rattlesnake Rd. After 0.2 mile, turn right onto Wheeler Rd. The entrance to the park is 0.8 mile down Wheeler Rd. on the left (east) side of the road.

Note: Transit between Jasper Park and Elijah Bristow State Park can be accomplished by using Wheeler Rd. instead of going back to Hwy. 58. From park to park, the distance using Wheeler Rd. (with a small segment of travel on Jasper Park Drive) is a little over 5 miles.

Elijah Bristow State Park is a developed park with accessible rest-room and picnic facilities, but there is no fee for access to the park or any of its facilities. This park is far enough away from well-traveled highways to provide a birding experience surrounded by bird song rather than traffic noise. Bristow is an 850-acre state park that offers a kiosk with maps along the entrance road. The large map will be of help in orienting yourself to the network of trails in the main park area, and also trails leading some 3 miles up the Middle Fork of the Willamette River all the way to Dexter Reservoir (Dexter is also accessible from Hwy. 58, see page 158).

The system of hiking trails in the park is extensive, but at the time of this writing the process of labeling and mapping the trails was not complete. Lack of attentiveness to one's physical location at this park could result in a long walk back to the parking lot from Dexter Reservoir. The trails can be quite muddy during the rainy months and for some time afterward as they dry out, so bring appropriate footwear for these conditions unless you can be certain that the trails are dry.

Visits to this park in spring and early summer can be quite productive for local breeding species, including Cassin's and Warbling Vireos, Bewick's Wren, Western Wood Pewee, Black-throated Gray and Orange-crowned Warblers, Swainson's Thrush, and Black-headed Grosbeak. Band-tailed Pigeons are also present.

Grassy areas bordering willows and other low shrubs along the entrance road are often good for Willow Flycatcher, Lazuli Bunting, McGillivray's Warblers, and others. The tall stands of mostly deciduous trees closer to the river can sometimes be quite good for Black-throated Gray Warblers, thrushes, flycatchers, and Hutton's, Cassin's, and Warbling Vireo.

Red-eyed Vireos are annual in this park. Listen for them singing anywhere along the streamside cottonwoods and other hardwoods. A half-mile stretch along the river near where a footbridge crosses Lost Creek has proved to be a good place to locate these uncommon vireos. Nesting has been reported here. But the uncommon Red-eyes along with many other species of passerines have also been found along the road near the park's picnic area, a good place to begin for birders unable to hike the trails.

Directions to the parks from Springfield:
The route to all three parks begins on Main Street. Take 42nd Street south from Main, and turn left (east) where it runs into Jasper Rd. Jasper Rd. goes east and then southeast and becomes Springfield-Creswell Hwy. Distance from Main Street to the town of Jasper is 5 miles, at which point turn right onto Parkway Rd. and cross the green bridge across the McKenzie River.

To go to Jasper Park: continue from the bridge on Parkway Rd. for 0.6 mile then turn left (east) onto the access road to the park. The park entrance is another 0.2 mile.

To go on to Bristow Park: from the access road to Jasper Park, follow Parkway Rd. another 0.8 mile. Turn left (east) here, onto Wheeler Rd. (See above for other details.)

To go to the east side of Mt. Pisgah from Parkway Rd.: from the access road to Jasper Park follow Parkway Rd. 0.8 mile and, instead of taking Wheeler Rd., turn right (east) onto Valley Rd. Go 0.7 mile on Valley to Edenvale, turn right (north) and follow this road 0.9 mile to Ridgeway. Turn left and follow Ridgeway to the gravel parking lot near the east side of the hill, about 2 miles.

Another way to reach the east parking area for Mt. Pisgah: from the bridge at Jasper take the immediate right turn off of Parkway onto Edenvale Rd. and follow its turns for a distance of 1.3 miles. At an intersection it then becomes Ridgeway Rd., which continues about 2 miles to the gravel parking lot of Pisgah.

Continuing on Parkway Rd. (southbound) takes you to Hwy. 58. Turn left (east) to go to Dexter Lake and beyond. Or, turn right (west) to return to I-5.

To return to Eugene this way, take northbound I-5 to the LCC exit, which, going north, is numbered Exit 189.

Highway 58: The Cascade Mountains

Barbara Combs

Travelers along Hwy. 58 southeast of Eugene toward Klamath Falls can find many birding opportunities. Lowland specialties such as Red-eyed Vireo and Bewick's Wren can be found close to Eugene-Springfield (the vireo mainly in the mid-valley parks of the previous section), while birds of higher-elevation habitats, such as Black-backed and Three-toed Woodpeckers, Clark's Nutcracker, and Mountain Chickadee can be found near the Willamette Pass.

Hills Creek Wetland, the town of Oakridge, Salt Creek Falls, Gold Lake, and Waldo Lake are all included in the Cascades Birding Trail. Visit http://www.oregonbirdingtrails.org/cascades.htm on the Internet for more information about the Cascades Birding Trail.

Dexter Reservoir

With contributions from Don DeWitt

Spring ***   Summer**   Fall ***   Winter ***

Travel about 13.9 miles southeast on Hwy. 58 from the I-5 exit south of Eugene. You will see a covered bridge on the left side of the road. Turn left (east) on Jasper-Lowell Rd. (which bypasses the covered bridge) and find a place to park in the wide area to the left just past the covered bridge. Birders and people fishing use this area and there is usually ample parking. Handicap access improvements are in progress here.

Dexter Reservoir is best in fall, winter, and early spring when waterfowl use it for resting and feeding. A number of Willamette Valley rarities have appeared here, including Sabine's Gull, Long-tailed Duck, Eurasian Wigeon, and a *Sterna* tern. The reservoir may also hold such hard-to-find species as Barrow's Goldeneye and Common Goldeneye. There is sometimes a Common Loon on the lake.

Fewer water birds are present in summer, but there is usually a population of Western Grebes to be seen somewhere on the lake. Any grebe that occurs in Oregon might be found here outside of the breeding season, although Red-necked Grebe is quite unusual.

Bald Eagles and Osprey nest in the area. The setting sun can interfere with viewing birds on Dexter Lake at this location, so plan to bird here during the first half of the day or when it is very cloudy.

Driving on across the causeway to Lowell gives you access to still more parks: the marina area to the left and a small day park to the right. It is possible to drive upstream along the West Boundary Rd. to the Corps of Engineers office area below the dam for another access point to the reservoir. Driving on up West Boundary Rd. takes you to the Lookout Point Dam and reservoir. See the Lowell entry below. (A long, slow drive on that unpaved road leads to Westfir. Not recommended for anyone with limited birding time and other sites to visit.)

Lowell

*Spring ****   *Summer****   *Fall ***   *Winter ***

From the covered bridge at Dexter Reservoir, the Lowell Service Center of the Middle Fork Ranger District is 0.5 mile away on the right side of Jasper-Lowell Rd., across from Lowell High School. If you arrive during office hours, you may be able to obtain advice about local road conditions and current bird sightings. A city park with rest-room facilities is another 0.2 mile down the road on the left.

Lookout Point Reservoir

To get to Lookout Point Reservoir, continue straight for another 0.1 mile past the ranger district office and turn right for access to the top of the dam. You may want to stop at a few pullouts along the way, including the Willamette project area. Look for various waterfowl at the dam, then continue southeast along the lakeside frontage road for access to a variety of small parks and boat landings that offer views of the reservoir. Some of the day use areas have accessible rest rooms.

Traveling through the woods on the side of the reservoir opposite Hwy. 58 provides excellent opportunities to view local breeding passerines in the spring and summer. Wrentit may be found at many areas along the road. Look also for Red-breasted Sapsucker, Pileated Woodpecker, Varied Thrush, and Red Crossbill. Harlequin Duck has been found on the rocks near the beginning of the reservoir. Common Merganser also nests in the area. The last developed site along the reservoir (a boat ramp area) is about 4.5 miles beyond the dam. Many birders may want to turn around and head back to Hwy. 58 at this point.

Another option is to continue along West Boundary (FS 5821) road to visit the Buckhead Wildlife Area's nature trail and return to Hwy. 58 via a bridge that has been a reliable spot to find American Dipper.

Buckhead Wildlife Area

Continue on FS Rd. 5821 and stay on it past its junction with FS Rd. 5824. At the junction with Rd. 5826, which is about 11.8 miles from the dam, stay to the right on Rd. 5821 and cross the railroad tracks. This portion of the road is full of potholes (as of spring 2005) for about 3.2 miles until you reach pavement. Soon after the paved road begins, turn right to go to the parking lot for the Buckhead Wildlife Area.

Alternate access to Buckhead Wildlife Area from Highway 58:
Travel southeast on Hwy. 58 about 18.7 miles from its intersection with Jasper-Lowell Rd. and turn east (left) toward Westfir just past the intersection of Deception Creek Rd. and Hwy. 58. Drive 0.4 mile, crossing over the green bridge. Turn left onto FS Rd. 19. Drive about 0.9 mile, turn left, and cross over another bridge. Turn left immediately after crossing the bridge.

Drive about 1.9 miles, first along Winfrey Rd., then on FS Rd. 5821 (also known as West Boundary Rd.) when the road name changes. Pass a tree nursery on the left side of the road before turning left into the Buckhead Wildlife Area parking lot.

A picnic table and an accessible rest-room facility are available here, but there is no water. The nature trail is a pleasant half-mile loop that passes through a small wet area and approaches the river before returning to the beginning of the loop. MacGillivray's Warbler nests here. Wrentit may also be found at this location. Chestnut-backed Chickadee makes its presence known incessantly. A short walk parallel to the power line right-of-way (to the right of the nature trail) leads to a small reedy pond. Mallards and other waterfowl may be found on this pond. It is also one of the best locations to find the area's elk.

Returning to Highway 58 at Westfir
Turn right when leaving the wildlife area. After 1.6 miles, note that the road name becomes Winfrey Rd. Stay toward the right after crossing the railroad tracks and drive another 0.3 mile through the small community of Hemlock. Turn right and go over the bridge to FS Rd. 19. Turn right again and travel about 0.9 mile to the green bridge.

Pull off the road onto the wide shoulder on the right side of the road before the bridge and search for American Dipper on the rocks in the river below and near the bridge. After completing your search, turn right onto the bridge and continue for about 0.4 mile to Hwy. 58. Here you may turn right to go back to Eugene, turn left to go to Oakridge and other points to the southeast, or turn right on Hwy. 58, then left immediately past the Main Middle Fork Ranger District Office, to bird on Deception Creek Rd.

Deception Creek Road (Forest Service Road 5850)

Spring ***   *Summer****   *Fall* **   *Winter* **

Note: There are no rest-room facilities on this road, but the Main Middle Fork Ranger District office does have public rest rooms.

The turnoff onto Deception Creek Rd. (FS Rd. 5850) is about 18.7 miles southeast of the Lowell-Jasper Rd. covered bridge. Turn right from Hwy. 58 if you are coming from the Eugene area. Pull out along the road where it is wide and there is good visibility in both directions. Slowly cruising along while keeping a sharp lookout along the road and roadside may produce views of Mountain Quail, Sooty Grouse, or Ruffed Grouse in any season. Early morning and dusk are best for these species.

Stop along the road where there is a safe place to pull out and check for such species as Gray Jay, Pileated Woodpecker, Townsend's Solitaire, Varied Thrush, Northern Pygmy-Owl, Olive-sided Flycatcher, Black-headed Grosbeak, Western Tanager, Red Crossbill, and Orange-crowned, Black-throated Gray, MacGillivray's, and Hermit Warblers. One such place is about 4.1 miles from Hwy. 58, where there is a dirt track to walk on and search for birds away from the roadside.

After about 8.5 miles, Deception Creek Rd. intersects with FS Rd. 2102, which provides access to Hills Creek Reservoir and is also good for quail and grouse. Turn left at this intersection and watch for birds along the roadside as you drive about 9.3 miles to the T intersection with FS Rd. 21. Turn left (north) to go back to Hwy. 58 or to bird around the reservoir.

To return to Highway 58:

Follow FS Rd. 21 about a mile to its intersection with FS Rd. 23. Turn left and take FS Rd. 23 about 0.5 mile to Hwy. 58. Turn left to go back to the Eugene area, or right to head toward the Willamette Pass and Klamath Falls.

To bird Hills Creek Reservoir:

Drive about 0.4 mile on FS Rd. 21 to the access road for the area below the dam. Turn right (southeast) on this road and park by the yellow gate. See below for more information about birding in this location.

Hills Creek Reservoir and nearby sites

Spring ***	Summer**	Fall **	Winter **

Coming from Eugene, travel about 6 miles past Deception Creek Rd. through the town of Oakridge. Turn right onto FS Rd. 23 (there is a sign that says Hills Creek Reservoir). After 0.5 mile, turn right on FS Rd. 21. Drive about 0.5 mile to the access road for the area below the dam. Turn left (southeast) and go to the yellow gate. Please do not block the gate when you park. To access birding areas on Army Corps of Engineers property, walk along the gravel road toward the powerhouse and past a second gate. Birders should not enter the fenced pastures, as these are private property.

Bird along Hills Creek and the small ponds at the base of the dam. Lark Sparrow, Brewer's Sparrow, Rock Wren, Ash-throated Flycatcher, Northern Mockingbird, and American Redstart are among the more unusual Lane Co. species that have been found here. Regulars

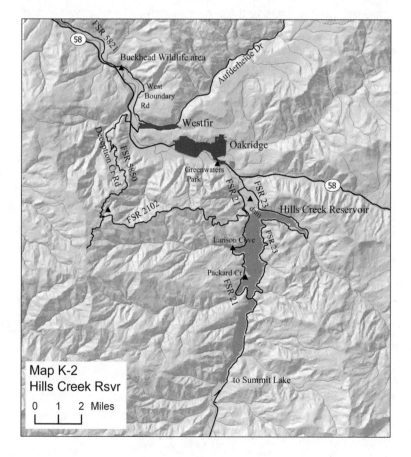

Map K-2
Hills Creek Rsvr

0   1   2 Miles

include Green Heron, Virginia Rail, Rufous Hummingbird, Spotted Sandpiper, Tree, Violet-green, Cliff, Barn, and Northern Rough-winged Swallows, Chestnut-backed Chickadee, Hutton's, Cassin's, and Warbling Vireos, Western Wood-Pewee, Swainson's Thrush, Willow and Olive-sided Flycatchers, Hermit, Yellow, MacGillivray's, Wilson's and Black-throated Gray Warblers, Yellow-breasted Chat, Western Tanager, Black-headed Grosbeak, Spotted Towhee, Dark-eyed Junco, and Song Sparrow.

After birding below the dam, go back up to FS Rd. 21 and turn left. Traveling around Hills Creek Reservoir and stopping along the way will yield good looks at many local species, including breeding Bald Eagle and Osprey in season. Some stops are *fee* areas, so watch signage carefully. Harlequin Duck may be present in the reservoir or along creeks. Pelagic species such as Leach's Storm-Petrel and Parasitic Jaeger have been blown into the area after a heavy storm at sea. Snow Goose has been seen here in early November. Loons may be found at times in the winter months, as well as Surf Scoter.

Short trips up less-traveled side roads can provide opportunities to listen to and view local species in a quieter setting. Larison Creek trail, for those who would like to get away from roads and traffic, begins about 2.8 miles from the dam access road. Its trailhead is on the north side of Larison Cove, on the opposite side from the boat ramp. It is 6.3 miles long and ends at FS Rd. 101, a primitive road. Old-growth habitat begins after about 1.6 miles, as the trail begins to climb above the portion of the creek that has been flooded for the reservoir.

Packard Creek Campground

Packard Creek Campground, about 4.5 miles past the access road for the dam, has accessible rest-room facilities. The boat ramp has a handicapped parking space with rest rooms and a nice view of the reservoir.

A decision point comes after about 10.5 miles from the beginning of the reservoir road (10 miles from the access road for birding below the dam), directly after the road crosses a narrow portion of the reservoir.

On to the Cascade Crest and Summit Lake?

A right turn here leads to some high-mountain birding areas, including Summit Lake, which is in Klamath Co. The distance to

Summit Lake is a little more than 30 miles. Exploration of wooded areas at the higher elevations can yield sightings of species such as Red-naped Sapsucker and Fox Sparrow. At times it is possible to find Green-tailed Towhees and Mountain Bluebirds in the higher-elevation areas when clear-cutting has provided suitable habitat. Exploration is the best way to find these areas, since they change over time as older clear-cut areas become overgrown with trees and these bird species move on to newer clear-cut (or burned) areas.

...or around the reservoir and back to Hwy. 58?

A left turn at this decision point will continue your journey around the reservoir, now on FS Rd. 23. This road will lead back to Hwy. 58 in about 13.6 miles. This a slow, winding gravel road.

Greenwaters Park

Along Hwy. 58 on the southeast edge of Oakridge, about 0.3 mile southeast of the bridge over Salmon Creek, lies Greenwaters Park. It makes a good rest stop, and may provide sightings of American Dipper and other local species along the Middle Fork of the Willamette River.

Road 5884

Note: There are no rest rooms or other facilities on this road.

This road is at a rather obscure turnoff about 14 miles southeast of the turnoff for Hills Creek Reservoir from Hwy. 58. Watch for it about 0.25 mile southeast of where a railroad bridge crosses Hwy. 58. Turn west over a short bridge, then climb up to a dead end about 9.3 miles from Hwy. 58. There are a number of spur roads in the area. Staying on the road that appears to be the most traveled will lead to the dead end described below.

The road is a good place to look for grouse and quail. Nashville Warbler inhabits the more open areas. Raptors may soar overhead. There are a few spur roads that can be explored, as well. The area at the dead end has an abundance of wildflowers in season that attracts a variety of hummingbirds. A Black-chinned Hummingbird was at this location one year in late summer.

Salt Creek Falls

Spring ***	*Summer* ***	*Fall* **	*Winter* *

Drive southeast on Hwy. 58 for about 6 miles after its intersection with Rd. 5884.

♿ Picnic tables and accessible rest-room facilities are available in the day use area at Salt Creek Falls; some falls viewpoints are accessible.

Visiting this *fee* area requires a day-use pass (which may be purchased on site) or a Northwest Forest (annual) Pass.

Salt Creek Falls is the only place in Oregon where Black Swift is easily observable during the breeding season. Sightings usually begin around Memorial Day weekend and last into at least mid-August. The best viewing time for Black Swift is early in the morning. Black Swifts normally leave roosting sites near or behind waterfalls before first light. Some birds may linger near the falls into the morning, especially on misty days. Later in the day, they are either soaring too high to be seen by the naked eye or foraging in distant areas. Near dark, they begin to return to the falls, but in breeding season this can be around 9:00 p.m., later than most daytime visitors would like to be out in this relatively remote area.

To view the swifts, walk to the lookout points for the falls from the parking lot. It often takes some time to spot the swifts. Especially when they are overhead, they may be in a mixed group of foragers, including swallows and Vaux's Swifts. Use caution when sorting out these high-flying species. Also found in the area are Hermit and Townsend's Warblers. Hermit Warbler often may be heard singing near the parking lot. Walking less than a half mile up the trail to Vivian Lake from the day use picnic area will allow escape from the noisy falls and easier listening for warbler songs.

Mule Prairie

There is a gravel road (FS Rd. 5893) that goes east from the access road to the parking lot, with a bridge at about 0.02 mile. Turn onto this road and stop by the bridge. American Dipper is often found here, and near other bridges in the area. Travel about 1.3-1.7 miles up this gravel road to any wide pullout on the left-hand side of the road. Walk down the hill (there is no trail) toward Hwy. 58. A swampy area down below has hosted Northern Waterthrush during the breeding season in some years. In winter, expect this road to be blocked by snow.

WALDO LAKE

Spring ***   *Summer****   *Fall ***   *Winter * (ski access only)*

Drive about 1.9 miles southeast on Hwy. 58 past Salt Creek Falls. Turn north up the paved FS Rd. 5897 to Waldo Lake, also a *fee* area. The road to Waldo Lake is impassable for passenger vehicles during the months it is covered by snow. Conditions vary from year to year, so check on road conditions before you go in fall to late spring. Barrow's Goldeneye may be found on the lake. Species such as Northern Goshawk, Hairy Woodpecker, Williamson's Sapsucker (unusual), Black-backed Woodpecker, Clark's Nutcracker, Gray Jay, Hermit and Varied Thrushes, Mountain Bluebird, Townsend's Solitaire, Hammond's and Olive-sided Flycatchers, Mountain Chickadee, Yellow-rumped (Audubon's) and Townsend's Warblers, Cassin's Finch, and Western Tanager can be found in areas near the lake and along nearby trails. Sooty Grouse are sometimes present along the paved road between Hwy. 58 and the camping area, especially near dawn or dusk. Careful checks of shrubby riparian areas could result in discovery of nesting Lincoln's Sparrow.

Several developed campgrounds along the lake may be used as a base of operations for those who want to spend more than a day exploring in the area. There are many trails to choose from, including trails up nearby mountains and to smaller lakes. It is possible to hike all the way around the lake (a distance of about 21 miles), but few birders will want to attempt this hike as a day trip.

Waldo Lake Trail

Access to the Waldo Lake Trail, one of Waldo Lake's best known birding spots, is located at the northeast corner of the lake near North Waldo Campground. To find the trail, travel all the way up Waldo Lake Rd. (about 11.2 miles) to a T intersection and turn right toward the North Waldo Campground. Drive toward the boat ramp and enter the upper parking lot on the right. There are accessible rest-room facilities just past the parking lot toward the lake. You will see a sign on the right side of the parking lot indicating the access point for the Waldo Lake Trail, which offers the possibility of Spotted Sandpiper, Mountain Bluebird, and Black-backed Woodpecker.

There was a large burn in this area in 1996, which killed many trees and left the landscape barren and open. After a few minutes of hiking up the Waldo Lake Trail through untouched green woods,

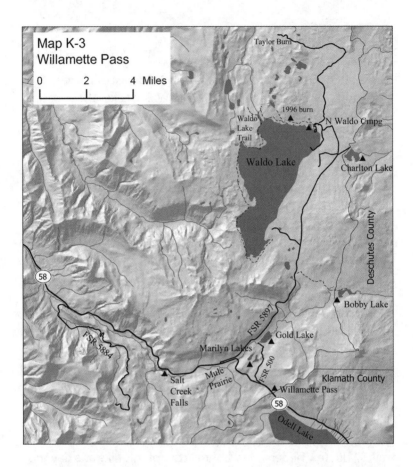

birders will reach this extensive area. It is a humbling experience to walk through a place where a forest fire created such a massive amount of destruction. The burn area is the best place to look for Black-backed Woodpecker and Mountain Bluebird. Stop often along the trail to listen for a very quiet tapping noise. Find the source of the noise, and you will probably find a Black-backed Woodpecker. Tree Swallows and Red-breasted Nuthatches also nest here.

Note: Hike in only as far as you think you can safely hike back out. This is not a loop trail unless you walk the entire 21 miles or so around the lake.

The Taylor Burn Rd., about 0.1 mile back toward Hwy. 58 from the parking lot, climbs to a location that used to harbor Boreal Owl, but, since the 1996 burn, none have been found there. Boreal Owl has also been reported from nearby Charlton Lake, so there may still be some owls in the area but finding them will require searching at high-elevation locations that look promising. A walk up the Taylor Burn Rd. offers other good birding opportunities and access to a different portion of the large burn area. Taylor Burn Rd. is steep and rutted in places, making it a difficult or impossible drive for a passenger vehicle that lacks high clearance and 4-wheel drive.

Bobby Lake Trail

The Bobby Lake trailhead is about 5.5 miles from Hwy. 58 along the Waldo Lake Rd. It is about 7.5 miles from the Taylor Burn intersection back toward Hwy. 58. The Bobby Lake Trail has been popular with birders searching for woodpeckers and other high-mountain species. It is a relatively flat round-trip hike of about 4.5 miles, but birders may want to do some additional hiking while at the lake.

Gold Lake

On Hwy. 58, the turnoff for Gold Lake is 2.6 miles southeast of the road to Waldo Lake. Watch for the signs for the Gold Lake Sno-Park (which is on the west side of the road), then look for a green road sign on the east side of the road. Turn east on Gold Lake Rd. (FS Rd. 500) and drive 2 miles to Gold Lake, another *fee* area. You may park in the day-use area parking lot, or find a campsite if you plan to camp. Accessible rest-room facilities area available in the developed portion of this recreation area.

Gold Lake Rd. becomes blocked by snow in the fall and may not be accessible by passenger vehicles until late spring in some years, so check local conditions if there is any question. Ski routes are available in the winter time, when Gray Jay may be one of the highlights of the trip.

Marilyn Lakes Trail

Walk straight through the picnic area from the day use parking lot to find a trail that goes to Marilyn Lakes. Sites along this trail, especially a large open area within 0.2 mile of its beginning, can produce breeding American Three-toed Woodpecker, Steller's Jay, Gray Jay, Hermit Warbler, Townsend's Warbler, Varied Thrush, and Olive-sided Flycatcher, depending on the season. Close looks at Golden-crowned Kinglet and Chestnut-backed Chickadee are possible at this location.

Gold Lake Campground and bog

Black-backed Woodpecker has nested in the campground, though the tree used for the nest is gone and there have been no recent reports of nearby nests. In late summer and fall of several different years, birders at Gold Lake have found White-winged Crossbill among the crossbill flocks feeding on the cone crop. There are several locations in the camping loop opposite the day use area where birders can set up a spotting scope to look out over portions of the lake. Barrow's Goldeneye, Bufflehead, Ring-necked Duck, Lesser Scaup, and Mallard may be found on the lake. Osprey nest there.

Solitary Sandpiper may nest occasionally in the bog area at the far side of the lake. The bog is most easily reached by canoe, but hikers may take a trail along the lake to the location. To find the trail, cross over the bridge just past the day use parking area to the northwest. It goes to a small auxiliary camping area. Walk along the campground road, keeping to the right, and turn right on the north side of the loop road to follow the trail along the lake.

At the bog, about 0.7 mile from the beginning of the trail, the area becomes very wet. Mosquitoes are abundant. Check for nesting Lincoln's Sparrow in brushy riparian areas. Western Wood-Pewee nests in trees along the lake, and this is a good area for woodpeckers.

Willamette Pass

Willamette Pass Ski Area is 1.8 miles southeast of Gold Lake along Hwy. 58. The lodge offers a very civilized rest stop and some interesting birding. Red-breasted Sapsucker and Chipping Sparrow nest there. Bald Eagles, probably from nearby Odell Lake, may soar by. Summertime gondola rides up to the top of the ski area offer high-elevation birding opportunities that have not been much exploited by birders to date.

Beyond the Willamette Pass are many fine birding possibilities. The Cascade Lakes Hwy., which goes from the Crescent cutoff road (an eastward turn off of Hwy. 58 about 15 miles southeast of the pass) to Bend, has many campgrounds and trails. Davis Lake, Wickiup Reservoir, and Hosmer Lake are popular sites for birding. If you missed Black-backed Woodpecker in Lane Co., the burned area at Davis Lake offers an excellent chance of success. When the north entrance to Crater Lake National Park off Hwy. 138 is open, it is sometimes possible to see Gray-crowned Rosy-Finch easily from the road around the lake where snowfields are still by the roadside. The Klamath Falls area, beginning with the Klamath Forest (recently renamed Klamath Marsh) Refuge about 50 miles southeast along Hwy. 97, is well-known for its rich birding opportunities.

Status and Distribution

Alan Contreras

Observers of Lane County birds quite naturally want to know not only where to go for the best birding experience, but what they may find in certain locations and where and when to seek certain birds of interest. The following species accounts provide basic information about the status, distribution, abundance, and movements of each species known to have occurred in Lane County.

Sources of information

Most of the information in this book comes from observers who have spent considerable time observing the birds of Lane County. This information is often published in Oregon Birds (Oregon Field Ornithologists); North American Birds (American Birding Association) and its predecessors; The Quail (Lane County Audubon Society); and (especially before 1977) Nature Notes (Eugene Natural History Society). Information from these sources is generally not cited specifically to the source to save space. Statements about status and lists of specific records without a cited source are from these field notes.

Additional sources include the Fern Ridge Reservoir checklist originally prepared by Steve Heinl and Matt Hunter (1987) and revised by Noah Strycker (2003) and checklists from the Willamette National Forest, Mt. Pisgah, and other "mini-sites." Records of unique events such as the Eugene and Cottage Grove "Spring Bird Counts" conducted in the 1970s were occasionally of use (e.g., for the account of Forster's Tern). Another example is the "Coast Birding Weekend" shorebird surveys of the late 1970s. These were in essence one-time or short-term data-collection efforts that have faded from the memories of most observers. Fortunately, much of the original data was preserved. Records of the Cascades Raptor Center were helpful for Long-eared Owl reports.

There can be no doubt that some records in obscure source material were missed in the preparation of this book. There can also be no doubt that the editor missed some records that should not have been missed, simply because of the vast amount of material gathered and sorted for the project. Observers who have information to add to the status of species as set forth in the book should send it to the Lane County Audubon Society (see page 347), which can provide it to those who might work on future editions. The data cutoff for this book, with a few exceptions, is Sep. 30, 2005. There may be records that occurred prior to that date that were not published until after that date, in which case they are usually not included.

For many years, authors of books about Oregon birds cited directly to North American Birds, Condor, Oregon Birds, and other journals because the most recent comprehensive book on Oregon birds was Gabrielson and Jewett's Birds of Oregon (1940), which was too old to include many modern records, though it did (and still does) serve as the principal baseline for historical status of Oregon birds.

I have departed somewhat from the practice of citing original sources, when known, because so much material is now gathered in a widespread, easily available source: Marshall et al.'s Birds of Oregon: A General Reference, issued by Oregon State University Press in 2003. Because Birds of Lane County is a small book with a regional audience, I decided to cite Marshall et al. as the source for some material rather than the original journal articles, because it is so much more readily available.

However, a regional guide such as this one also has opportunities to provide information at a greater level of detail regarding certain species or local conditions. For that reason, I use more specific Lane County data, in many cases, than is available in published form anywhere else. This includes museum specimen data, data from the Breeding Bird Survey and Christmas Bird Count (CBC), banding records, and the personal notes of many observers.

The Breeding Bird Survey has five currently active routes that are entirely or mostly in Lane County. These are almost all entirely within forested or wooded upland areas, so the data are quite useful for those species but not for valley floor species. Nonetheless, they give a good picture of abundance for forest species. The twenty most common breeding species (most abundant to least) in wooded and forested upland areas of the county, based on BBS data, are: Swainson's Thrush, American Robin, Hermit Warbler, "Oregon" Junco, Winter Wren, Wilson's Warbler, Varied Thrush, Steller's Jay, Pacific-slope Flycatcher, Song Sparrow, MacGillivray's Warbler, Red-breasted Nuthatch, Black-headed Grosbeak, Warbling Vireo, Hermit

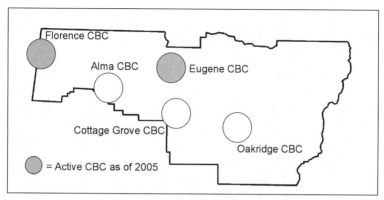

= Active CBC as of 2005: Oakridge CBC, Cottage Grove CBC, Alma CBC, Florence CBC, Eugene CBC, Cottage Grove CBC

Thrush, Chestnut-backed Chickadee, European Starling, Western Tanager, Golden-crowned Kinglet, and Rufous Hummingbird.

The data upon which this ranking is based are biased toward species that are easy to identify by sight and especially sound during daylight hours, so common species such as Western Screech-owl do not appear. Also, the absence of any BBS route on the Willamette Valley floor results in the absence of species such as Western Scrub-Jay and Red-winged Blackbird, to say nothing of House Sparrow.

A number of museums kindly allowed access to their specimens or provided data for their Lane County holdings. I owe special thanks to Dr. Pamela Endzweig of the University of Oregon Museum of Natural and Cultural History for her help over many years, including work on this project. Others who assisted with this project include Phil Unitt (San Diego Museum of Natural History), Kimball Garrett (Los Angeles County Museum of Natural History), Oregon State University Museum, Field Museum of Chicago, National Museum of Natural History (Smithsonian), American Museum of Natural History, Cleveland Museum, Burke Museum (University of Washington), Connor Museum (Washington State University) and the University of Puget Sound.

Codes for museums:

AMNH	American Museum of Natural History
CM	Cleveland Museum
FM	Field Museum
LA	Los Angeles County Museum
NMNH	National Museum of Natural History
OSU	Oregon State University Museum
SD	San Diego Museum
UO	University of Oregon Museum
UPS	Univ. of Puget Sound Museum
UW	Unversity of Washington Museum
WSU	Washington State University Museum

Abbreviations for most common sources

An abbreviated citation form is used for the most common sources used in this book. This form is used when data come from a database, general field notes in a newsletter or journal, or the two principal historical sources for data on central Lane County.

BBL   Data provided by the Bird Banding Laboratory

BBS   Data extracted from the breeding Bird Survey route database maintained by the U.S. Fish & Wildlife Service.

CBC   Data extracted from the Christmas Bird Count database maintained by the National Audubon Society in cooperation with Cornell University Laboratory of Ornithology.

ENHS   Eugene Natural History Society, field notes published in *Nature Trails* newsletter.

Gullion Gullion, Gordon. 1951. Birds of the Southern Willamette Valley, Oregon. *Condor* 53: 129-159

NAB   Field notes published in *North American Birds* and its predecessors *American Birds, Audubon Field Notes*, etc.

OB   Field notes and articles from *Oregon Birds*, including its predecessor *SWOC TALK*.

OBBA   Oregon Breeding Bird Atlas project.

Quail   Field Notes from *The Quail*, Lane County Audubon Society.

Shelton Shelton, Alfred C. A *Distributional List of the Land Birds of West-Central Oregon* (1917). The Oregon Field Ornithologists annotated reprint (2002) edited by Noah Strycker was used in preparation of this volume. Copies are available from OFO.

READING THE SPECIES ACCOUNTS

Sequence

The sequence of accounts will seem strange to most bird observers because it represents the recent major change in taxonomic sequence established by the American Ornithologists' Union (Banks et al. 2003). Thus the North American taxonomy now begins with waterfowl instead of loons and grebes. Confused readers can use the index of common names.

Content of accounts

Each account, except for vagrants, begins with a brief statement entitled Status, usually a sentence, of the status of the species in Lane County. This is followed by a sentence or two describing the species' preferred habitat.

For most species, the rest of this paragraph provides more detailed information about the status of the species by season, describing the timing of its movements. For breeding species, this information begins with the spring migration (unless resident), describes the timing of breeding activity, fall migration, and winter status. For nonbreeding species, this section usually begins with the fall migration, because for many nonbreeders (e.g., shorebirds and seabirds), this is the time of year that they are most common or most easily observed. It then covers winter status (if applicable), and spring and summer movements. Species that are mainly winter residents follow the same sequence as nonbreeders.

The second section, Distribution, describes in general terms in what parts of the county the species can be found, with information about variations by season, movements between areas, and the like.

The final section, Sites, refers the reader to specific sites if they are unusually reliable, with brief notes as to special circumstances at particular sites. Most of these sites are included in the Best 100 Birding Sites in Lane County section in this book.

Abundance

The following abundance scale is used, rather loosely, in the species accounts, usually in reference to a day in the field in appropriate habitat.

Abundant	Obvious flocks or large numbers easily found.
Common	Multiple birds easily observed, rarely missed.
Uncommon	Usually found but often in low numbers, requires effort to locate, sometimes missed.
Rare	Annual or regular in very small numbers, usually missed.
Casual	Irregular or not annual, usually more than 20 records in the county or region, expected to recur in the right season under the right conditions.
Vagrant	Not part of a pattern of regular occurrence, not expected to recur with any predictability, fewer than 10 county records.

Seasonality

Birds do not follow the human calendar, and some species don't seem to have any idea when they "should" nest from the point of view of humans. Thus Anna's Hummingbirds and some owls can begin nesting in Jan., adult shorebirds are pouring south in July, male Rufous Hummingbirds can be southbound migrants in early June, and Red Crossbills breed according to the timing and location of seed crops, not weather. The following general definitions may help you understand how I use traditional terms for seasonality.

Summer	Usually used for the months of June-Aug., which overlaps with but is not identical to the breeding season for most species.
Fall	Usually used to mean the months of Sep.-Nov., but sometimes used to refer to southbound migration, which begins in July for some species, mainly shorebirds.
Winter	Usually used to mean the months of Dec.-Feb.
Spring	Usually used to mean the months of Mar.-May, although sometimes used interchangeably with northbound migration, which begins by early Feb. in many species, notably waterfowl and in some years swallows, and extends into June for a few species, e.g. loons and kittiwakes.

Key to symbols used in headings

•	Breeds (180 species)
°	Probably breeds (18 species)
*	OBRC reports requested (** represents species not yet confirmed for Oregon by specimen or photo)
(I)	Introduced
[Species]	Not yet confirmed for the county but expected owing to patterns of occurrence in Oregon. Also used for a few single-observer sight records in the county, when there is only one report. Multi-observer sight records are treated as acceptable records for purposes of this book, although they are not confirmed by specimen, photo, or recording.

Order ANSERIFORMES

Family Anatidae - Subfamily Anserinae

Greater White-fronted Goose *Anser albifrons*

Status: Uncommon migrant; uncommon to rare in winter, quite variable from year to year. Fall birds are often seen as early as late Aug., with most movement in Sep. and early Oct. Very small flocks of fewer than 10 birds are the norm, and singles are often found, usually associated with flocks of Canada/Cackling Geese. Large flocks are generally flyovers, probably en route to and from wintering grounds farther south. Small numbers are sometimes found in winter. Spring movements are mainly in Apr. and very early May, but a few move as early as late Feb. Generally absent from mid-May through mid-Aug. Considered a common fall migrant in the 1940s, with a peak of 2,700 birds (Gullion), it is usually seen in smaller numbers today.

Distribution: Most are seen on the outer coast and the floor of the Willamette Valley. Small numbers can potentially be found in almost any open water, pasture, or short-grass habitat in the county in migration, and flyovers are often reported even from areas where there is no appropriate habitat on the ground, e.g., the high Cascades.

Sites: Dotterel Dike and Siuslaw deflation plain in fall, also shallow water and fields near Fern Ridge Res. Often seen overhead in spring and fall.

Emperor Goose *Chen canagica*

Status: Casual in winter, not a vagrant in the usual sense because one or two are in Oregon most winters as part of a regular pattern. Nine records: Nov. 10, 2004; Feb. 5-18, 2003 at Fern Ridge Res.; Jan. 4, 2002 (3 birds) at

Emperor Goose, Nov. 2003, Fern Ridge Res. (with Canada Goose in background). Photo by Sylvia Maulding.

181

the Siuslaw R. mouth; Dec. 12, 1993–Mar. 24, 1994 at Waite's pasture east of Florence; Feb. 26, 1989 at the south jetty of the Siuslaw; Nov. 21, 1981 through May 8, 1982 at Veneta sewage ponds; and Oct. 7, 1923 at Jasper (Gullion).
Distribution: Most in Willamette Valley or around Florence. Often settles in a single spot for months and becomes unwary.

Snow Goose *Chen caerulescens*
Status: Uncommon migrant, rare but regular most winters, although absent in some years. Typically present in very small numbers, often single birds embedded in flocks of Canada Geese or Cackling Geese. Arrives mid- to late Oct. when large flocks of Canada Geese arrive. Some move out of the area but one or two often winter. Spring movements are generally outside Lane County but small flocks are sometimes reported from late Mar. through Apr. Absent from mid-May through Sep. in most years, but has occurred as early as Aug. (2002).
Distribution: Mainly Willamette Valley lowland pastures, occasionally on the coast.
Sites: Vicinity of Fern Ridge Res.

Ross's Goose *Chen rossii*
Status: Rare, irregular migrant and winterer, more regular in recent years. Almost always singles, usually with flocks of Cackling or Canada Geese. Reported mid-Nov. through early Apr. First county record was Nov. 1951 (OSU F&W No. 2230) and the second was not until 1997, after which there have been several records of single birds.
Distribution: Usually on the Willamette Valley floor in pasturelands. Has also been found in coastal pastures.
Sites: Vicinity of Fern Ridge Res.

(Black) Brant *Branta bernicla* (*Branta orientalis*)
Note: All Lane County records are referable to the Black Brant, considered a separate species, *Branta orientalis,* by Browning in Marshall et al. 2003.
Status: Uncommon migrant, rare in winter. Most movement in fall is from mid-Sep. through Oct., but there appears to be some movement into early winter as birds arrive or relocate. Typically seen from Lane Co. shores as a flyby migrant, not often found on the ground. Regular migrant in very small numbers Mar.-May; nonbreeders are rare in summer.
Distribution: Coastal, mainly on and over the ocean, rarely within the Siuslaw estuary. Rare and irregular visitor inland, typically as single birds embedded in flocks of Canada or Cackling Geese in the Willamette Valley lowlands.
Sites: Siuslaw jetties and open coast.

Cackling Goose *Branta hutchinsii*
The smaller forms of Canada Goose were determined to be a separate species by the AOU in 2004. Cackling Goose occurs in Lane Co. in the same lowland habitats and locations as does the Canada Goose from late fall through mid-spring. It does not breed in Oregon.

• **Canada Goose** *Branta canadensis*
Status: Common to locally abundant migrant and winterer. Small numbers breed locally. Numbers have increased, probably because of introductions, improved wetlands around Fern Ridge Res. and the advent of grass seed farming in the past 40 years.
Distribution: Countywide, with large flocks wintering at Fern Ridge Res. and nearby pastures and fields. Local breeder from the outer coast to the high Cascades.
Sites: Largest winter flocks are around Fern Ridge Res., smaller flocks at Waite pastures, C & M Stables north of Florence.

Trumpeter Swan *Cygnus buccinator*
Status: Casual winter visitor. Most birds winter from northern Benton Co. locally northward, but now and then one reaches Lane Co. About a dozen records, 8 from Nov. through Feb. Unusual records, perhaps of injured or unhealthy birds, were May 2, 1998 (an immature at Fisher Butte) and June 27, 1991 near Noti.
Distribution: Reported from the Willamette Valley floor and the outer coast, with one record from the Coast Range (Triangle Lake, Dec. 10, 1964). There have been recent reports from the upper McKenzie Valley in summer and winter.
Sites: Check Tundra swan flocks in winter.

Tundra Swan *Cygnus columbianus*
Status: Common to locally abundant winter resident. Typically arrives rather late in fall, with outriders in mid-Oct. but no significant influx until late Nov. Also leaves fairly early in spring, with most gone after early Mar.. The main flock numbers 300-800 most years, with peak counts in excess of 1000.
Note: Bewick's Swan, a distinctive form with more yellow on the bill, has been reported once in the county, Jan. 12, 1990 at Fern Ridge Res. (Dave Jones).
Distribution: Rather local, with most birds feeding in grass seed and similar very short grass fields on the Willamette Valley floor, roosting at night on Fern Ridge Res. A small flock usually winters along the south jetty road near Florence, with outliers sometimes seen at the Sutton Creek outfall and Waite pastures east of Cushman. Occasionally reported elsewhere in the county, including montane lakes, mainly in migration.

Sites: Along Meadowview Rd. and other side roads north and east of the Eugene airport on both sides of Hwy. 99. Also in the flooded deflation plain east of South Jetty Rd. near Florence.

Subfamily Anatinae

•**Wood Duck** *Aix sponsa*

Status: Uncommon but widespread breeder, much less common and more local in winter.

Distribution: Breeds countywide where slow-moving or still water is available near snags for nesting. Local in the Cascades. Winters locally at lower elevations, mainly on the Willamette Valley floor. It can be hard to find in the Siuslaw Valley in winter (usually found from Duncan Island upriver, if at all) for reasons that are not clear, considering that it breeds there, winter conditions are the mildest in the county, and there is plenty of habitat.

Sites: Slow waters near Fern Ridge Res., backwaters of the Lower Siuslaw R. in summer, woodland ponds.

°**Gadwall** *Anas strepera*

Status: Uncommon to locally common (some years) winter resident. Rare but regular in summer at Fern Ridge Res.; probably breeds occasionally since the early 2000s. Not very visible in migration; generally present late Oct. through early Apr., with very few in summer.

Distribution: The only concentration in most years is at Fern Ridge Res., where a couple of hundred birds are present in some winters and much smaller numbers in other years. Smaller flocks (10-20) are sometimes seen elsewhere, especially on flooded grass fields on the valley floor, where a few pairs are often mixed in with flocks of American Wigeon or Northern Pintail. Also fairly regular in small numbers in the Siuslaw Valley in winter.

Sites: Mainly Fern Ridge Res., Delta Ponds.

*****Falcated Duck** *Anas falcate*

Vagrant. At least three records, presumably of the same bird. Oregon's first reported record was at Fern Ridge Res. (Kirk Park pond below the dam) on Feb. 14 and from Mar. 3-14, 2004 (OBRC 137.1-04-01). Falcated Ducks are occasionally kept in captivity but the OBRC accepted this as likely a wild bird owing to its association with a record-size flock of Eurasian Wigeon, occurrence only in winter, and other factors. Presumably the same bird was relocated at the ponds east of I-5 at Coburg (Premier RV Resort) on Jan. 2, 2005 and remained there through the winter. It reappeared in winter 2006. It may also have been in the area in the winter of 2002-03, according to the RV Park manager.

Falcated Duck. Photo by Peter Patricelli.

Eurasian Wigeon *Anas penelope*

Status: Rare but regular winter resident; numbers may be increasing. The highest single-site count was 12 in Jan.-Feb., 2004 at Kirk Park pond, but singles or numbers less than 5 are more typical even in a large flock of American Wigeon. Typically present from mid-Oct. through early Apr.; arrives and departs mainly with flocks of American Wigeon. First county record was Dec. 16, 1926 (Gullion), but there were no further reports through 1950.

Distribution: Can be in any flock of American Wigeon, thus wherever there are shallow bodies of water or flooded fields. Most are on the Willamette Valley floor and in the Siuslaw Valley.

Sites: Pond at Lane Memorial Gardens along Hwy. 126 west of Eugene, Stewart Pond in west Eugene in wet years, Kirk Pond, any large flock of American Wigeon.

° American Wigeon *Anas americana*

Status: Common to locally abundant winter resident; very small numbers may breed at Fern Ridge Res. Large winter flocks are present from late Oct. through late Mar., but migrants are sometimes seen as early as Aug. and the timing of arrival of significant flocks varies widely from year to year, perhaps due to weather conditions to the north of Oregon. Likewise, departure involves some straggling in spring, with some nonbreeders waiting until May before leaving. Formerly unheard-of in summer, but in recent years there have been a few at Fern Ridge Res., e.g., one on June 1, 2002. May breed.

American Wigeon. Drawing by Barbara Gleason.

Distribution: Widespread wherever there is shallow water or flooded fields, with most birds on the Willamette Valley floor and in the Siuslaw Valley. More likely than some ducks to use very small bodies of water if there is good short-grass forage nearby, for example ponds in golf courses or cemeteries.

Sites: Lane Memorial Gardens pond on Hwy 126 in west Eugene, Kirk Pond.

American Black Duck Anas rubripes

Vagrant, one record at Eugene, Dec. 25, 1984 (*Am. Birds* 39:201). The origin of unusual waterfowl is always a question. Black Duck is more likely to have come from an introduced (or escaped) northwest population than from the natural range in northeastern North America.

• Mallard *Anas platyrhynchos*

Status: Widespread and common, generally does not form large flocks, but pairs can be found almost anywhere there is shallow water and small groups sometimes form. In migration, single-sex flocks sometimes found.

Distribution: Countywide in shallow fresh and brackish water, avoids saltwater.

• Blue-winged Teal *Anas discors*

Status: Rare breeder and uncommon migrant, mainly in spring. Numbers vary widely from year to year; some years there are very few, other years scores are present. Earliest reports in Mar., with peak in Apr. and early May. In some years, many pairs remain into June and a few may breed at Fern Ridge Res., where some can be found all summer in most years. Bred in Eugene in 1965 (S. McDonald, p.c.). Bred at Fern Ridge Res. in 2002. Formerly considered a common fall migrant (Gullion) but not so today. Small numbers, generally gone by late Sep., but stragglers reported through Dec. Very rare mid-winter; few CBC reports.

Distribution: Most are at Fern Ridge Res. in spring, but pairs reported at many sites from the outer coast to montane marshes.

Sites: Mainly shallow marshes around Fern Ridge Res.

• Cinnamon Teal *Anas cyanoptera*

Status: Uncommon breeder, common migrant, especially in spring, using shallow freshwater habitats. First arrivals generally early, sometimes late Feb., with significant movements by mid-Mar. and peak numbers in Apr. Fall movements are obscure and fairly early, with most birds gone by late Sep. Stragglers appear throughout the fall, and in some years a few birds winter, mainly in shallow ponds, wet fields, and often narrow grassy ditches.

Distribution: Countywide in migration. Summer birds are mainly at Fern Ridge Res. and in coastal wetlands. Generally absent from Cascade sites in summer. Winter birds are mainly on the valley floor.
Sites: Widespread in migration, Fern Ridge in summer.

• Northern Shoveler *Anas clypeata*
Status: Fairly common migrant and winter resident. Small numbers summer and a few breed, mainly at Fern Ridge Res. Fall influx is apparent by Oct. and migrants depart by mid-Apr.
Distribution: Countywide in migration where shallow water is available. Mainly at Fern Ridge marshes in summer. Has also bred at Camas Swale in 1996 (fairly early; chicks were observed on Apr. 27). Winter distribution depends on availability of shallow fresh water, typically flooded fields.

° Northern Pintail *Anas acuta*
Status: Uncommon to locally abundant migrant and winter resident. First southbound migrants appear early, a few young and adults in eclipse plumage in July, with a steady movement by Aug. The arrival of significant flocks varies from mid-Sep. to late Oct., perhaps depending on weather conditions to the north. Winter numbers vary considerably from year to year. Departs early, with a noticeable drop-off in wintering birds by late Feb. and the bulk of migrants gone by early Apr. Rare in summer and not known to breed with any regularity, but a female with downy chicks was seen on the LCC ponds Aug. 1, 2001 (Larry McQueen, p.c.), and breeding at Fern Ridge Res. might be expected.
Distribution: Countywide in migration, with the earliest movements often coastal and offshore, as well as into montane lakes. The bulk of winter birds are on the valley floor wherever shallow water is available.

• Green-winged Teal *Anas {carolinensis} crecca*
Status: Common to abundant migrant and winter resident. Irregular local breeder. Early fall migrants are in Aug., with steady movement in Sep. (mainly late in the month) and winter flocks forming by late Oct. to early Nov. Departs in Mar. and Apr., with very few remaining by mid-May.
Note: The report of a possible Garganey on Aug. 20, 1997 at Gold Lake is thought to be of an eclipse plumage Green-winged Teal, which sometimes shows a Garganey-like face pattern in late summer.
Distribution: Fall movements are often coastal and over the ocean, sometimes with flocks of scoters or Northern Pintail. Under adverse conditions they can sometimes be seen resting on the ocean or between the Siuslaw jetties, which seems odd for a duck usually considered a bird of shallow fresh water. Irregular breeder at Gold Lake; not proven to breed elsewhere but possibly at Fern Ridge Res. Large winter flocks can be found

wherever there is shallow water on the valley floor, also in small ponds and coastal marshes and sometimes on mudflats, where they can be mistaken for shorebirds.

Common Teal {_Anas crecca_}

Status: Treated as a separate species from Green-winged (_carolinensis_) Teal by Browning in Marshall et al. (2003) and by some European taxonomists. Almost annual since the early 1990s as rare single birds in flocks of Green-wings. Arrives late, few are found before Jan. Latest in spring: Apr. 11, 1985.

Distribution: Shows an inexplicable preference for the Creswell sewage ponds over all other sites. Over half of the records from the entire county are from that site, including multiple birds. Unfortunately, that site was closed to the public in 2005. Otherwise found wherever Green-wings can be found.

Sites: Creswell sewage ponds (limited access), Stewart Ponds.

Canvasback _Aythya valisineria_

Status: Uncommon migrant and winter resident. Arrives during late Sep., departs during Mar. and Apr., rare by May. Very rare in summer: June 15, 1974 at Fern Ridge Res. (Lars Norgren) is the only record between May and Sep.

Distribution: Rather local. Tends to settle into a few preferred sites, generally lakes or ponds, and stays there most of the winter. Sometimes found in flooded fields with dabbling ducks.

Sites: Siltcoos Lake (from Darling's Resort at north end) in winter, Lane Memorial Gardens pond on Hwy. 126 in west Eugene.

• Redhead _Aythya americana_

Status: Uncommon to rare migrant and winter resident, highly local summer resident. A few are present in the county in most winters, but they are hard to find and sometimes absent. Beginning in the 1990s, 5-10 pairs summered at Fern Ridge Res. Breeding was confirmed there in 2003 (S. Maulding, p.c.) and 2004 (Don DeWitt, p.c.).

Distribution: Lakes, ponds, and sometimes flooded fields in lowlands and the coastal plain. Irregular and local. In recent years several pairs have summered in the Coyote Creek marshes at Fern Ridge Res. May have bred at Cougar Res. in 2005 (G. Crisman _fide_ B. Combs).

Sites: Fern Ridge Res. in summer, Siltcoos Lake in winter.

• Ring-necked Duck _Aythya collaris_

Status: Rare local breeder, common winter resident countywide. Prefers ponds and lakes with wooded shores, though also found in more open areas. Uses both shallow and deep-water habitats. Migrants arrive in late Sep. through mid-Oct., most leave during Apr. Flocks range from just a few to (rarely) hundreds.

Distribution: Bred at Gold Lake in 1994. Breeding probable at Triangle Lake and in the Cascades (OBBA); also reported in summer at Cottage Grove Res., Dorena Res., and at impoundments in the McKenzie Valley.

Sites: Widespread in winter.

Tufted Duck *Aythya fuligula*

Casual winter visitor. Two records: a male was found at Fern Ridge Res. on April 23, 2006, unusually late for this species (P. Sherrell, p.c.); Jan. 30, 2004 at Siltcoos Lake (*OB, Quail*). Almost annual in Oregon, so it is likely to occur again in late winter, probably with scaup, possibly with Ring-necked Ducks. Most Oregon records are in Feb. and Mar.

Greater Scaup *Aythya marila*

Status: Common but somewhat local winter resident and migrant. Numbers vary from single birds to flocks of hundreds, with some locations strongly favored. Uses fresh- and salt-water sites. A few nonbreeders found in summer, but most arrive in mid- to late Sep. and leave by May. More likely than some ducks to linger into late May and early June.

Distribution: Can occur on any sizable body of water, including larger rivers, but most regular at Fern Ridge Res. and on the outer coast. Tends to favor rivers and estuarine sites on the coast.

Sites: Kirk Park pond at Fern Ridge dam, Siltcoos Lake.

Lesser Scaup *Aythya affinis*

Status: Widespread and locally common migrant and winter resident. Nonbreeders rare in summer. The most recent summer record was June 1, 2002 at Fern Ridge Res. Prefers freshwater sites.

Distribution: Countywide, with most birds at larger lakes and some on large rivers.

Sites: Siltcoos Lake harbors the largest winter population and is a good place to compare scaup and other diving ducks.

*King Eider *Somateria spectabilis*

Casual in migration and winter on the ocean and possibly the lower Siuslaw estuary. Four records: Dec. 18, 2000 (flyby at Sea Lion Caves, probably this species, accepted as an eider by OBRC); Oct. 22, 1993 (OBRC 162-93-06, photo by Bill Stotz); July 1, 1987 near Florence (*Am. Birds* 41: 1478). See Supplemental Records (page 325).

*King Eider, Oct. 22, 1993 at
Florence. Photo by Bill Stotz.*

• **Harlequin Duck** *Histrionicus histrionicus*
Status: Uncommon local migrant and winter resident. Rare local breeder.
Some arrive very early (midsummer) after breeding, others arrive in Sep.
through Nov. Numbers begin dropping in Mar. and most depart by mid-
Apr. Sometimes seen in breeding areas as early as Mar., but most reports
in the Lane Co. Cascades are from Apr. and May.
Distribution: Occasional in winter at the Siuslaw jetties, otherwise found
along the rocky coast, mainly from Heceta Head northward. One on the
Oakridge CBC in 1975 was exceptional. Irregular local breeder on the
upper McKenzie R. and tributaries and perhaps rarely in the upper part
of the Middle Fork of the Willamette drainage, including Fall Creek. The
southernmost record is from Bryce Cr. east of Cottage Grove on May 5,
1999.
Sites: Late spring: upper McKenzie R. above the Hwy. 126-242 junction is
best bet. Winter: rocky coast from Klootchman overlook northward.

Surf Scoter *Melanitta perspicillata*
Status: Common to abundant migrant and winter resident. Nonbreeders
uncommon to rare in midsummer, numbers vary widely from year to year.
Substantial southbound movement sometimes as early as late Aug., with
rafts in the low thousands sometimes present Sep.-Nov. By midwinter, rafts
generally in the hundreds as birds disperse. Spring migration is also long
and diffuse, with most movement in Apr. but some birds staying through
the summer.
Distribution: Coastal, with most birds on the ocean in and just beyond
the surf line. Small flocks use coastal estuaries, sometimes going quite far
upriver, and also sometimes use lakes, especially during bad weather. Rare
but regular inland, mainly in fall migration (Oct. peak), on larger lakes and
occasionally small ponds. A few inland records in winter, east to Hills Creek
Res. (CBC).
Sites: Widespread on the coast. Easy to observe in winter between Siuslaw
jetties.

White-winged Scoter *Melanitta fusca*

Status: Common to abundant migrant and winter resident. Numbers quite variable year to year. Nonbreeders rare in midsummer (much less regular than Surf Scoter in summer), numbers vary widely from year to year. Southbound movement sometimes as early as July, with rafts in the hundreds sometimes present Sep.-Nov. In some years, peak movements briefly number in the thousands, e.g., 15,000 along the coast in Dec. 2002. Spring migration is also long and diffuse, with most movement in Apr.

Distribution: Coastal, with most birds on the ocean in and just beyond the surf line. Small flocks use coastal estuaries, generally not going far upriver, and rarely use lakes. Rare inland, mainly in fall migration or after major windstorms, mainly on larger lakes. One extraordinary record, July 10, 1989 at Fern Ridge Res. (*NAB* 43:1359).

Black Scoter *Melanitta nigra*

Status: Uncommon to rare and local in winter. Usually seen in singles or pairs, occasionally small flocks of fewer than 10 birds. Regular migrant in very small numbers, typically arriving late in fall (rare until Nov.) and departing in Apr. Rarely summers; two published records: June 22, 1998 and Aug. 14, 2004, both at Heceta Head.

Distribution: Coastal, exclusively on saltwater, rarely enters Siuslaw estuary further than a hundred yards or so. Generally in areas with rocky bottom.

Sites: Mainly north Lane Co. coast; Klootchman overlook is most regular.

Long-tailed Duck *Clangula hyemalis*

Status: Rare but regular migrant and winter resident. One or two birds are often present in winter, typically settling into an area for weeks or even months. Very rare in summer: July 5-12, 2003 (may have summered); June 25-28, 1997, and July 1994, all at Florence.

Distribution: Outer coast, almost always on saltwater, though it sometimes comes upriver as far as Florence. Very rare inland: one was at Dexter Res. on Nov. 30, 2004 and remained through early Dec. (D. Farrar, *OB* in press), and one spent about a week on the LCC ponds in early Nov. 1983 (David Fix, *fide* Larry McQueen).

Sites: Siuslaw jetties, Klootchman overlook, Brays Point overlook.

• Bufflehead *Bucephala albeola*

Status: Common to locally abundant migrant and winter resident, with the bulk of winter birds arriving en masse in late Oct. or early Nov. Mainly on larger, deep bodies of water and large rivers. Rare irregular breeder at montane lakes (can use very small ones) with timbered shores and available snags. Has bred at Waldo Lake and Gold Lake (L. Fish, p.c.) and at smaller lakes in that region of the Cascades (D. DeWitt, p.c.).

Distribution: Countywide in migration and winter wherever habitat available. Highest densities in the Siuslaw estuary.

Common Goldeneye *Bucephala clangula*

Status: Uncommon to locally rare migrant and winter resident. From mid-Sep. through Apr., can be found in very small numbers (typically fewer than 5 birds, highest recent count 22) on lakes and larger ponds, occasionally in larger, longer-term flooded fields.

Distribution: Mainly in the eastern half of the county, from Fern Ridge Res. to the Cascades. Most regular in any numbers at the Cascade lakes from Dexter Res. eastward, with a few on the valley floor and at Fern Ridge Res. Very small numbers reach the outer coast, where it is irregular and local, using estuaries and larger lakes, especially Siltcoos Lake.

Sites: Cascade foothill lakes in winter; regular at Dexter Reservoir.

• Barrow's Goldeneye *Bucephala islandica*

Status: A few pairs breed. Rare but regular winter resident. Mainly in lakes, sometimes uses smaller rivers (Common Goldeneye generally does not). No visible migratory movements, since east Lane Co. is at the southwest edge of the species' range.

Distribution: Eastern half of the county, irregular local breeder at high-elevation lakes. Winters mainly in lower montane areas. Found on 20 percent of Oakridge and Cottage Grove CBCs in 1970s-1980s. Rare and irregular to the valley floor, mainly from Eugene eastward. Very rare on the coast.

Sites: Waldo Lake and Gold Lake in summer. Try Hills Creek Res. in winter.

• Hooded Merganser *Lophodytes cucullatus*

Status: Local breeder. Uncommon to locally common winter resident. Uses a wide variety of still and slow-moving water habitats, including lakes, rivers, and flooded pastures. Generally avoids saltwater (with exceptions, mainly in migration) and fast-moving streams.

Distribution: Irregular breeder in Coast Range and sheltered fresh coastal waters, also irregularly in the high Cascade lakes. Bred at Fern Ridge Res. in 1947 and 1948 (Gullion), but not a regular breeder there today. Generally absent in summer from the Willamette Valley floor. Winters countywide on open waters.

Sites: Widespread. Often present in high numbers along Canary Rd. east of Siltcoos Lake in winter when pastures are flooded.

• Common Merganser *Mergus merganser*

Status: Uncommon but widespread breeder and winter resident. Common to abundant on Fern Ridge Res. in winter. Uses larger lakes and almost any size of river or large creek. Breeds mainly on streamsides, winters mainly on lakes and larger rivers.

Note: a male seen flying north off the Siuslaw jetties on June 1, 2003 had no dark bar on the white wing patch, suggesting that it may have been of the Asian subspecies *M. m. merganser* (*OB*, Will Russell, p.c.) The date and location are also quite unusual: Common Mergansers are rarely seen over the ocean, and spring movements are generally over by late Apr., by which time the species is on the breeding grounds. The subspecies *merganser* breeds east to northeastern Siberia.

Distribution: Countywide where proper water habitats available. Less regular on the valley floor in midsummer. Abundant at Fern Ridge Res. in winter.

Sites: Hundreds use Fern Ridge Res. in winter, Willamette R. in Eugene/Springfield.

Red-breasted Merganser *Mergus serrator*

Status: Locally common migrant and winter resident. A few arrive in late summer but most appear in Oct. and early Nov. Remains fairly late in spring, with some not departing until late May. Nonbreeders very rare in summer.

Distribution: Coastal, mainly in lower estuaries and the nearshore ocean. Does not usually go more than a mile or two up estuaries. Rarely uses coastal lakes. Very rare inland: 6 records, 2 on Oct. 21, 1996 at Lookout Point Res.; Mar. 13 and 15, 1994 on the Willamette R. at Eugene; Jan. 7, 1990 at Fern Ridge Res.; on the Cottage Grove CBC in 1984; 2 at Fern Ridge Res. in Dec., 1973; and 5 on Fern Ridge Res. on Apr. 21, 1958 (Tice 1998, *NAB* 12:379).

Sites: Lower Siuslaw estuary.

• Ruddy Duck *Oxyura jamaicensis*

Status: Rare irregular breeder, uncommon to locally common winter resident. Uses a variety of still-water locations, fresh and salt, but avoids lower estuaries and the open ocean.

Distribution: Small numbers countywide in winter, with most birds in lowland ponds and lakes and in coastal lakes. Abundant on Siltcoos Lake in winter. Has bred at Fern Ridge Res. since 2003 (owing to improved wetland habitat) and at LCC sewage treatment ponds in the 1980s; it still breeds occasionally at LCC (e.g., in 2005).

Sites: Siltcoos Lake in winter, Fern Ridge (impoundments) or LCC ponds.

Order GALLIFORMES

Family Phasianidae - Subfamily Phasianinae

(I) Chukar *Alectoris chukar*
Introduced to eastern Oregon. A few birds escape from game bird pens and appear at odd locations such as the Eugene airport, schoolyards, and parking lots. No self-sustaining populations exist in western Oregon.

(I) Gray Partridge *Perdix perdix*
Introduced to eastern Oregon. A few birds escape from game bird pens and appear in agricultural areas. No self-sustaining populations in western Oregon.

• (I) Ring-necked Pheasant *Phasianus colchicus*
Status: Uncommon introduced resident game bird. Local populations may or may not be self-sustaining; new birds are regularly released around Fern Ridge Res. for hunting purposes. Found mainly in edges of agricultural land, overgrown fields, and grain crops.
Distribution: Willamette Valley floor. Rare on the outer coast, where it is sometimes found in dense dune grass or the edges of upriver pastureland.
Sites: Regular in Fern Ridge Res. wildlife areas.

Subfamily Tetraoninae

• Ruffed Grouse *Bonasa umbellus*
Status: Uncommon resident, mainly in woodlands and younger forests containing both deciduous and coniferous trees with some openings. Somewhat secretive.
Distribution: Countywide; least common on the valley floor and in high-elevation monocultural fir and pine forests.
Sites: Deception Creek Rd. off Hwy. 58. Check forest roads in Coast Range and Cascades early in the morning.

• Sooty Grouse *Dendragapus obscurus*
Status: Uncommon resident, mainly in fir, spruce, and lodgepole pine forests. Somewhat secretive.
Distribution: Mostly in heavily forested areas in eastern Lane Co., but also locally to the outer coast where sufficient habitat exists. Generally absent from the valley floor, but can be present on heavily forested adjacent hills, e.g., Spencer Butte in south Eugene.
Sites: Waldo and Gold lakes. Can be heard calling on Spencer Butte in spring; Horsepasture Mtn. is a good place also.

Subfamily Meleagridinae

• (I) **Wild Turkey** *Meleagris gallopavo*

Status: Locally common introduced resident game bird, numbers increasing in recent years. Uses open woodlands and nearby fields, especially where oaks are present.

Distribution: Mainly in foothills and small valleys adjacent to the Willamette Valley floor, also the Mohawk Valley and Coburg Hills. West locally in the Coast Range to Walton and Triangle Lake.

Sites: Hillside roads east of Coburg; Cloverdale road south of Hwy. 58, Mt. Pisgah.

Family Odontophoridae

• **Mountain Quail** *Oreortyx pictus*

Status: Uncommon resident. Found largely in forested areas with openings and often steep slopes. More often heard than seen.

Distribution: Countywide except in agricultural lands of the valley floor. Most common in the Coast Range and at middle elevations in the western Cascades. Sometimes seen along the edges of wooded areas on the outer coast, even near the ocean.

Sites: Forest roads around Oakridge and Lookout Point Res., Coburg Hills, Herman Cape Rd. north of Florence.

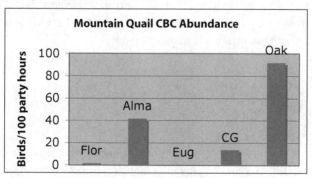

• (I) **California Quail** *Callipepla californica*

Status: Uncommon to locally common resident. Uses rural hedgerows, orchards, open deciduous woodlands. Lane Co. populations originated with introductions in the 1880s; native north to the Rogue Valley and perhaps the south Umpqua Valley.

Distribution: Mainly the Willamette Valley floor and adjacent tributary valleys with open ground. East locally to Leaburg in the McKenzie Valley and Hills Creek Dam in the valley of the Middle Fork of the Willamette,

Mountain Quail. Illustration by Barbara Gleason.

irregular farther upriver in each valley. Irregular and local within the Coast Range and in the Siuslaw Valley; rare on the outer coast. Absent from the forested Cascades.

(I) Northern Bobwhite *Colinus virginianus*
A few birds escape from game bird pens and appear in agricultural areas. Also released for hunting, mainly on the east side of Fern Ridge Res. No self-sustaining populations in western Oregon.

Order GAVIIFORMES
Family Gaviidae

Red-throated Loon *Gavia stellata*
Status: Uncommon to common migrant and winter resident. Briefly abundant during spring and fall migration. Nonbreeders rare in summer. Open water.
Distribution: Mainly on the ocean and in lower estuaries. Occasionally found on coastal lakes. Rare in migration and winter on inland lakes, absent most years. During peak of passage, thousands can be seen flying along above or just beyond the surf line. Timing of this movement varies but is usually in Apr. and from late Oct. through late Nov. Peak movements can be compressed into a few days during these periods.
Sites: Coast.

Arctic Loon Gavia arctica

Vagrant. One sight record, July 12, 1998 at Florence (A. Contreras). OBRC has not yet acted on the record.

Pacific Loon *Gavia pacifica*

Status: Uncommon to abundant migrant and winter resident. Can be briefly abundant close offshore (often just beyond the surf line) during peak of migration, timing of which varies. Fall peak is typically rather late, in late Oct. to late Nov. Usually uncommon to rare in winter, but numbers vary widely from year to year. Spring peak movement is very late, generally in May, with significant numbers still moving in early June (late June in some years). Summer nonbreeders are rare but regular. Open water.

Distribution: Ocean and lower estuary waters. Rare on coastal lakes, very rare away from outer coast. It has occurred as far east as Hills Creek Res. (Oakridge CBC) and Cougar Res. (Oct. 26, 1992, Al Prigge, p.c.), and on smaller lakes such as the Walterville EWEB pond (C. Jobanek, 1974).

Sites: In some years, easy to see between Siuslaw jetties.

• **Common Loon** *Gavia immer*

Status: Uncommon to common migrant and winter resident. Rare but regular in summer as a nonbreeder at both coastal and interior locations, east to the west Cascade reservoirs. Movements are more spread out with fewer intense peaks than for smaller loons, with small numbers moving by Sep. and the bulk of movement in late Oct. and early Nov. Fairly common in winter; usually the most common loon. Spring movements begin fairly late, with many birds still present in Apr. and a few still moving by late May.

Oregon's only breeding record was at Lower Eddeeleo Lake in the Waldo Lake Wilderness in 1991, but there is evidence strongly suggestive of breeding at Waldo Lake in 1948 (Marshall et al. 2003).

Distribution: Primarily coastal, with a few migrants at inland lakes every year and one or two wintering on larger lakes such as Fern Ridge Res., occasionally east to Hills Creek Res. (Oakridge CBC and observations in 2004 and 2005, D. Farrar, p.c.) and probably other lower Cascade reservoirs. Regular in small numbers during fall migration on lakes in the High Cascades. More regular on fresh water than the smaller loons.

Sites: Easy to view in winter between Siuslaw jetties.

Yellow-billed Loon *Gavia adamsii*

Casual. Five records, all from the Florence area except as noted: Feb. 2-24, 2002 (presumably the same bird again on Apr. 5 at the same location); Dec. 24, 2001; Jan. 9, 1994; Nov. 15, 1993 (OBRC 008-93-30); Dec. 31, 1989

Yellow-billed Loon: Florence, February 24, 2002. Photo by Noah K. Strycker.

(Fern Ridge Res., Eugene CBC, OBRC 008-89-21) and May 11, 1983 near the south jetty of the Siuslaw (David Fix, p.c.). Generally prefers shallow water in estuaries.

Order PODICIPEDIFORMES
Family Podicipedidae

• **Pied-billed Grebe** *Podilymbus podiceps*
Status: Uncommon local breeder. Numbers increase significantly in winter. Open water, usually fresh with significant tall emergent vegetation.
Distribution: Breeding is largely limited to shallow marshes on the valley floor and in nearby lower valleys, mainly at Fern Ridge Res. Has bred at Cottage Grove Res. in limited habitat (Gullion). Also breeds at Siltcoos Lake and possibly at other coastal lakes with emergent vegetation. High numbers sometimes found on Dorena Res. in fall. Siltcoos Lake has a large winter population, with scores of birds often visible at a time.
Sites: Summer: Fern Ridge marshes. Winter: Darling's resort and the Westlake boat ramp are good places to observe many at Siltcoos Lake.

Horned Grebe *Podiceps auritus*
Status: Uncommon but visible migrant and winter resident. Open water, salt or fresh. Begins arriving in very late Aug. and early Sep., but arrivals are spread out until Nov., by which time most winter birds have settled in.
Distribution: Mainly coastal, both on the nearshore ocean and in estuaries. A few use coastal freshwater lakes. Small numbers are usually found at Fern Ridge Res. in winter, and they are occasional on other large lakes and reservoirs.

Sites: Easy to observe in the lower Siuslaw estuary in winter, also Dexter Res.

Red-necked Grebe *Podiceps grisegena*
Status: Uncommon migrant and winter resident. Open water, mainly larger bodies of water.
Distribution: Almost all coastal in winter. Most of these are on the ocean near the surf line or in lower estuaries. A few are seen at inland lakes during migration, especially in late fall. There are surprisingly few records from Fern Ridge Res.
Sites: Easiest to observe in the lower Siuslaw estuary (often between the jetties) from mid-autumn to early spring.

Eared Grebe *Podiceps nigricollis*
Status: Uncommon to rare migrant and rare but regular local winter resident. Arrives fairly late, typically in Oct., usually departing in Apr. Rare to late May (May 29, 2001 is latest). May be increasing slightly in winter.
Distribution: Can appear on any body of water in migration; generally avoids rivers and never uses fast-moving streams. Tends to appear on small, shallow, permanent bodies of water such as sewage ponds. One or two often winter in the lower Siuslaw estuary, a relatively recent phenomenon.
Sites: Unpredictable. Sometimes in the lower Siuslaw estuary in fall, but does not always winter there. Irregular at Creswell and LCC sewage ponds.

• Western Grebe *Aechmophorus occidentalis*
Status: Local breeder. Uncommon to locally common in migration and winter. Fall movements are protracted and generally thin, from Sep. through Nov. Spring movements are hard to detect but appear to be in Mar. and early Apr. Paired adults are at Fern Ridge Res. by late Mar.. However, in some years nonbreeders summer on the ocean, so the end of spring movements is hard to determine. Found in deep open water, salt or fresh.
Distribution: Has bred at Fern Ridge Res. since at least the early 1990s. Found in migration and winter on most sizable bodies of deep water. Common to locally abundant in winter in offshore rafts just beyond the surf line.
Sites: Breeders with young can easily be seen west of Perkins Peninsula at Fern Ridge Res. Easily observed in winter at Fern Ridge or the Siuslaw estuary.

• **Clark's Grebe** *Aechmophorus clarkii*
Status: Local breeder. Rare, often unreported, in migration and winter.
Distribution: Two to four pairs have bred at Fern Ridge Res. in recent years.
Should be looked for in migration and winter on most sizable bodies of
deep water. Single birds are sometimes found with Western Grebes in
coastal flocks.
Sites: Breeders with young can sometimes be seen west of Perkins
Peninsula.

Order PROCELLARIIFORMES

Family Diomedeidae

Laysan Albatross *Phoebastria immutabilis*
Status: Presumed regular in migration and winter (as they are off Lincoln
Co.), but offshore access is so limited that records are essentially absent.
Two records: Oct. 7, 2000 and Apr. 15, 1958.
Distribution: Far offshore.
Sites: Accessible only by boat offshore.

Black-footed Albatross *Phoebastria nigripes*
Status: Uncommon to common offshore (based on regularity on Lincoln
and Coos Co. pelagic trips). It has been seen as close as 5 miles offshore in
Lane Co. (B. Combs, p.c.).
Distribution: Far offshore. Has been seen from land on rare occasions in
Coos and Lincoln Cos., so could be seen from land in Lane Co.
Sites: Accessible only by boat offshore.

* Short-tailed Albatross *Phoebastria albatrus*
Very rare wanderer from the western Pacific Ocean. One was tracked by
radio off the Lane Co. coast as it moved down the coastline offshore in fall
2003 (Rob Suryan, p.c.). Seabird researchers observed one on July 12, 2005
at the edge of Heceta Bank, just north of the Lane-Lincoln Co. line (report
by David Ainley to OBRC).

Family Procellariidae

Northern Fulmar *Fulmarus glacialis*
Status: Uncommon to common offshore migrant. Generally present
from July through Apr., but varies widely. Fall movement typically peaks
in Oct. but sometimes as late as mid-Dec. Spring movements essentially
unknown.

Distribution: Movements and population size moving off Oregon varies widely from year to year, and visibility from shore can be excellent (rarely) or nil depending on conditions.
Sites: Pelagic. Sometimes visible from shore (e.g. jetties, Sea Lion Caves, Heceta Head).

[Murphy's Petrel Pterodroma ultima]
Casual offshore. Unconfirmed offshore reports in Mar. and May. See Marshall et al. (2003) for status.

[Mottled Petrel Pterodroma inexpectata]
Present off Oregon in very small numbers, mainly from late fall through early spring. Not confirmed from Lane Co. but treated as provisionally present based on multiple sightings in immediately adjacent areas. See Marshall et al. (2003) for status.

Streaked Shearwater Calonectris leucomelas
Casual offshore. One sight report accepted by the OBRC, Sep. 13, 1996 over Heceta Bank, 53 miles offshore (Force et al. 1999, OBRC 088.1-96-01).

Pink-footed Shearwater *Puffinus creatopus*
Status: Uncommon migrant, mainly in summer and fall, rare in winter, density based on pelagic trips off Lincoln and Coos Cos.
Distribution: Offshore, rarely visible from land.
Sites: Pelagic.

Flesh-footed Shearwater *Puffinus carneipes*
Status: Probably rare offshore as it is off Coos and Lincoln Cos. See Supplemental Records.

Buller's Shearwater *Puffinus bulleri*
Status: Uncommon to common offshore from late summer through fall, as it is off Coos and Lincoln Cos. Peak count is 150-200, an exceptional total, off south Lane Co. on Sep. 5, 2005 (D. and A. Heyerly). A record Jan. 7, 2001 at the mouth of the Siuslaw R. was unusual in midwinter.
Distribution: Almost entirely offshore beyond sight of land.
Sites: Pelagic.

Sooty Shearwater *Puffinus griseus*
Status: Common to abundant offshore, with the bulk of passage from mid-July through mid-Sep. Small numbers reported year-round; rarest in winter.
Distribution: Mainly offshore beyond sight of land, but often close to shore in late summer.

*Sooty
Shearwaters.
Illustration
by Barbara
Gleason.*

Sites: Watch from coastal headlands, especially Aug.-Sep. Sometimes close to shore during foggy conditions in early fall.

Short-tailed Shearwater *Puffinus tenuirostris*
Status: Uncommon to abundant offshore. Most are reported from late Sep. through early Dec., with a peak in Nov.
Distribution: Pelagic, but sometimes visible from shore. Difficult to distinguish from Sooty.
Sites: Same as Sooty.

**Black-vented Shearwater *Puffinus opisthomelas*
Casual fall vagrant to Oregon from California. One Nov. report offshore, unconfirmed.

Family Hydrobatidae

Fork-tailed Storm-Petrel *Oceanodroma furcata*
Status: Probably common offshore, at least July-Oct., during and after the breeding season. Few reports.
Distribution: Heceta Bank and perhaps other locations offshore. Nearest known breeding colonies are in Tillamook Co. and Curry Co., but reported off Lane Co. by pelagic trips out of Newport.
Sites: Offshore.

Leach's Storm-Petrel *Oceanodroma leucorhoa*
Status: Probably common offshore, at least July-Oct., during and after the breeding season, but few reports. Occasionally seen at the mouth of the Siuslaw R., e.g., on June 22, 1998. During severe storms (notably Nov. 9, 1975 and Nov. 15, 1981), good numbers were blown inland to Fern Ridge Res. and other lakes. At least 15 birds were at Fern Ridge in 1975. After the

overnight storm of Nov. 8-9, 1975, birds were found as far inland as the Cascades east of Oakridge and were seen flying across Interstate 5. These were extraordinary conditions, with steady onshore winds in excess of 90 mph for several hours overnight, gusting to at least 130 mph (the Cape Blanco wind gauge only went that high, and was carried away overnight after reaching that number).

Distribution: Heceta Bank and perhaps other locations offshore. Nearest known breeding colonies are in Tillamook Co. and Coos Co., but reported off Lane Co. by pelagic trips.

Sites: Offshore.

Order PELECANIFORMES

Family Pelecanidae

American White Pelican *Pelecanus erythrorhynchos*
Status: Irregular and very local, occasionally common during summer. This species had been reported at Fern Ridge Res. as far back as the 1940s (Gullion), when it was considered abundant, with a peak count of 109. From the early 1950s through the 1990s, it was rare and irregular. Only since the early 2000s have significant numbers been present again at Fern Ridge Res. (e.g., 44 on June 23, 2001, 40 on July 14, 2004). At least 70 and perhaps as many as 100 were present at Fern Ridge in the last week of Aug., 2005 (D. Farrar). These birds are apparently nonbreeders (they do not breed at Fern Ridge), perhaps augmented by postbreeding wanderers from eastern Oregon or elsewhere. Rare in winter, only present since the early 2000s. One coastal record, collected near Florence on June 2, 1915 (*UO 1342*).

Distribution: Regular only at Fern Ridge Res. Could appear in late spring through early fall at larger bodies of water elsewhere in the county.

Sites: Fern Ridge Res.

Brown Pelican *Pelecanus occidentalis*
Status: Uncommon to common, May through Nov. In some years birds are present earlier in spring and later in fall; the earliest recent record was on Feb. 1, 2000. Status is changing, with more birds in Oregon nearly year-round and breeding attempted at the mouth of the Columbia R. Large numbers are remaining in fall, witness the 105 roosting on the rocks at Heceta Head on Sep. 11, 2000.

Distribution: Nearshore coastal, where they feed near the surf line and in lower estuaries. Generally do not go far up rivers or use freshwater lakes.

Sites: Lower Siuslaw estuary, Heceta Head.

Family Phalacrocoracidae

• **Brandt's Cormorant** *Phalacrocorax penicillatus*

Status: Uncommon to locally abundant breeding resident. Least common from mid-autumn through late winter. Local breeding birds depart in fall, possibly to Puget Sound and southern British Columbia waters, where winter numbers increase.

Distribution: Outer coast, mainly in rocky areas, especially during the breeding season from Mar. to early Sep., when hundreds gather in colonies on cliffs. Can be found in the lower Siuslaw estuary (roughly from the North Fork downriver) but generally does not go up rivers very far or use freshwater lakes.

Sites: Excellent views at breeding cliffs north of Sea Lion Caves.

• **Double-crested Cormorant** *Phalacrocorax auritus*

Status: Uncommon to common resident countywide in more open waters and adjacent snags; considerable seasonal movement among sites. A significant influx from late Sep. through mid-Nov. is especially noticeable on the outer coast and at Fern Ridge Res., as well as along the Willamette and McKenzie rivers in lowland areas. Small numbers move onto smaller lakes and reservoirs at this time.

It was considered rare in the Willamette Valley in the 1960s, and single birds were considered worth mentioning in field notes through the 1970s. Only since the 1980s have numbers been noticeable, and only since the late 1990s have roosts of many score been found with regularity. On the Eugene CBC, none were found from 1952 until a single bird appeared on the 1971 count (there were a couple of records in the 1940s). It did not become annual on the Eugene CBC until 1986, after which numbers increased steadily (see chart).

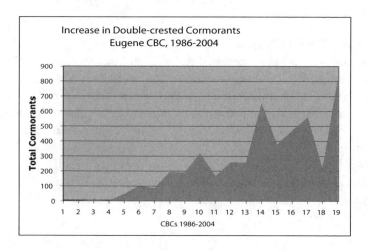

Increase in Double-crested Cormorants
Eugene CBC, 1986-2004

Double-crested Cormorant. Illustration by Barbara Gleason.

Distribution: Breeds locally along the outer coast, but more breed in estuarine settings than on cliffs or islands. There are many summer reports away from the coast, but no proof of breeding inland. Generally absent from smaller lakes and reservoirs from late spring through Aug., but widespread in open water from Sep. through Apr.

Sites: Widespread. Roosts move somewhat, with the most recent addition being a roost in Island Park, Springfield, established in 2000 and used mainly from Oct. through Apr., and a winter roost in the cottonwoods north of the footbridge at the Valley R. Center in Eugene.

• **Pelagic Cormorant** *Phalacrocorax pelagicus*

Status: Common resident. Breeds on cliffs and sometimes on human-made structures.

Distribution: Outer coast, mainly in rocky areas but also uses lower estuaries, especially in winter. More likely than Brandt's Cormorant to travel upriver into fresher water in winter.

Sites: Scattered. A few are easily visible on the edges of the Brandt's Cormorant colony just north of Sea Lion Caves.

Magnificent Frigatebird, July 29, 1983,
at Newport, seen later that day at
Florence. Photo by Al Prigge.

Family Fregatidae

* **Magnificent Frigatebird** *Fregata magnificens*
Status: Vagrant from the south. Two records: Mar. 4, 1987 (an adult female over the mouth of Big Creek, *NAB* 41:478) and July 29, 1983 (OBRC 128-83-02) at Florence.

Order CICONIIFORMES

Family Ardeidae

• **American Bittern** *Botaurus lentiginosus*
Status: Uncommon and local breeder. A few remain in winter.
Distribution: Wherever there are sizable marshlands or areas with extensive emergent vegetation. Most often found at Fern Ridge Res., where it is fairly easy to find along the marshes in summer and a few remain in winter. Also regular in small numbers in the wetter, more densely vegetated parts of the Siuslaw deflation plain (where it has bred). Occasional elsewhere, e.g., Lily Lake.
Sites: Easiest to see along the diked impoundments at Fern Ridge Res. Also fairly regular at the Dog Pond and along Dotterel Dike off the South Jetty Rd. at Florence. Easiest to find early in the morning, especially at the South Jetty Rd. sites.

Least Bittern *Ixobrychus exilis*
Status: Very rare vagrant; nearest site where it is known to breed is Upper Klamath Lake. One was found June 14, 1968 at Fern Ridge Res. (*NAB* 22:471, by L. McQueen). Another was seen and well described in Eugene in spring, 1970 (Dave Brown, p.c.). May occur rarely at Fern Ridge Res. marshes, but has not been systematically sought there.

• **Great Blue Heron** *Ardea herodias*
Status: Uncommon but highly visible breeder and winter resident. Locally common at or near breeding colonies. More are in the county in winter than in summer.

Distribution: Along waterways, lakes, and ocean shorelines countywide. Often concentrates where prey is available, e.g., narrow channels and shallow waters. Sometimes hunts rodents, amphibians, and reptiles in open fields.

Great Egret *Ardea alba*
Status: Uncommon to locally abundant, varies widely by season. Mainly along lakes, estuaries, and larger slow-moving rivers. Generally does not use oceanfront areas exposed to surf as the Great Blue Heron does, but uses calm saltwater areas. Most abundant from midsummer through fall, with local concentrations during winter.

Generally absent in May and June, but becoming more omnipresent. One recent record was May 28, 2002 and one was found in June, 2005 (both at Fern Ridge Res.), and the success of recent breeding colonies at Coos Bay suggests that the species may eventually breed in Lane Co. Early summer records are becoming more regular throughout western Oregon and even southwest Washington, where the species was once very rare. This is a fairly recent addition to the region's avifauna; the first county record was May 3, 1947 (Gullion).

Distribution: Peak numbers (20-40 birds) use the Siuslaw estuary from mid-July through early Sep., after which coastal numbers drop significantly and peak counts of 60 or more loosely clustered are at Fern Ridge Res. In fall, single birds and small groups are sometimes found in fields, along ponds and rivers countywide.

Sites: Siuslaw estuary in late summer, Fern Ridge Res. in fall and winter.

Snowy Egret *Egretta thula*
Status: Very rare and irregular, most in fall and winter, fewer than 10 records.

Distribution: Records are Sep. 16, 2001 along the lower North Fork of the Siuslaw R.; Nov. 18, 1995 near Florence; Aug. 19, 1994 at the mouth of the Siltcoos R.; Aug. 31, 1992 near Florence; Aug. 21, 1997 along the Siuslaw R. and Aug. 31 of the same year at Fern Ridge Res., possibly the same bird, since this is the pattern followed by Great Egrets. Also one on Dec. 27, 1987 near Florence. One spring record: May 28, 1988. Lane Co. records are probably of birds dispersing from California breeding colonies, but this is speculation.

*[Little Blue Heron *Egretta caerulea*]
One report, Aug. 23-24 1992 at Florence, was not accepted by the OBRC, and may have been an immature Snowy Egret, which is quite similar. However, Little Blue Heron has occurred a few times in Oregon.

Cattle Egret *Bubulcus ibis*

Status: Rare and irregular fall and winter visitor, less regular in recent years. Two late-summer records: Aug. 21, 1997, and June 10 - July 15, 2004 at Fern Ridge Res. Most records are in Nov.-Dec. Sometimes uses sites with heavy human influence, e.g., one spent several weeks in the Alvadore area, feeding in small open lots and pastures; another was seen entering a barn on the North Fork of the Siuslaw.

Distribution: Mostly coastal pastures, but also on the Willamette Valley floor.

Sites: No regular sites in recent years.

• Green Heron *Butorides virescens*

Status: Uncommon but widespread breeder, usually along still and slow-moving waters but occasionally away from water (e.g., in large trees south of downtown Eugene). Almost all depart in winter. Arrivals are typically in early Apr., departures are not noticed.

Distribution: Countywide along fresh or brackish water; generally absent from the high Cascades and central Coast Range. Uses protected saltwater in estuaries but avoids the open coast.

Sites: Often visible along Amazon creek in Eugene and west of Eugene.

° Black-crowned Night-Heron *Nycticorax nycticorax*

Status: Rare but regular, highly local at roost sites but otherwise seen in and near marshes countywide, mostly in Willamette Valley lowlands. Essentially unreported on the coast, rarely in the high Cascades. May breed occasionally but not proven. Records from May 25, 1998 near Junction City; June 17, 1998 near the Delta Ponds; and May 5, 1999 (5 birds in the R. Rd. area) suggest possible local breeding.

Distribution: Most records are from Aug. and early fall at or near Fern Ridge Res.; present there occasionally from June-Oct. In some years winter roosts are located on the valley floor, sometimes in suburban areas. May be a postbreeding arrival from breeding sites east of the Cascades, but this is speculation. The presence of a migrant on Aug. 12, 2003 at Gold Lake suggests some movement from eastern Oregon.

Sites: Irregular, but Fern Ridge Res. and wetlands north and west of Eugene have the most reports.

Family Threskiornithidae - Subfamily Threskiornithinae

White-faced Ibis *Plegadis chihi*
Status: Rare but recently regular as a spring migrant from late Apr. through early June. The first Lane Co. record was fairly recent, May 24, 1981. The earliest spring report is from Apr. 22, 1995. These birds may represent pioneers or migratory overshoots from populations breeding in eastern Oregon, but this is speculation. Found largely in wet grassy or shallow marshy areas. Very rare in fall, 2 records: Sep. 2, 1998 at Fern Ridge Res. and Nov. 9, 1996 near Coburg. A single bird on Aug. 1, 2002 at Fern Ridge Res. could have been a nonbreeder or a postbreeding wanderer.
Distribution: Almost all records are from the Fern Ridge Res. area.
Sites: Shallow grassy marshes around Fern Ridge Res.

Family Cathartidae

• Turkey Vulture *Cathartes aura*
Status: Fairly common and highly visible breeder and migrant. Concentrates where carrion is available. Spring arrivals are typically early, in late Feb. Fall movements are extended; most obvious in mid- to late Sep. Rare but increasing in winter, with a small winter roost (5-17 birds) southeast of Fern Ridge Res. in the 2000s.
Distribution: Countywide breeder. Concentrates in roost sites and along ridges in migration.

Order FALCONIFORMES

Family Accipitridae - Subfamily Pandioninae

• Osprey *Pandion haliaetus*
Status: Uncommon but highly visible breeder. Some breed in cities where tall trees or platforms are available near water. Uncommon but widespread migrant. Rare in winter; 1 to 3 birds have been wintering along the Willamette and McKenzie rivers on the valley floor since the 1990s. Spring migrants begin appearing in mid-Mar.
Distribution: Breeds countywide from the coast to the Cascade lakes near water. Mostly absent from Coast Range. Migration is fairly early in fall, with most obvious movement (small numbers) in Sep., often along the outer coast.
Sites: Obvious around Fern Ridge Res. and along the Willamette and other major rivers and lakes.

Subfamily Accipitrinae

• **White-tailed Kite** *Elanus leucurus*

Status: Rare local breeder, uncommon but highly visible in fall and winter. This is a fairly recent arrival to Lane Co.; the first record was in Dec. 1968 at Fern Ridge Res. It slowly expanded in the 1970s and was considered regular at most seasons, most visible in winter, by the 1980s.

First breeding record in the county was in 1981 in the Upper Siuslaw R. Valley at Lorane. Uncommon and local from late summer through winter. Prefers isolated perches above open grasslands, pastures, marshes, and estuary edges except in breeding season, when it apparently moves slightly upslope into foothills and small canyons bordering pasturelands and drier fields for nesting. Quite secretive during the breeding season from Mar. through Aug. Breeding season can be variable; see Marshall et al. (2003).

Distribution: Mostly on the Willamette Valley floor and the lower Siuslaw estuary. A winter roost, sometimes in excess of 20 birds, forms at Fern Ridge Res.

Sites: Easiest to see in grassy areas near Fern Ridge Res. from Sep. through Mar. Usually visible on islands or pasture trees in the Siuslaw estuary east of Florence.

• **Bald Eagle** *Haliaeetus leucocephalus*

Status: Local breeder in small numbers countywide where there are large trees near water. Numbers slowly increasing. Uncommon migrant near water, sometimes forms concentrations in winter where fish or rodents are concentrated. An extraordinary concentration of over 60 birds at Fern Ridge Res. in late winter 2004 may have been related to unique conditions at the reservoir (a die-off of small carp) or in the region. Also gathers during lambing season to feed on afterbirth and dead sheep. As many as 11 birds have been seen feeding together on the ground in such situations (P. Peterson, p.c.). Has bred at or near Fern Ridge Res. irregularly since 1959-61 (L. Fish, p.c.)

Distribution: Countywide, mainly near water and in open fields when prey or carrion is available.

Sites: Widespread, Fern Ridge Res. in winter.

• **Northern Harrier** *Circus cyaneus*

Status: Local breeder in small numbers. Migrant in open areas countywide, rare in montane openings unless meadows are present. Locally common in winter.

Distribution: In breeding season, present in small numbers on the Willamette Valley floor where extensive marshes or grasslands are

present, mainly around Fern Ridge Res. Sometimes breeds in the south jetty deflation plain near Florence. Winters in marshland and agricultural areas with overgrown fields. Sometimes forms roosts, e.g., at Fern Ridge Res. Winter numbers higher than breeding numbers.
Sites: Southeast side of Fern Ridge Res., South Jetty Rd. near Florence.

• **Sharp-shinned Hawk** *Accipiter striatus*
Status: Uncommon breeder, also often seen in migration. Winter resident, often raiding bird feeders.
Distribution: Countywide at all seasons, generally in forested areas in the breeding season, when it is also hard to find on the coast.

• **Cooper's Hawk** *Accipiter cooperii*
Status: Breeds in forested areas and sometimes in urban areas. Winters, also seen in migration.
Distribution: Countywide; mainly in forested areas in the breeding season, when it is hard to find on the coast. In migration and winter, can appear anywhere. Sometimes found in very open agricultural areas in winter, unlike Sharp-shinned Hawk.

Sharp-shinned Hawk. Illustration by Barbara Gleason.

• **Northern Goshawk** *Accipiter gentilis*
Status: Rare to uncommon resident breeder. Rarely reported in winter but that probably has more to do with the habits of observers than those of Goshawks. During the years of the Oakridge CBC, the species was reported on 40 percent of counts (6/15). Generally not reported as a migrant. Status not well known owing to use of heavily forested areas, especially at higher elevations.
Distribution: Breeds mainly in the higher Cascades and along the Calapooya Divide between Lane and Douglas Co. Very rare and irregular breeder and migrant in the Coast Range, only confirmed breeding once in Lane Co. (T. Mickel, p.c.). Rare on the valley floors or the outer coast at any season; most often reported there in winter: Alma CBC 3/15, Cottage Grove CBC 4/14, Eugene CBC 14/62.
Sites: Horsepasture Mtn. above McKenzie Bridge.

• **Red-shouldered Hawk** *Buteo lineatus*
Status: Rare but increasing resident breeder. Uncommon around Fern Ridge Res. Some additional influx in winter. First county record was in 1977, and has been annual since the late 1980s, with multiple birds often reported since the late 1990s.
Distribution: Lowlands and adjacent small valleys in the western half of the county. Most often reported from wooded or swampy areas on the Willamette Valley floor and westward (especially around Fern Ridge Res.), occasionally in openings or open streamsides in the Coast Range and western Cascades. Increasing around Florence and in the Siuslaw Valley.
Sites: Wooded areas near Fern Ridge Res.

Swainson's Hawk *Buteo swainsoni*
Status: The true status of this species in the county has been misunderstood for decades. This is a rare but regular migrant, mainly in mid-spring and early autumn. There are 12 published spring records that have an ascertainable date, of which 10 are between Apr. 20 (1916, a dark phase specimen from Eugene, *UO 1631*) and May 9, a clear pattern of occurrence. The other two records are from Mar. 9, 1948 and the third week of Mar. 1996 at Fern Ridge Res. (Marian Matthews). In the early 1970s one was observed south of Cottage Grove in Apr. (A. Contreras).

There are at least 6 fall records: Sep. 13-17, 2004 (3 birds near the Eugene airport); Aug. 30, 2001, Aug. 6, 1998 at Belknap Springs; Oct. 9, 1993 at Waldo Lake; Sep. 1, 1949 and Nov. 30, 1945. The last two are from the generally excellent records of Ben Pruitt, as published in Gullion. Pruitt had an unknown number of additional fall records that fell between these two dates. He lived in the Thurston area when it was entirely rural, a natural location for fall records of this species.

Immature Swainson's Hawk, Dec. 6, 2005, west of Junction City. Photo by Sylvia Maulding.

Two unexpected winter records, an immature present from Dec. 12, 1968 through Jan. 19, 1969 at Fern Ridge Res., was seen by many observers (L. McQueen, A. Contreras et al.). An early Dec. bird appeared west of Junction City in 2005, with definitive photos obtained. This bird may have been present since earlier in fall, based on a distant observation by another observer. It remained through at least late February 2006.

Note: Some darker Red-tailed Hawks are mistakenly reported as Swainson's Hawks.

Distribution: Records are from the Cascades, Willamette Valley floor, Mt. Pisgah, over Skinner Butte and Fern Ridge Res.

• Red-tailed Hawk *Buteo jamaicensis*

Status: Uncommon but highly visible resident breeder. Additional influx in winter. In some winters, single individuals of the dark "Harlan's" form are found, mainly in the Willamette Valley lowlands.

Distribution: Countywide except inside the most solid areas of forest. Uses a wide variety of semi-open habitat from coastal headlands to forest openings and agricultural areas.

Ferruginous Hawk *Buteo regalis*
Rare fall and winter visitor, possibly from eastern Oregon. Seven records: March 4-12, 2001, Sep. 3-10, 2001 at the Eugene airport; Oct. 27, 1997 at Camas Swale; an immature Sep. 28-29, 1992 at Erickson and Pine Grove roads near Lorane; Dec. 31, 1972-Jan., 1973 near the Eugene airport; and Dec. 28, 1952 on the Eugene CBC. There have been a few additional unpublished reports, mainly from open country north of the Eugene airport.

Rough-legged Hawk *Buteo lagopus*
Status: Uncommon irregular winter resident. Typically arrives in mid-Oct. and remains through early Apr. Earliest recent arrivals were Oct. 2, 2000 and Oct 8, 2001. Numbers vary widely from year to year, with lows under 5 and peak numbers approaching 20.
Distribution: Mostly in the open agricultural lands of the Willamette Valley north of the Eugene-Springfield area. In peak years a few reach the outer coast, where they are usually found in the deflation plain of the Siuslaw and occasionally in other very open areas. Rare east to montane prairies in the west Cascades (7/15 Oakridge CBC).
Sites: Valley floor north of the Eugene airport.

• Golden Eagle *Aquila chrysaetos*
Status: Rare irregular local breeder. Rare but regular in very small numbers in winter.
Distribution: Has bred irregularly in the Coburg Hills and along the Cascade summit ridges. Generally absent or hard to find in summer. A few birds sometimes winter west to the valley floors, mainly along the eastern edge of the valleys from Cottage Grove north to the Coburg area, and along the south side of Fern Ridge Res.

Family Falconidae - Subfamily Falconinae

• American Kestrel *Falco sparverius*
Status: Uncommon but visible breeder, fairly common migrant and winter resident. More common and more widespread in winter than in the breeding season.
Distribution: Breeds mainly in open areas on the valley floors and lower river valleys. Generally does not breed on the coast or in the high Cascades. Winters more widely, including forest openings and open areas on the outer coast, where it is sometimes hard to find. Sparse in the Coast Range in winter (Alma CBC 4/15). Winter numbers on the Willamette Valley floor are much higher than breeding numbers.

° **Merlin** *Falco columbarius*

Status: Very rare and irregular in summer in the high Cascades. A few summer records suggest the possibility of occasional breeding: a pair at Scott Lake in summer 1975 (M. Patterson, p.c.) and birds seen in the summers of 2001 and 2003 (Gold Lake). Uncommon but widespread migrant and winter resident, mainly on the valley floor and coast. Latest recent record in the lowlands is May 3, 2002.

Winter birds include darker *suckleyi*, often seen on the coast and originating in Alaska or British Columbia (Gullion, specimen in Elmira now lost, noted by Jewett), and paler birds that may represent *columbarius*. The palest subspecies, *richardsonii*, is very rare in Oregon. Merlin specimens from Oregon are scarce; I am aware of none extant from Lane Co.

Distribution: Uses a wide variety of open and semi-open habitats. Most often reported on the outer coast hunting along estuaries or the oceanfront, at Fern Ridge Res., and within urban Eugene-Springfield, where it hunts in more open neighborhoods and along the treetops. Rarely reported from montane or heavily forested areas, but was found on 6 of 15 Oakridge CBCs, suggesting fairly regular presence in river valleys to 1000 feet elevation or so.

Sites: Easiest to find around Fern Ridge Res. and on the outer coast; can be difficult elsewhere.

Gyrfalcon *Falco rusticolus*

Casual, 3 records: Sep. 23-24, 2003 north of Florence; Dec. 1973-Jan. 1974 and Dec. 17, 1971, both near the Eugene airport. Likely to occur again in the valley or on the outer coast; annual (2-3 birds) in western Oregon in past several years.

• **Peregrine Falcon** *Falco peregrinus*

Status: Rare local breeder. Rare but highly visible migrant and winter resident. Found mainly near water in migration and winter, owing to its preference for waterfowl and shorebirds.

Both dark *peali* and paler *anatum* are known to occur in the county, *peali* only in migration and winter. There are a few reports of *tundrius*, but the exact status of this subspecies in the county is unknown, due to its similarity to *anatum*.

Distribution: Local breeder in mid to high Cascades. Could breed on cliffs of the outer coast but not proven in Lane Co. Most migrants and winter birds are found around Fern Ridge Res., on the outer coast and along major waterways.

Sites: Outer coast, Fern Ridge Res., and wetlands around west Eugene in winter.

Prairie Falcon *Falco mexicanus*
Status: Rare but regular winter visitor, one or two records each year, mostly Oct.-Apr., earliest until 2005 was Sep. 4, latest May 4. Earliest recent arrival in the valley was Aug. 28, 2005 at Fern Ridge Res. (D. Irons, p.c.), which was 2 weeks earlier than the previous recent early date of Sep. 10, 2001.
Distribution: Mainly on the floor of the Willamette Valley north of Eugene-Springfield, also Fern Ridge Res., but has also been seen in clear-cuts in valley foothills and occasionally along the Cascade summit in early fall.

Order GRUIFORMES

Family Rallidae

• **Virginia Rail** *Rallus limicola*
Status: Fairly common but local and secretive breeder in marshlands countywide. Uncommon to rare in winter (interior), depending in part on the severity of the winter. Locally common in winter in a few sites on the outer coast. Most inland birds leave in winter, but coastal populations increase.
Distribution: Countywide, but habitat is limited outside lowlands. Most common in summer in the large marshes at Fern Ridge Res. Has bred at Triangle Lake. Also present year-round in the Lily Lake swamp north of Florence and in small marshes at coastal lakes. Probably breeds much more widely than is known, owing to its somewhat secretive habits and willingness to use small patches of habitat. In winter, regular in flooded grassy areas and willow bogs of the Siuslaw deflation plain.
Sites: Relatively easy to find along the wet edges of Royal Ave. and the dike network at Fern Ridge Res., especially in late summer when young birds are active.

• **Sora** *Porzana carolina*
Status: Fairly common but local breeder in marshes and wet meadows. Rare in winter, most winter birds are coastal. Spring arrivals sometimes appear during Mar., but most arrive in early Apr. Unclear whether it breeds in coastal marshes or only winters there.
Distribution: Countywide breeder where there is sufficient marsh vegetation; almost all of this habitat is on the valley floor around Fern Ridge Res. These interior birds leave in winter. A few winter in marshes on the coast.
Sites: Fern Ridge Res. (especially along Royal Ave.) in summer, Baker Beach Rd. swamp in winter (irregular).

• American Coot *Fulica americana*

Status: Uncommon breeder in lakes with significant emergent vegetation on the valley floor. Could breed in similar habitat countywide, but currently does not. It is unclear why it does not breed at coastal lakes such as Siltcoos that appear to have appropriate habitat.

Distribution: In breeding season from Apr. through Aug., found mainly at Fern Ridge Res., with small numbers at other lakes that have emergent vegetation. Can appear on any still water in migration. Winters on most lakes and even large ponds in the lowlands, and locally in the Coast Range (Triangle Lake), west Cascades (Dexter Res.), and on coastal lakes, where it is fairly common at Siltcoos Lake and uncommon to rare at other lakes, for reasons that are not clear.

Family Gruidae - Subfamily Gruinae

• Sandhill Crane *Grus canadensis*

Status: Common migrant but seen mainly overhead; not often seen on the ground. Does not breed except on an occasional basis at Mink Lake basin in the high Cascades. Early spring migrants are sometimes seen as early as mid-Feb., regular by Mar., and most are past before Apr. Fall migrants move during an extended period from mid-Sep. through early Nov. Very rare in winter, a few records of single birds at Fern Ridge Res. or in open fields.

Distribution: Most often reported in migration at Camas Swale along I-5 north of Creswell, or as flocks flying over on the eastern side of the Willamette Valley.

Sites: Irregular, check Camas Swale in migration. Because of preferred migration routes, often seen from Mt. Pisgah.

Order CHARADRIIFORMES

Family Charadriidae - Subfamily Charadriinae

Black-bellied Plover *Pluvialis squatarola*

Status: Locally common migrant and winter resident. Southbound migrants begin arriving in early July; peak numbers are present in Sep. Winter peak is normally a couple of dozen birds, but in some years many more are present; record count is 132 near the Eugene airport on Jan. 2, 2000. Peak of passage in spring is late Apr., but birds are often seen quite late, with stragglers into early June and an occasional nonbreeder staying the summer. Uses mudflats, wet short-grass pastures, and grass-seed fields.

Distribution: Most common on mudflats of the Siuslaw estuary, with small numbers at the Siltcoos estuary. Small numbers use Fern Ridge Res. and occasionally nearby fields. Fall migrants were formerly uncommon there because the reservoir level covers all mudflats until Oct., by which time most birds have gone through. However, new impoundments have created mud habitat throughout migration, and plovers and other shorebirds are now more regular.

Sites: Easiest to see along the Siuslaw estuary and at Fern Ridge Res.

American Golden-Plover *Pluvialis dominica*
Status: Rare migrant, mainly in fall. Very few birds migrate through Oregon, and numbers in the county in a given year range from a couple to at most a dozen birds in a season. Fall birds have been seen from July through Oct., but most records are from very late Aug. and Sep. Latest recent record was Oct. 16, 2004. Peak fall count of golden plovers (undifferentiated by species) is 12 on Sep. 9, 1983 in the south jetty deflation plain (S. Heinl, p.c.). Spring reports are from Apr. and early May, with rare reports to mid-May and a single early June record of a golden-plover of uncertain species (June 5, 1989 at the south jetty deflation plain, S. Heinl, p.c.). Prefers drier grassy or mixed grass and sandy/gravelly areas over mudflats, but does use mudflats.

Distribution: Mostly coastal. Also occurs occasionally at Fern Ridge Res.

Sites: South jetty sites near Florence (especially Siuslaw deflation plain).

Pacific Golden-Plover *Pluvialis fulva*
Status: Rare migrant, mainly in fall from Aug. to early Oct. Has wintered in Linn Co. and one was found Jan. 2, 2005 at Fern Ridge Res. (CBC; D. Irons, N. Strycker et al.). Very rare in spring; the only recent records are May 9, 2003 and May 14, 1998, both at Florence. Uses drier habitats than Black-bellied, e.g., open sand, gravel, or these mixed with short grass.

Pacific Golden-Plover, south jetty Siuslaw R., Sep. 24, 2000. Photo by Luke Bloch.

Snowy
Plover on
beach.
Illustration
by Barbara
Gleason.

Distribution: Almost all coastal. Also reported from Fern Ridge Res. and could appear in wet short-grass fields or pastures.
Sites: South jetty sites near Florence (especially Siuslaw deflation plain).

• Snowy Plover *Charadrius alexandrinus*
Status: Rare local breeder, rare migrant, and uncommon and highly local winter resident. Open dry sand.
Distribution: Breeds at the mouth of the Siltcoos R. and in the Baker Beach area between Sutton Creek and Lily Lake. Winters in both of these areas. Very rare migrant inland: Aug. 18, 2003 and Sep. 7, 1970 (*ENHS* 4:8, Sep. 1970), both at Fern Ridge Res.
Sites: Mouth of Siltcoos R. or Lily Lake beaches in winter. *Note*: this area is closed to the public during the breeding season, Apr. 15-Sep. 15.

Semipalmated Plover *Charadrius semipalmatus*
Status: Uncommon to locally common migrant; rare and irregular in winter. Occurs on mudflats, occasionally in wet pastures or on open sand. First southbound migrants appear in early July, with peak of passage in Aug. and Sep. A steady movement of small numbers continues throughout Oct., with occasional stragglers into Nov. Rare and irregular in winter, with just as many reports at Fern Ridge as on the coast. Numbers quite variable. Sometimes completely absent, but a flock of 17 (with 9 Snowies) at the mouth of the Siltcoos R. on Jan. 23, 2000 (J. Carlson, *Quail*) suggests that either local wintering or early spring movements of sizable groups happens occasionally. Spring movements are apparent by late Mar., with peak of passage mid-Apr. to mid-May. Very rare in June.

Semipalmated Plovers have bred twice and attempted to breed in other years at the north spit of Coos Bay in areas used by breeding Snowy Plovers (Marshall et al. 2003). It is possible that they might attempt to breed in coastal Lane Co. in the future. Any June sightings in appropriate habitat should be checked with care for possible nesting.

Distribution: Primarily coastal in fall, with flocks of dozens sometimes present on mudflats of the Siuslaw R., some roosting in the deflation plain east of the South Jetty Rd. Small numbers can be found at the Siltcoos mouth, with a few present on beaches, especially at creek mouths. A few sometimes winter on the mudflats at Fern Ridge Res., sometimes moving into wet pastures and grass-seed fields, especially if muddy.

Sites: Mudflats by Siuslaw jetties.

• **Killdeer** *Charadrius vociferus*

Status: Fairly common and highly visible widespread breeder, migrant, and abundant winter resident. Breeds in a variety of open habitats with some semblance of cover, including gravel pans, riverbanks, grassy or muddy areas around buildings, and sometimes in unlikely small patches of gravel and grass in the midst of human activities. Highly vocal, thus easily detected. Migrants often move during hours of darkness, when they can sometimes be heard calling overhead, even in cities. Abundant in winter, mainly in grass-seed fields and similar wet short-grass settings.

Distribution: Breeds countywide, very local in the high Cascades and Coast Range owing to limited habitat. Winters on open ground, mainly on the valley floor, on the outer coast and locally at reservoirs that have been lowered for the winter. Wintering flocks in grass-seed fields and other wet short-grass habitats from northern Lane Co. to the central Willamette Valley are often the largest local concentrations in the United States.

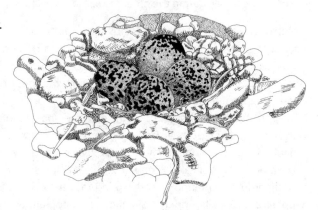

Killdeer nest. Illustration by Barbara Gleason.

Eurasian
Dotterel near
Florence. Photo
by Craig Miller.

*Eurasian Dotterel *Charadrius morinellus*

Vagrant from Alaska or east Asia. One record, the only one for Oregon, Sep.
24-26, 2000 on the sand flats of the Siuslaw deflation plain (OBRC 269.1-
00-01). The bird was in the company of an American Golden-Plover.

Family Haematopodidae

• **Black Oystercatcher** *Haematopus bachmani*

Status: Uncommon local resident breeder in rocky areas of the outer
coast. Sometimes found bathing in the mouths of small creeks where they
meet the ocean, loosely associated with flocks of gulls.
Distribution: A few pairs breed on the rocky headlands from roughly Sea
Lion Caves northward. Most easily observed on the low rocky points of the
northern coast, where they forage on rocks and bathe in creek mouths.
Sites: Stonefield Beach and Bob Creek.

Family Recurvirostridae

• **Black-necked Stilt** *Himantopus mexicanus*

Status: Rare local breeder, confirmed in 2002, possibly earlier; rare migrant.
Found in mudflats with pools of water, shallow marshes with open areas.
Arrives very late Mar. to early Apr., a few remain through midsummer in
years when they breed. The latest record is Aug. 25, 2004. First record was
June 2, 1968 at ponds along Coburg Rd. (*ENHS*).
Distribution: Breeds locally in shallow marshes at the southeastern
corner of Fern Ridge Res., south of Royal Ave. Spring migrants occasionally
reported elsewhere on the valley floor. No coastal records.
Sites: Fern Ridge Res., east and south sides.

American Avocet *Recurvirostra americana*

Status: Rare migrant, very rare until the early 1980s, almost annual (every year except 2000) since 1996. About 20 records involving about 50 birds, about 2/3 late spring to early summer, 1/3 in fall. Mudflats and shallow marshes. Usually single birds, but an astonishing 24 were at Fern Ridge Res. on Sep. 3, 2003. Ten were there on Apr. 10, 1988, and 3 were at Florence on Sep. 21-22, 2001. A rare early spring migrant was at Fern Ridge Res. Feb. 9-14, 1996. There are no records between June 24 and Aug. 18, which suggests that breeding is not being attempted in the county.

Distribution: Mainly on the valley floor in spring and early summer. In addition to the greater Fern Ridge area, birds have been seen at Cottage Grove Res. (June 24, 1981), the Walterville pond (Apr. 20, 1982), Creswell (Aug. 24, 1996), and Stewart Pond (Nov. 27, 2003, the latest fall record for the county). Several records from the Siuslaw estuary, mainly in Apr. and late Aug.

Family Scolopacidae - Subfamily Scolopacinae

Greater Yellowlegs *Tringa melanoleuca*

Status: Uncommon to locally common migrant, uncommon to rare in winter. Small sheltered mudflats, flooded pastures, shallow ponds. Generally avoids large open mudflats. Present in the county nearly year-round, with southbound migrant adults appearing in very late June. A steady buildup of adults in midsummer is followed by immatures in early fall. Flocks of 5-20 birds sometimes winter; in recent years counts of up to 70 have been found.

Distribution: Countywide in migration, but most movement is on the valley floor and the outer coast. Winter birds are mostly in flooded fields and larger ponds on the valley floor and in wet coastal pasturelands.

Sites: Meadowlark Prairie and Canary Rd. in winter, edges of Fern Ridge Res. and Dotterel Dike in fall.

Lesser Yellowlegs *Tringa flavipes*

Status: Uncommon to rare migrant, very rare but becoming more regular in winter. Uses shallow ponds, flat riverbanks, flooded pastures. Much less common than Greater Yellowlegs, and numbers vary more from year to year. Southbound migrants begin arriving in early July, with no significant peak. Small numbers continue moving throughout the fall, tapering off in Oct., with very few seen after Nov. 1. One of few migrant shorebirds to be seen more often inland than on the outer coast.

This species was formerly unheard-of in winter, but that is changing. One to three birds have wintered around Fern Ridge Res. (sometimes in ponds along Hwy 126 west of Veneta) in most years since 1997. The peak winter count is 6 birds on Jan. 17, 2005 at Stewart Pond. This species has become more regular in winter in the Coos Bay area as well, but not yet around Florence, where one record, Jan. 22, 1997 is the only winter report. **Distribution:** Mostly on the valley floor and the outer coast (not on beaches). **Sites:** Small ponds around Fern Ridge are best.

° **Solitary Sandpiper** *Tringa solitaria*

Status: Very rare and irregular probable breeder at Gold Lake Bog (Sawyer 1981, Marshall et al. 2003). Adults were found defending territory there June 28, 1981 and occasionally thereafter. Four birds, two of which appeared to be juveniles, were found there on July 25, 1981. Another was seen there July 18, 2003. The area should be checked each summer for proof of breeding.

In migration, uses small ponds and the quietest edges of backwaters in fresh and brackish water. Generally avoids mudflats and open pastures. Willing to use astonishingly small ponds and little holes, even large puddles.

Uncommon to rare migrant, regular in very small numbers. Unlike most shorebirds that migrate through Oregon, Solitary Sandpipers are more often reported in spring than in fall, with a very clear window of most movement between approximately Apr. 20 and May 10. Some birds appear in early Apr. and there are reports through late May, but the vast bulk of records are from the late Apr.-early May window.

Fall movements are so sparse as to be unclear, but most reports are from Aug. and early to mid-Sep., with none after Sep. Latest recent record was Sep 17, 2005 north of Florence (B. and Z. Stotz, p.c.). An unusual record was July 13-14, 2004 at Fern Ridge. **Distribution:** Except for the Gold Lake records in summer, this species occurs mainly on the valley floor and the coast (estuary backwaters but not beaches or open mudflats). **Sites:** Ponds at Meadowlark Prairie, ponds around Fern Ridge Res., farm ponds, lower Siltcoos R.

Willet *Catoptrophorus semipalmatus*

Status: Rare but somewhat regular migrant, mostly in late summer. About 15 records. Not annual, but reported fairly often in Aug. (8 records since 1994), with stragglers as late as mid-Oct. Almost always single birds. Very rare in spring, with about 5 records in mid- to late May. Three of these are from Florence; one on May 22, 2000 and another May 16-17, 2003 are the only Fern Ridge Res. records and the only interior Lane Co. records of which I am aware.

Distribution: Almost all records are on the outer coast, in the lower Siuslaw estuary and the Siltcoos mouth. It is unclear why this obvious species does not occur more often in spring at Fern Ridge Res. in a pattern similar to that shown by Black-necked Stilt, Black Tern, Wilson's Phalarope and (in smaller numbers), American Avocet and Long-billed Curlew, which have a similar breeding range in eastern Oregon.

Sites: Lower Siuslaw estuary is best bet.

Wandering Tattler *Heteroscelus incanus*

Status: Uncommon to rare migrant on rocky parts of the outer coast. Southbound movements are thin and start fairly late; the earliest fall record is of two collected July 10, 1934 (*SD* 21004 & 21008) and arrivals are more typically in late July, with a peak in Aug. and a steady trickle through late Sep., after which they are quite rare. The latest recent records are Oct. 20, 2000 and Oct. 21, 2004. Highest count is 22 at the Florence jetties on Aug. 2, 1996, three times the usual migration counts there. Spring movements are thin and extended, beginning in very late Mar., peaking in mid-May and extending through very early June. Numbers vary from year to year. An exceptionally early record was Feb. 11, 2002 (north jetty, David Smith). No winter records.

Distribution: Exclusively on low rocky outcrops and jetties on the outer coast.

Sites: Siuslaw jetties.

Note: Any tattler seen on mudflats or beaches ought to be carefully examined in case it proves to be a Gray-tailed Tattler (*Heteroscelus brevipes*), a rare Asian vagrant that has probably occurred in Oregon a couple of times. The best way to distinguish Gray-tailed is its call notes; see standard field guides and Paulson (1983, 2004).

• **Spotted Sandpiper** *Actitis macularia*
Status: Uncommon but easily detected breeder; rare but regular in very small numbers in winter. Uses streamside gravel bars, edges of mudflats, and other relatively flat, semi-open water's edge habitat. Often feeds on log booms and similar large floating wooden objects, especially when high tides cover all mud margins. Does not venture far out on mudflats. Fall migration is not easy to detect because the species does not form flocks, but observations by Vjera Arnold suggest that local breeders depart by late Sep., while the small number of winter birds do not arrive until late Nov. It sometimes seems absent in Oct. Migration is a little easier to see in spring, when breeders begin to arrive along rivers and lakesides in lowlands by late Apr. and at higher elevations during May as snow levels allow.
Distribution: Countywide in breeding season, with highest densities along rivers with wide, flat gravel pans. Winter birds (very few) found at lower elevations, most regular in the lower Siuslaw estuary and along the Willamette R. in Eugene/Springfield. May be more regular at higher elevations in winter than is generally thought, since it was found on 11 of 15 Oakridge CBCs, with a peak count of 9, higher than is often found on lower-elevation counts.
Sites: Willamette R. banks in summer, mud and log booms adjacent to Old Town Florence in winter.

Whimbrel *Numenius phaeopus*
Status: Uncommon to common migrant, does not breed. Has not been found in winter, but winters occasionally at Coos Bay, Bandon, and Newport, so could occur on the Siuslaw in winter. Usually found on open mudflats and sometimes beaches, less often on rocks; generally avoids dense grass.
  Southbound movements begin in mid-July, with an extended, somewhat variable peak between early Aug. (adults) and mid-Sep. (juveniles). Small numbers pass through until late Oct., after which it is rare (Nov.) to absent (winter). Spring movements start by very late Mar., with most birds moving from mid-Apr. to early May. Stragglers (sometimes small flocks) into early June are fairly regular.
  Oregon's highest fall coastal count (240 on Aug. 24, 1997 at Florence) and highest fall inland count (15 at Fern Ridge Res. on Aug. 2, 2001) are both from Lane County.
Distribution: Almost all coastal, with occasional inland reports at Fern Ridge Res. Fern Ridge records (1-9 birds, and the flock of 15) are mostly from mid-May and Sep., with an early record Aug. 8, 1947, 9 together on Aug. 24, 1977 (*OB* 3(5): 41) and an unusual record June 13, 1948 (Gullion).

Most coastal birds are within a mile of the ocean; whimbrels do not travel far up rivers.

Sites: Lower Siuslaw estuary and adjacent areas.

Long-billed Curlew *Numenius americanus*

Status: Rare but regular migrant. Reports range from Apr. through early Nov., with a single winter record, Jan. 3-4, 2000 near the Eugene airport. Most reports are in Apr. and early summer, but it is not clear if the latter are migrants or (perhaps more likely), nonbreeding year-old birds or postbreeding dispersants. Fall peak is in Aug. and early Sep., but with few records. Long-billed Curlews breed early in the Great Basin and eastern Washington and some birds stage for migration by mid-June.

Distribution: Most reports are from the valley floor, especially around Fern Ridge Res. Very rare on the outer coast.

*Hudsonian Godwit *Limosa haemastica*

Vagrant. Two records: Aug. 5-8, 1995 at the Siuslaw deflation plain and Sep. 18, 1990 at the Crab Dock Cove (OBRC 251-90-11).

*Bar-tailed Godwit *Limosa lapponica*

Vagrant. One record, Sep. 17-23+, 2004 at Florence.

Marbled Godwit *Limosa fedoa*

Status: Uncommon migrant, mainly in fall. Found largely on open mudflats. First southbound birds appear in early July, with an extended movement in low numbers (variable from year to year) through Oct. Stragglers are seen into early Nov. in some years, latest record Nov. 17, 1975.

Although this species winters with some regularity at Coos Bay, there is only one winter record in Lane County, Feb. 20, 1999. This may have been an early spring migrant. Spring movements are thin and extended, and typically begin in very late Mar., with most movement in Apr. and early May. Some are reported through the end of May.

Distribution: Mostly coastal. There are a few records at Fern Ridge Res., mostly of single birds, from late May through Nov. 1. One was near Creswell on May 24, 1998.

Sites: Florence, Crab Dock Cove.

Ruddy Turnstone *Arenaria interpres*

Status: Uncommon to rare migrant, rare and irregular in winter. Found on mudflats, coastal rocks, jetties, piers. May be decreasing. Southbound movements are typically the most obvious, and occur rather abruptly with a short peak in mid-July. Numbers are very low after early Aug., with single birds the norm by Sep. (some years none are seen) and stragglers through

Hudsonian Godwit, Sep. 1990. Photo by Bill and Zanah Stotz.

Bar-tailed Godwit, Sep. 23, 2004 at Florence. Photo by Diane Pettey.

the fall. Rare and irregular in winter, fewer reports today than in the 1980s. Numbers are also low in spring, with movement fairly early, late Mar. and early Apr., some still moving through early May.
Distribution: Almost all on the outer coast. See Supplemental Records.
Sites: Siuslaw mouth.

Black Turnstone *Arenaria melanocephala*
Status: Uncommon to locally common migrant and winter resident. Rocky shorelines and jetties. Sometimes uses log booms and piers, especially during severe weather or very high tides. First southbound migrants typically appear the second week of July, with a steady movement of small numbers thereafter. It is not known whether these early arrivals are the same birds that remain to winter or whether they continue southward to be replaced by successive waves.

Winter numbers are typically a couple of dozen birds at favored locations, often with Surfbirds. Spring movements are likewise obscured by the presence of a local wintering population. A significant drop in numbers is apparent after mid-Apr., with small numbers often present through mid-May.

Distribution: Rocky areas of the outer coast, occasionally on adjacent mudflats. During severe weather or high tides, sometimes goes far up estuaries and roosts on log booms or even in wet pastures. Extremely rare inland; one record of a bird in a field near Coburg on Dec. 19, 1974 (Randy Floyd, *fide* Larry McQueen) and one at the Creswell sewage treatment plant on Oct. 23, 1995 (S. Nelson).

Sites: Siuslaw jetties, Heceta Head, Stonefield Beach, Bob Creek.

Surfbird *Aphriza virgata*

Status: Uncommon and somewhat local migrant and winter resident. Rocky shorelines on the outer coast. Unlike Black Turnstone, tends to avoid log booms, pilings, and piers. Typically arrives in mid-July and remains through mid-Apr., with small numbers through early May. Flocks typically number fewer than 20 birds, often mixed with turnstones, but flocks in excess of 40 birds are sometimes reported.

Distribution: Outer coast, on Siuslaw jetties and rocky shorelines. Less ubiquitous than Black Turnstone, it can be absent in some areas, concentrating in a few flocks. It is also more restricted to the very outer coast and major rock formations, and does not usually come into estuaries as Black Turnstone sometimes does.

Sites: Siuslaw jetties, Heceta Head, Stonefield Beach, Bob Creek.

Red Knot *Calidris canutus*

Status: Uncommon to rare, rather irregular migrant. Numbers vary from a few very small flocks (fewer than 10 birds) to none from year to year. Most Red Knots stage out of Grays Harbor, Washington, and appear to leapfrog over Oregon to reach California estuaries. Found mainly on open mudflats, wet-sand beaches. Generally does not go far up estuaries. Southbound movements are weakly defined but include records from mid-July through

Surfbird, a regular winter denizen of the Siuslaw jetties. Photo by Noah K. Strycker.

early Oct. One winter record, Dec. 27, 1987 at Florence. Spring movements are equally thin and occur from early Apr. through early May.
Distribution: Mainly outer coast. Sometimes feeds on open beach with Sanderlings. Rare inland; one record on Oct. 14, 2003, at Fern Ridge Res.
Sites: Crab Dock Cove, Siltcoos mouth.

Sanderling *Calidris alba*
Status: Common to abundant migrant and winter resident. Almost all on flat sand beaches, going back and forth along the water's edge, with a few using mudflats. Sometimes roosts on rocks and mixes with flocks of turnstones. Winter numbers on outer beaches can run to hundreds per flock. Spring movements are almost purely coastal, masked by wintering populations, which begin to drop in late Apr. By late May all birds are gone.
Distribution: Almost all are on beaches of the outer coast, especially near creek outfalls. Rare but regular as a fall migrant at Fern Ridge Res. from early Aug. through mid-Oct. (one Nov. record), somewhat dependent on water levels. Strycker (2003) lists one Apr. and two May records at Fern Ridge Res. Older spring records there include birds on May 16, 1969, May 3, 1975, and May 5, 1975 (all *ENHS*).
Sites: Almost any beach away from dogs.

Semipalmated Sandpiper *Calidris pusilla*
Status: Rare but regular fall migrant, usually single birds embedded in flocks of Least or Western Sandpipers. Peak count is 5 (S. Heinl, p.c.). Records from early July through mid-Sep.; earliest was June 29, 1969 (*ENHS*). Seems to peak in Aug., but records are limited. No records later than mid-Sep. No spring records known from the county and few from Oregon.
Distribution: Mainly coastal, but reported annually from Fern Ridge Res. in recent years (Strycker 2003, D. Farrar, p.c.). There is also one record from Stewart Pond, Eugene, on Aug. 23, 1998 (D. Heyerly, p.c.).
Sites: Siuslaw mudflats, Fern Ridge Res., Siltcoos mouth.

Western Sandpiper *Calidris mauri*
Status: Common to locally abundant migrant; rare to uncommon in winter. Mudflats, wet sandy areas, occasionally in wet pastures. First southbound migrants (adults) typically appear in the last day or two of June; by the first week of July they are widespread in small numbers on tidal flats and locally inland where habitat is available (habitat is limited except in low-water years). Adults continue to move through in Aug., supplanted by immatures by late Aug. and Sep., when numbers are at their highest, sometimes flocks of hundreds or the low thousands are found in preferred locations. Numbers drop dramatically in the last half of Oct.

Very few birds winter in the county, with a couple sometimes present in flocks of Least Sandpipers and Dunlin on the coast, occasionally at Fern Ridge Res. Spring movements are highly compressed, beginning in early Apr. and mostly over by early May. A few sometimes straggle to early June, probably nonbreeders.

Distribution: Mainly mudflats on the outer coast, with small numbers higher up coastal estuaries and a few on beaches, sometimes mixed into flocks of Sanderlings (early in the season) or Dunlin (late fall).

Sites: Lower Siuslaw estuary, south jetty deflation plain, Siltcoos mouth.

*Red-necked Stint *Calidris ruficollis*

Asian vagrant. Two records, both at the mouth of the Siltcoos R.: 2 adults on Sep. 3, 2001 (J. and J. Carlson) and a juvenile on Sep. 19, 2004 (D. Farrar, A. Contreras; *Oregon Birds*, 31:24).

Least Sandpiper *Calidris minutilla*

Status: Common to locally abundant migrant, uncommon winter resident. Found mainly on mudflats, but also in wet short-grass fields, occasionally on wet beaches. First southbound migrants appear in early July, with a peak movement of immatures in late Aug. and Sep. Significant numbers are still passing through in Oct., and smaller numbers winter regularly. Numbers build in spring beginning with outriders in late Mar., with peak movement in the last week of Apr. and very early May. Unlike Western Sandpiper, rarely straggles past late May.

Distribution: The bulk of movement is coastal, with small flocks at Fern Ridge Res. and very small groups occasional at sewage ponds, farm ponds, flooded fields, and other limited or temporary sites. Sometimes seen in fall along margins of high-elevation lakes, where Western sometimes occurs but is less common.

Sites: Siuslaw estuary and deflation plain, Siltcoos mouth, Fern Ridge Res.

Baird's Sandpiper *Calidris bairdii*

Status: Uncommon to rare fall migrant countywide. Uses mud margins, open grassy areas (either wet or on sand flats) and the wet margins of alpine lakes and montane snow fields. In this latter high-elevation habitat it is the most likely fall migrant peep. Numbers vary from year to year, with peak years offering small flocks of 5-10 birds and off years providing hardly any birds at all.

Movement is usually from mid-July to mid-Sep. (earliest July 6, 2001), with a few to late Sep. Rare after early Oct. Unusually late records include Oct. 16, 2004 at the Siltcoos mouth and Nov. 20, 1995 at Fern Ridge Res. (Marshall et al. 2003). There are no valid winter records in Oregon. The only spring record from Lane Co. is of 7 seen May 2, 2004 at Fern Ridge

Res. (Bruce Newhouse and Peg Boulay). It is a very rare spring migrant elsewhere in Oregon.

Distribution: Countywide in very small numbers. One of few shorebirds that may be at least as common or more so at higher-elevation lakes and wet alpine meadows and gravel pans in the eastern part of the county than on the outer coast.

Pectoral Sandpiper *Calidris melanotos*

Status: Uncommon fall migrant, rare to absent spring migrant. Numbers vary considerably from year to year. Uses grassier areas than most shorebirds, though it will also feed on mudflats. Sometimes seen on open gravel or sandy areas, especially if any grass is present. Fall movement has timing unlike any other regular migrant, with a slow, thin movement beginning in July and running through mid-Sep., followed by a significant peak from mid-Sep. through mid- or sometimes late Oct., after which remaining birds depart *en masse* without any winter stragglers. Rare in early Nov.; latest Nov. 17, 2002 near Junction City.

Rare to absent in spring in western Oregon, with sparse records from mid-Apr. through mid-June in coastal Lane Co. Appears to be absent in some years, usually absent inland, few spring records at Fern Ridge Res.; small numbers in late Apr., 2002 and, very unusual, June 5, 2003. One was at Stewart Pond, Eugene, May 10, 2002.

Distribution: Mostly on the outer coast, but significant flocks sometimes appear at Fern Ridge Res. in fall. Because this species migrates late in fall, it can take advantage of the autumn drawdown of the reservoir that migrants moving mainly in Aug. and early Sep. cannot. There is little coverage of eastern Lane Co. lakes in fall, but this species probably occurs there in small numbers.

Sites: Dotterel Dike, Dog Pond, Siuslaw jetties and deflation plain, south and east sides of Fern Ridge Res.

Sharp-tailed Sandpiper *Calidris acuminata*

Status: Very rare but recently almost annual in late fall, usually embedded in flocks of Pectoral Sandpipers. Although the species is thought of as a late fall migrant, Lane Co. has multiple records in late Aug. as well.

Eleven records: Sep. 29-Oct. 1, 2004 (2 birds) at Fern Ridge Res.; Sep. 24, 2003 on South Jetty Rd. near Florence; Oct. 21-Nov. 19, 2003 at Fern Ridge Res.; Sep. 28-Oct 7, 2002 at Fern Ridge Res.; Sep. 4, 2001 at Fern Ridge Res.; Sep. 13, 1997 at the Siltcoos mouth; Sep. 14, 1991 at Dotterel Dike along the South Jetty Rd. near Florence; Aug. 28, 1987 at Fern Ridge Res. (Steve Heinl notes); 2 on Aug 22-23, 1973 at the Lane Community College sewage ponds (*NAB* 28:95, Contreras 1988). Note: *NAB* mentions 1 at LCC,

but 2 were present, as correctly reported in Roberson (1980). Additional records are one Oct. 26-29, 1969 near Perkins Peninsula Park (Eric Forsman, Al Larrabee, Gordon Murphy; *NAB* 24:85). See Supplemental Records.
Distribution: As many records inland as on the outer coast, possibly a result of coverage or better habitat in the new impoundments at Fern Ridge Res.
Sites: Fern Ridge Res. or Florence area.

Rock Sandpiper *Calidris ptilocnemis*
Status: Rare winter resident, present most years, but less regular in 2000s. One or two birds typically winter on the rocky parts of the outer coast. Arrives very late, usually not until early Oct., departs early Apr. Always with Surfbirds or Black Turnstones. An unusual report of a single bird June 27, 2000 (David Bailey, *NAB* 54:416) at the sandy mouth of the Siltcoos R. should be considered valid based on the experience of the observer, and may be the only midsummer record for Oregon.
Distribution: Siuslaw jetties, rocky outcrops on the north Lane Co. coast.
Sites: Siuslaw jetties, rocky points from Heceta Head northward.

Dunlin *Calidris alpina*
Status: Common to abundant migrant and winter resident. Mainly on mudflats, but often uses flooded grass-seed fields and other flooded short-grass pastures and fields in midwinter. Some use the outer beaches, often joining flocks of Sanderlings. Sometimes appears on rocks, log booms, or piers, especially during very high tides or adverse weather conditions. The timing of southbound migration is variable, with very small numbers of adults (often just single birds in flocks of Westerns) appearing in very late July and early Aug. The bulk of southbound and wintering birds arrive rather late, with no obvious movement until mid-Sep.; most birds arrive in early Oct. on the outer coast.

Hundreds and sometimes thousands of birds winter on the mudflats at Fern Ridge Res., with smaller flocks at other large lowland reservoirs with extensive mudflats. Numbers in the southern Willamette Valley typically peak in late winter, when birds tend to use flooded fields. These peaks can exceed 10,000 birds under good conditions. Studies in California have shown that such birds may be coming inland from the coast prior to their northward migration.
Distribution: Mainly on mudflats of the outer coast and in the vicinity of Fern Ridge Res., with late winter movement into wet agricultural lands of the valley floor. Radio tracking has shown that some birds roosting at Fern Ridge at night forage during the day as far away as the outer coast and the northern Willamette Valley (Daniel Farrar, p.c.).
Sites: Siuslaw estuary, Fern Ridge mudflats.

Curlew Sandpiper *Calidris ferruginea*

Vagrant from Asia. Two records. One was seen Sep. 17-18, 2000 at Florence (B. Stotz, Z. Stotz, R. Freeman). Another, seen briefly, was at the mouth of the Siltcoos R. on Sep. 29, 2001 (H. Herlyn, p.c.). This was probably the same bird seen the next day, and for several days thereafter, at the north spit of Coos Bay, as it was also accompanied by a small flock of Pectoral Sandpipers. It is accepted here as a Lane Co. record, although it was too brief a sighting to be submitted to the OBRC.

Stilt Sandpiper *Calidris himantopus*

Status: Rare irregular migrant in early fall. Found on mudflats and the edges of shallow ponds and backwaters. Seven records: Aug. 25, 2004 along Dotterel Dike in the deflation plain of the Siuslaw; Sep. 19, 1998 at Fern Ridge Res.; Sep. 13, 1997 at the Siltcoos mouth; Aug. 23, 1997 at the Siltcoos mouth; Aug. 23, 1994 at the Siltcoos mouth; Sep. 15, 1985 at the Siltcoos mouth and Sep. 1, 1977 (2 birds) at Fern Ridge Res.

Distribution: All records are coastal (Florence area and mouth of the Siltcoos) or at Fern Ridge Res.

Buff-breasted Sandpiper *Tryngites subruficollis*

Status: Rare irregular migrant in early fall. Generally found near the outer coast in drier semi-open grass or gravel flats or the drier, grassier parts of beaches, though there is one record of a bird on the mudflats upriver from Florence. All records are between Aug. 18 and Sep. 15; most are within a few days of Sep. 1 and the great majority are in the first 10 days of Sep. In peak years, small flocks are sometimes found. The high count is 14 birds in the Siuslaw deflation plain on Sep 11, 1985 (S. Heinl, p.c.). In some years none are found.

Stilt Sandpiper near Florence. Photo by Diane Pettey.

Distribution: Coastal, although it could occur at Fern Ridge Res.
Sites: Most records are from the Siuslaw deflation plain.

Ruff *Philomachus pugnax*

Status: Rare irregular fall migrant from Asia and Alaska. There is also one record involving 2 birds that wintered in 2002-03, last seen Mar. 19, 2003. Most records are from late Aug. to mid-Sep. The chart below omits the wintering record. Generally found in somewhat sheltered parts of mudflats or shallow ponds, often in or near grassy areas.
Distribution: Coastal and Fern Ridge Res. The 2 birds that remained during much of the winter 2002-03 appeared in various small wetlands in west Eugene and north to the Junction City area.
Sites: Irregular. Siuslaw deflation plain and nearby areas.

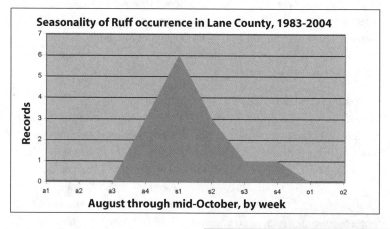

Ruff (female), near Florence. Photo by Diane Pettey.

Short-billed Dowitcher *Limnodromus griseus*

Status: Common fall and uncommon spring migrant. Mostly on mudflats and in shallow wetlands, sometimes in grass high enough to hide the birds. This species typically appears earlier in its southbound movement than does Long-billed, with the first adults around the first of July. Peak of passage is extended, from mid-July through mid-Sep., with juveniles dominating after late Aug. A significant drop occurs in late Sep.; rare after early Oct. No winter records for Lane Co., but there are a few reports of birds identified by call note in Coos Co.

Spring movements are much less apparent, beginning in early Apr., peaking in late Apr. and early May and concluding before the end of May.

Distribution: Largely coastal, with small numbers at shallow wetlands on the Willamette Valley floor.

Sites: Coastal mudflats are best.

Long-billed Dowitcher *Limnodromus scolopaceus*

Status: Common migrant in spring and fall, uncommon and numbers quite variable in winter. Uses mudflats and shallow wetlands, flooded pastures. First adults begin arriving in mid-July, with peak numbers of juveniles in Sep. and Oct. In some years, many winter in the Siuslaw Valley and nearby wet pasturelands; in other years hardly any can be found. A few can be found in most winters in wetlands and flooded pastures around Fern Ridge Res. and in west Eugene. Spring movements are mainly in late Apr. and early May, and are largely coastal. A few birds straggle into June, when it is hard to tell whether they are going north or south.

Distribution: Coastal mudflats, wetlands, occasionally wet pockets within outer beaches in migration. In winter, more common in wet pastures and fields on the valley floor than on the coast.

• Wilson's Snipe *Gallinago delicata*

Status: Irregular local breeder. Uncommon but widespread migrant in marshes, wetlands and pasture sumps countywide. Migratory patterns not well known, but migrants away from breeding areas are seen beginning in early Aug. Migratory movements are rather thin until late Sep. and Oct., after which lowland populations build considerably, with concentrations of dozens and (on rare occasions) over 100 birds forming in preferred habitat. These winter flocks are usually in extensive shallow wetlands or in wet, grassy sumps of pastures. Single birds can be found in almost any unfrozen marsh, grassy pond edge, or grassy ditch countywide in winter.

Spring movements are masked by the large wintering population, but it is likely that some local birds begin leaving in Mar.. By mid-Apr. lowland populations have dropped significantly.

Distribution: Highly local as a rare breeder, with confirmed breeding at Fern Ridge Res., Triangle Lake, and some marshes along the Cascade summit, including Gold Lake Bog. Countywide as a migrant, mainly in lowlands but also in wet montane meadows. Widespread below the regular freezing level in winter.

Subfamily Phalaropodinae

• **Wilson's Phalarope** *Phalaropus tricolor*
Status: Status has fluctuated over time. From 1947-49, this was a fairly regular spring migrant at Fern Ridge Res. (Gullion). It was much less regular in the 1960s-80s. Today it is rare but regular as a breeder at Fern Ridge Res. First proven to breed at Fern Ridge in 2002 (S. Maulding, p.c.), annual since then, probably owing to improved wetland habitat. Arrives on breeding territory late Apr. or early May, departs mid-Aug. Rare irregular migrant elsewhere in the county late Apr. through Sep. Three birds at Fern Ridge Res. on Oct. 19, 2000 were quite late, and they apparently were migrants from another location.
Distribution: Breeder in marshes at Fern Ridge Res. Migrant (rare but regular away from breeding area) mainly at marshes on the valley floor and on the outer coast.
Sites: Mainly marshes in southeast part of Fern Ridge complex.

Red-necked Phalarope *Phalaropus lobatus*
Status: Uncommon to common migrant, most common in spring. Often found in sewage ponds, calmer patches of nearshore ocean, sloughs and backwaters along the outer coast. Spring movements are mainly in late Apr. and early May, with stragglers as late as early June in some years. Numbers vary considerably from year to year. Fall movements are extended from July through Oct. but rarely involve very many birds. Small flocks of fewer than 20 are the norm. Variation in numbers from year to year is unpredictable and may relate to food supply or weather conditions.
Distribution: Mainly coastal, especially in spring. Some occur inland, especially after bad weather. Fall movements are more evenly divided, with some on shallow interior lakes and some on the outer coast and offshore.

Red Phalarope *Phalaropus fulicarius*
Status: Uncommon, sometimes abundant, offshore migrant. Most of this movement is invisible from shore, but during storms with high winds from the west, major coastal incursions sometimes occur, mainly in Nov. and early winter. During such events, they can be found almost anywhere, with most birds on coastal lakes and ponds, but also on wet roadways,

in parks, and even in forest clearings, e.g,. the Clay Creek recreation site in the middle of the Coast Range. Severe storms sometimes blow them far inland to the interior valleys. Mortality can be very high under severe weather conditions. They sometimes appear in odd situations, for example a breeding-plumage female at Eugene on Jan. 1, 1997 (*OB*), a breeding-plumage female with a flock of Red-necked Phalaropes on the Creswell sewage ponds on May 15, 1996, and at Fern Ridge Res. in May (Strycker 2003).
Distribution: Highly pelagic, sometimes onshore or inland at ponds and lakes after late fall storms.
Sites: Outer coast after high winds.

Family Laridae - Subfamily Stercorariinae

South Polar Skua *Stercorarius maccormicki*
Rare to uncommon offshore migrant, status poorly known owing to limited coverage offshore. Records known to be in Lane Co. waters are Oct. 6, 2002 (30 miles offshore), Oct. 6, 2001 (Heceta Bank), Apr. 8, 1992, and Sep. 9, 1989. One winter record, a live beached bird Dec. 23, 1988. (S. Heinl, Florence CBC).

Pomarine Jaeger *Stercorarius pomarinus*
Status: Common offshore migrant, rarely seen from shore, therefore few Lane Co. records. Spring migration is mainly from late Mar. through May; fall movements from July through Nov., with a peak in late Sep. and Oct. Recent records at Cape Arago under storm conditions suggest that this species is present offshore in small numbers through at least mid-Dec. One was seen on the Florence CBC in 1983. Sometimes seen from shore, and under extreme conditions can be blown inland, e.g., the 2 birds blown in to Fern Ridge Res. on Nov. 9-10, 1975. One additional inland record, Sep. 19, 1998 at Fern Ridge Res.
Distribution: Offshore. Very rare inland migrant.
Sites: Pelagic.

Parasitic Jaeger *Stercorarius parasiticus*
Status: Rare (coast and inland) to common (offshore) migrant, mostly in fall. Movements in fall are from mid-July to mid-Nov., peaking in Sep. Rare in winter, one was seen on the Florence CBC on Dec. 20, 2004 (Randy Moore, John Sullivan). Spring movements are thin from shore, from late Mar. through early June. Few records.
Distribution: Offshore. Rare inland migrant; records at Fern Ridge Res. Sep. 13-18, 2004, Sep. 11, 2000, Nov. 11, 1981, Oct. 25, 1979, and Aug. 29-Sep. 4, 1977 (2 birds, see *OB* 3(5): 41), Nov 10-14, 1975.
Sites: Best bet is the Siuslaw jetties.

Parasitic Jaeger, Sep. 17, 2004 at Fern Ridge dam. Photo by Sylvia Maulding.

Long-tailed Jaeger *Stercorarius longicaudus*

Status: Uncommon offshore migrant, mainly in fall. Very rare onshore and inland.

Distribution: Offshore, rarely seen from shore. The only recent records along the coast are Aug. 31, 1992 and Sep. 22, 1990, both at Florence.

Four records at Fern Ridge Res.: July 21, 1987; Aug. 30-Sep 1 (first bird) and Sep. 3 (second bird) 1977; the earlier bird lost its long central tail feathers while at Fern Ridge, one of which was recovered by observers, which allowed the second bird, found Sep. 3 with its tail feathers intact, to be distinguished from the first (Egger, 1977); and Sep. 20-25, 1973. The timing of these records suggests that overland movements in this species may be earlier in the season than for the other jaegers.

Sites: Pelagic.

Subfamily Larinae

* [Laughing Gull *Larus atricilla*]

Vagrant. One record, not reviewed by the OBRC, of a bird seen offshore over Heceta Bank by Richard Rowlett on Sep. 17, 1996 (*NAB*).

Franklin's Gull *Larus pipixcan*

Status: Rare but regular in migration, nearly annual, with records of single birds from early May through early Nov.; latest record Nov. 22, 1970 (*ENHS*). Most records are in July and early Nov., with relatively few in between, suggesting two distinct patterns of postbreeding movement, perhaps of adults and immatures, though most reports seem to be of adults. On rare occasions, small groups are found, e.g, 3 at Fern Ridge Res. on Nov. 1, 1969 (*ENHS*) and four on Sep. 6, 1971 (*ENHS*). Typically found in flocks of other small gulls.

Distribution: Records are largely from the outer coast and Fern Ridge Res., with one record from the Junction City area.

[* Little Gull *Larus minimus*]

Has not yet been reported in Lane Co., but has occurred in adjacent counties and can be expected in Lane Co.

Bonaparte's Gull *Larus philadelphia*

Status: Common, sometimes abundant, migrant, with a few birds present in midwinter and occasionally midsummer. The bulk of movement in spring is in late Apr. and early May, with hundreds of birds sometimes seen passing coastal headlands. A few nonbreeders, often in a rather ragged state of molt, sometimes summer on the coast. Fall movements begin in July, but few birds are found until Aug., and the bulk of movement is in Oct. and Nov.

Distribution: Most movement is coastal, but small numbers migrate inland regularly, and large flocks sometimes occur inland, especially under storm conditions. About 1000 were at Fern Ridge dam after the extraordinary overnight windstorm on Nov. 9-10, 1975, though a few dozen is more normal in migration, and in some years very few appear.

Sites: Siuslaw jetties at any season, Fern Ridge spillway in Nov. and early Dec.

Heermann's Gull *Larus heermanni*

Status: Uncommon to common postbreeding visitant, moving north in early summer and south in late autumn, roughly paralleling the movement of Brown Pelicans. Small numbers begin appearing as early as mid-Apr., but significant movements are unusual before mid-June. This pattern has changed in recent years, with more birds moving early, as is also true of pelicans.

Southbound movements are long and slow, peaking in Sep. and Oct. and trailing off through Nov. Very rare in winter: one on Jan. 2, 1998 at Florence is the only known record.

Distribution: Near-shore coastal, with most birds using beaches and the lower Siuslaw estuary, rarely coming upriver past Florence. Very rare inland: Nov. 19, 1994; Oct. 31, 1985; Nov 10, 1975; and Nov 9, 1974, and Nov. 9, 1973—all at Fern Ridge Res. (latter *ENHS*); Nov. 15, 1981 on the Willamette R. rocks in Glenwood.

Sites: Siuslaw jetties, Stonefield Beach, Bob Creek.

Mew Gull *Larus canus*

Status: Common to abundant migrant and winter resident. Uses a variety of coastal habitats including open water, wet beaches, creek mouths, and mudflats. Prefers wet areas. Also found inland at larger lakes, mainly at low elevations, and in flooded grass-seed fields, pastures and other open short-grass settings. Fall movements are fairly late, with very small numbers trickling in from late July or early Aug. to early Sep., a slight increase in late Sep. and a major influx in late Oct. Sometimes numbers do not reach full winter levels until early to mid-Nov.

Abundant all winter on the coast, but leaves fairly early, usually during late Mar. and early Apr., at which time large numbers often appear inland in flooded fields for a couple of weeks. Nonbreeding stragglers sometimes remain into early summer.

Distribution: Mostly coastal in fall and winter, moving onto the valley floor in early spring. Some winter at Fern Ridge Res., where numbers vary from year to year, often feeding nearby in wet fields.

Ring-billed Gull *Larus delawarensis*

Status: Common to abundant migrant and winter resident. Somewhat local, showing a strong preference for freshwater locations, wet pastures and open urban spaces such as playing fields and even parking lots, where they eagerly accept handouts. Rare but regular on the outer coastal beaches and lower estuaries, typically one or two birds in late fall mixed in with other more common coastal gulls. Most birds arrive by Nov., remaining through Apr., with a few nonbreeders, sometimes in a state of suspended or partial molt, occasionally remaining in the summer.

Distribution: More common inland than on the coast; the most common small gull in the Willamette Valley most of the winter, except when large flocks of Mew Gulls stage in early spring. Some winter in the Siuslaw Valley, mainly at upriver wet pasture sites such as Waite pastures, Canary Rd., and the lower North Fork of the Siuslaw, depending on local conditions. Also sometimes found in numbers on mudflats at the confluence of the North Fork and main stem of the Siuslaw.

California Gull *Larus californicus*

Status: Common to locally abundant migrant, uncommon and local winter resident. Postbreeding movements are extended and complex. The earliest movement is westbound over the Cascade ridgeline and down the Columbia, with large numbers moving as soon as early July and sizable movements throughout July and into Aug.

This movement results in flocks of hundreds roosting on beaches and mudflats on the Lane Co. coast during late summer. By late Sep. these groups begin to thin out and a massive southbound migration occurs during Oct., with the bulk of movement quite visible above the surf line. By Nov., numbers have dropped significantly, with small packets of migrants still found roosting and moving south. By early Dec. only a small number of wintering birds are left. This species can be local and hard to find in some winters, with more birds at Fern Ridge Res. than on the outer coast.

By late Mar., a northward and eastward movement has begun, and birds become hard to find in Lane Co. by May. A few nonbreeding stragglers can be found in June in some years.

Distribution: Countywide in fall migration, with a general downslope movement. Abundant on beaches and the lower Siuslaw estuary in late summer and early fall. Mainly on the valley floor in winter, with small numbers on the outer coast.

Sites: Widespread in fall migration.

Herring Gull *Larus argentatus*

Status: Uncommon migrant and winter resident, occasionally abundant for brief periods in fall and winter, probably owing to weather and sea conditions. Most birds in Oregon are adults. A few can be found on coastal beaches from early Aug. (rarely July) through early fall, with numbers building in Oct. and Nov., during which time flocks of a few dozen are sometimes encountered for brief periods. Peak movement is in late Nov. After late fall and winter storms, flocks of 40 or 50 are occasionally seen. The flock of over 800 found in the flooded deflation plain of the Siuslaw on Nov. 26, 2004 is by far the largest group recorded in the county, although similar numbers sometimes occur in Siletz Bay, Lincoln Co. Spring movements are mainly offshore and along the outer beaches from late Mar. through early May. This species is rarely found as a nonbreeder in summer, e.g,. the one at Florence on the unlikely date of June 16, 2002.

Distribution: Most birds are coastal, but small numbers can be found wherever gulls gather on the valley floor, including flocks within the Eugene-Springfield urban area.

Sites: Siuslaw jetties and adjacent roost sites, Stonefield, and Bob Creek.

Thayer's Gull *Larus thayeri*

Status: Uncommon to rare migrant and winter resident. Found on beaches, lakes, mudflats. The proportion of first-year birds to adults wintering in Lane Co. is significantly higher for Thayer's Gull than for Herring Gull; in large flocks there are sometimes more first-year than adult birds, especially inland. Peak counts can be very low, a few birds within even large gull flocks. The largest number reported is 300 sheltering from bad weather in the Crab Dock Cove, lower Siuslaw R. on Dec. 4, 2004 (W. Hoffman, p.c.), but normal peak counts are less than 20 birds. Movements are generally similar to those of Herring Gull, but typically arrives later in fall. First reports are usually in Oct., last reports in spring typically in late Mar. and Apr., though movements are poorly known.

Distribution: Essentially the same as for Herring Gull, except that numbers in the Willamette Valley are more variable from year to year.

Western Gull. Sometimes mistakenly called a Herring Gull, the northern (occidentalis) subspecies of Western Gull has much blacker wingtips than mantle. Photo by Noah K. Strycker.

Sites: Siuslaw jetties and Siltcoos mouth. Also often easy to find in winter at Stonefield Beach and Bob Creek, where they can be compared to Herring Gulls at bathing sites.

** Lesser Black-backed Gull *Larus fuscus*

Vagrant to Oregon from Europe or northeastern North America. One Oregon record, possibly the same bird seen twice, an adult at Fern Ridge Res. Mar. 17-21, 2001 (OBRC 050-01-02) and Nov. 17-23, 2001. There is one earlier report from Oct. 23, 1982 (B. Bellin).

• Western Gull *Larus occidentalis*

Status: Common to abundant resident. Found on coastal beaches, headlands, mudflats, and in open parts of urbanized areas. This is the principal large, dark-backed gull of the Lane Co. coast, and the largest gull present from May through Sep. Breeds locally on steep headlands such as Parrot Rock at Heceta Head, cliffs near Sea Lion Caves and perhaps elsewhere. Numbers increase in winter.

Note: Hybridizes with Glaucous-winged Gull in northwestern Oregon, Washington, and British Columbia; the hybrids are common in winter on the northern Oregon coast, where they can have a variety of colors and patterns. Some second-generation hybrids may breed occasionally in the county.

Distribution: Mainly coastal, including upper estuaries. Prefers beaches, mudflats, and open saltwater settings; does not use flooded pastures much on the coast. Rare but regular in the Willamette Valley in winter (usually late Nov.-Feb.); half a dozen birds are typically scattered in gull flocks at Fern Ridge Res., flooded fields, and in urban Eugene-Springfield.

Glaucous Gull, North Jetty tidal flat of Siuslaw R., Feb. 23, 2003. Photo by Noah K. Strycker.

• Glaucous-winged Gull *Larus glaucescens*

Status: Has bred at Heceta Head (1975, in Marshall et al. 2003) but is not known to breed in the county today. Common winter resident. It has apparently increased inland since the 1950s, when it was considered a straggler around Eugene (Gullion). Uses open beaches, mudflats, estuaries, wet pastures, parking lots. Arrives late, with most movement not until mid-Nov. By early Dec., common along the outer coast and uncommon to common in the Fern Ridge-Eugene area, where its large size and pale coloration help it stand out from the smaller Ring-billed, California, and Mew Gulls. Nonbreeders occasionally summer on the coast.

Distribution: Coastal, using a wide variety of habitats. Also on the valley floor, mainly at low elevations near water.

Glaucous Gull *Larus hyperboreus*

Status: Rare but regular winter visitor. First known record for Lane Co. was Oct. 25, 1958 at Florence (Leroy Fish, p.c.). Habitat use is varied, similar to that of Glaucous-winged Gull. One or two, almost all first-winter birds, reach Lane County in most winters, arriving fairly late (mid-Nov. to early Dec.) and remaining until late Mar. or early Apr. (little data available). Mainly coastal, but occasionally found along the Willamette R. in Eugene. The earliest fall record in recent years is Oct. 13, 2003 at Heceta Head; the latest recent spring record was Apr. 23, 2005.

Distribution: Most records are from the outer coast, but there are a number of records for the valley floor, where it is not annual.

Sites: Most regular at Siuslaw jetties.

Sabine's Gull *Xema sabini*

Status: Rare migrant. Mainly pelagic, rare at interior lakes. Reported from late Mar. through late Nov., mainly in Apr.-May (coastal) and from Aug. through Oct.

Distribution: Mostly offshore, rare but regular from shore, rare inside the lower Siuslaw estuary. Rare but somewhat regular inland, mainly in fall. At least 9 records for Fern Ridge Res.: May 6, 2005; Sep. 19, 2001; 3 on Sep. 8, 2001; May 19-22, 1996; Oct. 21, 1981; Nov. 10, 1977; Nov. 11, 1975; Sep. 18. 1973; 1 each on Oct. 6 and 7, 1969 (*ENHS*).

Singles were at Dexter Lake Sep. 8-12, 2004 and Sep. 9, 1998.

Sites: Mainly pelagic.

Black-legged Kittiwake *Rissa tridactyla*

Status: Uncommon but sometimes quite visible migrant and winter resident. Highly pelagic, but reported fairly often foraging in lower estuaries or roosting on beaches, typically single birds. Usually quite approachable when resting. Present offshore from Aug. through May, sometimes early June, but most Lane Co. reports are from Sep. through mid-winter.

Distribution: Mostly coastal. Rare in the interior, almost always after major storms, with most records at Fern Ridge Res., usually the dam area. Sometimes appears inland at unexpected times of year, e.g,. at Fern Ridge on Mar. 4, 1998 and Jan. 20, 1996.

Sites: Outer coast at jetties and gull roosts.

Subfamily Sterninae

Caspian Tern *Sterna caspia*

Status: Uncommon to common migrant and nonbreeding summer visitor. Highly visible in late summer, as family groups from breeding colonies elsewhere linger around estuaries, young squealing for food. Northbound migrants are sometimes reported in early Mar. (earliest was Mar. 3, 2004); by the last week of Mar. they are regular. Few are present in early summer, but as young leave the breeding grounds, numbers increase noticeably by early July and they remain fairly common through mid-Sep., after which migrants leave the northwest. Rarely reported after mid-Oct.

Distribution: The largest numbers are on the outer coast and in lower estuaries, but there is also a steady movement through Fern Ridge Res. from midsummer through mid-Sep.

Sites: Siuslaw jetties in late summer, Siltcoos mouth.

Elegant Tern *Sterna elegans*

Status: Rare irregular postbreeding visitor in warm-water "El Niño" years; sometimes arrives in small flocks, but absent in most years. About a dozen occurrences, all in the past 20 years on the outer coastal beaches and the lower Siuslaw estuary, from late June (exceptional) through Sep., with most records in Aug. and early Sep.

The birds found June 22, 1998 at the mouth of the Siuslaw may be the earliest in the season found in Oregon. The latest for Lane Co. are Sep. 20, 1987 and Sep 19, 2000. Peak count is 70, July 18, 1996 at the Siuslaw jetties (Tom Mickel, p.c.).

Distribution: Coastal beaches and lower estuaries.

Sites: Siuslaw mouth.

Common Tern *Sterna hirundo*

Status: Uncommon irregular migrant, mainly in fall. Most often reported from late Aug. through Sep., typically in small flocks of fewer than 20 birds; rare to Oct. (Oct. 9, 1985; S. Heinl, p.c.). Latest records are Nov. 5, 1985 from the north jetty of the Siuslaw (S. Heinl, D. Fix) and Nov. 11, 1975 at Fern Ridge Res., the day after a severe windstorm from the coast. Spring status poorly known; this species is considered a fairly common coastal migrant in northwestern Oregon, but is not often reported in coastal Lane Co. However, large flocks sometimes appear, e.g., 120 on May 11, 2002 at Florence. One found at Florence on July 19, 1994 was unusual (Marshall et al. 2003).

Distribution: Mostly on the outer coast and the lower mile of the Siuslaw estuary; somewhat regular in fall at Fern Ridge Res.

Sites: Siuslaw estuary.

Arctic Tern *Sterna paradisaea*

Status: Rare to uncommon migrant offshore, true status not well known owing to limited offshore observation. Most often reported from late Aug. through early Oct., but in some years there are no reports, probably owing to a combination of observer absence, weather and sea conditions, and the general pelagic nature of the species in migration. Latest record is Nov. 5, 1985 from the north jetty of the Siuslaw (S. Heinl, D. Fix). Spring movements are thought to be from late Mar. through early May, but there are few Lane Co. records. No confirmed inland records.

Recent reports include Sep. 21 and 22, 2000 at the Siuslaw jetties and 7 on Aug. 20, 1997 at the Siltcoos mouth.

Distribution: Outer coast and offshore.

Forster's Tern *Sterna forsteri*

Status: Uncommon to rare migrant and nonbreeding summer visitor. Open water and mudflats. Found from late Apr. through early Oct., most birds in fall, numbers vary from year to year.

Distribution: Fairly regular in late spring at Fern Ridge Res.; also sometimes seen at east end of Dorena Lake in May (e.g., 11 there on May 13, 1972); could occur as a migrant at any inland lake in the county. Sometimes reported at

lakes in the high Cascades in summer, perhaps owing to nearby breeding in Klamath and Lake Cos. Rare but regular as a fall migrant at Fern Ridge Res.; rare fall migrant on the outer coast.
Sites: Fern Ridge Res.

* **Least Tern** *Sterna antillarum*
Vagrant. Two Lane County records: June 8, 1997 (OBRC 074-97-05) and Aug. 19, 1973 (4 birds, OBRC 074-73-01), both at Florence. Fewer than 10 Oregon records.

• **Black Tern** *Chlidonias niger*
Status: Common local breeder, rare migrant. Arrives very early May (most birds in mid-May), departs in last half of Aug. Earliest recent report was Apr. 13, 2003, quite early, the latest is Sep. 3, 2003 (3 juveniles). Primarily found over marshes and adjacent open water, usually not a "deep-water" tern. Has probably bred at Fern Ridge occasionally in the past; Ben Pruitt was dived on by adults in the marshes in 1948 (Gullion) and a few were present on May 23, 1972 (*ENHS*).
Distribution: Breeding colony is at the southeast corner of Fern Ridge Res., mainly around the mouth of Coyote Cr. and in adjacent impoundments. Probably breeds in Long Tom marshes in the southwest corner of the reservoir. Has bred at Fern Ridge since 1992, when 12 nests were found (Papish 1992). In 2004 about 50 pairs were present. When lake levels were low in 2005, bred in impoundments in Fisher and Coyote Units. Has also been seen in May at the east end of Dorena Lake, rarely elsewhere over marshy areas. Not reported from the coast.
Sites: Southeast part of Fern Ridge Res.

Black Tern.
Illustration
by Barbara
Gleason.

Family Alcidae

• **Common Murre** *Uria aalge*

Status: Uncommon to abundant local breeder, migrant, and winter resident. Breeds at Heceta Head. Most Oregon birds breed on the northern and southern coast. Common during postbreeding period and migration close to shore. Winter numbers vary considerably, but small flocks are often visible from shore.

Distribution: Strictly coastal, mainly on the ocean, with small numbers regular in Aug. and Sep. inside the lower Siuslaw estuary.

Sites: Easiest to view between the Siuslaw jetties in late summer.

*****Thick-billed Murre** *Uria lomvia*

Vagrant. One record, a specimen found beached Jan. 30, 1933 near Florence (OSU #10,483).

• **Pigeon Guillemot** *Cepphus columba*

Status: Uncommon to locally common breeder, uncommon migrant, and rare but regular winter resident. Breeds on cliffs and occasionally on pilings and other human structures. Most common from Mar. through Aug. at or near breeding sites. Numbers drop in Sep. and only solitary stragglers are present after early Oct. In some years, a few of these winter.

Distribution: Exclusively coastal, using only the ocean and the lower Siuslaw estuary.

Sites: Easy to observe on cliffs north of Sea Lion Caves Apr.-Aug.

*****Long-billed Murrelet** *Brachyramphus perdix*

Vagrant or rare visitor from northeast Asia, status poorly known. One record, July 30, 1998 north of Heceta Beach. A murrelet seen in Aug. 1997 at Leaburg Res. may have been this species. See Marshall et al. (2003) for more information about the status of this poorly known species.

• **Marbled Murrelet** *Brachyramphus marmoratus*

Status: Uncommon breeder, migrant, and winter resident. Breeds in old-growth forests within 30 miles of the ocean, usually much closer. Thereafter, found in family groups or small clusters on the ocean, typically close to shore just beyond the surf line. Occasionally enters the lower Siuslaw estuary.

Distribution: Coastal, usually close to shore. Much easier to find from Sea Lion Caves northward than off the sandy beaches of south Lane Co. Breeders difficult to find in forested habitat.

Sites: Waters adjacent to Klootchman, Stonefield, Brays Point, and Bob Creek in mid- to late summer.

* Xantus's Murrelet *Synthliboramphus hypoleucus*
Vagrant from the south. Two records: July 23, 1991 off Brays Point (OBRC
025/026-91-01, treated as Xantus's or Craveri's) and Aug. 31, 1985, 12 miles
offshore (OBRC 025-85-03). Has occurred in coastal Oregon a number of
times (small flocks have been seen offshore on rare occasions) and is likely
to occur again, probably in late summer.

Ancient Murrelet *Synthliboramphus antiquus*
Status: Uncommon to rare migrant and winter resident. Numbers vary
widely from year to year. In peak years, small flocks of 5 to 15 birds can
be found at multiple locations offshore, often visible from shore. In most
years only a few pairs or singles are found, and in some years there seem
to be none using Lane Co. waters.
    Movements are fairly late in fall, with peak of passage generally in Oct.
to early Nov. and peak numbers sometimes not apparent until Dec. Spring
movements are essentially invisible, perhaps farther offshore, but seem to
be in Mar. or Apr.; after mid-Apr. there are few reports. Very rare in summer;
3 breeding-season reports in Lane Co.: May 22, 2001 near Florence, and
July 1997 and June 22, 1998, both at Heceta Head.
Distribution: Exclusively coastal, mainly offshore, and nearshore beyond
the surf line, occasionally inside the Siuslaw jetties but rarely into estuarine
waters. This species occasionally wanders in fall and ends up on inland
lakes and reservoirs. To date, this has not been reported in Lane Co., but it
could occur in the future.

° Cassin's Auklet *Ptychoramphus aleuticus*
Status: Common offshore migrant and winter resident, occasionally
visible from land. Has bred at Conical Rock at Heceta Head and possibly on
Parrot Rock there as well (1967, see Marshall et al. 2003). Has been seen in
the Heceta Head area in the summers of 1998, 1999, and 2000, suggesting
that the site may still be in use. No recent breeding records, but habitat is
difficult to check. Suitable habitat on the rocks at Heceta Head has largely
weathered away in the past 20 years.
Distribution: Largely pelagic, difficult to see from land and infrequently
reported.
Sites: Mainly pelagic.

[* Parakeet Auklet *Aethia psittacula*]
Multiple reports and washups from the northern and southern Oregon
coast, likely to be reported eventually in Lane Co.

• **Rhinoceros Auklet** *Cerorhinca monocerata*

Status: Uncommon very local breeder (inside Sea Lion Caves), uncommon migrant and postbreeding visitor, uncommon to rare and irregular in midwinter.

Distribution: Coastal, using the nearshore ocean and occasionally the lower Siuslaw estuary, mainly in late summer and early Sep. More common from Florence northward than off the dune beaches.

Sites: Easy to observe on the water off Sea Lion Caves Apr.-July; also fairly regular between Siuslaw jetties in late summer.

Horned Puffin *Fratercula corniculata*

Status: Casual visitor from northern waters; has occurred at all times of year. Specimen records include 2 washups Mar. 15, 1919 (Gabrielson and Jewett 1940), 4 washups Feb. 21, 1959 (Leroy Fish, p.c.), live birds seen from shore on Jan. 25-26, 2005 between the Siuslaw jetties (photo by D. Pettey), June 5, 2003, Aug. 9, 1991, Aug. 5, 1969, and Jan. 8, 1933.

Distribution: Coastal, outer beaches, and oceanic.

• **Tufted Puffin** *Fratercula cirrhata*

Status: Rare irregular breeder at rocks off Heceta Head, has decreased steadily in past 30 years and may not breed there every year now owing to erosion of soil necessary for burrows. Mainly from Florence jetties northward, rarely seen elsewhere along the Lane Co. coast

Distribution: Exclusively oceanic. Parrot Rock at Heceta Head in summer.

Sites: Heceta Head (irregular).

Order COLUMBIFORMES

Family Columbidae

• (I) Rock Pigeon *Columba livia*

Status: Common resident breeder in urban areas, under major bridges and perhaps locally on cliffs. Sometimes found at rural barns. Formerly known as Rock Dove and, in its captive state, as domestic or racing pigeon.

Distribution: Mainly urban except where kept locally.

• Band-tailed Pigeon *Patagioenas fasciata*

Status: Uncommon to locally common (in fall concentrations), widespread in woodlands, especially those containing a mix of Douglas-fir and oaks. Sometimes seen on coastal mudflats near forest edges in late summer and fall—the species often comes to salt licks and other sources of salt. Most leave in winter, returning in mid-Mar. (late Feb. some years). Remains fairly late in fall, with reports into mid-Nov. Small numbers winter in Portland and the interior Rogue Valley, but usually not in Lane Co.

Distribution: From sea level to the mid-level Cascades (essentially within the range of Douglas-fir), rare in pine- and true fir-dominated forests of the Cascade summit ridges. Most common in Coast Range.

Sites: Lower Siltcoos R.

* Eurasian Collared-Dove *Streptopelia decaocto*

Vagrant that has invaded much of the U.S. and has recently reached Oregon. One sight record in Lane Co., probably in 2001 (B. Combs, p.c.). More records are expected.

* White-winged Dove *Zenaida asiatica*

Vagrant from the southwest. One record, Oct. 24, 1998, observed from Autzen Stadium, Eugene.

• Mourning Dove *Zenaida macroura*

Status: Common resident breeder. Most common in open deciduous woodlands, farmland, shrubby areas. Concentrates in flocks in winter.

Distribution: Most are on the valley floor and in foothill areas. Absent in breeding season from the high Cascades and the Coast Range, except in openings with adequate cover and food supply. Rare and local on the coastal slope and outer coast, except for small numbers that winter mainly within Florence, apparently eating at bird feeders.

Order CUCULIFORMES

Family Cuculidae - Subfamily Coccyzinae

Yellow-billed Cuckoo Coccyzus americanus

Vagrant. One record, collected June 30, 1915 near Florence (Gullion). The specimen may have been lost.

Order STRIGIFORMES

Family Tytonidae

• Barn Owl *Tyto alba*

Status: Uncommon local resident breeder. An owl of open country, usually found in large open pasturelands and fields with few trees or structures. Often located at night by its loud hissing screech emitted in flight. During the day, it can sometimes be found by checking in old barns, silos, and the like.

Distribution: Willamette Valley floor and locally in adjacent foothills where open agricultural land is available for foraging. May occur locally in larger agricultural openings in the eastern part of the Coast Range. Rare on the outer coast; does not seem to use the Siuslaw valleys on a regular basis, although most available habitat is inaccessible owing to its physical location or ownership. Has been seen around the Davidson mill at Mapleton. Occasionally found in winter roosting in dense cover along South Jetty Rd. and in overgrown Christmas tree plantations on the valley floor. Occasional in cities and towns.

Family Strigidae

° Flammulated Owl *Otus flammeolus*

Status: Possible rare local breeder in pines along the Cascade summit. One record to date, found on the Oregon Breeding Bird Atlas project in the vicinity of Horsepasture Mtn. near the Three Sisters.

Distribution: Pine forests east of the Cascade summit. Lane Co. is barely touched by its range. However, it occurs in small numbers west of the Cascade summit in Douglas Co.

• Western Screech-Owl *Megascops kennicottii*

Status: Uncommon but widespread resident; actual numbers probably much higher than usually thought owing to nocturnal habits and few observers seeking them. When a concerted effort was made on the Florence CBC in 1988 (Fix 1988), 48 were found, mostly in one evening

*Western Screech-owl. Illustration by
Barbara Gleason.*

along the North Fork of the Siuslaw, showing how common they can be in preferred habitat. Most common in open woodlands with some deciduous component and adjacent openings for hunting. Prefers areas with adjacent agricultural land, probably owing to the abundance of rodent prey.

Distribution: Mostly on the valley floor and in the Coast Range, with some present in river valleys extending into the Cascades, but generally not in dense evergreen forests. Also present in coastal valleys, though often absent on the immediate outer coast.

Sites: Widespread. A couple of pairs can usually be found on the University of Oregon campus in Eugene.

• **Great Horned Owl** *Bubo virginianus*
Status: Uncommon, widespread, highly visible resident, found in a wide variety of habitats from dense forests to open country with scattered trees. Breeds early, with birds on nests by Feb. No significant seasonal movements.
Distribution: Countywide, no concentrations.

Snowy Owl *Bubo scandiaca*
Status: Rare irregular winter visitor, absent most years. First record appears to be Nov. 9, 1946 at Fern Ridge dam (Gullion). In years when these huge northern owls reach Oregon, birds are sometimes found on the Willamette Valley floor (in open country and sometimes around farm buildings) or in

dunes of the outer coast. In peak years, birds arrive in late Nov. or Dec. and remain through early spring. Occurs every 3 to 5 years, usually one or two birds in such years. The most recent years in which birds reached Lane Co. are 1996, 1997, 2000, and 2001. Latest spring record is Apr. 3, 1974 near the Eugene airport (*ENHS*).
Distribution: Valley lowlands and the outer coast.

• Northern Pygmy-Owl *Glaucidium gnoma*
Status: Uncommon but visible resident, some seasonal movement. Prefers dense evergreen forests with small openings, wooded canyons. Anecdotal data suggest that there is some downslope movement in winter, although the actual origin of lowland birds in winter is not known. Absent from open areas of the valley floor. Relatively easy to call out in daytime. Quite easy to find in the Coast Range in winter; Alma CBC found 10 birds twice.
Distribution: Countywide except the open Willamette Valley floor.

Burrowing Owl *Athene cunicularia*
Status: Rare irregular migrant and winter visitor since at least the mid-1940s. Absent many years. Found in open country, usually around some kind of shelter such as a culvert, driftwood, or even a small tree suitable for roosting. Records from Sep. through Mar., but most reports after mid-Oct. Latest spring record is Mar. 31, 1987.
Distribution: Willamette Valley floor and coastal dunes. Has been found near Creswell (Oct. 30, 1949, Gullion) but is more often found in open areas of the valley floor. More rare on the coast.

Burrowing Owl: Near Junction City, Jan. 3, 2004. Photo by Noah K. Strycker.

• **Spotted Owl** *Strix occidentalis*

Status: Uncommon to rare local breeder countywide. Highly associated with old-growth evergreen forests, especially for breeding and roosting. Mainly away from the edges of the valley floor. Difficult to locate owing to habitat preferences, but often approachable when found. No noticeable seasonal movements.

Distribution: Countywide in older evergreen forests.

• **Barred Owl** *Strix varia*

Status: Uncommon recent resident. First record was in July 1981 in the Cottage Grove Ranger District, Willamette National Forest. Found in a variety of forest types, usually with a significant component of conifers. Has occurred in wooded areas of the south hills of Eugene. No significant seasonal movements.

Distribution: Countywide. Least regular in the high Cascades, the valley floor, and on the outer coast, but recently regular at Cape Mtn. north of Florence. Increasing and spreading into most wooded habitats.

• **Great Gray Owl** *Strix nebulosa*

Status: Uncommon to rare resident of high-elevation meadows and occasionally clear-cuts within evergreen forests.

Distribution: Higher Cascades, mainly above 3000 feet. Most reports are from the upper Aufderheide Dr. and in the southeast part of the county; see Goggans and Platt (1992). Rarely reported at lower elevations, but has reached eastern Springfield, Mt. Pisgah, Jasper area, and south Eugene. A report from the Coast Range near Triangle Lake in Mar. and May, 1998 could not be confirmed.

• **Long-eared Owl** *Asio otus*

Status: Rare, poorly known breeder in Lane Co. There are about 20 records for the county, a significant portion of which are of specimens or birds found injured. True status of this species is very hard to determine, but most records come from the McKenzie Valley and nearby lowlands of the upper Willamette Valley. Winter records in the Willamette Valley are mainly in lowland thickets, e.g., dense stands of ash or young evergreens.

Distribution: Two calling birds in mid-Apr. 1989 suggest breeding in east Lane Co. (Marshall et al. 2003). An immature bird near McKenzie Bridge on Oct. 1, 1994 had left the nest but was not capable of sustained flight. One was collected near McKenzie Bridge on July 8, 1914 (USMNH 259689), and one was heard near there on May 14, 2003. An adult female was found near Jasper on Apr. 4, 1999. A still-downy juvenile found near Creswell (Barbara Mooney) was delivered to the Cascades Raptor Center on May 19, 1994. Another was brought to the Cascades Raptor Center from an unknown location June 30, 2000. One was found Jan. 12, 2004 in the Willow Creek area of west Eugene. Although they are not usually found in urban areas, one was brought to the Cascades Raptor Center from Hendricks Park in Eugene on Oct. 24, 1990.

Not reported west of the Fern Ridge Res. area except for one collected near Mercer Lake north of Florence in Dec. 1917 (OSU 6788).

° **Short-eared Owl** *Asio flammeus*

Status: Bred in small numbers at Fern Ridge Res. as recently as the late 1970s; not known lately but found in summer some years and might breed. Found in marshes, overgrown fields and pastures, dense dune grass. Rare migrant in open country, uncommon to rare in winter. Usually found from Oct. through Apr.

Distribution: Most regular at east side of Fern Ridge Res. Also reported elsewhere on the valley floor and on the outer coast.

Sites: End of Royal Ave. at dusk in winter.

° **Boreal Owl** *Aegolius funereus*

Rare local resident and probable breeder above 5000 feet in the vicinity of Waldo Lake. First reported there Oct. 25, 1989, found occasionally since. Part of this area is within the North Waldo Burn (Taylor Burn); the impact of that burn on the species is unknown. Also reported on the Deschutes Co. side of South Sister. Uses montane meadows and rocky forest openings, generally within open forest of spruce and fir. True status poorly known, but probably resident in very small numbers along the Cascade summit ridgeline, which apparently constitutes the very southwestern edge of the species' range.

• **Northern Saw-whet Owl** *Aegolius acadicus*

Status: Uncommon (perhaps more accurately, not often reported) but widespread breeder, winter resident, and probably migrant. Uses a variety of forest types containing a significant evergreen component. In winter, often found in dense stands of 20-40-year-old evergreens.

Banding reports and occasional field observations suggest that some seasonal migration occurs, but it is not clear which populations are involved or how far they go. Principal fall movement is in Oct.

Distribution: Countywide except on the open valley floor; least common along the Cascade summit in broken lodgepole pine forests.

Order CAPRIMULGIFORMES

Family Caprimulgidae - Subfamily Chordeilinae

• **Common Nighthawk** *Chordeiles minor*

Status: Uncommon to rare but widespread breeder and migrant. Found flying over a wide variety of habitats, but often concentrates around shallow or slow-moving water where insect prey is most dense. Breeds on the ground in open areas (e.g., gravel bars, abandoned logging landings). One of the latest spring arrivals, it is not usually seen until mid-May, with most not arriving until late May or early June. Small flocks form in late Aug. and early Sep. as they move south. Most are gone after mid-Sep., but stragglers are sometimes found as late as early Oct. Latest known is Oct. 12, 1962 (G. Morsello, *AFN* 17:60).

Note: There is a published report of a nighthawk seen in Eugene mid-Apr., 1974 (*ENHS*). Nighthawks are quite distinctive as a genus, but any nighthawk seen before mid-May should be carefully scrutinized; Lesser Nighthawk migrates earlier than Common and breeds to north-central California.

Distribution: More common in the Cascades and the Coast Range than on the valley floor or in the urban Eugene-Springfield area, where the species was seen regularly through the 1970s but is quite uncommon today.

Sites: Widespread in the Cascades.

Subfamily Caprimulginae

Common Poorwill *Phalaenoptilus nuttallii*

Status: Rare but regular wanderer from southern or eastern Oregon. About a dozen records, all from Apr.-June and Oct.-Nov., except for a recent record, Aug. 21, 2002 near Hills Creek Res. Several records have come from southeastern Lane Co. Breeds just across the Cascade summit in Deschutes and Klamath Cos., and may breed in the Diamond Peak area of Lane Co., where 2 were heard calling on June 27, 1992 (T. Mickel, p.c.).

Distribution: Most records are from Eugene eastward. See Contreras (2002, 2003b) for more detail on these records.

Sites: Irregular. Check rocky slopes near the Cascade summit.

Order APODIFORMES

Family Apodidae - Subfamily Cypseloidinae

• **Black Swift** *Cypseloides niger*
Status: Uncommon to rare, highly visible under good conditions at breeding site but extremely local and often hard to see. Seen mainly around waterfalls at high elevations. Also seen in migration, mainly on the outer coast and on the valley floor. Spring movement is largely in the second week of May in the lowlands, with birds appearing at Salt Creek Falls by the last week of May. Fall movements are poorly known, but usually absent from breeding areas by mid-Aug. Migrates in small numbers through Sep., mainly on the coast, and rarely reported. Latest record available is Oct. 11, 1997 in Eugene (J. Gilligan).
Distribution: Breeds regularly at Salt Creek Falls east of Oakridge. Probably breeds at a waterfall in the Swift Crk. basin northwest of Diamond Peak. A pair was observed carrying nesting material at a waterfall near Blue Lake west of Diamond Peak on June 16, 1998; the observer saw birds carrying food behind the same falls on June 25, 2000. This location is about 7 miles south of the Salt Creek Falls site. May also breed at Proxy Falls off Hwy. 242; seen there in July 2003. Seen in migration on the outer coast and occasionally in the Willamette Valley and adjacent valleys. Migratory patterns are obscure and birds sometimes appear when and where not expected, including Heceta Head on June 15, 2003, Fern Ridge Res. on May 30, 1971 (*ENHS*), the Siuslaw deflation plain on June 10, 2000 and, inexplicably, in Eugene on July 16, 2000.
Sites: Salt Creek Falls in June and July. Note: Vaux's Swifts also occur in the general area of the falls.

Subfamily Chaeturinae

• **Vaux's Swift** *Chaetura vauxi*
Status: Common migrant and breeder, seasonally abundant at roost sites. Absent in winter. Found in older forests, in towns, and in small numbers in most habitats where suitable breeding trees or structures are available. Outriders appear around the first of Apr. (earliest Mar. 30, 2004), with most movement the second week of Apr. Common and visible through Sep. By late Sep., forms large migrant flocks that roost in spectacular numbers (15,000 or more). Latest fall records are typically around Oct. 10, with stragglers for another week after that in some years. Latest known is Oct. 22, 1998.
Distribution: Countywide from sea level to timberline. First migrants are in the lowlands (typically in the Willamette Valley).

Vaux's Swifts.
Illustration by
Barbara Gleason.

Sites: The most well-known roost site in Lane Co. (most heavily used in fall) is the disused chimney at Agate Hall (17th and Agate streets) on the University of Oregon campus. The university has reinforced this old chimney specifically to protect the swift roost.

Subfamily Apodinae

White-throated Swift *Aeronautes saxatalis*
Casual wanderer into the county, presumably from populations in eastern Oregon. One recent record: May 4, 2000 at Spencer Butte (B. Newhouse, mistakenly placed at Skinner Butte in one published account). See Supplemental Records.

Family Trochilidae - Subfamily Trochilinae

Black-chinned Hummingbird *Archilochus alexandri*
Status: Rare but somewhat regular visitor, perhaps related to populations in eastern Oregon. About 10 records from Mar. 18 through Aug., half of which are between Apr. 10 and May 13.
Distribution: Most records are from the Eugene area eastward, mainly in the Cascades. The nearest breeding populations are in central Oregon.

• Anna's Hummingbird *Calypte anna*
Status: Uncommon widespread breeder. Uses gardens, lush evergreen shrubbery with flowers or feeders nearby, open urban landscapes with pockets of cover, coastal sumps with dense cover. No obvious seasonal migration, but appears to withdraw into urban areas in winter, except on the coast.

Distribution: Mostly in urban areas and on the outer coast. Generally absent from the Cascades and Coast Range, except in major Cascade river valleys to about 1200 feet elevation.
Sites: Urban feeders, Skinner Butte.

Costa's Hummingbird *Calypte costae*
Status: Casual wanderer from breeding populations to the south. About 10 records, mainly in winter and spring. The only record between May and Dec. is Sep. 2-12, 1993 at Florence.
Distribution: Most reports are at feeders in urban areas.

• Calliope Hummingbird *Stellula calliope*
Status: Rare irregular breeder. Found in montane meadows, urban plantings, and gardens. Rare but regular spring migrant; reports mainly from the Eugene area and occasionally from the Coast Range in late Apr. and early May. Most recent records have fallen between Apr. 12 and May 12. Earliest records are Mar. 29, 2002 and Mar. 30, 2003 in Eugene. Essentially unreported in fall, thus one at Tokatee Golf Course along Hwy. 126 on Oct. 29, 2004 is noteworthy not only for the location but for the late fall date. This may be the only fall record for the county.
Distribution: Spring migrants are rare but regular in the Eugene area, mainly in flower gardens and flowering trees along ridges. Irregular local breeder in the higher parts of the Cascades.
Sites: Skinner Butte, east side of Mt. Pisgah, ridgeline near Hendricks Park, hummingbird feeders.

• Rufous Hummingbird *Selasphorus rufus*
Status: Uncommon but widespread and highly visible migrant and breeder. Locally common for brief periods in migration. Uses flowering forbs, shrubs, and trees, hummingbird feeders. Very early migrant using a distinctive route. First arrives on the outer coast during mid-Feb., using salmonberry or red flowering currant if available. Moves up the coast until late Feb. and early Mar., at which time some appear inland, typically a week to 10 days behind coastal movements. Does not reach montane areas until late Mar. and Apr.

Breeds early, and males are southbound by June, often using high-elevation montane meadows that have begun to flower after snowmelt. Females and young remain through the summer, trickling out in small numbers through Sep. and early Oct., with highest numbers using montane meadows. Latest recent records are Oct. 8, 2003 and Oct. 6, 2004. Very rare in winter at feeders; one wintered in Leaburg in 2002-03.

Distribution: Countywide, least common as a breeder along the Cascade crest, but often seen there in migration.

[Allen's Hummingbird *Selasphorus sasin*]

Not known to breed north of central Coos Co., but wanderers have been confirmed by in-hand measurement from Corvallis and Astoria, so may occur occasionally in Lane Co., though extremely difficult to identify: some Rufous Hummingbirds have largely green backs.

Order CORACIIFORMES

Family Alcedinidae - Subfamily Cerylinae

• Belted Kingfisher *Ceryle alcyon*

Status: Uncommon but widespread and highly visible (and audible) breeder and winter resident. Winter numbers are distinctly higher than breeding numbers, especially on the outer coast, which suggests at least some migratory or downslope movement.

Distribution: Countywide where habitat permits; least common at small streams within dense forests. Requires banks for nesting, so some montane streams not suitable; least common in the high Cascades. Also nests in road-cut banks near water.

Order PICIFORMES

Family Picidae - Subfamily Picinae

Lewis's Woodpecker *Melanerpes lewis*

Status: Rare but regular migrant, mainly in late summer and fall through Oct.; rare winter resident. Status of this species has changed considerably in the past 60 years. Gullion (1951) reports that flocks of 70 in the fall and 30 in the spring were considered normal peak counts around Eugene in the mid-20th century. Small flocks of 3-4 birds could be found in fall and winter around Eugene in the late 1960s. Today a single bird on the valley floor is worth mentioning and flocks are unheard of.

Eugene CBC results show this change to some extent. However, it seems that the species has a cycle of winter abundance. It was absent in the early 1940s, regular for 10 years from the mid-1940s through mid-1950s, then largely absent until the late 1960s, when it was around for a few years. On only 2 CBCs between 1971 and 2000 was the species recorded at all. In 2001 and 2002, 2 birds were recorded, consistent with the slight increase noted elsewhere in west Oregon and the same as the median found 1945-1956, though during that period there were counts as high as 24 and 38, unimaginable today. Shelton (1917) considered it "irregular" in the Eugene area.   It is therefore reasonable to conclude that although migratory numbers are clearly down from mid-century, the number of wintering birds has been quite variable for at least a century.

Most reports in recent years have been of birds in the Cascades and the foothills west to Mt. Pisgah near Springfield in late summer and fall. Most of these do not winter in the county; it is not clear where they go. Latest spring records are May 27, 1998 in Alvadore and May 20, 2002 near Cottage Grove.

Distribution: Mainly in the Cascades and their foothills, with some records to the valley floor as far west as Fern Ridge Res. Unrecorded west of Fern Ridge.

Sites: Montane burns and snag fields in late summer; east side of Mt. Pisgah in fall migration.

• Acorn Woodpecker *Melanerpes formicivorus*

Status: Uncommon and highly local resident, restricted to oak stands; has declined from the 1970s through early 2000s. It was not present in Lane Co. at the time of Shelton's initial list for the region (1917) but by 1920 had arrived (UO specimens from Eugene and Cottage Grove, 1920; Neff 1928). Gullion (1951) notes that by mid-20th century its northern range limit was at Richardson Butte near Alvadore. Northwestern Oregon near Banks, Washington Co., today represents the edge of the species' range (it is rare and local in southern Washington).

Distribution: Formerly easy to find within Eugene in stands of oaks, rare today. Most regular in oak stands around Fern Ridge Res. and on valley foothills. The easternmost record is from Hills Creek Res. on Sep 10, 2003.

Sites: Oaks along Royal Ave. at eastern edge of Fern Ridge Res.; also sometimes in Perkins Peninsula Park.

° Williamson's Sapsucker *Sphyrapicus thyroideus*

Status: Rare irregular probable breeder. Rare but somewhat regular in late summer and early fall. Pine forests at high elevations. Eugene CBC record from 1948 is generally considered inaccurate.

Distribution: Restricted to Cascade summit pine forests and mixed pine-fir, rare and irregular, mainly in the southeast corner of the county in the vicinity of Waldo Lake. Found at Scott Lake near the McKenzie Pass in Oct. 2002. Breeding record reported in the OBBA was of a male Williamson's apparently paired with a female that was either a Red-breasted Sapsucker or a hybrid Red-breasted X Red-naped Sapsucker.

Sites: Waldo-Gold Lake area.

Yellow-bellied Sapsucker: Florence, Jan. 11, 2004. Photo by Noah K. Strycker.

* Yellow-bellied Sapsucker *Sphyrapicus varius*

Vagrant from the east. Two records confirmed by photos: an immature south of Fern Ridge Res. along Halderson Rd. Jan. 1-12, 1997 (OBRC 402-97-12) and an adult male in Florence Dec. 19, 2003-Jan. 27, 2004 (OBRC 402-03-18). In addition, there is one unconfirmed report from Kirk Park (Fern Ridge dam area) on Feb. 9, 2005 (D. Bontrager, N. McKechnie et al.).

• Red-naped Sapsucker *Sphyrapicus nuchalis*

Status: Rare irregular breeder, mainly in montane forests dominated by mountain hemlock, true fir, and pine. Rare migrant in montane areas, mainly in fall but also recorded from Apr., June and July.

Note: Hybrids between this species and Red-breasted Sapsucker are fairly common in the central and southern Cascades at high elevations. The CBC record of 3 Red-naped at Oakridge in 1975 is possible, although a family group of hybrids is more likely. May have interbred with Williamson's Sapsucker near Waldo Lake in 1998.

Distribution: Cascade summit region. Has bred west to Salt Creek Falls, noted in fall to Horsepasture Mtn. and at an unusually low elevation at Cougar Res., Oct. 4, 1991. Very rare to the valley floor: one record, Apr. 16, 1982 at Skinner Butte. Alma CBC records (11 years) should be treated as referring to Red-breasted Sapsucker.

Sites: Most often reported in the Gold Lake area.

• Red-breasted Sapsucker *Sphyrapicus ruber*

Status: Uncommon but widespread breeder, fairly easy to find in preferred habitat. Uses a variety of forests and woodlands, avoids the interior of dense evergreen forests but uses openings, snags, and streamside corridors within such forests. Also fond of orchards and urban plantings

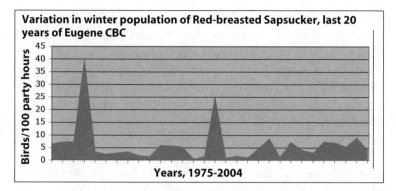

Variation in winter population of Red-breasted Sapsucker, last 20 years of Eugene CBC

Birds/100 party hours

Years, 1975-2004

such as decorative birches. Some migratory movement, not well known. Numbers increase in the lowlands in winter, but the source of these birds is not known. Winter numbers vary widely, e.g., from none to 13 on the Alma CBC in the Coast Range. Likewise, montane numbers decrease in winter, but it is not known whether these birds remain in Oregon or migrate southward.

Distribution: Countywide; least common in Cascade summit pine stands and in shore (lodgepole) pines on the outer coast.

• Downy Woodpecker *Picoides pubescens*
Status: Uncommon but easily located resident. Found in open woodlands, forest edges, towns, and small isolated stands of mature trees. In the Coast Range, mainly in riparian areas. Often comes to suet feeders. Sometimes found feeding on shrubs and even large forbs; often uses mullein. Mostly absent from dense higher-elevation evergreen forests in the Coast Range and Cascades.

Distribution: Countywide in suitable habitat.

• Hairy Woodpecker *Picoides villosus*
Status: Uncommon but widespread resident, mainly in more heavily wooded areas than Downy Woodpecker. Much less regular than Downy inside towns; rare at urban feeders.

Distribution: Countywide, least easy to find on the valley floor and in cities and towns. Generally more common than Downy in heavily wooded areas.

[White-headed Woodpecker *Picoides albolarvatus*]
This species has never been confirmed in Lane Co., but breeds just over the Cascade crest in northwest Deschutes and northwest Klamath Cos. It may occur in Lane Co. in the not-too-distant future, most likely as a dispersing bird in late summer or fall. See Supplemental Records.

• American Three-toed Woodpecker *Picoides dorsalis*

Status: Uncommon to rare local resident breeder along the Cascade crest, mainly in mixed lodgepole pine and true fir forests. Uses both very dense stands and more open, park-like areas, especially favoring recent burns. More willing to forage and nest in fairly young trees than are some other woodpeckers. Recently split from the Three-toed Woodpecker of Eurasia.

Distribution: Limited to pine-fir-mountain hemlock forests along the Cascade crest. Known to occur in the vicinity of Scott Lake, Melakwa Lake, Waldo Lake, and Gold Lake. Distribution is highly affected by the availability of recently burned forests, where it prefers to feed. For this reason, in some years the species concentrates, leaving other areas essentially void, while during periods of infrequent burns, it is more widespread in lower numbers.

Sites: North Waldo Burn (Taylor Burn) north of Waldo Lake has been a regular site in 2000s.

• Black-backed Woodpecker *Picoides arcticus*

Status: Uncommon and somewhat local breeding resident. Found mainly in forests containing lodgepole pine; at higher elevations often mixed with true fir and spruce. Highly attracted to recent burns and concentrates there. Sometimes found in lower-elevation conifer forests, mainly in winter. Found as low as the Oakridge CBC in 1974 (2 birds).

Distribution: Essentially limited to pine-fir-mountain hemlock forests of the Cascade crest.

Sites: Has been regular in North Waldo Burn (Taylor Burn) in 2000s.

• Northern Flicker *Colaptes auratus*

Status: Common and widespread breeding resident. Numbers increase in winter with an influx (peak in Oct.) from elsewhere, sometimes including "yellow-shafted" birds or, more commonly, "yellow x red-shafted" intergrades, usually in mid- to late fall. Uses a variety of habitats from stunted coastal pines to openings in heavy timber and subalpine parkland. Also uses more open areas as long as there are scattered trees for perching.

Distribution: Countywide, least common in dense higher-elevation coniferous forests. Somewhat local on the outer coast in summer, very common there late fall and winter. A few breed in urban areas.

• Pileated Woodpecker *Dryocopus pileatus*

Status: Uncommon and more often heard calling from a distant ridgeline than seen up close. Found mainly in more heavily wooded areas, rare in cities and towns, but sometimes seen in south Eugene near forested ridges. Rare and local in high-elevation lodgepole pine forests, where it is found mainly in pockets of older trees mixed with fir and deciduous trees.

Distribution: Countywide; irregular along the Cascade summit ridges.

Order PASSERIFORMES

Family Tyrannidae - Subfamily Fluvicolinae

• **Olive-sided Flycatcher** *Contopus cooperi*

Status: Uncommon breeder and migrant, may be declining. Breeds in coniferous forests, often in older trees. Found in migration in a wide variety of wooded habitats; rarely in open country. One of the later arrivals in spring, often not found until early May at low elevations, mid-May in the high Cascades. Earliest reported arrival is Apr. 21, 1974 (*ENHS*). Stragglers are sometimes found into early June, and the breeding season can be protracted, with departure not until late Aug. The latest obvious movements are usually in the first week of Sep., after which it becomes quite rare; absent after Sep. Latest recent report was Sep. 17, 1987.

Distribution: Countywide in migration, but more restricted as a breeder, when it is hard to find on the valley floor and local on the outer coast.

• **Western Wood-Pewee** *Contopus sordidulus*

Status: Common migrant and breeding resident. Uses a variety of fairly open forest types, usually with a significant deciduous component. Outriders appear in very late Apr. (earliest in recent years was Apr. 23, 1986), with significant influxes in early May. Common on breeding grounds until late Aug., after which they seem to melt away: a quiet pewee in fall is much harder to detect than a calling one in spring. Some migrants are seen through Sep., rarely into early Oct. (late stragglers are usually on the outer coast). The latest recent date was Oct. 2, 1980.

Note: Early spring reports of this species should be visually identified, since its calls are often given by European Starlings in late winter and spring.

Distribution: Countywide, with earliest migratory movements in spring in the valley lowlands and on the outer coast.

• **Willow Flycatcher** *Empidonax traillii*

Status: Fairly common but somewhat local in two superficially different but structurally similar habitats: dense riparian willows at lower elevations and shrub-stage regenerating clear-cuts, usually at higher elevations.

Arrives quite late in spring, with early migrants seen in the last half of May but the bulk of movement in early June. Reports from Apr. should be viewed with skepticism unless heard calling. The earliest record of a calling bird in recent years was May 3, 1997. Also departs rather early, with numbers dropping after mid-Aug. (perhaps due in part to difficulty in detection), but a steady trickle through Sep. and a few records in early Oct. Latest record in recent years was Oct. 2, 1986.

Distribution: Countywide within a rather specialized habitat niche. Rare and local in high-elevation pine forests.

Sites: Local. A few are usually visible and audible from the boardwalk nature trail at the west side of Perkins Peninsula Park.

Least Flycatcher *Empidonax minimus*

Casual/vagrant. This species is a rare migrant and very rare local breeder in eastern Oregon. One record of a calling bird, May 2, 1992 (quite early for this species) at Homestead Ridge in extreme southeast Lane Co., T24S R2E SEC 15 NE SE near Rd. 3818 (Ron Maertz, p.c.).

• Hammond's Flycatcher *Empidonax hammondii*

Status: Common breeder and migrant in coniferous forests, especially Douglas-fir, spruce, and true fir. Prefers forests with some openings in or below the canopy. Also seen in migration in a variety of habitat, including lowland shrubbery, woodlots, cemeteries, parks. Generally not found in pine forests unless they contain a significant admixture of fir or spruce. Often appears fairly early, with outriders in early Apr. and a steady buildup throughout the month. Peak numbers are not very obvious in many years, perhaps because migrants move upslope as soon as they arrive in the lowlands, where most observers are located. Latest fall records in recent years were Sep. 27, 1997 in the Coast Range and Sep. 29, 2002 near the mouth of the Siltcoos R.

Distribution: Countywide, with most breeders in the Coast Range and in the Cascades, except for the highest-elevation pine-dominated ridges. Regular in the valley lowlands in spring migration, but does not remain long and rarely breeds. Fall movements are not visible and may be along higher ridges.

Sites: Migrants are apparent at Skinner Butte in late Apr. and early May.

Gray Flycatcher *Empidonax wrightii*

Status: Casual in spring, presumably migrants that ended up on the wrong side of the Cascades. About a dozen records, most in a narrow seasonal window between Apr. 26 and May 7: May 4, 2006 at Green Island (R. Robb, p.c.); Apr. 25, 2005 at Mt. Pisgah (D. DeWitt, p.c.); Apr. 21, 2005 below Hills Creek Dam (D. Farrar, p.c.); May 24, 2004 on the University of Oregon campus; Apr. 28, 2004 at Mt. Pisgah; May 7, 2002 at Lane Community College; May 2, 2001 along the Willamette R. in Eugene; Apr. 29-30, 2001 at Skinner Butte; Apr. 26, 2001; Apr. 30, May 1, 10 and 17, 1991 at Skinner Butte (all the same bird?); and May 4-5, 1986 at Skinner Butte. The only record from the Cascades besides the Hills Creek bird was at Box Canyon Guard Station along Aufderheide Dr. on May 22, 1994 (T. Mickel, p.c.). However, this is probably owing to poor coverage in the higher Cascades in mid-spring.

Distribution: Most records to date have been on the valley floor, but it is likely that good coverage of montane oasis sites such as Hills Creek Dam during the period late Apr.-early May would result in more records.

• Dusky Flycatcher *Empidonax oberholseri*

Status: Locally common to uncommon breeder in drier open montane forests and taller brushfields. Uncommon migrant, mostly east of the valley floor. Outriders arrive in very late Apr., with the principal movement in mid-May, later along the Cascade summit. Fall movements far less obvious, but generally reported only through late Aug., with only a few stragglers in early Sep., e.g., Sep. 16, 2000 and Sep. 8, 2003. Latest recent record is Sep 28, 1998 (2 birds) in the Coast Range.

Distribution: Mainly in the mid- and high Cascades (generally above 3000 feet), with small numbers of migrants locally in the central Coast Range, where it is irregular and probably does not breed. Can be found anywhere in migration, but generally not reported on the outer coast or the coastal slope of the Coast Range.

• Pacific-slope Flycatcher *Empidonax difficilis*

Status: Common and easily heard (fairly easy to see). Found in moist forested areas, especially in mixed coniferous-deciduous forests such as the Douglas-fir and maple-alder dominated forests of the Coast Range and lower Cascades. Arrives fairly early, with reports from early Apr. and a significant influx by the end of Apr. Remains relatively late in fall, often reported through Sep. and multiple records in early Oct. Latest recent record was Oct. 6, 2002 at Craig Lake near McKenzie Pass. One was seen by an experienced observer on Jan. 30, 1998 at Finn Rock (*OB*, Kurt Cox). There are a couple of other reasonably documented winter records for Oregon.

Distribution: Most common in the coastal forest belt, Coast Range, and lowland forests fringing the Willamette Valley and western Cascades. Found throughout the Cascades, with most birds in riparian areas and mixed forest, rare in pine-dominated areas along the Cascade summit, where it tends to be found locally along streams and lakes where there is some deciduous tree cover.

• Black Phoebe *Sayornis nigricans*

Status: Rare local breeder, expanding northward. Reported from Lane Co. every year since at least 1984. Not migratory in the usual sense, but the few that are present in summer are usually augmented by several arrivals in winter, apparently from the south. Uses trees and shrubs around ponds, along slow-moving streams, in the edge of marshes, and along pastures. Breeds under bridges and on other flat structural features.

Distribution: Has bred at Creswell (1997) and near Ada junction southeast of Siltcoos Lake (2003). It is likely to expand as a breeder along coastal lakesides and on the valley floor. Has also been found at Fern Ridge Res. (Fisher Unit and Coyote Unit), East Regional Park in Cottage Grove, Lily Lake swamp on the coast, Gillespie Butte in Eugene, and in a few other sites, generally along water. A record July 10, 2005 in Eugene (R. Robb) may have been a local breeder, a nonbreeder, or a postbreeding dispersant. One unusual record was on July 8, 1988 at Gold Lake Bog.

Sites: Currently regular only along Fiddle Creek Rd. from Ada junction eastward, but likely to expand.

° Say's Phoebe *Sayornis saya*

Status: Rare regular migrant and winter visitor; has attempted to breed (McKenzie High School). Occurs at all seasons except midsummer (the breeding attempt excepted), with most reports from early spring (late Feb. through early Apr.) and Oct. through early winter.

Distribution: Mostly on the valley floor, generally on the east side, with multiple spring records from the Mt. Pisgah area. Casual to the outer coast: Oct. 30, 2004 at Florence, Mar. 16, 2004 at Florence, and Apr. 21, 2001 at Heceta Head.

Subfamily Tyranninae

° Ash-throated Flycatcher *Myiarchus cinerascens*

Status: Rare but fairly regular spring migrant and rare summer resident; breeding probable but not proven. Appears mainly in oak-dominated habitats. Most records are between early May and mid-autumn. Generally not reported after Sep.; latest interior record was Oct. 16, 1998 at Fern Ridge Res. Three very late records: Dec. 5, 2002 at Lily Lake (B. and Z. Stotz); Nov. 25, 1992 and Dec. 16, 1990 (photographed by Greg Hamann), both at Florence. Late fall birds should be carefully scrutinized, as Dusky-capped Flycatcher is a rare late-fall vagrant to northern California and has occurred once in Oregon.

Distribution: Summer residents on Mt. Pisgah and west of Eugene may have bred. Most spring and summer records are from hilly areas around the

Two views of a Tropical Kingbird: South Jetty Rd., Florence, Nov. 10, 2002. Photos by Noah K. Strycker (left) and Sylvia Maulding (right).

southern end of the valley. Has occurred at Oakridge (May 13, 1980) and Hills Creek dam pond (June 18, 2005, A. Prigge, p.c.) and better coverage in montane areas in spring would probably result in additional records. **Sites**: Irregular. Recently somewhat regular on south side of Mt. Pisgah and off Cantrell Rd. just east of K. R. Nielson Rd.

Tropical Kingbird *Tyrannus melancholicus*
Rare but regular late fall postbreeding visitor. Six or seven records to date: Nov. 9-15, 2002; Sep. 30, 2000; Nov. 18, 1996; Nov. 18, 1995; Nov. 3, 1973 (seen briefly but probably this species) near Lane Community College (*ENHS*, A. Contreras and E. Schultz); Sep. 30, 1973. All but the LCC bird were coastal.

Two kingbirds seen Dec. 31, 1972 on the Eugene CBC by four observers who knew the difference between kingbirds and other flycatchers (Larry Daggett et al.) were reported as Westerns, but were probably Tropicals.

* Cassin's Kingbird *Tyrannus vociferans*
Vagrant. One of Oregon's 2 records was an immature collected Aug. 4, 1935 at Mercer Lake (Marshall et al. 2003).

• Western Kingbird *Tyrannus verticalis*
Status: Uncommon breeder and migrant. Found mainly in semi-open areas with high nest sites; often nests on utility towers or the eaves of multistory farm buildings. Arrives mainly in early May, but there are often outriders in the latter half of Apr. Two unusually early records, if correctly identified: Mar. 27, 2002 and Feb. 28, 1947 (Gullion). Most depart in late Aug., with a few through early Sep. and stragglers to mid-Oct. The latest recent record was Oct. 28, 2000.

Note: Any kingbird seen after the third week of Sep., especially on the coast, should be examined with care in case it is a Tropical Kingbird.

Distribution: Almost entirely in the Willamette Valley and its lower foothills. Rare on the outer coast.

Sites: Usually visible along K. R. Neilson Rd. south of Fern Ridge Res., also along Central Rd. in that area, also the east side of Mt. Pisgah.

Eastern Kingbird *Tyrannus tyrannus*

Rare but possibly increasing as an early-summer wanderer. The first county record was at Fern Ridge Res. on June 5, 1965 (*AFN* 19: 573). About 10 records to date, all in June except for July 5, 1971 at Lane Community College and July 14-17, 1996 at the lower Siltcoos R. Five of these records have been in the past dozen years. Reports are from a wide variety of locations, from the outer coast to Mt. Pisgah and Fall Creek dam.

Family Laniidae

Loggerhead Shrike *Lanius ludovicianus*

Status: Rare nonbreeding migrant; rare and irregular winter visitor. Formerly a more regular spring migrant. Appears every few years, mainly in mid-spring and fall, but also occasionally found in winter.

Distribution: Mainly on the Willamette Valley floor, including Fern Ridge Res. Rare to the outer coast; the only recent record there is Apr. 7, 1997 in the Siuslaw deflation plain.

Northern Shrike *Lanius excubitor*

Status: Uncommon winter resident and migrant; numbers vary from year to year, especially on the coast. Mainly in open country with considerable shrub growth. Arrives in mid-Oct., most leave in late Mar., with stragglers throughout Apr. Rare in early May at Fern Ridge Res. (May 1, 1974 *ENHS*). Recent more typical late spring dates are Apr. 10, 1999 at Fern Ridge and Apr. 16, 1999 at the Siltcoos R. mouth.

Distribution: Mainly the valley floor, especially in marshlands around Fern Ridge Res.; also fairly regular but local on the outer coast.

Sites: Easiest to find around Fern Ridge Res. and, in most years, along the South Jetty Rd. near Florence.

Family Vireonidae

• **Cassin's Vireo** *Vireo cassinii*

Status: Uncommon but widespread breeder and migrant. Found in woodlands and forests, typically with a mix of coniferous and deciduous trees. Arrives fairly early in spring, with a few birds typically arriving in the last few days of Mar. (earliest Mar. 22, 1974, *ENHS*) and a steady movement beginning in early Apr. Present through Aug., with a regular movement of very small numbers throughout Sep. Rare in early Oct.; most late records are coastal.

Distribution: Countywide, local and irregular breeder on the outer coast and mostly absent from the Coast Range, does breed in pines to the Cascade summit. Migrant countywide, more regular on the coast in fall than in spring.

Sites: Widespread away from the coastal slope.

* **Blue-headed Vireo** *Vireo solitarius*

Vagrant. One record: Sep. 13, 2003 in Alton Baker Park, Eugene (D. Irons, submitted to OBRC).

• **Hutton's Vireo** *Vireo huttoni*

Status: Uncommon but widespread resident and breeder. Found mainly in fairly dense forests (generally second-growth, not very large trees) that include both coniferous and deciduous trees, especially where Douglas-fir and oaks are marbled together. Non-migratory but winter birds tend to join flocks of kinglets and chickadees, where their more robust appearance, tangible bill, and less frenetic behavior help distinguish them from Ruby-crowned Kinglets. Begins singing early in spring (sometimes by late Feb.), which can make them fairly easy to locate.

Distribution: Countywide. Most common at low to mid-elevations; can be fairly easy to find in the Coast Range. Progressively less common eastward into the Cascades, roughly as far east as Cougar and Hills Creek reservoirs,

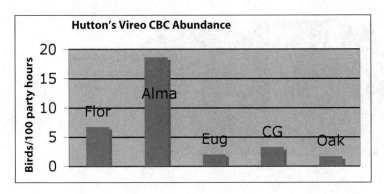

where the last oaks are available, and absent in the pine belt along the summit ridges. Rather local on the valley floor, generally where sizable stands of trees remain.

• Warbling Vireo *Vireo gilvus*
Status: Fairly common breeder and migrant. Uses a variety of deciduous woodlands and mixed forests that contain sizable deciduous trees. Especially common in riparian areas; also found in dry brush fields at high elevations in the Cascades (T. Mickel, p.c.). Typically arrives in a significant wave in mid- to late Apr., with very few outriders. Gullion notes the earliest record in the 1940s as Apr. 12; the earliest recent record was Apr. 1, 2003 at Eugene. Usually remains through very early Sep., with stragglers through late Sep., rarely to early Oct. Recent late dates are Sep. 23, 2001 and 2002, Sep. 21, 1986, Sep. 17, 2003, and Sep 15, 2004.
Distribution: Countywide. Least common in high-elevation coniferous forests, but in such habitat is easy to find in deciduous pockets, especially near water.

• Red-eyed Vireo *Vireo olivaceus*
Status: Rare but regular local breeder, not reported in migration. Lane Co. represents the extreme southwest corner of the species' regular northwest breeding range.

Note: One female Red-eyed Vireo mated with a male Cassin's Vireo at Jasper Park in June 1997, producing eggs but no young (photos, *OB* 24:33).

Found almost exclusively in very tall deciduous trees in or near riparian areas. Generally arrives very late in spring, with earliest birds in very late May and most not on territory until early June. An unusual early record was Apr. 21, 1974 (*ENHS*). Essentially invisible as a fall migrant; birds may move east instead of south, although this is not known for certain. Generally not found after the third week of Aug. The only recent late-season report was Aug. 28, 1996.

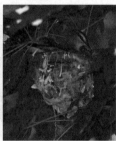

Bliss but no babies: Harold and Maude at their nest in Jasper Park. Photos by Roger Robb.

Distribution: Breeds regularly from Jasper Park locally upriver along the Middle Fork of the Willamette, in some years as far as Oakridge, but mainly lower in the valley. Has bred near Shore Lane on the northeast shore of Fern Ridge Res. May have bred along the Long Tom R. east of Veneta and in the lower McKenzie R. drainage (B. Combs, p.c.). Reported west of Veneta in July, 2004; there are previous reports from this area.
Sites: Jasper Park, Elijah Bristow State Park.

Family Corvidae

• **Gray Jay** *Perisoreus canadensis*
Status: Fairly common resident in higher-elevation coniferous forests. Most common in true fir, mixed fir-lodgepole pine, and sometimes dense pine forests. Rather quiet and sometimes overlooked, unless an incautious camper leaves a sandwich unguarded.
Distribution: Most common above 2000 feet in the Cascades, but found to sea level locally in the Coast Range, mainly north of Florence on the outer coast, more widespread in the interior Coast Range. In these areas, they use Douglas-fir, Sitka spruce, and coastal lodgepole pines. Generally absent on the valley floor and the lower foothills, with small numbers along the Calapooya Divide and rarely as low as the Cottage Grove area.
Sites: Waldo Lake, Gold Lake.

• **Steller's Jay** *Cyanocitta stelleri*
Status: Common resident breeder. Found mainly in coniferous forests, but also found to the valley floor in mixed woodlands that include or are near a stand of coniferous trees. Seasonal movements are very limited, but in some years there is a significant movement into lowland areas in Oct.
Distribution: Countywide; least common on the open valley floor (often absent away from conifers) and in open pine stands along the Cascade crest.

Blue Jay *Cyanocitta cristata*
Status: Casual in fall and winter. About a dozen records since 1978, two of which wintered in Springfield. Found mainly in urbanized areas and at feeders. A few remained until mid-spring.
Distribution: Most reports are from the fall (mainly Oct.), and are limited to the valley floor and river valleys to the eastward, except for the most recent record, Oct. 30, 2005 at Waldo Lake (C. Coury, B. Hughes; *fide* V. Arnold). There are no records from the Coast Range westward except for one at Florence Oct. 19, 1995.

• **Western Scrub-Jay** *Aphelocoma californica*

Status: Common resident breeder. Found in a variety of urban and agricultural areas, around farms and in riparian areas. Most common where oaks are present.

Distribution: Common throughout the interior lowlands, open foothills where considerable deciduous woodlands are found, river valleys in the western Cascades (in the upper valleys, mainly in towns), and locally into the eastern slope of the Coast Range. Absent from high-elevation coniferous forests and the western Coast Range, with one recent unusual record, Oct. 6, 2002 near the McKenzie Pass. In recent years, one or two have been found in Florence on a regular basis year round (bred in 2002), and a few have been found in fall on the outer coast, possibly part of a seasonal movement.

Sites: Widespread in the interior valleys.

Pinyon Jay *Gymnorhinus cyanocephalus*

Casual wanderer, presumably from populations in central Oregon. The only county record is 30-50 birds at Waldo Lake on Sep. 24, 2000 (Kit Larsen, *Quail*).

• **Clark's Nutcracker** *Nucifraga columbiana*

Status: Uncommon but widespread, highly visible (and audible) resident breeder. Found in high-elevation forests, mainly pines. Also sometimes found at campgrounds, especially along the Cascade summit, and in lava fields with sparse pine incursions.

Distribution: Mostly along the Cascade crest above 3500 feet. Rare but regular wanderer west as far as Spencer Butte and the Eugene airport, mainly in fall and early winter. Can appear at odd times and places, e.g., May 13, 2000 at Coburg. Three coastal records: 1 in north Florence, Nov. 2, 2004 (D. Pettey); 1 collected Nov. 11, 1913 at Oceanview (SD #24075); and 1 collected Sep. 30, 1930 at Heceta Head (SD #24066). The site name Oceanview does not appear on modern maps or in McArthur's Oregon Geographic Names, but the San Diego Museum records list the site as in Lane Co.

Sites: Easiest along Cascade summit, e.g., Hand Lake Trail.

Black-billed Magpie *Pica hudsonia*

Casual wanderer, presumably from populations in eastern Oregon. Most records are from earlier decades; seems less likely to enter the area today, perhaps because of changes in land use in Central Oregon, especially in western Deschutes Co., where it is distinctly less common than in the 1960s and early 1970s (A. Contreras, p.c.).

The most recent record was on Apr. 14, 2000 near Triangle Lake (C. McQuoid). One was reported near Blue R. on Sep. 30, 1985. Prior published records were Sep. 27, 1947 at Pleasant Hill and Oct. 28, 1946 near Elmira (both Gullion 1951). Shelton (1917) notes that there were several records from the McKenzie Valley and that it had been recorded near Eugene. See Supplemental Records.

• American Crow *Corvus brachyrhynchos*
Status: Common to abundant resident breeder. Uses a variety of habitats, generally a mixture of open ground and woodlands. Also common in cities and towns, sometimes abundant at winter roosts on the valley floor and in the lower Siuslaw estuary.
Distribution: Widespread from the outer coast to the western Cascades, where it becomes somewhat local in river valleys. Rare but increasingly regular in openings along highway corridors in the higher Cascades. Generally absent from the Cascade summit region.

• Common Raven *Corvus corax*
Status: Fairly common resident breeder. Mainly in heavily forested areas during the summer, but fairly common on the valley floor from late autumn through mid-spring. Often attends lambing on the valley floor, and found around sheep and cattle carcasses.
Distribution: Countywide; least common on the open valley floor except in winter and early spring. Seen to and above timberline in the Cascades. In recent years, found inside the Eugene-Springfield urban area occasionally.

Family Alaudidae

° Horned Lark *Eremophila alpestris*
Status: Uncommon to rare, mainly in migration and winter. Rare in summer, might breed occasionally on the valley floor along the northern edge of the county. Singing birds have been noted in recent years around the Eugene airport. Found in open grasslands, grassy beach edges, open gravel pans, montane meadows. Fall movements are weak and occur mainly in Sep. and Oct. Spring movements are essentially invisible.

E. a. strigata is resident in the Willamette Valley, but it is unclear if Lane Co.'s breeding population stays in the county in the winter. Lane Co. is, however, the southernmost known breeding population of *strigata*, since Jackson Co.'s population seems to have disappeared. At least one pair of *strigata* probably bred on the unusually dry Fern Ridge mudflats in 2005; an adult with a single juvenile was found there Aug. 27, 2005 (D. Farrar).

The only winter record that has been identified to subspecies is one flock of 80 in the winter of 2003-04 in a clover field next to the Eugene airport. This flock was made up entirely of *E. a. merrilli* (and possibly *lamprochroma*; the two are not safely separable in the field), the subspecies that breeds east of the Cascades. The subspecies *E. a. alpina/arcticola* is probably a rare winter visitor and passage migrant in spring and fall. Several have been well described from Mt. Pisgah in fall migration. They are found farther north in the Willamette valley at about the rate of 1 per 100 larks.

Distribution: Mainly on the valley floor north of the Eugene area; also on hilltops (especially Mt. Pisgah) in fall migration and occasionally in winter. Found occasionally in the Siuslaw deflation plain and other open areas on the outer coast. Very few reports from the high Cascades, though the sighting of a bird in juvenal plumage on Twins Peak suggests that there may be a small breeding population above treeline nearby. The subspecific identification of Oregon Cascades breeders has yet to be determined.

Sites: Irregular. Most often reported around the Eugene airport at all seasons.

Family Hirundinidae - Subfamily Hirundininae

• **Purple Martin** *Progne subis*
Status: Local colonial breeder, generally either common or absent. Found mainly in snags or nest boxes above or adjacent to water, although several small snag-nesting colonies were found in clear-cuts away from water in the Coast Range and low Cascades in 2002 (T. Mickel, p.c.). Arrives fairly early in spring, with a few in the last few days of Mar. and most in early Apr. Fairly obvious through early Sep., when it sometimes occurs away from breeding areas in migration. Rare but regular as late as early Oct.

Pair of Purple Martins at Florence. Photo by Diane Pettey.

Distribution: Most breeders are around Fern Ridge Res. and in the Florence-Cushman area, with small numbers elsewhere on the valley floor, mainly around lakes. A few use nest boxes at Dorena and Cottage Grove reservoirs. A few may breed locally in snags within forested areas west of the high Cascades. Late fall birds are mainly on the outer coast.
Sites: Snags at Fern Ridge, locally around Florence, sometimes on the Cushman railroad bridge.

• **Tree Swallow** *Tachycineta bicolor*
Status: Common to locally abundant breeder and migrant, rare in winter. Found mainly near water, where they breed in snags and nest boxes. Arrives very early in spring, with the first outriders usually reported in early Feb., a steady movement through Feb. and a significant surge in early Mar. Early movements are almost exclusively along major waterways.

In mid-July, begins to form large local flocks while numbers drop at breeding sites through Aug. By early Sep., essentially gone from breeding sites but still found in large migrant flocks, mainly along major waterways. Latest recent records are Oct. 9, 2000 (an exceptional 200 birds, mixed Tree and Violet-greens, at the Siltcoos mouth) and Oct. 18, 2003. Very rare in winter, mainly on the valley floor along open water.
Distribution: Countywide; least common in the high Cascades except around lakes where snags are available. Early spring and late fall movements mainly coastal and at Fern Ridge Res.

• **Violet-green Swallow** *Tachycineta thalassina*
Status: Common breeder and migrant. Very rare in winter. Found mainly near water and in cities and towns, locally in cliff colonies. Arrives slightly later than Tree Swallow in spring, with the first reports typically in the last half of Feb. Numbers increase dramatically during Mar., but these early birds seem to be largely migrants. Local breeding often does not begin until around the first of Apr., sometimes late Apr.

By late July, most urban birds have departed and large flocks have formed along rivers and lakeshores from the high Cascades to the coast. By the end of Aug., flocks are moving south and to the coast, but most birds are gone from breeding areas. Migrants are easy to find along the coast in Sep., with small numbers inland. By early Oct., they are rare, and by the end of Oct., absent.
Distribution: Countywide, with most in cities and towns, on human-made structures, in holes in cliffs. Least common in the high Cascades, except near cliffs and river canyons. Most early spring and late fall movements are along major rivers and lakes.

• **Northern Rough-winged Swallow** *Stelgidopteryx serripennis*
Status: Uncommon but widespread breeder and migrant. Found mainly along rivers, especially those with vertical banks suitable for nest holes, but also uses road-cut banks in the Coast Range and low Cascades. Less common along lakes, generally absent in urban areas except along major waterways. Arrives later than Tree and Violet-green Swallows, with small numbers in late Mar. and the principal movement in early Apr. Breeders begin departing in late Aug. without forming large flocks. This relatively obscure movement continues through Sep. Absent in winter, no records after Sep.

Distribution: More common in lowlands along rivers with vertical dirt banks, with most birds at the Willamette R. and its lower tributaries. Small numbers are found along rivers and streams countywide, except in the high Cascades, where rare and local.

° **Bank Swallow** *Riparia riparia*
Rare but regular in migration, mainly at Fern Ridge Res. First reported in the county in 1947 (Gullion). About 30 records involving 35-40 birds, mostly in May and Aug. The bulk of movement seems to be of postbreeding birds in late summer. Most May records are in the past 10 years, suggesting possible local breeding. May records are from Cottage Grove, Creswell, and Fern Ridge Res. An Apr. 14, 1974 record from Cougar Res. is the easternmost from the county (*ENHS*).

Note: observers should be careful not to confuse immature Tree Swallow with Bank Swallow. See field guides.

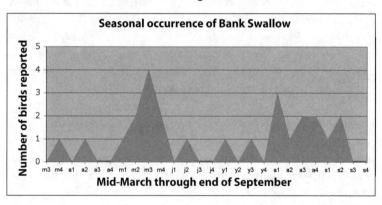

Seasonal occurrence of Bank Swallow
Number of birds reported
Mid-March through end of September

• **Cliff Swallow** *Petrochelidon pyrrhonota*
Status: Locally common to abundant breeder and migrant. Found in colonies, mainly on bridges, human-made structures, and drier cliff sites. Generally absent from moist cliffs, which are used by Violet-green Swallows. Arrives fairly late for a swallow, with early migrants in late Mar. and a major push in early Apr. The earliest recent spring report is Mar. 11, 2005 at Eugene (D. DeWitt, p.c.), the earliest since one on Mar. 15, 1980 and probably the earliest ever found in the county. Fairly common through Aug., with movement away from colony sites by late July. Regular through mid-Sep., with late-season migrants mainly coastal. A few sometimes moving through Oct. Latest record is Oct. 27, 1975.
Distribution: Countywide, but rather local since it is relatively selective in nesting habitat. Essentially absent in the high Cascades except for small numbers at local colonies. Early migrants mainly along major waterways.

• **Barn Swallow** *Hirundo rustica*
Status: Common breeder and migrant. Uses human structures, natural clefts for breeding. Arrives rather late for a swallow, with the first movements in early Apr., quickly building to peak numbers. Present in numbers later than any other swallow, with significant numbers still moving throughout Sep., small numbers in early Oct. and stragglers to early Dec. A few winter records. In recent years, small northward movements have been detected in Jan., for reasons that are not clear.
Distribution: Countywide; least common in heavily forested areas and away from human habitation. A few are present along the Cascade summit ridges, perhaps using montane rock features for nesting.

Family Paridae

• **Black-capped Chickadee** *Poecile atricapillus*
Status: Common resident breeder. Found mainly in deciduous woods and shrubbery, in towns, willow patches, riparian areas, and in coniferous forests where there is a substantial intermixture of maple, alder, or willow.
Distribution: Countywide except in dense evergreen forests; generally absent in the Cascades above 3000 feet except in larger shrubby openings.

• **Mountain Chickadee** *Poecile gambeli*
Status: Common resident breeder in coniferous forests (almost exclusively lodgepole pines) along the Cascade crest. More local down to about 3000 feet. Only minor seasonal movement except in peak invasion years.
Distribution: Mainly in pine-dominated forests along the Cascade crest in summer. Fairly regular to lower Cascades in winter (12/15 on Oakridge CBC,

often with more than a dozen birds) and may move along the Calapooya Divide with some regularity (7/14 on Cottage Grove CBC, 5 counts with 5 or more birds). In some years, invades lowlands as far as the outer coast, sometimes beginning in late summer, more typically mid-autumn, and remaining for the winter. Probably more regular in the western Cascades in southern Lane Co. than in the northern part of the county, owing to the greater abundance of pines farther south.

Sites: High elevations, west locally to Bohemia Mtn. and ridges east of Oakridge.

• Chestnut-backed Chickadee *Poecile rufescens*
Status: Common to locally abundant (winter flocks), resident breeder in coniferous forests. Also found in mixed forests containing a significant evergreen component. Least common in pines in the Cascades, but common in coastal pines.

Distribution: Countywide, generally absent in pure pine stands along the Cascade crest. Especially common in Coast Range and western Cascades.

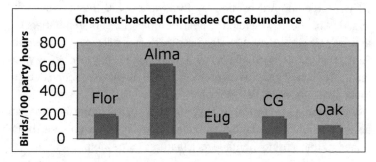

[Oak Titmouse *Baeolophus inornatus*]
Reports from Mt. Pisgah (Don Payne) and Fern Ridge Res. lack available details and are 75 miles north of the northern edge of the usual range. However, the Mt. Pisgah report in particular was in appropriate habitat that has also supported Blue-gray Gnatcatcher and Ash-throated Flycatcher.

Family Aegithalidae

• Bushtit *Psaltriparus minimus*
Status: Uncommon to seasonally common breeding resident. Found mainly in somewhat open park-like settings with a mix of taller trees, open space, and shrubs, including urban areas.

Distribution: Countywide except in pine-dominated forests along the Cascade crest. Generally hard to find in the higher Cascades except along major rivers and locally in regenerating clear-cuts with sufficient tall vegetation. Forms flocks in fall and winter, so can be locally quite common when encountered in the field or at suet feeders.

Family Sittidae - Subfamily Sittinae

• **Red-breasted Nuthatch** *Sitta canadensis*

Status: Fairly common breeding resident, also a migrant, sometimes staging large invasions. Found in wooded areas dominated by evergreens. Sometimes locally common in migration and in peak invasion periods.

Distribution: Countywide, with significant seasonal and cyclic variation, especially on the outer coast and in valley lowlands. In these areas, can be all but absent in some years, common in others.

• **White-breasted Nuthatch** *Sitta carolinensis*

Status: Uncommon and declining local breeder. Strongly associated with stands of large oaks. Formerly fairly common in urban Eugene and nearby areas, but today rather difficult to find. Eugene CBC formerly recorded many of them (high count is 88 in 1967) but today fewer than 10 is normal.

Distribution: Most are on the valley floor and adjacent hillsides with oak cover. Most often reported from oak stands near Fern Ridge Res., e.g,. along Royal Ave. or in Perkins Peninsula Park. A few are reported in the Willamette (Middle Fork east locally to Oakridge in 1970s, may have declined) and McKenzie valleys. Very rare on the coastal slope and interior of the Coast Range (Alma CBC 1/11) and on the outer coast. Two records on Florence CBC, both at a feeder along the North Fork of the Siuslaw.

Sites: Oaks at the west end of Royal Ave. at Fern Ridge, nearby Fisher Rd. and Perkins Peninsula Park.

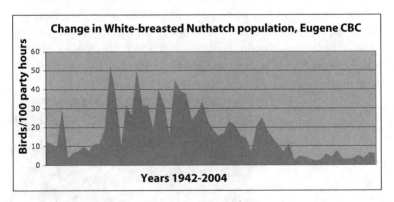

Change in White-breasted Nuthatch population, Eugene CBC

Birds/100 party hours

Years 1942-2004

Pygmy Nuthatch *Sitta pygmaea*

Possible irregular visitor; unconfirmed. One was reported on Jan. 22, 2005 (an all-time record invasion year for Red-breasted Nuthatches to the coast) at a bird feeder located on Cougar Mtn. between Cottage Grove and Creswell (Marilyn Miller, p.c.). One was reported on the Oakridge CBC in 1978. There are two reports from the Cottage Grove CBC (one in 1971 and two in 1972), but details are unavailable. This species is very rare west of the Cascade summit.

Family Certhiidae - Subfamily Certhiinae

• Brown Creeper *Certhia americana*

Status: Uncommon but widespread resident breeder. Found mainly in forests and woodlands containing larger trees. In migration and winter, sometimes found in habitat unsuitable for breeding. A noticeable fall movement is sometimes underway in Oct. The origin of these migrants and the exact nature of these movements is poorly understood. Several subspecies migrate through Oregon, in addition to local breeders that winter to the south.

Distribution: Countywide in relatively small numbers.

Family Troglodytidae

• Rock Wren *Salpinctes obsoletus*

Status: Rare but regular local breeder. Uses rock quarries, dam faces, rocky hilltops. Very few pairs breed in the county annually. Usually arrive in early Apr. and sometimes remain through early Dec. (Gullion 1951); some late fall and winter birds may be migrants unrelated to local breeding pairs. These birds are not always in breeding habitat, e.g., the one on Oct. 20, 1974 at the Salt Creek bridge near Oakridge (*ENHS*). This species is mainly known as a resident of eastern Oregon, where it is easy to find in canyons, talus slopes, and cliffs. Lane Co. represents a fringe population.

Rock Wren: Top of Spencer Butte, May 9, 2003. Photo by Noah K. Strycker.

Distribution: Has bred occasionally on top of Spencer Butte south of Eugene (Holbo 1979, Gullion 1951, Shelton 1917). Also found occasionally on dams and quarries east of the Willamette Valley lowlands and along the edge of lava fields near McKenzie Pass. There are a few records from rocky road-cuts and quarries in the Coast Range during breeding season (T. Mickel, p.c.), and 3 reports (2 in Apr., 1 in Sep.) from a quarry near Fern Ridge Dam (Strycker 2003). The only coastal record was at Tenmile Cr. (Stonefield beach area) on May 13, 1990.
Sites: Local. Cascade dams, Scott Lake rock quarry are most regular.

Canyon Wren *Catherpes mexicanus*
Status: Casual wanderer from eastern Oregon, found on rock faces, dams.
Distribution: Records of this species are exceptionally obscure, but are included here as a baseline. At least 5 records: July 9, 1992 in the Oakridge Ranger District (R. Davis, *fide* Matt Hunter); July 1991 at T24S, R5E S 30 near Tumblebug Cr. in the Cascades (*fide* Matt Hunter); Nov. in the late 1980s or early '90s at Cougar Res. and in summer in the Coal Cr. drainage T24S R3E S27, by Gary McAtee *fide* Matt Hunter. Reported from Spencer Butte in the early 1950s (Dave Brown, p.c.). In addition, Mar. and Aug. records have been heard of second-hand, but even less information is available.

• Bewick's Wren *Thryomanes bewickii*
Status: Fairly common resident breeder. Found in a variety of dense shrubby situations, blackberry tangles, large scrub willow patches. Found regularly in urban areas where dense cover available.
Distribution: From the outer coast to the lower Cascades, generally absent from the higher Cascades. Reaches east of Oakridge and the McKenzie Bridge region in riparian areas, not regular at higher elevations or within forested areas.

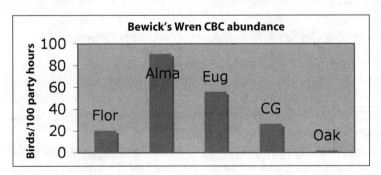

Bewick's Wren CBC abundance

Bewick's Wren.
Illustration by Barbara
Gleason.

• House Wren *Troglodytes aedon*

Status: Uncommon to locally common breeder and migrant. Most common in regenerating clear-cuts and in other settings containing stumps or snags with cavities to contain nests. Also uses nest boxes. Most arrive in early Apr., but in some years a small number appear during late Mar. Two specimens taken Mar. 2, 1920 (UO 1624, 1625) establish the earliest known arrival date. Numbers decrease after Aug., with migrants found occasionally throughout Sep. Rare as late as early Oct., mainly coastal. Latest recent record was Oct. 19, 2002.

No confirmed records between mid-Oct. and early Mar., but there are multiple sight records, and may have occurred in winter in mild years. Sight records by experienced observers include Dec. 30, 1984 at Eugene (Roger Robb), and Feb. 20, 1993 (Dennis Arendt, Ram Papish).

Distribution: Most common in the Coast Range and in foothills around the valley floor, local on the outer coast. Local along the Cascade summit, where it occurs mainly in deciduous pockets within coniferous forests.

• Winter Wren *Troglodytes troglodytes*

Status: Common resident breeder. Abundant in the Coast Range and western Cascades in winter. Found mainly in dense undergrowth within forests in summer, more widespread in winter, including lowland blackberry patches and shrubby areas.

Distribution: Countywide. Most common in heavily forested areas. Local on the valley floor; absent from some lowland areas in summer.

*Winter Wren.
Illustration by Barbara
Gleason.*

• **Marsh Wren** *Cistothorus palustris*
Status: Locally common to abundant breeder and winter resident. Found in marshes and grassy wetlands in summer. In winter, also found in thick dune grass and shorter wet grass fields. Can be found in almost any tall grassy habitat in migration.
Distribution: Most common in major marshes such as at Fern Ridge Res., around coastal lakes, montane lake margins. Can be found countywide in migration.
Sites: Widespread. Easiest to see at Fern Ridge marshes in spring and summer.

Family Cinclidae

• **American Dipper** *Cinclus mexicanus*
Status: Uncommon resident breeder, somewhat local. Found along fast-moving rivers and creeks.
Distribution: Found in the Coast Range (mainly north of the Siuslaw Valley) and the Cascades above the valley floor, wherever rivers and streams are fast-moving and contain exposed rocks. Rare to the valley floor in winter, most records from Island Park (Springfield) and the nearby Willamette R. Regular breeder in the Mohawk Valley above Marcola (T. Mickel, p.c.). Rare to absent from streams in the Calapooya Divide from Cottage Grove Reservoir west to the upper Siuslaw and Smith rivers (OBBA). Distribution in this area is poorly known.

Family Regulidae

• Golden-crowned Kinglet *Regulus satrapa*
Status: Common to abundant resident, breeding in coniferous forests. Some move into lowlands in winter, forming small flocks with other forest and woodland species. Generally remains in or near conifers.
Distribution: Countywide. More on the valley floor in winter than in summer.

° Ruby-crowned Kinglet *Regulus calendula*
Status: Abundant migrant and winter resident. Rare probable local breeder in pine and pine-fir forests above 4000 feet along Cascade summit ridges. Common migrant, with first southbound birds usually seen in mid-Sep. and a major incursion in late Sep. and early Oct. Spring movement is mainly in Apr., after which they are distinctly less common, but some migrants can be found through late May, even early June, which gives a false impression that the species may be breeding locally in lowland areas. Frequently sings in migration and even in late winter, which adds to the false impression of local breeding.
Distribution: Countywide in winter, mainly below 2000 feet. Abundant in lowlands, especially on the outer coast.
Sites: Widespread in winter.

Family Sylviidae - Subfamily Polioptilinae

° Blue-gray Gnatcatcher *Polioptila caerulea*
Casual summer visitor, nested unsuccessfully at Mt. Pisgah in 1997, a peak year. Six birds were found in the Thurston area in spring 1949 (Pruitt 1950). Fewer than 20 records, all in the southern Willamette Valley and the western McKenzie Valley, from Apr. 24 (1997) through July 27 (1997). One was in Alton Baker Park in Eugene, an unlikely location, on June 5, 1997. One was along Willow Creek in west Eugene Apr. 25-May 10, 1997, as well. One was at Mt. Pisgah on June 10, 1990.

Family Turdidae

• Western Bluebird *Sialia mexicana*
Status: Uncommon local resident breeder. Some movement into nonbreeding areas in winter. Numbers fell significantly in the mid-20th century owing to habitat loss and competition from introduced birds such as the House Sparrow and European Starling. The establishment of nest-box programs in the 1970s helped save the species. Today it is reasonably easy to find. The graph on the facing page is from the Eugene CBC.

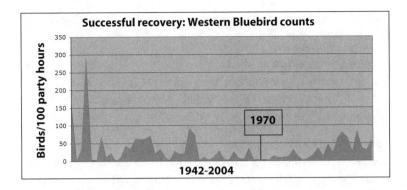

Successful recovery: Western Bluebird counts

Birds/100 party hours

1970

1942-2004

Distribution: Most common in foothills around the Willamette Valley (especially in oaks), locally common in regenerating clear-cuts and natural openings with snags in the high Cascades and Coast Range. Multiple recent reports on hillsides within Eugene. Rare on the outer coast.
Sites: Widespread in valley foothills.

• Mountain Bluebird *Sialia currucoides*
Status: Uncommon but highly visible breeder along the Cascade summit in open areas with scattered trees, and occasionally at mid-elevation clear-cuts (e.g., above Hills Creek Res.; B. Combs, p.c.). Thought to be present in breeding range from mid-Apr. through mid-Oct. (including migrants), but in fact there is not much information available owing to the relative inaccessibility of the habitat in spring.
Distribution: Cascade summit ridges. Rare west to the valley floor, mainly in fall and winter. No coastal records.
Sites: North Waldo Burn (Taylor Burn), Waldo Lake area, Three Sisters.

• Townsend's Solitaire *Myadestes townsendi*
Status: Uncommon but widespread breeder in high-elevation forests, mainly where there are openings, especially on steeper terrain. Most winter east of the Cascades but a few remain at lower elevations. Uncommon irregular breeder in the Coast Range.
Distribution: Breeds mostly in broken and open forests above 3000 feet in the Cascades or at any elevation in the Coast Range, where it is mainly found in steep, slash-bearing clear-cuts in the summer (T. Mickel, p.c.). This species is more regular as a Coast Range breeder north and south of Lane Co., perhaps because the Coast Range of Lane Co. is relatively low and densely forested, without major rock formations, cliffs, or other incursions, which create the steeper open areas that this species seems to prefer. Appears to have been more regular on the valley floor around Eugene in the 1960s-70s than it is today, perhaps because of changes in forest practices.

Rare but regular in winter and early spring to the valley floor, Coast Range, and occasionally to the outer coast.

[Veery *Catharus fuscescens*]

Vagrant, perhaps an overshoot from eastern Oregon breeding areas, although it was a little early for such a bird. One sight record, May 31, 2003 on Skinner Butte in Eugene (Ted Floyd, p.c.; *Quail*).

• Swainson's Thrush *Catharus ustulatus*

Status: Common breeder and migrant. Found in forested areas, especially moist riparian zones; least common in pine stands. Earliest spring reports are typically in the last few days of Apr., with a major influx in the first half of May. The earliest known arrival in Oregon was Apr. 2, 1972 in Eugene (Marshall et al. 2003). After they stop singing in late summer, difficult to detect except as calling nocturnal migrants.

Postbreeding movements begin in July (banding data *fide* D. Farrar). Significant southbound movement begins in late Aug., with a steady movement in much of Sep.; peak of passage is the middle half of Sep. Irregular to very early Oct. Recent sight records by experienced observers have been as late as Oct. 4, 2000 and Oct 2, 2003. Stragglers with reasonably certain identification have occurred to Oct. 24, 1996 (bird in hand, Eugene), and more doubtful sight records are made through Nov., when confusion with duller subspecies of Hermit Thrush is likely. This problem with Hermit Thrush also applies to early records in spring.

Distribution: Countywide; least common in pure lodgepole pine stands along the Cascade crest.

• Hermit Thrush *Catharus guttatus*

Status: Fairly common breeder and migrant. Breeders are found primarily in high-elevation coniferous forests, including small stands and fairly open stands. Winter birds are found mainly in dense wooded or shrub cover, with concentrations on the outer coast and fewer in the interior valleys. Lane Co. breeders winter to the south; birds wintering in Lane Co. are from

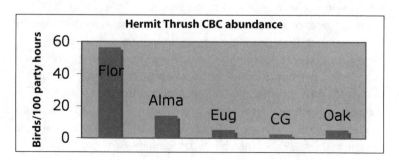

Alaska and Canada (Marshall et al. 2003). Winter population size varies somewhat from year to year.

Spring movements are obscured by the presence of wintering birds, but some movement occurs by late Mar., continuing through May. Breeding birds generally depart higher elevations by early Sep.; wintering birds arrive mainly from late Sep. through Oct.

Distribution: Breeders: mostly above 2000 feet in the Cascades, more common at higher elevations. Mainly on higher ridgelines in the Coast Range, but increasingly in lower habitats there (T. Mickel, p.c.). Winter: found mostly in coastal parks and campgrounds with dense cover, but present in small numbers throughout lowlands.

• American Robin *Turdus migratorius*

Status: Common to abundant breeder, migrant, and winter resident. Uses a wide variety of semi-open habitats, breeding in towns as well as woodlands and open forests to timberline. Tends to avoid drier areas. Seasonal movements can be quite noticeable, with local breeders moving south or to the lowlands while more northerly populations enter the area for winter, sometimes in large flocks. However, these movements are poorly understood.

Distribution: Countywide, with breeders at all elevations up to timberline and winter birds mainly in lowlands.

• Varied Thrush *Ixoreus naevius*

Status: Uncommon widespread breeder, uncommon to abundant in winter, mainly at lower elevations. Arrives in lowlands from mid-Sep. to early Oct., varies somewhat from year to year. Departs for montane areas by mid-Apr. to early May. Uses dense coniferous forests and woodlands, rarely found far from heavy cover, unlike the robin. Often feeds in dense ground litter underneath evergreens, barely visible in the dim light. In winter, also found in orchards and urban yards with dense cover and a food source. Most active in winter at dawn; can be exceptionally quiet and hard to find during the day.

Winter numbers vary from year to year for reasons that are not well known. Some birds may be from more northerly populations.

Distribution: Countywide as a breeder, except on the valley floor and lower foothills. Most common above 3000 feet in the Cascades; uncommon and more local in the Coast Range, where it occurs mainly on higher ridges with older trees. Absent as a breeder from valleys within the Coast Range and on the coastal plain, except where stands of older conifers reach the coastline. Uncommon in the pine belt along the Cascade summit, found mainly where fir or spruce are intermixed.

Sites: Widespread above valley floor.

Family Timaliidae

• **Wrentit** *Chamaea fasciata*

Status: Common but hard to see in dense coastal scrub such as thickets of salal, salmonberry, or blackberry. Also found inland in early-stage regenerating clear-cuts with dense brush cover, and locally in dense shrubby areas. No seasonal movements, but some dispersal in Aug., which results in birds appearing briefly in unusual habitat such as urban yards.

Distribution: From the outer coast eastward to the Cascades. Generally absent from the open valley floor. In eastern Lane Co., found mainly from the McKenzie Valley southward. Mostly at lower elevations in the western Cascades; rare but regular eastward into the western high Cascades, mainly in regenerating clear-cuts and natural brush fields. Absent from the Cascade summit ridges. By the mid-20th century it had been reported from Cottage Grove, Walterville, and Crow; today it is more widespread and the range continues to expand.

Sites: Coastal parks with dense shrubbery have the most birds that are easily accessible; Zumwalt Park at Fern Ridge Res.

*Common but hard to see:
a Wrentit emerges. Photo
near Florence by Diane
Pettey.*

Family Mimidae

Gray Catbird *Dumetella carolinensis*

Vagrant. Two records: July 17-20, 1997 near Westfir (Don Munson et al.; *Quail*) and at the Dog Pond along South Jetty Rd. near Florence, Sep. 4, 2005 (A. Contreras, H. Reinhard). A report on Oct. 12, 1964 in Eugene (*AFN* 19: 70) has been withdrawn by the observer.

Northern Mockingbird *Mimus polyglottos*

Status: Rare but regular wanderer to the county, mainly in fall and winter. Records from every month, rarest in summer (only 2 July records). Has not bred.

Distribution: Most records are from cities and towns on the valley floor or from the outer coast, with a number from Fern Ridge Res. One record at Oakridge, 1980 CBC.

Sage Thrasher *Oreoscoptes montanus*

Casual wanderer from eastern Oregon. About a dozen records, all but one since 1950, from Mar. through July; 7 mid- to late Apr. records represent the peak of occurrence. One Dec. 20-21, 2003 on K. R. Nielson Rd. south of Fern Ridge Res. is the only winter record.

All records are from the Willamette Valley except for one at Badger Mtn. near Noti on May 1, 1980 (T. Mickel) and one collected near Oakridge on July 6, 1916 (UO 1,925).

Sage Thrasher: K. R. Nielson Rd., West Eugene, Dec. 21, 2003. Photo by Noah K. Strycker.

* Brown Thrasher *Toxostoma rufum*
Vagrant. One record, June 13, 1993 in Springfield (OBRC 705-93-17).

Family Sturnidae

• (I) European Starling *Sturnus vulgaris*
Status: Abundant introduced species. First appeared in 1947, common by 1949. Most common in urban areas and agricultural lands. Generally absent in dense forests, rare in subalpine areas. Most withdraw from higher elevations in winter, forming large flocks in the valley lowlands and locally on the outer coast.
Distribution: Countywide. Very local in the western and high Cascades owing to the lack of suitable cavities for nesting.
Sites: Widespread pest.

Family Motacillidae

** Eastern Yellow Wagtail *Motacilla tschutschensis*
Vagrant. One sight record: Aug. 31, 1997 at the mouth of the Siltcoos R. (Hendrik Herlyn, Rich Hoyer; OBRC 696-97-01). First Oregon record.

* White Wagtail *Motacilla alba*
Vagrant. One record, of the *lugens* subspecies formerly called Black-backed Wagtail (Banks et al. 2005), Feb. 3 through Mar. 31, 1974 in the parking lot at Autzen Stadium in Eugene (OBRC No. 695.1-74-01). First Oregon record.

[* Red-throated Pipit *Anthus cervinus*]
Vagrant from Asia. Has not yet been definitively reported in the county, but may have occurred and should be sought. Has occurred in Curry and Deschutes Cos. An observer familiar with the species heard the distinctive call note of Red-throated Pipit at the north jetty of the Siuslaw on Sep. 23, 2000 (Steve Summers, p.c.).

• American Pipit *Anthus rubescens*
Status: Rare local breeder above timberline in open areas. Fairly common migrant on open mud flats, large gravel pans, sandy areas, and short-grass areas. More noticeable as a migrant in fall than spring. Small numbers can be seen after late Aug. (earliest Aug. 17, 1946; Gullion) with the major movement beginning in mid-Sep., peaking in late Sep. and early Oct., and not dropping off until the end of Oct., after which small numbers remain to winter. Timing of fall movements varies somewhat from year to year. Spring movements begin early, in late Feb., and are most noticeable in Apr. Rare later in spring; a record on June 5, 2003 at the mouth of the Siltcoos R.

"Black-backed" White Wagtail at Eugene. Photo Feb. 17, 1974 by Larry McQueen.

was probably a late spring migrant rather than a postbreeder.

Distribution: Breeds above timberline, known only from the Three Sisters region and the Diamond Peak area. Countywide in migration, within its rather limited habitat. At higher elevations, fall migrants are usually along muddy lake margins and dry lakebeds. Winters mainly on the Willamette Valley floor and along the outer coast.

Sites: Deflation plain at the Siuslaw south jetty, Fern Ridge Res., Eugene. airport.

Family Bombycillidae

Bohemian Waxwing *Bombycilla garrulus*

Status: Rare irruptive winter visitor, absent most years. Occasionally invades in numbers, more often as a few birds within Cedar Waxwing flocks. Records from mid-Nov. through Mar. Major invasion winters of 1968-69 and 1981-82 brought sizable flocks to the valley floor.

Distribution: Records are from the Willamette Valley floor and nearby lowlands. Rare as far east as Oakridge (2 CBC records, 1976 and 1977). One coastal record, Feb. 21, 1987 at Florence.

• Cedar Waxwing *Bombycilla cedrorum*

Status: Common widespread breeder, fairly common in migration, uncommon to rare and highly local in winter. Uses open woodlands, fruit-tree plantings in towns (especially in winter), riparian deciduous corridors. Seasonal movements are poorly known, but becomes more obvious in spring after mid-Apr., is easily found through the summer and is seen in small flocks through Sep. and locally through Oct.

Distribution: Countywide, rare and local along the Cascade summit, where it is present mainly in deciduous pockets near water. Rare and irregular in winter from the Coast Range westward. Locally common on the valley floor, mainly in flocks and often in plantings bearing fruit. Much less common in winter. Uncommon and irregular eastward in major river valleys (found on 9 of 15 Oakridge CBCs)

Sites: Widespread in summer.

[Family Ptilogonatidae]

* [Phainopepla *Phainopepla nitens*]

There are published reports but no confirmation of this vagrant occurring in Lane Co. in Florence (2002-03) and Eugene (2001).

Family Parulidae

Tennessee Warbler *Vermivora peregrina*

Casual in migration and winter. About a dozen records, mostly in May, Sep., and Dec. One on Aug. 6, 1986 on the Winchester Lake trail in the high Cascades may have summered locally. Oregon is just west of the normal migration route of this species.

• Orange-crowned Warbler *Vermivora celata*

Status: Common breeder and migrant, rare annual winter resident. One bird collected in winter proved to be of the subspecies *V. c. celata* (Gabrielson and Jewett 1940). In breeding season, uses younger open woodlands with dense undergrowth, also montane brushfields and brushy clear-cuts. Winters mainly in heavy undergrowth near water, especially in grassy sumps with red alder, willow, blackberry, and standing water (locally referred to as "kack"). Also winters in dense urban plantings.
Distribution: Breeds countywide, local in pine-dominated areas along the Cascade summit.

• Nashville Warbler *Vermivora ruficapilla*

Status: Uncommon breeder and migrant, very rare and irregular in winter. Breeds on drier brushy hillsides and brushy patches within forested areas. First spring migrants are typically in early Apr., with a small peak in the last half of Apr. Fall movements are quiet and obscure, taking place mostly in the first half of Sep. There are a few winter records from the valley lowlands and the outer coast.
Distribution: Breeds from the Cascade foothills eastward. Does not breed regularly in the Coast Range. Rare breeder in hills south of Eugene. Almost all movement occurs from the valley floor eastward. Rare and irregular as a migrant west of the Willamette Valley.

* Virginia's Warbler *Vermivora virginiae*

Vagrant. Three records: Aug. 9, 1988 in the Coast Range near Mapleton (OBRC 644-88-06); May 5, 1985 in Eugene (Van Truan, p.c., not accepted by the OBRC but included here based on communication with the observer); Nov. 8, 1979 west of Eugene (OBRC 644-79-02).

* Lucy's Warbler *Vermivora luciae*

Vagrant. One record, Oregon's first, on the North Fork of the Siuslaw R. from Dec. 27, 1986 through Jan. 25, 1987 (Bond 1987, OBRC 643-86-01).

Northern Parula *Parula americana*

Vagrant. Two records: Aug. 21, 1993 at Florence (D. Arendt) and June 23, 2002 on the Herman Cape Rd. north of Florence (D. Pettey, K. Hollinga).

• Yellow Warbler *Dendroica petechia*

Status: Uncommon to locally common breeder, uncommon migrant, absent in winter. Found mainly in riparian areas with dense undergrowth, especially willows. Arrival is typically in late Apr., but early outriders are fairly regular from the beginning of Apr.; the earliest known is from Mar. 18, 1989 (B. Combs). Numbers drop beginning in late Aug., after which migrants can be found, mainly through mid-Sep., with stragglers to very early Oct., mainly coastal.

Distribution: Most breeders are east of the Coast Range, with greatest densities around Fern Ridge Res. and locally along major rivers. Rare at higher elevations in the Cascades, where limited mainly to lakeshores. Rare and local on the outer coast as a breeder. Migrates countywide in riparian corridors, wetland shrubbery, towns.

Sites: Easy to see at the boardwalk nature trail on the west side of Perkins Peninsula Park at Fern Ridge Res.

Yellow Warbler. Illustration by Barbara Gleason.

Chestnut-sided Warbler *Dendroica pensylvanica*
Vagrant, 2 records: Sep. 15, 1981 (OBRC 659-81-10) and May 26-31, 1979 (OBRC 659-79-05), both at Florence.

* Magnolia Warbler *Dendroica magnolia*
Vagrant, 2 records: Apr. 25, 1991 at Blue R. Ranger District in the Cascades (OBRC 657-91-18), and June 4, 1981 in the Coast Range (OBRC No. 657-81-05).

• Yellow-rumped Warbler *Dendroica coronata*
Status: Common widespread breeder and migrant; uncommon to abundant local winter resident. Breeds in older coniferous forests. Winters in evergreen thickets (especially wax myrtle) on the outer coast, locally inland at low elevations. Most abundant (though very local) in winter, widespread at relatively low densities in summer.

Distribution: The two populations in Lane Co. are "Audubon's" Warbler, the yellow-throated subspecies that breeds, and "Myrtle" Warbler, the white-throated subspecies that winters mainly on the outer coast.

Audubon's Warbler breeds countywide except on the open valley floor, with peak numbers in higher-elevation coniferous forests and smaller numbers breeding locally to the outer coast. Least common and very local in the Coast Range. It migrates countywide and winters in small numbers, mainly at inland locations but in small numbers on the coast. Fall migrants move earlier than do Myrtles, peaking in late Sep. Spring migrants are obvious by late Mar., peaking in Apr.

Myrtle Warblers arrive in Lane Co. (mainly on the outer coast) after mid-Sep., peaking in Oct., after which significant numbers winter, mainly within a mile or two of the coast, or farther inland if there is good cover, especially broadleaf evergreens such as wax myrtle. Spring departure dates for coastal Myrtle Warblers are poorly known but are probably during Apr.

• Black-throated Gray Warbler *Dendroica nigrescens*
Status: Uncommon but widespread breeder and migrant. Mainly uses the edges of coniferous and mixed coniferous-deciduous forests. Arrives fairly early in spring, with outriders sometimes found in the last few days of Mar. and a major movement in early to mid-Apr. Southbound movements are apparent from late Aug. through mid-Sep., with small numbers found through mid-Oct. with some regularity. Very rare migrant through early Dec., may have wintered (L. McQueen).

Distribution: Breeds countywide, least common along the Cascade summit in pine-dominated forests. Late fall migrants are mainly coastal.

Black-throated Green Warbler Dendroica virens

Vagrant. Two records: Dec. 7-14, 2001 in Eugene (OBRC 667-01-10) and May 10, 1978 in Eugene (Larry McQueen).

• Townsend's Warbler *Dendroica townsendi*

Status: Uncommon breeder, migrant, and winter resident. Found largely in coniferous forests, using older trees in summer and a variety of age classes in winter. Migration patterns are poorly understood owing to the overlapping movements of different populations. Montane breeders are at the southern limit of their range and their arrival dates are essentially unknown, but probably during early May, which is when northbound birds reach sites in eastern Oregon. Some interbreeding with Hermit Warbler occurs. A hybrid specimen was collected June 27, 1998 along Roaring R. Ridge near Oakridge (UW 60,419).

Coastal wintering birds are thought to originate with breeding populations on the Queen Charlotte Islands, British Columbia (Marshall et al. 2003). They appear to arrive fairly late in fall, perhaps in mid-Oct., but actual reports from the outer coast are few until CBC season in Dec. Cascade breeders begin moving out of breeding areas by mid-Aug., but appear to use montane rather than coastal routes.

Distribution: Countywide as a migrant, though not often encountered in migration. Breeders occur in the high Cascades, usually in small numbers, south at least to Waldo Lake and the Diamond Peak area. Winter birds are most common on the outer coast, where single birds are often embedded in flocks of kinglets and chickadees. Pure flocks of Townsend's Warblers sometimes occur, with counts of up to 30 birds near Florence (rarely). Much less regular in winter in the Coast Range (Alma CBC 2/11) and the western Cascades (Oakridge CBC 2/15). Regular in small numbers on the valley floor in winter, usually embedded in flocks of chickadees and kinglets, occasionally in small flocks (up to 20 birds). One found June 14, 2002 along the lower Siltcoos R. was unexpected and was probably a nonbreeder or very late northbound migrant.

Sites: Somewhat local, but when located tend to remain in the same area in winter. A couple usually winter on the UO campus in Eugene, typically north of 13th St. or in the cemetery. Breeders are uncommon but are sometimes seen in the McKenzie Pass or at Gold or Waldo lakes.

• **Hermit Warbler** *Dendroica occidentalis*
Status: Common widespread breeder, uncommon migrant. Found mainly in older coniferous forests, especially dense Douglas-fir with complex understories. Also uses younger coniferous forests (fir or mixed fir-lodgepole pine) with less understory. Very rare in winter, almost always in flocks of Townsend's Warblers. About 5 winter records since 1970; one spent the winter of 1983-84 in Pioneer Cemetery in Eugene.

First arrivals are typically in early Apr., but significant movements occur mainly in late Apr. and very early May. Three birds found near Eugene in Mar. 2000 may have been local winterers or very early spring migrants. Departs fairly early; fall movements are poorly known but appear to be largely at higher elevations during late Aug. and very early Sep. Stragglers are rare later in fall; the most recent was Oct. 3, 2000.

Distribution: Countywide except in the valley lowlands and in the coastal pine belt. Most common in the Coast Range and the Cascades, especially the middle elevations below the summit ridges.

Palm Warbler *Dendroica palmarum*
Status: Rare but regular fall migrant, rare and less regular in winter. One singing bird July 25-26, 1974 at Jasper Park (Dan Gleason, George Jobanek, L. McQueen, ENHS) was very unusual, one of only 3 midsummer records from the state (not mentioned in Marshall et al. 2003). Has been found as early as Sep. 5 (Siltcoos R. in 2000, Oregon's earliest fall report), but typically arrives in early Oct. (2-3 birds a year). Single birds are occasionally found in winter, mainly around Florence (CBC 4/21) but occasionally on the valley floor (Stewart Pond wetlands in west Eugene, Fern Ridge Res., Alton Baker Park, and near Junction City). Spring movements are hard to detect, but 3 records in mid-Apr. (Florence [2] and Eugene) suggest that this may be the time that they move.

Distribution: Mainly on the outer coast, with a few records on the Willamette Valley floor. Early arrivals are typically very close to the ocean (e.g., along South Jetty Rd.), winter birds are usually farther inland (e.g., the edges of Old Town Florence), suggesting that birds work their way inland into what is usually better habitat as the season moves along.

Sites: Most regular (fall) in shrubs near the south jetty, Florence.

Blackpoll Warbler *Dendroica striata*
Vagrant or casual fall migrant. Four records: Sep. 27, 2000 at McKenzie Pass; Sep. 30, 1999 at Scott Lake near McKenzie Pass; Sep. 15, 1988 at Kirk Park below Fern Ridge Dam (OBRC No. 661-88-21); and July 21, 1983 at Florence (M. Markley, OB), an unusual time of year but seen by an experienced observer. In addition, a warbler arriving off the ocean at the mouth of the

Siltcoos R. on Sep. 20, 2003 was almost certainly of this species (H. Herlyn, A. Contreras). This species may occur with greater regularity than is actually reported.

Black-and-white Warbler *Mniotilta varia*
Vagrant or casual fall migrant and winter visitor. At least 7 records: Sep. 22, 2002 in Santa Clara; Sep. 6, 2001 in Springfield; Sep. 5, 1994 at Skinner Butte; Aug. 19, 1994 at the lower Siltcoos R.; July 9, 1994 at Bloomberg Park near Lane Community College; Feb. 25 through Apr. 8, 1989 at Skinner Butte (NAB 43:530); and Sep. or possibly Oct 1970 in the University of Oregon cemetery (Clarice Watson).

American Redstart *Setophaga ruticilla*
Casual visitor. Three records: June 13, 2005 below Hills Creek Dam (D. Farrar, V. Arnold, P. Sherrell, D. Arendt); June 27, 2003 near Creswell (Hydie Lown, Sally Nelson); and Dec. 28, 1997 at the University of Oregon (Kit Larsen).

Ovenbird *Seiurus aurocapilla*
Vagrant. Three records: June 10, 2003 along Cape Mtn. Rd. north of Florence; June 11, 1995 at Elmira; and May 31, 1992 along Rd. 770 off Mill Creek Rd., McKenzie R. Valley (Matt Hunter).

• Northern Waterthrush *Seiurus noveboracensis*
Rare and extremely local breeder, casual migrant. One or two pairs usually breed east of Salt Creek Falls (Mule Prairie) in dense willow riparian habitat. They have used this area since at least 1983 (Larry McQueen, p.c. and published records). Birds typically do not appear at the site until early June and depart by the end of July. However, they are essentially impossible to locate after they stop singing in very early July. A singing bird was found near the confluence of Skookum Cr. and the North Fork of the Middle Fork of the Willamette R. in the early 1990s (Marshall et al. 2003).

Not reported in migration. One was at the Lily Lake swamp along Baker Beach Rd. north of Florence on Oct. 19 and Nov. 30, 2002 (N. Strycker et al., Quail, OB) and probably wintered in the area.
Sites: Salt Creek east of the falls (Mule Prairie).

** Mourning Warbler *Oporornis philadelphia*
Vagrant. One record: July 12, 1984 at Hills Creek Reservoir (OBRC 679-84-02).

• MacGillivray's Warbler *Oporornis tolmiei*
Status: Common breeder and migrant, very rare winter holdover. Breeds in dense shrubs, generally near water but sometimes on hillsides, and in brushy clear-cuts. First arrivals are in early Apr., with the bulk of movement

in mid- to late Apr. and early May. Fall departure is mainly in Sep.; by the end of the month very few can be found. However, stragglers sometimes occur late in fall, e.g., Oct. 4, 2003 and Nov. 14, 1986 (the latter in Florence). The winter records are extraordinary but some are well documented. A female wintered near Stewart Pond in west Eugene from Dec. 28, 2001 through Feb. 22, 2002 (Marshall et al. 2003). One was seen Feb. 21, 2002 at the Owosso bridge along the Willamette R. (Quail). One was at Meadowlark Prairie wetlands west of Eugene on Dec. 29, 2001 (Quail). In Jan., 1969, one was found in a Eugene building (L. McQueen, ENHS). Two were reported in Eugene on Dec. 31, 1967.

Distribution: Countywide. Very few can be found on the valley floor in summer. Local in the high Cascades, mostly along watercourses, in shrub growth in wet meadows, and in brushy clear-cuts. Late fall records mainly coastal.

• **Common Yellowthroat** *Geothlypis trichas*

Status: Common to abundant breeder in marshes and moist tall-grass habitats. Arrives early in spring, with outriders in late Mar. and significant movements in very early Apr. Abundant on territory by mid-Apr. Generally departs rather late, fairly easy to find through Oct. in preferred habitat, and stragglers into early winter are rare but regular. Several winter records, mainly at Fern Ridge Res.

Distribution: Largely from the valley floor and the lower McKenzie and Middle Fork Willamette westward, with pockets of occurrence upstream where habitat allows, and locally at montane lakes and seasonally wet meadows. Most abundant around Fern Ridge Res., other marshes on the valley floor, and in coastal marshes.

* Hooded Warbler *Wilsonia citrina*

Vagrant, one record: July 20-21, 1974 at Washburne Wayside Park north of Junction City (OBRC No. 684-74-01).

• Wilson's Warbler *Wilsonia pusilla*

Status: Common breeder and migrant, very rare winter holdover. Found mainly in riparian undergrowth where taller trees such as red alder and maple are found. Widespread but less abundant in upland sites with dense undergrowth and some tree cover.

This species has one of the most extended spring migrations of any Lane Co. bird. Arrives fairly early, with outriders as early as very late Mar. and a steady movement of small numbers through mid-Apr. Peak of passage begins in late Apr., but sometimes extends well into May. A few birds can even be found moving through nonbreeding habitat in early June, mainly at higher elevations. Departs in fall in a rather leisurely fashion from mid-Aug. through mid-Sep., with a thin movement sometimes continuing through late Sep. and stragglers regular in Oct. Rare to midwinter, with the latest record Jan. 2, 1993 at Eugene.

Distribution: Countywide, with highest densities in the Coast Range, along coastal streams and in the western Cascades. Fairly common on the valley floor where habitat allows, uncommon and local along the Cascade summit ridges.

* [Canada Warbler *Wilsonia canadensis*]

Vagrant. A female was reported May 4, 1973 in Walterville by George Jobanek (Jobanek 1973). The record occurred several years before the establishment of the OBRC and has not been reviewed.

• Yellow-breasted Chat *Icteria virens*

Status: Uncommon and local breeder and migrant. Found in dense brush and riparian tangles mainly at lower elevations. Among the latest spring migrants, with movement not starting until early May (rarely late Apr.), and most birds not arriving until mid- to late May. Does not remain long, as they generally cannot be found after late Aug. Fall movements are essentially invisible, owing in part to the species' habitat preferences: a silent chat is an invisible chat. The only recent reports are Sep. 12, 2001, Sep. 17, 2003 at Lane Community College, and Sep. 20, 2002 near Creswell. Gullion lists Sep. 30, 1940 as the latest mid-20th-century date.

Although the species is thought of as a summer-only resident, there are 2 winter records and 1 very early spring report. One wintered at Florence from Dec. 27, 2001 through Jan. 28, 2002 (photo, Contreras 2003a). Another was at Dexter on Feb. 15, 1973. See Supplemental Records.

Distribution: Mainly in the lower valleys. Found from the central Coast Range (local) eastward to about 1200 feet along the McKenzie and Middle Fork of the Willamette, depending on the availability of habitat. Some habitat that looks adequate is not used, even in the heart of the Willamette Valley. Absent from the coastal slope except as a rare wanderer. Also absent from the higher Cascades; bred in recent years as far east as Hills Creek dam.

Sites: Behind Lane Community College (not currently accessible), east side trail at Mt. Pisgah, Bloomberg Park, Fisher Butte at Fern Ridge Res.

Family Thraupidae

• **Western Tanager** *Piranga ludoviciana*
Status: Common breeder and migrant, very rare in winter. Breeds mainly in coniferous forests; migrants can be found in any wooded area. The main movement begins in late Apr., but builds through mid-May. Occasionally found as early as late Mar. (earliest Mar. 16, 1972). Fall movements are inconspicuous and extend through Sep., with a few stragglers in Oct. and rarely into early winter. Latest recent records were Oct. 8, 2003 and Oct. 31, 2005 (S. Gordon, p.c.). One was in Eugene on Dec. 30, 1973 (*ENHS*). CBC records include one at Florence Dec. 17, 2001 and singles at Eugene in 1983 and 1995.

Distribution: Countywide. Least common on the valley floor where habitat is limited (but occurs there during migration), and on the outer coast, where it generally does not breed in shore pines.

Family Emberizidae

• **Green-tailed Towhee** *Pipilo chlorurus*
Status: Very rare local breeder. Absent in migration except at breeding sites.

Distribution: Mainly in the extreme southeastern corner of the county along the Cascade summit ridges near Waldo Lake and Emigrant Pass where dry brushfields are available. Recent records are Aug. 25, 2002 at the Rigdon Lake trailhead in North Waldo Burn (Taylor Burn); Aug. 24, 2002 at Waldo Lake; Aug. 28, 2000 at Horsepasture Mtn. east of Cougar Res.; Aug. 10, 1999 at Craig Lake near McKenzie Pass; and Sep. 20, 1997 at Marilyn Lakes near Gold Lake. Most of the records are in a time period that suggests a regular small-scale postbreeding movement across the Cascade summit. Bred in the 1980s in the Emigrant Pass region but current status there is unclear.

The only lowland records of wanderers are May 29, 2005 and Mar. 25, 2000, both at Skinner Butte, and one caught by a cat in June 1971 (*ENHS*) near the South Willamette Dump (no longer in operation, off W. 52nd Ave in south Eugene).

• Spotted Towhee *Pipilo maculatus*
Status: Common breeding resident, migrant, and very common winter resident. Several populations involved. Local breeding birds (*P.m.oregonus*) are widespread but not abundant, using dense brushy cover, often on the edges of forests. Migrants, possibly including other subspecies, appear in a variety of brushy habitats. Winter populations are quite high in good cover in valley lowlands, with few remaining in montane regions.
Distribution: Countywide; uncommon and local in the high Cascades where habitat is limited.

[California Towhee *Pipilo crissalis*]
Casual wanderer from southwest interior Oregon. One unconfirmed sight record on July 15, 1998 at Mt. Pisgah. This is appropriate habitat but the bird could not be relocated.

American Tree Sparrow *Spizella arborea*
Status: Rare irregular winter visitor. Present every 2-3 years, usually one or two birds. Found in lowland sparrow flocks in grassy areas with some small shrubs. All but three records from early Nov. through early Mar. Three exceptional records: Oct. 6, 2005 at the Dotterel Dike near Florence, possibly the earliest fall record for Oregon (A. Contreras); May 15, 1971 at Eugene (Clare Watson); and May 17, 1947 at Thurston (Gullion).
Distribution: Largely the valley floor; very rare on the outer coast (Florence CBC: 1/ 21).
Sites: Irregular, most around Fern Ridge Res.

• Chipping Sparrow *Spizella passerina*
Status: Common but declining breeder and migrant, rare in winter. Mainly in open areas within woodlands, forest edges, oak savannah. Arrives early in spring, with a noteworthy movement in late Mar. Remains through mid-autumn, with many Oct. records. Rare in winter; Eugene CBC finds it about 1 year in 6. Often found in filbert orchards in winter, for reasons that are not known.

Note: The similar Clay-colored Sparrow is about as likely in winter as is Chipping Sparrow.
Distribution: Mostly in the Willamette Valley and its adjacent foothills, with small numbers present locally in the Cascades and Coast Range

where open grassy habitat is available within forested areas. Rare on the outer coast at all seasons. A Spizella sparrow seen on the outer coast in fall or winter may well be a Clay-colored.

Sites: Widespread. Often easy to see at Perkins Peninsula Park and the east side of Mt. Pisgah.

Clay-colored Sparrow *Spizella pallida*

Status: Casual fall and winter visitor, about 10 records. Two records are from Sep., 6 from midwinter. The latest in spring is Apr. 2, 1996 at Florence.

Distribution: Valley lowlands and the outer coast. Sometimes found with other sparrows but also with juncos and by itself.

• Brewer's Sparrow *Spizella breweri*

Status: Rare irregular breeder, rare but regular fall migrant. Highly local. Uses open brushlands and low shrubbery; its preferred sagebrush is not available in Lane Co.

Distribution: Rare irregular breeder in the extreme southeastern corner of the county near Emigrant Pass. May be dependent on the availability of regenerating clear-cuts. One was at Fall Creek dam on Mar. 31, 2004, and one at Lane Community College on Apr. 29, 2002. Probably bred at Fern Ridge Res. (singing bird found May 23, 1972, *ENHS*) and probably bred again in 1985 (Heinl 1986). Found again there in May 2003.

Irregular early fall migrant in very small numbers on the east side of Fern Ridge Res. (Royal Ave.), where it must be distinguished with care from Chipping Sparrows. Also found in fall at Hills Creek Res. (3 birds on Aug. 27, 2004).

Sites: Irregular. Check Royal Ave. gate area in late summer.

• Vesper Sparrow *Pooecetes gramineus*

Status: Uncommon breeder and migrant, very rare irregular winter resident. Found in grasslands, overgrown pastures, tree farms. Arrives fairly early, within a few days either side of Apr. 1. Hard to find after Aug., with no distinct fall migratory movement, but there are several records from Sep. to Nov. 1 at Mt. Pisgah (D. DeWitt, p.c.). Very rare in winter, the only recent records are Jan. 11, 2004 and Dec. 17, 1998 at Fern Ridge Res., and Feb. 20, 1997 at the Creswell sewage ponds.

Distribution: Willamette Valley floor and adjacent lower foothills where habitat is available. Essentially absent from the Cascades, Coast Range and outer coast.

Sites: Fairly regular along Cantrell Rd. south of Fern Ridge Res.; east side of Mt. Pisgah.

Lark Sparrow: South Eugene High School track, May 4, 2003. Photo by Noah K. Strycker.

Lark Sparrow *Chondestes grammacus*

Status: This species reaches the edge of its breeding range in southwest Oregon and has occasionally bred in Douglas Co. It occasionally appears in Lane Co. but has not bred. Has occurred in every season, but roughly half of the 20+ records have been between Apr. 15 and May 23. In early May of 1992, flocks of 2 and 6 birds appeared at Tokatee Golf Course and in the "central Cascades," respectively. A recent record Apr. 30, 2004 at Hills Creek Res. suggests that better coverage of montane openings in spring would reveal a pattern of occurrence.

The earliest record in spring was Mar. 8, 1998. One late fall record, Nov. 26, 1983 at Heceta Head (*NAB* 38:239) is one of only two from the coast; the other was Sep. 20, 1997. It may be worth noting that these are the only fall records for the county (latest in summer is Aug. 17, 1948, Gullion). Very rare in winter, and not recently: 2 records on the Eugene CBC, Dec. 30, 1945 and Dec. 29, 1946.

Distribution: Mainly the Willamette Valley floor and montane openings.

Black-throated Sparrow. Mercer Lake, north of Florence, Apr. 26, 1977. Photo by Edith Diehnel.

Black-throated Sparrow
Amphispiza bilineata

Status:Casual spring migrant, presumably overshoots from populations in the Great Basin. Eleven records between Apr. 26 and June 19, 9 of which are from May, mostly the first half of the month.

Distribution: Records have come from all over the county, mainly at lower elevations.

Sage Sparrow *Amphispiza belli*

Casual spring migrant. Five records: Mar. 26, 2002 along Edenvale Rd. near Pleasant Hill; Apr. 26-27, 1996 in the West Coyote Unit south of Fern Ridge Res.; Apr. 14, 1984 at Fern Ridge Res.; Apr. 26, 1976 (location not known); and Apr. 27, 1973 at Roosevelt Middle School, Eugene, singing from a softball backstop (Sayre Greenfield, p.c.).

*Lark Bunting *Calamospiza melanocorys*

Vagrant. Three records: June 11-30, 2001 along Cantrell Rd. south of Fern Ridge Res. (OBRC 605-01-19); Aug. 26, 1992 at Florence (Dave Stejskal, Joe Kaplan); and June 17, 1983 at Bob Creek Wayside along Hwy. 101 north of Florence (OBRC 605-83-04). One observed along Gimpl Hill Rd. southwest of Eugene on June 21, 2001 (Joan Bray) may have been a different bird than the one on Cantrell Rd. several miles to the west, since the Cantrell bird remained in the area.

Lark Bunting south of Fern Ridge Reservoir, June 2001. Photo by Owen Schmidt.

• Savannah Sparrow *Passerculus sandwichensis*

Status: Common to locally abundant breeder and migrant. Locally common winter resident. Uses grasslands, the drier parts of marshes, overgrown pastures. Also uses beach grass, especially in migration.

This species has a complex pattern of occurrence in the county. Breeding birds in the Willamette Valley and the outer coast are *brooksi*; breeders along the southern Cascade summit (rare and local in Lane Co.) are probably *nevadensis*, although the true status of these populations is poorly known. Spring movements are heavy and highly compressed, involving a huge surge, especially along the outer coast, in late Apr., with only minor movement before or after this period. These are probably more northerly breeding populations. Fall movements are likewise somewhat compressed into mid-Sep.

Winter populations are quite limited and local. Uncommon to rare on the outer coast, almost exclusively in beach grass on and behind the outer dune line. Uncommon but sometimes locally abundant on the Willamette Valley floor, where it often forms sizable flocks (20-100+ birds) in winter. **Distribution**: Willamette Valley floor and the outer coast; rare in montane wetlands as a migrant and possible local breeder. **Sites**: Easy to observe from late spring through early fall on the east side of Fern Ridge Res. Winters in variable numbers along the access road north from the Fisher Unit parking lot at Fern Ridge Res.

• **Grasshopper Sparrow** *Ammodramus savannarum*

Status: Rare local breeder, very rare in winter. Undetected as a migrant. Found in open grasslands with a few small shrubs; quite selective about its habitat. Present in breeding areas from early May through mid-Aug.; essentially undetectable when it is not singing.

One mid-autumn record: Oct. 26, 2000 at Fern Ridge Res. Four winter records: 1982, 1991, and 1992 on the Eugene CBC; the latter 2 near areas where they breed. The bird found Jan. 1-9, 1982 (Marshall et al. 2003, OB) in Alton Baker Park was later found dead (SD 41,684). Another was found at Fern Ridge Res. on Jan. 10, 2004.

Distribution: The breeding population is mainly along the east shore of Fern Ridge Res. Occasionally occupies other breeding areas, e.g., along Cantrell Rd., depending on habitat conditions. One was found singing in June 1996 near Coburg. **Sites**: Local on east side of Fern Ridge Res.

• **Fox Sparrow** *Passerella iliaca*

Status: Uncommon local breeder, common to locally abundant in winter. Breeders occur in montane brushfields, often associated with regeneration after fires or clear-cuts. Winter birds are mainly in low-elevation undergrowth, especially salal, salmonberry, and blackberry thickets.

Breeding birds are probably part of the *megarhyncha/fulva* complex, which arrives in breeding areas by mid-Apr. and remains through early Sep.

Winter birds are almost all from the chocolate-brown *fuliginosa/chilcatensis* group that breeds in Alaska and British Columbia. These begin arriving in small numbers in the second half of Sep., with the bulk of arrivals starting around Oct. 1. The earliest fall report of a dark northern migrant in recent years was Aug. 26, 2000. They remain until late Apr., by which time numbers begin to drop. The latest recent date for a wintering lowland bird is May 7, 2003. Red forms (*iliaca* group, an OBRC review subspecies) are rarely reported and are not annual.

Distribution: Breeders are found in the higher parts of the Cascades where there are sizable brushy openings in forested areas. Winter birds are found throughout the lowlands, Coast Range, and outer coast, with significant numbers reaching into the western Cascades along the McKenzie Valley east to McKenzie Bridge and the Middle Fork of the Willamette at least to Oakridge. Greatest densities of winter birds are along the outer coast and nearby coastal hills. These populations are sometimes the densest on the continent in winter, based on CBC data.

• Song Sparrow *Melospiza melodia*

Status: Common to locally abundant widespread resident (*morphna*). Found in dense undergrowth in a variety of settings from the edges of marshes to openings in high elevation forests. Some influx of northern birds (*caurina* from southern Alaska and possibly others) occurs in fall, especially on the outer coast, where they can sometimes be found foraging along jetties, perhaps having just arrived. Winter numbers are also augmented by what are thought to be downslope movements, although this is poorly understood.

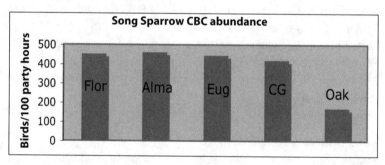

Distribution: Countywide in the breeding season, including urban areas where habitat is sufficient.

Least common in summer at very high elevations, where open pine-dominated forests with little undergrowth do not provide much habitat. In winter, few are at higher elevations, but densities on the valley floor and in coastal lowlands can be very high and are similar from the coast to the Cascade foothills, one of few species of which this is true.

• Lincoln's Sparrow *Melospiza lincolnii*

Status: Uncommon and local breeder (*lincolnii*), uncommon and local in winter (*gracilis*). In summer, breeds in high-elevation bogs with a mix of emergent vegetation, generally wet meadows with patches of willows. Winters in lowland areas with tall grass adjacent to shrubs, brush, blackberries, or similar dense cover, especially if moist. Winter numbers vary somewhat from year to year.

Migrants typically arrive in small numbers after early Sep. (first birds sometimes in the few days of Sep.), with a major push at the end of Sep. They move out during late Apr. and early May. The latest recent report was May 7, 2005 (V. Arnold, p.c.). Arrival on montane territories is generally unobserved owing to snowpack, but is probably in early May, with fall movements apparently at high elevations into Sep., and generally unreported until migrants reach the lowlands in mid- to late Sep.

Distribution: Breeds locally along the Cascade crest at Gold Lake Bog and other wet meadows, sparingly north near the Cascade summit in similar settings. Rare to lower elevations, breeds very locally in the higher western Cascades. Winters almost entirely on the floor of the Willamette Valley and in adjacent major river valleys; also winters in the Siuslaw Valley and sparingly in coastal bogs with sufficient grass cover.

Sites: Fisher Butte grasslands in winter.

Swamp Sparrow *Melospiza georgiana*

Status: Rare migrant and winter visitor, casual in late spring. Found in grassy sumps with standing water, often with dense brush adjacent. Arrives in late Oct. or early Nov. Generally absent after early Mar., but actual spring departure unknown. The latest recent reports were Apr. 1, 1990 and Apr. 4, 1987. One singing territorial bird in a bog in Mule Prairie along Salt Creek east of the falls on May 17, 1992 (Marshall et al. 2003) is anomalous.

Distribution: Mainly coastal lowlands and around Fern Ridge Res., but a few reports elsewhere from the valley floor. Quite selective about habitat.

Sites: Most regular in sumps near Fern Ridge Res. and around Florence.

White-throated Sparrow *Zonotrichia albicollis*

Status: Uncommon to rare migrant and winter resident. Found mainly in the edges of open woodlands where there is some brushy area or open space nearby, but sometimes found in relatively dense deciduous wooded areas. Arrival is extended. First arrivals typically in the first week of Oct., but few are seen until Nov., when the principal pulse seems to arrive. Timing of the arrival of noticeable numbers varies from year to year, as does the number of birds involved, perhaps because of weather or food conditions to the northeast. It is unusual in Sep., but in 1973 several arrived on Sep. 22 (*ENHS*) and one was reported Sep. 30, 2000.

Departs during Apr.; occasional stragglers to the first 10 days of May. The latest record known is May 27, 1996 at Skinner Butte (A. Prigge, p.c.). Sometimes moves out of wintering areas before departing, singing from unlikely places for a day or two. Winter numbers vary somewhat from year to year; sometimes forms small flocks of fewer than half a dozen birds.

Distribution: Countywide at lower elevations, with most birds on the valley floor or the outer coast and lower Siuslaw Valley.

Sites: Local. Often visits bird feeders.

Harris's Sparrow *Zonotrichia querula*

Status: Rare irregular winter visitor. Not quite annual. Typically found with other *Zonotrichia* sparrows or juncos, tending to stay near trees and willing to fly high into them in the manner of a junco, rather than staying fairly low as a White-crowned Sparrow would. When it occurs, generally arrives very late in fall, usually Nov. or early Dec., but sometimes remains fairly late in spring. The earliest recent report was Oct. 11, 1997. Has remained until early May in Lane Co. Elsewhere in Oregon, has remained to late May and even early June.

Distribution: Lowland valleys. Usually does not reach the coast, but has occurred at Florence.

• White-crowned Sparrow *Zonotrichia leucophrys*

Status: Common to abundant breeder (*pugetensis*), migrant, and winter resident. Found in open shrubby areas, generally not in woodlands. Breeds most abundantly in coastal scrub, more locally inland, but fairly common except in the drier part of the high Cascades. Sometimes breeds in residential areas when habitat is available. Significant fall (mainly Sep.) and spring (mainly Apr.) movements involve multiple populations; small numbers of *gambelii* can be found in winter in the county (Marshall et al. 2003).

Distribution: Primarily in lowlands, but locally in clear-cuts in the Coast Range and locally in the Cascades to near timberline. Most common on the coast at all seasons, with some winter concentrations on the Willamette Valley floor. Breeding status in the high Cascades not well known. Reported as a breeder from the Diamond Peak area at 6,000 ft. (T. Mickel, p.c.), subspecies uncertain.

Golden-crowned Sparrow *Zonotrichia atricapilla*

Status: Locally common migrant and winter resident. Uses dense brush near open ground, often near woodlands. Arrives on high Cascade ridges in early Sep. (rarely by late Aug.), when first-year birds move south. The earliest report is Aug. 26, 1947. First appears in valley lowlands in early to mid-Sep., with continued influx into early Oct. Often remains fairly late in spring, with no real movement until mid-Apr. (by which time they are often singing), some still present to mid-May and stragglers sometimes reported until early June.

Distribution: Mainly lowlands of the valley and outer coast; most abundant on the valley floor. Fall migration along Cascade ridges ends by early Oct., after which they are rarely found in the high Cascades. Winters locally within the Coast Range in very small numbers (Alma CBC: median 6,

Golden-crowned Sparrow. Illustration by Barbara Gleason.

high 37, missed on about half of counts). Winters east in the McKenzie and Middle Fork Willamette valleys to about 1200 feet (regular in moderate numbers on Oakridge CBC).

• Dark-eyed Junco *Junco hyemalis*

Status: Common to abundant breeder, migrant, and winter resident ("Oregon" form). Breeds in low shrubbery (usually on the ground), generally under or adjacent to a canopy of coniferous trees but sometimes within deciduous stands. Although some breed on the valley floor and to sea level on the outer coast, a significant influx of wintering birds occurs around the first of Oct., with these birds leaving the lowlands during late Mar. and Apr. A few individuals of the "Slate-colored" form are reported each year, mainly in late fall and winter.

Distribution: Countywide. Numbers on the valley floor are low in summer, but breeds in areas with low shrubbery under an evergreen canopy, e.g., on the University of Oregon campus. Winter numbers highest from valley floor eastward.

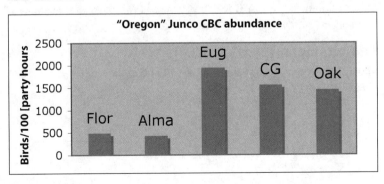

Lapland Longspur: South Jetty Rd., Florence, Apr. 20, 2003. Photo by Noah K. Strycker.

Lapland Longspur *Calcarius lapponicus*

Status: Rare but regular migrant in fall and spring, rare winter visitor. Does not seem to be annual in midwinter, but status difficult to determine. Early fall reports are from mid-Sep., but most regular in Oct. and early Nov. Spring movements are less often reported, but appear to be mainly from late Apr. and early May. Latest records May 24, 1989 and June 1, 1999, both on the outer coast.

Distribution: Mainly on the outer coast within a mile of the ocean, with most records from the Siuslaw jetties, the deflation plain, and the mouth of the Siltcoos. Also Fern Ridge Res. (reported from the dam and Royal Ave. in Sep. and Oct.) and the valley floor, sometimes mixed into flocks of Horned Larks or American Pipits.

Sites: Most likely on the outer coast; also Mt. Pisgah and gravel-topped dikes at Fern Ridge Res.

* Smith's Longspur *Calcarius pictus*

Vagrant. One record, Oregon's first, was at the mouth of the Siltcoos R. on Sep. 24, 2000 (Herlyn et al. 2001). This record is still under review by the OBRC.

* Chestnut-collared Longspur *Calcarius ornatus*

Casual migrant in Oregon. One Lane Co. record: May 1, 1976 at Royal Ave., Fern Ridge Res. (OBRC 538-76-01).

* Rustic Bunting *Emberiza rustica*

Vagrant to Oregon from Asia. One was in Eugene Mar. 31-Apr. 17, 1994 (OBRC 535.1-94-02)

Snow Bunting *Plectrophenax nivalis*
Status: Rare but regular late fall migrant and winter visitor. Not annual. Typically found in open areas on sand or gravel, beach wrack, open dirt fields, short-grass hilltops. Arrives in Nov., unreported after Feb. Lane Co. is at the extreme southwestern corner of the species' winter range, and in some years it does not reach this far south. Numbers are typically very small, one or two birds, alone or with Horned Larks, pipits or longspurs. Largest flocks are fewer than 10 birds.

Distribution: Most records are from the outer coast within a mile of the ocean, typically near the Siuslaw jetties. Has also been found at Stonefield Beach wayside south of Cape Perpetua. Also reported from Fern Ridge Dam (Nov. 17-30, 1996), Mt. Pisgah (Nov. 4-10, 2002), and the flatlands north of the Eugene airport.

Sites: Irregular, most likely in coastal dunes.

Family Cardinalidae

Rose-breasted Grosbeak *Pheucticus ludovicianus*
Status: Casual wanderer to Oregon and Lane Co. About 20 records, mainly from May and June, with two Dec. records and single records in Mar. and Apr.

Distribution: Reported mainly from cities and towns at feeders; also on the coast.

Rose-breasted Grosbeak, June 2, 1991, Vida. Photo by Frances Burns, courtesy OBRC.

• **Black-headed Grosbeak** *Pheucticus melanocephalus*
Status: Common breeder in a variety of woodlands and forest edges. Avoids the interior of densely forested areas. Arrives mainly in very early May (a few outriders in Apr.) and remains through late summer. Early arrivals Mar. 26, 1973 and Mar. 28, 1975 (*ENHS*) were exceptional. Departure timing is poorly known, but numbers drop by late Aug., and Sep. migrants are relatively few. In 2005, a significant movement occurred throughout Eugene in the last half of Aug. Occasional stragglers into early Oct. Latest recent record is Oct. 10, 2004.
Distribution: Countywide, least common along the Cascade summit.

* **Blue Grosbeak** *Passerina caerulea*
Vagrant to Oregon and Lane Co. Two sight records: June 3, 2000 at Sea Vue Motel on the northern coast (Renee LaChance) and Dec. 21, 1980 (OBRC 597-80-02) near the Eugene airport (A. Contreras, B. Combs, E. Schultz; CBC).

• **Lazuli Bunting** *Passerina amoena*
Status: Uncommon but highly visible migrant and breeder. Found in fairly open areas with a mix of low shrubbery and trees, often on hillsides. Sometimes found in grassy areas with a mix of shrubs and saplings. Arrives within a few days either side of May 1, with the bulk of movement in early May. In cold, wet years, arrival can be delayed until mid-May. Has been recorded as early as Mar. 15, 1947 (Gullion). Departure is poorly known, but difficult to find after July except at high elevations, migrants rarely reported after Aug. but a few stragglers have been found through early Oct. The latest record was Oct. 8, 1983.
Distribution: Mainly from the Willamette Valley floor eastward, especially south of the McKenzie Valley. Rare and local in the Coast Range including its eastern foothills; essentially absent on the outer coast. A report May 9, 2004 at Florence was highly unusual. Local along the Cascade summit ridges, mainly on brushy south-facing slopes.

* **Indigo Bunting** *Passerina cyanea*
Status: Casual visitor, mainly in late spring and summer. Very rare in winter. About a dozen county records, most from May through July. One attempted to breed with a Lazuli Bunting at Bloomberg Park near Lane Community College in 1994 and 1995.
Note: there are at least 2 Lane Co. reports of hybrids between this species and Lazuli Bunting.
Distribution: Mainly from the Eugene-Springfield area.

* Dickcissel *Spiza americana*

Vagrant. One sight record: Nov. 24, 1979 in Alton Baker Park in Eugene (David Fix, p.c.). This record was filed with the OBRC but the committee was not asked to consider it owing to the observer's opinion that the record did not have complete details. However, the description is sufficient to support its inclusion here as a sight record.

Family Icteridae

Bobolink *Dolichonyx oryzivorus*

Casual wanderer to the county. Sep. 29, 2003 in the south jetty deflation plain; June 1 and Sep. 1, 1980 (*NAB*), possibly the same bird, at Fern Ridge Res.; and one reported in June, 1979 along I-5 near Coburg.

• Red-winged Blackbird *Agelaius phoeniceus*

Status: Common to locally abundant breeder and migrant. Somewhat local in winter, usually in large flocks. Status of populations using Lane Co. is not well known, movements are little noted. Winter flocks begin to break up by late Feb., and during Mar. males can be seen on territories along every shrubby ditch, marsh, and wet pasture in the lowlands. Flocks re-form after the breeding season, becoming noticeable in July and highly concentrated by Sep.

Distribution: Breeds countywide; highly visible throughout the lower valleys and on the coast, more local within wooded areas. Winters mainly on the Willamette Valley floor and in river valleys, with small flocks in the Siuslaw Valley and very locally (mainly at feeders) on the outer coast. Generally absent from the central Coast Range and high Cascades in winter.

Red-winged Blackbird. Illustration by Barbara Gleason.

Tricolored Blackbird *Agelaius tricolor*
Casual visitor. Four reports: Aug. 13, 2005, July 13, 2003, Jan. 6, 1999, and Apr. 6, 1996, all at Fern Ridge Res.

• **Western Meadowlark** *Sturnella neglecta*
Status: Uncommon local breeder, probably declining. Found in fields, grasslands, and overgrown pastures (breeding) and also in dense beachgrass (winter). Locally common in migration and winter where flocks form. No significant seasonal movements, although the origin of winter flocks is essentially unknown.
Distribution: Essentially limited to the floor of the Willamette Valley and wider adjacent river valleys as a breeder. Probably a rare breeder on the outer coast in dense beach grass. Absent from the Coast Range and the Cascades except as rare migrants, but has bred in grassy areas around Oakridge (LCBBA).

• **Yellow-headed Blackbird** *Xanthocephalus xanthocephalus*
Status: Common to locally abundant breeder in marshes, especially at Fern Ridge Res. Bred in Springfield in 1947 (Gullion), but does not do so today. Arrives around the first of Apr., remains in numbers through mid-Sep., then most depart. Rare through early winter; recent records Dec. 28, 1999; Dec. 5, 1987.
Distribution: Marshes around Fern Ridge Res., occasionally at nearby ponds and marshes.
Sites: Southeast part of Fern Ridge Res.

• **Brewer's Blackbird** *Euphagus cyanocephalus*
Status: Common to abundant resident breeder. Found in a variety of urban areas, farmyards and pastures, riparian areas. Sometimes becomes remarkably unwary in towns and cities, especially in large parking lots. Seasonal movements are poorly known, but clearly less widespread in winter, when it forms flocks, large and small.
Distribution: Countywide as a breeder, from the outer coast to timberline. Much more restricted in winter, when it leaves high elevations and most of the Coast Range, gathering mainly on the Willamette Valley floor. However, it is not known whether winter birds are local breeders. Can be rare and local on the outer coast in winter, found mainly around farmyards and feeders.

* **Common Grackle** *Quiscalus quiscula*
Vagrant, 3 records: Aug. 11, 2004 at Florence; Apr. 21, 1994 at Eugene (OBRC 511-94-14); and May 1-June 19, 1987 at Veneta (OBRC 511-87-04).

Common Grackle, Aug. 11, 2004 at Florence. Photo by Diane Pettey.

* Great-tailed Grackle *Quiscalus mexicanus*

Vagrant, 3 records involving 4 or 5 birds. Two summered at Fern Ridge Res. in 2000 from at least June 9-July 12; one (possibly different from the Fern Ridge birds) was in Eugene on June 23, 2000; and one was at Fern Ridge Res. on June 27, 1992 (OBRC No. 517-92-12). One was north of Florence on May 8, 2000.

• Brown-headed Cowbird *Molothrus ater*

Status: Common breeder, rare, irregular, and local in winter. Found in urban areas, around farmyards, in riparian corridors. Spring birds arrive fairly early, with a significant influx in late Mar. and early Apr. Obvious and widespread through Aug., depart through Sep. and rare after early Oct. Avoids dense forests.

Distribution: Countywide except along the Cascade summit, where rare and local, largely limited to riparian areas and lakeshores where potential host species are available. Most common in lowlands and coastal valleys. Very rare in winter anywhere except the Willamette Valley floor , where it is rare to uncommon, with numbers varying from nearly zero to several dozen. Occasionally forms winter flocks.

Hooded Orioles. Top, Eugene in 1979. Photo by Larry McQueen. Bottom, Florence in 1986. Photo by Mary Forrester.

Baltimore Oriole: Florence, Jan. 5, 2003. Photo by Noah K. Strycker.

* Hooded Oriole *Icterus cucullatus*
Casual visitor. Apr. 28-30, 1996 at Eugene (Francine Delmore, photos); June 2 and 5-7, 1986 at Florence (OBRC No. 505-86-08); May 1, 1985 at Eugene (OBRC 505-85-07); and Dec. 24, 1978 through Mar. 1979 in Eugene (OBRC 505-79-02). See Supplemental Records.

* Baltimore Oriole *Icterus galbula*
Vagrant. Three records: Dec. 2002-Jan. 10, 2003 at Florence (OBRC 507-03-09); May 12, 1994 at Eugene; and May 27-June 13, 1986 at Fern Ridge Res. (OBRC 507-86-02).

• Bullock's Oriole *Icterus bullockii*
Status: Uncommon, somewhat local, breeder and migrant. Extremely rare in winter. Found mainly in tall trees along waterways and within cities and towns. Arrives in the last few days of Apr., with most movement in early May. Departs in early Sep., with a few records of stragglers to winter: Nov. 30, 1985 at Sutton Beach; Dec. 30, 1979, Feb. 5, 1999. A pair wintered at Florence in 1982-83.
Distribution: Mainly on the Willamette Valley floor and in the lower valley of the Middle Fork of the Willamette. A few are sometimes found in valleys within the eastern Coast Range and in the lower Cascades up to Hills Creek Res. Generally absent on the outer coast and in the higher Cascades.

Family Fringillidae - Subfamily Fringillinae

* Brambling *Fringilla montifringilla*
Vagrant. Two records: Oct. 25-31 1990 at Florence (OBRC 514.1-90-03) and April 7-14, 2006 at Eugene (Mark "Rudi" Rudolph).

Subfamily Carduelinae

• Gray-crowned Rosy-Finch *Leucosticte tephrocotis*
Status: Bred historically and probably still does in very small numbers above timberline on the Three Sisters and possibly (unknown) on Diamond Peak.
Distribution: Mainly in the Three Sisters wilderness. Rare in fall and winter (usually late Oct. and Nov.) to open hilltops and occasionally the valley floor.
Sites: Three Sisters.

Brambling at Florence, Oct., 1990. Photo by Pat Moynahan.

Brambling at Eugene, April 2006. Photo by Mark "Rudi" Rudolph.

° **Pine Grosbeak** *Pinicola enucleator*

Status: Rare irregular winter visitor and possible rare local breeder.

Distribution: High Cascades. Records of an adult male on May 29, 1971 at a Springfield feeder (ENHS); Mar. 5, 1995 at Elmira; and July 22, 1996 in the Cook Cr. drainage near Blue R. (Matt Hunter, p.c.) suggest the possibility of occasional local breeding or at least summering. Three records involving multiple birds from the Oakridge CBC and 4 birds collected by A. C. Shelton on Feb. 17, 1915 on Horsepasture Mtn. south of McKenzie Bridge (UO 1170-1173) suggest that the species occurs with some regularity in very small numbers in the high Cascades in winter, where observer coverage is limited. One record from the Coast Range, Dec. 19, 1977 (T. Finnell, photos, Alma CBC); no coastal records.

• **Purple Finch** *Carpodacus purpureus*

Status: Uncommon widespread breeder, uncommon and somewhat local in winter, when numbers vary from year to year, especially on the coast. Found in forests with a significant coniferous component, mainly around edges and openings. In winter, sometimes visits feeders. Migratory movements are subtle and poorly known. A small but noticeable spring movement occurs in Mar. and Apr., when birds appear in areas where they did not winter and do not breed. Fall movements are usually undetected.

Distribution: Countywide as a breeder, local on the valley floor and usually absent in pine-dominated areas of the Cascade summit ridges. Winters mainly at lower elevations but also locally into the western Cascades (was common on the Oakridge CBC). Uncommon to rare and local in winter on the outer coast, mainly at feeders.

• Cassin's Finch *Carpodacus cassinii*
Status: Uncommon local breeder in high-elevation pine forests, casual in winter to lower elevations. Somewhat irruptive, with the only significant recent lowland movement in the mid- to late 1970s. Two males and one female were near Fern Ridge Res. on Jan. 6, 1973 (L. McQueen, p.c.). Clare Watson observed one at her Eugene feeder in Nov., 1973 (ENHS). Found on the Oakridge CBC in 1973, 1974, 1975, and 1984, and Cottage Grove in 1972 and 1979. Singles appeared at feeders in Eugene during the 1970s. Less often reported in winter since that time, with single birds in 1989 (L. McQueen, p.c.) and Dec. 30, 2001 (Dave Irons). Additional reports are from Walterville in Feb. 1996 and Apr. 10, 2000, Creswell on Jan. 1, 1997, and Eugene on Jan. 21, 1998.

It is possible that some of these reports represent misidentified Purple or House Finches. However, several factors suggest that a genuine irregular small-scale movement of Cassin's Finch occurs. First, almost all reports are from mid-winter. Second, there are no reports at all west of the Eugene area, which suggests an easterly origin. The fact that the slightly upslope Oakridge and Cottage Grove CBCs reported the species more than once fits a natural pattern for birds with an eastern origin, as would two reports from Walterville. Alma and Florence CBCs have never reported the species. Finally, montane species erupt into the lowlands of western Oregon with some regularity.
Distribution: Pine-dominated Cascade summit ridges in summer (most reports in the Waldo Lake area owing to ease of access). Rare and irregular to the western Cascades and valley lowlands. No records west of the Willamette Valley.
Sites: Waldo-Gold Lake area.

• House Finch *Carpodacus mexicanus*
Status: Common to locally abundant breeding resident. Most common in towns and around farm buildings, but can be found in most habitats except for dense forests and open country. In fall, sometimes seen on the outer coast in flocks in dense beach grass and coastal scrub; by winter coastal flocks generally depart the outer beaches and settle into dense shrub growth.

Distribution: Countywide, mainly at lower elevations, rare and local in the higher Cascades, mainly around buildings.

• Red Crossbill *Loxia curvirostra*

Status: Common resident breeder with substantial irregular seasonal movements tied to the availability of cone crops. Most regular in higher-elevation coniferous forests in summer, though a few can be found to sea level if food supplies allow. Winters throughout the county except for purely deciduous areas of the valley floor.

Distribution: Countywide except in summer, when generally absent below about 500 feet. However, breeding can occur at any time of year and location when food allows. In 2005, small flocks and singles remained in the Eugene area (even the lowlands) into late June, and immatures that were probably of local origin were seen.

White-winged Crossbill *Loxia leucoptera*

Status: Rare, highly irregular irruptive that can occur at any time of year, but most records are in Aug.-early Oct. and mid-winter. No records Feb.-May. Found where Red Crossbills are, usually at high elevations but can occur to sea level in irruption years (2 were on the Florence CBC on Dec. 20, 2004).

Distribution: Most records are from the Waldo Lake area, perhaps owing to ease of access. Other records include Craig Lake near McKenzie Pass and even relatively low on June 28, 1997 at McKenzie Bridge and 5 on the Eugene CBC in 1965. However, they could occur anywhere there is a good cone crop, especially spruce cones, in irruption years.

Sites: Irregular. Try spruce stands and fire pits along the Cascade summit late summer and fall.

Common Redpoll *Carduelis flammea*

Casual winter visitor; 4 records: Jan. 6-8 2000 in Eugene; Dec. 16, 1989-Feb. 14, 1990 in Florence; one on the 1997 Florence CBC; and Dec. 16, 1914 (collected) in Eugene (Shelton 1917). Shelton indicates that the 1914 specimen was deposited with the UO Museum, but the museum, which holds Shelton's specimens, has no record of this.

• Pine Siskin *Carduelis pinus*

Status: Common to abundant breeder; irruptive migrant and winter resident. Breeds in conifers, mainly above the valley lowlands. Movements are erratic and tied to the location and seasonality of food crops. In some years, hundreds descend to the lowlands and the outer coast. In other years few to none leave the higher mountains.

Distribution: Countywide, local in winter owing to a tendency to form large flocks as the season progresses.

• Lesser Goldfinch *Carduelis psaltria*

Status: Common breeder, somewhat local, in towns and cities, woodland edges with adjacent shrubbery, open oak woodlands. Seasonal movements are limited, and seem to include some concentration in urban areas, but this is poorly known.

Distribution: Mainly the Willamette Valley floor and adjacent foothills, especially from Eugene-Springfield south and east. Rare local breeder in the McKenzie and Middle Fork Willamette valleys. Casual to the outer coast in winter.

Sites: Most regular in urban areas; Skinner Butte.

* Lawrence's Goldfinch *Carduelis lawrencei*

Vagrant. One was in Florence Dec. 24, 1991 to Jan. 11, 1992 (OBRC 531-91-02).

• American Goldfinch *Carduelis tristis*

Status: Common to abundant resident breeder and winter resident. Breeds in open woodlands, forest edges, hedgerows containing trees; also in towns and cities. Seasonal movements are largely concentrations, with widespread breeders congregating for winter.

Distribution: Countywide except for dense forests; absent from the high Cascades and local in the Coast Range, mainly in larger openings. Most common in and around the Willamette Valley, adjacent valleys and the Siuslaw valleys. Concentrates in more open areas (e.g., hedgerows along pastures) and in urban areas in winter.

• Evening Grosbeak *Coccothraustes vespertinus*

Status: Uncommon but widespread breeder, briefly common in migration, especially in spring, when scores gather to eat elm and maple seeds. Breeding is mainly in higher-elevation conifers, usually absent from the valley floor from June through Aug.

Lawrence's Goldfinch, Florence. Photo by Bill & Zanah Stotz.

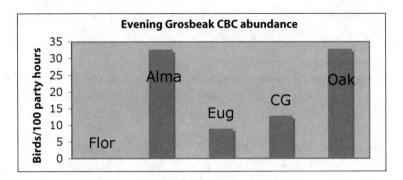

Distribution: In summer, mainly the Cascades and higher foothills and the central Coast Range. In winter, quite variable from year to year, with many remaining in the mountains some years and invading the lowlands every few winters. Rare and irregular on the outer coast in winter.

Family Passeridae

• (I) **House Sparrow** *Passer domesticus*
Status: Locally common resident breeder, mainly in towns, cities and around farmyards.
Distribution: Countywide except away from human habitation, where rare. It is absent from most of the Cascades and the central Coast Range.
Sites: Residential areas and around farm buildings on the valley floor.

Supplemental Records

A small number of records were discovered for which insufficient information could be obtained by the time the book went to the publisher. These records may be correct (most of them probably are) and more detail may be available at a later date.

King Eider: A record, April 12, 1981

Flesh-footed Shearwater: Specific records are known but unpublished

Ruddy Turnstone: One report at Fern Ridge Res. in 2004

Sharp-tailed Sandpiper: A record, Aug. 22, 1969. Another on Sep.14, 1991

White-throated Swift: A record, Sep. 25, 1973

White-headed Woodpecker: A record from the Oakridge area in the 1970s

Black-billed Magpie: Records from March 17, 1979, Nov. 10 1934, and May 20, 1922

Yellow-breasted Chat: March 27, 1989

Hooded Oriole: June 17, 1998

References and Basic Information

A VERY SHORT HISTORY OF LANE COUNTY ORNITHOLOGY

Alan Contreras

Birds have been in the arbitrary political unit that we now call Lane County, Oregon far longer than any people have. For this reason birds appear among stories and legends of the first humans to settle in Oregon. This publication has nothing to say about these early times because it has a different purpose and focus. Nonetheless, some sense of the historic setting relative to the birds we discuss seems appropriate.

Lane County was largely untouched by the earliest European explorers who paid significant attention to the natural world. Lewis and Clark passed well to the north in 1805-06, David Douglas wrote mainly of plants (we remember him in the Douglas-fir) during his visit of 1825-26, John Kirk Townsend did not come so far south in 1834-35, and John C. Fremont spent most of his productive time east of the Cascade summit in 1843 (and in any event wrote little about birds).

The first exploration party to spend significant time in the area we now call Lane County was the Pacific Railroad Survey of 1855, in which the Williamson-Newberry party crossed the Cascades near Diamond Peak, came down the Middle Fork of the Willamette and proceeded north through the Willamette Valley. However, the 1857 Pacific Railroad Report that resulted from the trip did not specifically mention Lane County birds. The excellent reports of Mearns, Merrill, Bendire, and others in the post-Civil War years were almost all from east of the Cascades, providing the solid baseline that we have for the Klamath basin and central Harney County area. O.B. Johnson's 1880 list of birds of the Willamette Valley published in the *American Naturalist* was actually birds of the area from Salem to Portland, and does not seem very accurate.

A. R. Woodcock's 1902 *Annotated List of Birds of Oregon* issued by what was then the Oregon Agricultural College at Corvallis was largely a compendium of Woodcock's own records from the Corvallis area (apparently quite accurate) and a set of reports that he gathered from observers around the state and a few publications such as Lyman Belding's 1890 *Land Birds of the Pacific District* (itself a rather shallow compilation). Some of the material Woodcock gathered was of doubtful accuracy, and none of any utility was from Lane County.

This lack of published information changed abruptly, and rather spectacularly, with the publication of Alfred Cooper Shelton's *Distributional List of the Land Birds of West-Central Oregon* by the University of Oregon in 1917. Even today, the accuracy and precision of Shelton's list is astonishing, especially when compared to material issued only a few years previously. In order to fully understand why this happened, it is necessary to consider what was happening elsewhere in the scientific world of the American West. As set forth in a splendid biography by Barbara Stein (*On Her Own Terms*, University of California Press, 2001), philanthropist and field researcher Annie Alexander had donated the funds necessary to establish the Museum of Vertebrate Zoology at the University of California in Berkeley in 1908. Joseph Grinnell, whose commitment to systematic zoology underpins so much of western ornithology, was named (in effect by Alexander herself) to direct the museum.

Alfred Cooper Shelton was born in 1892 in Santa Rosa, California, and developed a strong interest in birds as a teenager. He was elected to the Cooper Ornithological Club, the principal western ornithological organization, at seventeen and went to the University of California to study under Grinnell. Shelton was chosen to be the first collector of birds in the Eugene area by the Biological Survey in 1914, with a joint appointment at the University of Oregon. For a more detailed overview of Shelton's life and work, see the excellent biography by George Jobanek included in the splendid Oregon Field Ornithologists reprint of Shelton's 1917 list issued in 2002. One of the delightful symmetries of Lane County ornithology is that the 2002 reprint was prepared by a fifteen-year-old Lane County observer, Noah K. Strycker, who subsequently issued a revised checklist of the birds of Fern Ridge Reservoir and wrote some species accounts for *Birds of Oregon: A General Reference* (Marshall et al. 2003). It seems that Lane County ornithology is in good hands.

Shelton's list, based mainly on his own three years of systematic collecting of bird specimens, did not include water birds or coastal species, but in other respects it was a remarkable jump into modern ornithology. There were no more significant publications from the county until *Birds of Oregon* (Gabrielson and Jewett 1940), but that publication included data from several Lane County collectors (specimen ornithology was the norm until the mid-20th century), most notably including Overton Dowell of the Florence area, from whom came Oregon's first record of Cassin's Kingbird, and also from visiting observers such as Florence Merriam Bailey, author of the *Handbook of Birds of the Western United States* (1902 and subsequent editions).

When Gordon Gullion published his "Birds of the Southern Willamette Valley" in *Condor* in 1951, the most obvious transition was that most of the records were of birds that had not been collected: Lane County ornithology had moved into the modern era in which carefully collected sight records, rather than collected birds, formed the basis for statements about the local status of birds. Gullion's publication is, in effect, the status baseline that has been used for over fifty years for the southern Willamette Valley.

By the 1940s, a core group of people interested in the natural world was active in the Eugene area, and has conducted the Eugene Christmas Bird Count every year since 1942 (there was one earlier count). In the early 1960s, Lane County observations began appearing with some regularity in *Audubon Field Notes*, the national journal of notable field records (it is now called *North American Birds* and is issued by the American Birding Association). The Eugene Natural History Society grew out of this interest, and began publishing a regular newsletter in 1967. The Oakridge Audubon Society was established in 1972, serving all members of the National Audubon Society in Lane County. This chapter eventually became the Lane County Audubon Society, and is based in Eugene today.

One of the more noteworthy events in the ornithological history of Lane County was the establishment of the Southern Willamette Ornithological Club (SWOC) in 1974 by George "Chip" Jobanek, Aaron Skirvin, and nine others. This was the first modern organization in the state that focused on birds alone. Its newsletter, *SWOC Talk*, began that year and in 1977 became *Oregon Birds* and was transferred to the brand-new Oregon Field Ornithologists. SWOC continues to meet each month today, over thirty years later, as an informal discussion group with occasional programs, and its members' field notes appear in both *The Quail* (Lane County Audubon Society) and *Oregon Birds*. This book came to be as the result of discussions at a SWOC meeting.

It is tempting to consider ourselves as the pinnacle of all possible achievement and to regard history as what trails behind us as we make our grand way through the world of modern ornithology. In fact, ornithology has become a very broad and complex subject and there is a great deal to be learned all the time about the birds of our region. Most readers of this book are not professional biologists but can still participate in bird counts, surveys, banding, and other activities that allow us to learn more about the birds of Lane County.

I hope that this short history has made clear that, ultimately, it is what we choose to do as observers, and our attention to quality and detail in our records, that add to knowledge. It is also clear from this book that most of us enjoy observing birds under all sorts of conditions for all sorts of reasons, and that this joy is good in itself.

SEASONAL INFORMATION

Average Arrival – Spring

Spring migration in Lane County extends over four entire months and has two principal peaks. The earliest movement is typically of Tree Swallows in early Feb., with Sandhill Cranes, Violet-green Swallows, Rufous Hummingbirds, Turkey Vultures, and Cinnamon Teal coming later in Feb. or very early March. One unusual but almost annual species, Say's Phoebe, also comes in this early period.

The graph below shows the two principal peaks of species arrival diversity during spring migration. The first of the "summer" insect eaters other than swallows have a principal peak around April 1, while the second wave of arrivals tends to be about a month later, varying from year to year but usually the last few days of April or the early days of May, which is also the peak of shorebird movement.

Almost all of the regular breeding species have arrived by the second week of May, with the last arrivals usually Red-eyed Vireo and Common Nighthawk, which sometimes do not appear until the first few days of June. Willow Flycatcher is very late in some years, too.

The following checklist shows the average arrival date in spring for many common migrants. Seven additional columns allow observers to keep their own records of arrivals, and ten additional rows allow for more species to be added. Arrival dates for migrant shorebirds are poorly known and more attention should be paid to them.

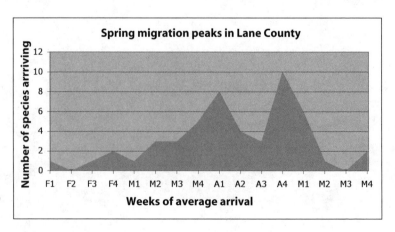

Spring Arrival Dates in Lane County

Avg. Arrival*	Species	Records						
2/5	Tree Swallow							
2/20	Sandhill Crane							
2/22	Turkey Vulture							
2/24	Rufous Hummingbird							
3/5	Cinnamon Teal							
3/8	Say's Phoebe							
3/9	Violet-green Swallow							
3/13	Green Heron							
3/15	Osprey							
3/20	Virginia Rail							
3/20	Orange-cr. Warbler							
3/22	Band-tailed Pigeon							
3/26	Cliff Swallow							
3/26	C. Yellowthroat							
3/29	Evening Grosbeak							
3/31	Chipping Sparrow							
4/1	N Rough-w. Swallow							
4/2	Barn Swallow							
4/3	Vesper Sparrow							
4/3	Yellow-head. Blackbird							
4/6	Sora							
4/6	Cassin's Vireo							
4/6	Black-thr. Gray Warbler							
4/6	Brown-headed Cowbird							
4/8	Wilson's Warbler							
4/10	Vaux's Swift							
4/12	Purple Martin							
4/13	Nashville Warbler							
4/18	Hammond's Flycatcher							

4/19	House Wren							
4/20	MacGillivray's Warbler							
4/22	Pacific-slope Flycatcher							
4/22	Western Kingbird							
4/22	Warbling Vireo							
4/23	Western Tanager							
4/24	Hermit Warbler							
4/25	Bullock's Oriole							
4/27	Olive-sided Flycatcher							
4/27	Yellow Warbler							
4/28	Black-headed Grosbeak							
4/29	Blue-winged Teal							
5/2	Lazuli Bunting							
5/4	Western Wood-Pewee							
5/5	Black Tern							
5/5	Swainson's Thrush							
5/6	Yellow-breasted Chat							
5/6	Grasshopper Sparrow							
5/11	Willow Flycatcher							
5/31	Common Nighthawk							
5/31	Red-eyed Vireo							

* Average arrival during the period 1994-2004, based on records kept by Tom Mickel for The Quail, Lane County Audubon Society.

Arrivals and Departures - Fall

Fall arrival and departure data for Lane County are very poorly known. Many species depart very quietly, some as early as August, and some move south using montane routes that do not get much coverage. Please keep your own records and help expand knowledge of fall movements.

DEPARTURES

Latest	Species	Late Records							
	Green Heron								
	Turkey Vulture								
	Blue-winged Teal								
	Cinnamon Teal								
	Osprey								
	Virginia Rail								
	Sora								
	Sandhill Crane								
	Black Tern								
	Band-tailed Pigeon								
	Common Nighthawk								
	Vaux's Swift								
	Rufous Hummingbird								
	Olive-sided Flycatcher								
	Western Wood-Pewee								
	Willow Flycatcher								
	Hammond's Flycatcher								
	Pacific-slope Flycatcher								
	Say's Phoebe								
	Western Kingbird								
	Cassin's Vireo								
	Warbling Vireo								
	Red-eyed Vireo								
	Purple Martin								

Tree Swallow							
Violet-green Swallow							
N. Rough-w. Swallow							
Cliff Swallow							
Barn Swallow							
House Wren							
Swainson's Thrush							
Orange-cr. Warbler							
Nashville Warbler							
Yellow Warbler							
Black-thr. Gray Warbler							
Hermit Warbler							
MacGillivray's Warbler							
C. Yellowthroat							
Wilson's Warbler							
Yellow-breasted Chat							
Western Tanager							
Chipping Sparrow							
Vesper Sparrow							
Grasshopper Sparrow							
Black-headed Grosbeak							
Lazuli Bunting							
Yellow-head. Blackbird							
Brown-headed Cowbird							
Bullock's Oriole							
Evening Grosbeak							

FALL ARRIVALS

Fall arrivals are better known than postbreeding departures, but there are still limited data for many species. For some, such as shorebirds, it is difficult to determine whether a bird seen in June is a late spring migrant, an early southbound migrant, or a nonbreeder that came to a convenient place in Lane County and stopped for a while. Some species of scoters, grebes, and ducks make such stopovers annually, as do shorebirds and gulls in smaller numbers.

Given the limited available data, no averages are shown. If observers keep good records, these data may become available in future years. Report your arrivals and past dates for the field notes in *The Quail*, newsletter of the Lane County Audubon Society.

Earliest	Species	Early Records							
	Gr. White-fr. Goose								
	Snow Goose								
	Cackling Goose								
	Canada Goose								
	Tundra Swan								
	Gadwall								
	Eurasian Wigeon								
	American Wigeon								
	Northern Shoveler								
	Northern Pintail								
	Green-winged Teal								
	Common Teal								
	Canvasback								
	Redhead								
	Ring-necked Duck								
	Greater Scaup								
	Lesser Scaup								
	Harlequin Duck								
	Surf Scoter								
	White-winged Scoter								
	Black Scoter								
	Long-tailed Duck								
	Bufflehead								
	Common Goldeneye								

Red-br. Merganser								
Ruddy Duck								
Red-throated Loon								
Pacific Loon								
Common Loon								
Horned Grebe								
Red-necked Grebe								
Eared Grebe								
Great Egret								
Rough-legged Hawk								
Merlin								
Prairie Falcon								
Sandhill Crane								
Black-bellied Plover								
Amer. Golden-Plover								
Pacific Golden-Plover								
Semipalmated Plover								
Greater Yellowlegs								
Lesser Yellowlegs								
Solitary Sandpiper								
Willet								
Wandering Tattler								
Whimbrel								
Marbled Godwit								
Ruddy Turnstone								
Black Turnstone								
Surfbird								
Red Knot								
Sanderling								
Semipalmated Sandp.								
Western Sandpiper								
Least Sandpiper								
Baird's Sandpiper								
Pectoral Sandpiper								
Rock Sandpiper								
Dunlin								
Short-billed Dowitcher								
Long-billed Dowitcher								

Wilson's Snipe								
Wilson's Phalarope								
Red-necked Phalarope								
Red Phalarope								
Bonaparte's Gull								
Mew Gull								
Ring-billed Gull								
California Gull								
Herring Gull								
Thayer's Gull								
Glaucous-winged Gull								
Glaucous Gull								
Black-legged Kittiwake								
Common Tern								
Arctic Tern								
Forster's Tern								
Ancient Murrelet								
Northern Shrike								
American Pipit								
Townsend's Warbler								
Palm Warbler								
Am. Tree Sparrow								
Fox Sparrow								
Lincoln's Sparrow								
Swamp Sparrow								
White-throated Sparrow								
Harris's Sparrow								
Golden-cr. Sparrow								
Lapland Longspur								
Snow Bunting								
Gray-cr. Rosy-Finch								
Pine Siskin								
Evening Grosbeak								

Gazetteer

by Vjera Arnold

Alton Baker Park: Lane Co. park (400 acres) in Eugene and Springfield, located on the north side of the Willamette R.

Alvadore: Town on the north side of Fern Ridge Res.

Amazon Creek: Canal from south Eugene to Fern Ridge Res., often with bicycle path paralleling it.

Amazon Flats: Older name for Meadowlark Prairie, used in some older field notes.

Aufderheide Memorial Drive: Connector that runs through Willamette National Forest between Oakridge and Cougar Res.

Autzen Stadium: University of Oregon's football stadium, adjacent to Alton Baker Park.

Baker Beach: Beach adjacent to Lily Lake, about 7 miles north of Florence.

Bloomberg Park: Small park near Lane Community College.

Bob Creek: Wayside on Hwy. 101, north Lane Co. coast.

Bohemia Mtn.: Peak southeast of Cottage Grove, highest point in the Calapooya Divide.

Brays Pt.: Overlook off Hwy. 101, north of Stonefield Beach.

C & M Stables: Along Hwy. 101 north of Florence, just south of Baker Beach Rd.

Calapooya Divide: The ridge and hill complex extending from southwest of Cottage Grove in a shallow arc south and southeast of Cottage Grove, dividing the Willamette and Umpqua drainages.

Camas Swale: Marshy and agricultural area north of Creswell and west of I-5.

Canary Rd.: Road leading north and east of Siltcoos Lake, south of Florence.

Cape Perpetua: Cape with a visitor center, just north of the Lane Co. line, on Hwy. 101.

Clay Creek: Recreation area in the middle of the Coast Range, south of Hwy. 126.

Cottage Grove: Small city 20 miles south of Eugene.

Cottage Grove Res.: Reservoir south of Cottage Grove.

Cougar Res.: Off Hwy. 126, at the north end of Aufderheide Drive.

Coyote Creek: Creek running through the Coyote Units in south Fern Ridge.

Coyote Units: East and west wetland units in southern Fern Ridge, south of Hwy. 126.

Crab Dock: Small pier and adjacent cove near the north end of South Jetty Rd., Florence.

Craig Lake: Small lake near McKenzie Pass.

Creswell sewage ponds: Previously open to the public, now inaccessible.

Cushman: Hamlet off Hwy. 126, east of Florence.

Darling's Resort: Private resort and store at the north end of Siltcoos Lake.

Deflation plain: Sand flats partly covered with grass and shrubs, east of South Jetty Rd., Florence.

Delta Ponds: Pond complex along Delta Hwy. near Valley River Center in Eugene.

Dexter Res.: Large reservoir in the lower western Cascades, off Hwy. 58 between Pleasant Hill and Oakridge.

Diamond Peak: Cascade peak in southeast Lane Co.

Dog Pond: Small pond near the west end of the east-west portion of South Jetty Rd.

Dorena Res.: Reservoir east of Cottage Grove.

Dotterel Dike: Dike with a walking trail leading east into the deflation plain from Parking Lot No. 3 along South Jetty Rd., Florence.

Duncan Island: Island in the Siuslaw R. between Florence and Mapleton.

East Regional Park: 56-acre park near Cottage Grove.

Elijah Bristow State Park: Park along the Willamette, east of Springfield, north of Hwy. 58.

Emigrant Pass: Pass in the extreme southeastern corner of the county, accessible via Hills Creek Res.

Fall Creek dam: Dam and reservoir in the western Cascades north of Hwy. 58 and Dexter Res.

Fern Ridge Res.: Reservoir, dam, wetlands, and parks west of Eugene.

Fiddle Creek Rd.: Spur east of Canary Rd. at Ada junction, east of Siltcoos Lake and south of Florence.

Finn Rock: A monolith off Hwy. 126, near Ben and Kay Dorris State Park. Also a small community.

Fisher Unit: Wetland unit in Fern Ridge north of W. 11th (Hwy. 126) and south of Royal Ave.

Gillespie Butte: A small butte in northern Eugene.

Glenwood: The area between Eugene and Springfield, bordered to the north by the Willamette R.

Gold Lake and Bog: Lake and bog in the Cascades, north of Hwy. 58 at Willamette Pass.

Hand Lake: A lake that is a short hike from Hwy. 242, near the Cascade summit.

Heceta Bank: Offshore bank where concentrations of pelagic species can be found feeding.

Heceta Head: Lighthouse park north of Florence with protected beach, tidepools, and large rocks that seabirds breed on.

Hills Creek Pond: Pond below Hills Creek dam.

Hills Creek Res.: Southeast of Oakridge.

Horsepasture Mtn.: Peak rises to 5660 ft. east of Cougar Res.

Island Park: Small park in Springfield, bordered on the south by the Willamette R.

Jasper Park: Park east of Springfield, north of Hwy. 58, along the Willamette R.

Kirk Park and pond: Formal name for the park and used casually for the pond next to Fern Ridge dam.

Tokatee Klootchman: Overlook on Hwy. 101 in north Lane Co.

Lane Memorial Gardens: Cemetery on W. 11th (Hwy. 126) with a public-accessible pond.

Lane Community College and Ponds: Sewage ponds and trails off I-5, just south of Eugene/Springfield.

Leaburg Res.: Along Hwy. 126 just east of the hamlet of Leaburg.

Lily Lake: Small lake about 7 miles north of Florence.

Lower Eddeeleo Lake: Lake in the Waldo Lake Wilderness.

Marilyn Lakes: Lake reached from a trail at Gold Lake.

Meadowlark Prairie: Wetlands (122.5 acres) west of Eugene, bordered by Greenhill Rd. and Royal Ave.

Melakwa Lake: Lake in the Cascades near Scott Lake, also a Boy Scout camp.

Mercer Lake: Lake off Hwy. 101 north of Florence and southest of Sutton Lake.

Mink Lake: Lake in the high Cascades.

Mt. Pisgah: Also known as the Howard Buford Recreation Area. Large park on the southwest edge of Springfield; the only place in the county with extensive dry prairie and oak savanna habitat.

Mule Prairie: Riparian area just east of Salt Creek Falls.

Noti: Small town in the Coast Range, off Hwy. 126.

Old Town Florence: Area of town along the northern edge of the Siuslaw R., east of Hwy. 101.

Perkins Peninsula Park: Park on the southwest edge of Fern Ridge Res.

Redhead Pond: Westernmost pond formed by dikes in Fisher Unit at Fern Ridge Res.

Richardson Butte: North of Fern Ridge near Alvadore.

Royal Ave.: East access into Fern Ridge. Before the reservoir was made, this was the old road that crossed this area.

South Willamette dump: Now-closed dump off W. 52nd and Willamette St.

Salt Creek Falls: Tallest waterfall in Lane Co., off Hwy. 58, east of Oakridge.

Scott Lake: High Cascades lake off Hwy. 242.

Sea Lion Caves: Tourist attraction north of Florence, with viewpoints nearby.

Siltcoos estuary: Estuary south of Florence, with trails and beach access.

Siltcoos Lake: Large lake south of Florence.

Siuslaw jetties: Only jetties in Lane Co.; both north and south can be reached from Florence.

Skinner Butte: Low hill between downtown Eugene and Willamette R.

Skookum Creek: Creek near Aufderheide Drive.

Smith R.: River in southwest Lane Co., drains into the Umpqua in Douglas Co.

South Jetty Rd.: Access road for the dunes, deflation plain, and south jetty. Turnoff is just south of Florence.

Spencer Butte: Peak on the south side of Eugene.

Stewart Pond: Small wetland complex in west Eugene north of W. 11th St. (Hwy. 126).

Stonefield Beach: Rocky beach north of Florence, mouth of Tenmile Creek.

Sutton Creek and Lake: Off Hwy. 101, north of Florence.

Taylor Burn: Extensive burn from 1996, north of Waldo Lake.

Triangle Lake: Lake and community in the Coast Range, off Hwy. 36.

Tumblebug Creek: Creek in the Cascades.

Waites pasture: Pasture along Hwy. 126, east of Florence, where the river swings away from the road.

Waldo Lake: Largest Cascade lake, off Hwy. 58.

Walterville Pond: Small pond off Hwy. 126, 6 miles west of Leaburg.

Washburne Wayside: Wayside along Hwy. 99, north of Junction City.

Westfir: Small town near Oakridge.

Westlake boat ramp: Access point for west side of Siltcoos Lake.

Willow Creek: Wetland complex bordered by Bailey Hill Rd. and W. 18th St. in Eugene.

Zumwalt Park: Park on the southwest side of Fern Ridge.

REFERENCES

Banks, R. C., C. Cicero, J. L. Dunn, A. W. Kratter, P. C. Rasmussen, J. V. Remsen, Jr., J. D. Rising, and D. F. Stotz. 2005. Forty-sixth Supplement to the Check-List of North American Birds. *Auk* 122(3):1026-1031.

Banks, R. C., C. Cicero, J. L. Dunn, A. W. Kratter, P. C. Rasmussen, J. V. Remsen, Jr., J. D. Rising, and D. F. Stotz. 2003. Forty-fourth Supplement to the American Ornithologists' Union Checklist of North American Birds. *Auk* 120(3): 923-931.

Bond, C. 1987. Oregon's first Lucy's Warbler. *Oregon Birds* 13: 292-293.

Contreras, 2003a. Winter records of Yellow-breasted Chat in Oregon. *Oregon Birds* 29: 124-125.

Contreras, A. 2003b. Additional Lane County records of Common Poor-will. *Oregon Birds* 29:93.

Contreras, A. 2002. Status of the Common Poor-will, *Phalaenoptilus nuttallii*, in Lane County, western Oregon. *Oregon Birds* 28: 119-120.

Contreras, A. 1988. A review of the status of the Sharp-tailed Sandpiper in Oregon. *Oregon Birds* 14:383-387

Courtney, S. P., J. A. Blakesley, R. E. Bigley, M. L. Cody, J. P. Dumbacher, R. C. Fleischer, A. B. Franklin, J. F. Franklin, R. J. Gutiérrez, J. M. Marzluff, L. Sztukowski. Sep 2004. Scientific evaluation of the status of the Northern Spotted Owl. Sustainable Ecosystems Institute Portland, Oregon. http://naum.sei.org/owl/finalreport/OwlFinalReport.pdf Accessed 16 Aug 2005.

Egger, M. 1977. Long-tailed Jaegers at Fern Ridge. *Oregon Birds* 3(5): 49.

Fix, D. 1988. A record of 48 Western Screech-Owls on the Florence CBC. *Oregon Birds* 13:278.

Force, M. P., R. A. Rowlett, and G. Grace. 1999. A sight record of a Streaked Shearwater in Oregon. *Western Birds* 30: 49-52.

Goggans, R., and M. Platt. 1992. Breeding-season observations of Great Gray Owl in the Willamette National Forest, Oregon. *Oregon Birds* 18: 35-41.

Gullion, G. 1951. Birds of the Southern Willamette Valley, Oregon. *Condor* 53:129-149.

Heinl, S. 1986. Field notes: western Oregon summer 1985. *Oregon Birds* 12: 133-137.

Herlyn, H., A. Contreras, and L. Bloch. 2001. A sight record of Smith's Longspur from Lane County, Oregon. *Oregon Birds* 27: 12.

Holbo, K. 1979. Observations of a Rock Wren nest: Spencer Butte, Lane County. *Oregon Birds* 5(5): 1.

Jobanek, George. 1997. *An annotated bibliography of Oregon bird literature published before 1935*. Oregon State University Press.

Jobanek, George (Chip). 1973. A list of the birds of Walterville, Oregon. Issued Sep. 3, 1973. Privately circulated.

Loy, W. 1976. *Atlas of Oregon*. University of Oregon Press.

McAtee, G. 2001. A new Black Swift nest site near Blue Lake, Lane County, Oregon. *Oregon Birds* 27:15.

Marshall, D., M. Hunter, and A. Contreras. 2003. *Birds of Oregon: A General Reference*. Oregon State University Press.

McArthur, L. A., and L. L. McArthur. 2003. *Oregon Geographic Names*. Seventh Edition. Oregon Historical Society Press.

Neff, J. 1928. *Common woodpeckers in relation to Oregon agriculture*. Free Press of Marionville, Missouri.

Papish, U. 1992. Black Terns Nest at Fern Ridge Reservoir, Lane County, Oregon. *Oregon Birds* 19:97-98.

Paulson, D. 2005. *Shorebirds of North America*. Princeton University Press.

Paulson, D. 1993. *Shorebirds of the Pacific Northwest*. University of Washington Press.

Pruitt, B. 1950. Gnatcatchers in Oregon. *Condor* 52:40.

Roberson, D. 1980. *Rare Birds of the West Coast*. Woodcock.

Strycker, N. 2003. *Birds of Fern Ridge Reservoir*. A seasonal checklist. U.S. Army Corps of Engineers.

Shelton, A. 1917. *A distributional list of the land birds of west-central Oregon*. University of Oregon, 1917. Reprinted, edited, and with supplementary annotations by N. Strycker, historical commentary by G. Jobanek, as Oregon Field Ornithologists Special Publication No. 14 (2002).

Tice, B. 1998. Inland observations of Red-breasted Mergansers in Oregon. *Oregon Birds* 24: 82-85.

PRINCIPAL CONTRIBUTORS

Vjera Arnold grew up in Springfield, Oregon. She started birding when she was 14 by going to Island Park and Alton Baker three or four times a week. She was a board member for Oregon Field Ornithologists while she was still in high school. In 1999 she was a member of American Birding Association's Tropicbirds, a youth birder team that competed in Point Reyes, California. She is a recent graduate of Eugene Bible College.

Dave Brown started birding around Eugene in the 4th grade in 1944 because his teacher at Dunn School was interested in birds. He studied skins at the University of Oregon Museum with Arnold Shotwell, and also learned how to stuff specimens. He was raised on West 34th St., just off Willamette Street, and spent much of his time hiking around Blanton Heights and Spencers Butte. At that time, this was outside the city limits and there were two dairies nearby. He lives near Alvadore today.

Barbara Combs has field notes dating back to 1956, when her second grade teacher in New Jersey enrolled her class in Junior National Audubon. Her undergraduate degree is from Oberlin College. Among her favorite classes was ethology, which she took as a master's degree student at Bucknell University. Her ethology professor, Douglas K. Candland, provided much enlightenment on how to avoid common writing mistakes and inspired her to work at becoming a better writer. She moved to Oregon in 1974 and received her Ph. D. in Psychology in 1980 from the University of Oregon. She authored nine of the species accounts in *Birds of Oregon: A General Reference* and has participated in a number of bird-related research activities since moving to Oregon. Now retired from her job as a senior policy analyst with the Oregon Public Utility Commission, she has been spending more time pursuing her personal interests.

Alan Contreras started birding in Eugene when he was a grade school student in 1967. He is co-editor of *Birds of Oregon: A General Reference* (Oregon State University Press, 2003), author of *Northwest Birds in Winter* (Oregon State University Press, 1996) and the author of a poetry collection, *Night Crossing* (CraneDance, 2004). He was born in Tillamook County and grew up in small towns around Oregon, settling in Eugene. He is a graduate of the University of Oregon and its law school, and works as administrator of the Oregon Office of Degree Authorization.

Don DeWitt began bird watching in 1996 along with his wife Linda and then two-year-old granddaughter Deshaunah. Birding while hiking at Mt. Pisgah led eventually to an article for *Oregon Birds* magazine (for which he also serves as an assistant editor). A "big year" birding effort in Lane County in 2000 became the subject for another article in *Oregon Birds*. Don's current interest is observing birds on his daily walks and jogs along trails and bikepaths near his Eugene home.

Barbara B. C. Gleason has been creating artwork since she could hold a crayon and she now uses pen, paper, paint, and computers, often integrating design with illustration. Her specialty in scientific illustration often features birds, as she began birding in the early 1970s in Massachusetts. She has also been involved in teaching, bird monitoring, and other bird-oriented citizen-science projects over the past 30 years, working with both children and adults. She and husband Dan Gleason authored *Birds from the Inside Out* (CraneDance, 3rd Edition, 2001).

Daniel Farrar could not have identified a Robin when in high school, let alone a juvenile Red-necked Stint mixed in a flock of Westerns. A class at Elmira High School and a trip to Malheur National Wildlife Refuge changed that. Raised in Veneta, he has always had deep ties to Fern Ridge. He is currently a student at the University of Oregon and an assistant biologist with the Corps of Engineers at Fern Ridge Reservoir, and operates the Fern Ridge banding site.

Steve Gordon is a fifth-generation Oregonian with a BS in geography from the University of Oregon. He worked 33 years in planning in Oregon, with over 20 years on natural resources and wetlands planning, the latter resulting in the successful west Eugene wetland plan and a 3,000-acre open space area. He began birding seriously in 1974 and was a charter member of Oregon Field Ornithologists and served for two years as Editor of *Oregon Birds*. He leads many field trips and has authored numerous local articles about birding. Most recently, along with Cary Kerst, he co-authored *Dragonflies and Damselflies of the Willamette Valley, Oregon,* the first Oregon guide to this group of colorful aquatic insects. His love of dragonflies is a direct result of his birding and wetlands experience.

Hydie Lown grew up in Rhode Island in a birding household and remembers being able to distinguish Laughing Gulls from Common Terns by age seven. At age ten, she spent many winter hours standing next to the bird feeder waiting for chickadees and titmice to take sunflower seeds from her outstretched hand. She met her husband Don in 1988 at Braddock Bay Hawk Lookout on the south shore of Lake Ontario near Rochester, NY. Hydie and Don birded their way across the country in 1995 and now live near Creswell. Hydie holds a Bachelor of Science degree from Eastern Oregon University.

Kit Larsen's interest in birds started when, as a child, he would trap wild birds under a mulberry tree, using papaya as bait. He has been an Oregon resident since 1972. He has served the Oregon Field Ornithologists as a board member and treasurer. He is retired, having worked as a systems analyst at the University of Oregon, working with database and GIS systems.

Tom Mickel grew up in Eugene, Oregon and started birdwatching while at Oregon State University in the early 1970s. He became "hooked" after going on a shorebird field trip with Tad Finnell in the late 1970s and has birded ever since. He has worked and birded in the Coast Range since 1976 and has written the *Quail* field notes for Lane County Audubon Society since 1994.

Diane Pettey is an active birder and leader for Elderhostel, Lane Community College, and Lane County Audubon birdwatching tours on the central Oregon coast. She grew up in a small town in the northern Mojave Desert, where family outings, hikes, and Sierra Nevada backpacking trips with her third-grade teacher sharpened her knowledge and love of natural history. Residing in Oregon since 1989, Diane now makes her home in Florence.

Paul Sherrell has had an interest in birds since his college days in the 1960s. A major in biology and an ornithology class contributed to this interest. Active birding, however, did not begin until the mid 1980s. Paul has been especially active birding Lane County.

Bill Stotz started birding at feeders in the 1960s. He and Zanah have four children, two of whom have become ornithologists. Bill served as president of Oregon Field Ornithologists in 1990 and is active in Florence-area birding groups.

Noah K. Strycker is a recent graduate of South Eugene High School and a student at Oregon State University. He authored several species accounts in Birds of Oregon: A General Reference (Oregon State University Press, 2003). Noah edited the annotated reprint of Alfred C. Shelton's 1917 Distributional List of the Birds of West-Central Oregon (Oregon Field Ornithologists, 2002). He was chosen Young Birder of the Year by the American Birding Association in 2005.

CONTACT INFORMATION

Bureau of Land Management Eugene District Office, P.O. Box 10226 (2890 Chad Dr.), Eugene, OR 97440-2226 • (541) 683-6600

Cascades Raptor Center, 32275 Fox Hollow Road - P.O. Box 5386 , Eugene, OR 97405 • 541/485-1320
info@eRaptors.org • www.eraptors.org

Eugene Natural History Society, PO Box 3082, Eugene, OR 97403
biology.uoregon.edu/enhs/

Lane County: http://www.co.lane.or.us/

Lane County Audubon Society, P.O. Box 5086, Eugene, OR 97405
(541) 485-BIRD
audubon@efn.org • www.laneaudubon.org/index.htm

Oregon Climate Service, Strand Agriculture Hall 326, Oregon State University, Corvallis, Oregon, USA, 97331-2209
Main Office: (541) 737-5705
Weather Observations: (541) 737-3714
http://www.ocs.oregonstate.edu/index.html

Oregon Department of Fish and Wildlife, 3406 Cherry Avenue N.E., Salem, OR 97303
Main Phone (503) 947-6000 or (800) 720-ODFW
http://www.dfw.state.or.us/

Fern Ridge Wildlife Area, 26969 Cantrell Road, Eugene, OR 97402
(541) 935-2591
http://www.dfw.state.or.us/wildlifearea/fernridge.htm

ODFW Mapleton Satellite Office, Mapleton Ranger District, P.O. Box 352, Mapleton, OR 97453
(541) 991-7838 Fax: (541) 997-2958

ODFW Springfield Field Office, 3150 E Main Street, Springfield, OR 97478-5800
(541) 726-3515 Fax: (541) 726-2505

Oregon Field Ornithologists, P.O. Box 10373, Eugene, OR 97440
www.oregonbirds.org

Oregon Bird Records Committee, Harry Nehls, Secretary, Oregon Bird Records Committee, 2736 S.E. 20th. Ave., Portland, OR 97202
www.oregonbirds.org/obrc.html

UO Museum of Natural & Cultural History, 1680 E. 15th Ave., Eugene, OR, 97403
mnh@uoregon.edu • natural-history.uoregon.edu/

US Army Corps of Engineers, 26275 Clear Lake Rd, Junction City, OR 97448
541-688-8147

Willamette National Forest, Federal Building, 211 East 7th Avenue, P.O. Box 10607, Eugene, OR 97440
(541) 225-6300 • Fax: (541) 225-6223 • TTY: (541) 465-6323
http://www.fs.fed.us/r6/willamette/

Cottage Grove Ranger District, 78405 Cedar Park Road, Cottage Grove, OR 97424
Deb Schmidt, District Ranger
(541) 767-5001

Middle Fork Ranger District, 46375 Highway 5, Westfir, OR 97492
Chip Weber, District Ranger
(541) 782-2283

McKenzie River Ranger District, 57600 McKenzie Highway, McKenzie Bridge, OR 97413
Mary Allison, District Ranger
(541) 822-3381

CHECKLIST OF THE BIRDS OF LANE COUNTY

About 403 species have been reported and probably have occurred in Lane County. Most of these are known to occur in the county. A few hypothetical or speculative species that appear in the main text do not appear here. Species marked with an asterisk are considered very rare in Oregon and a report with details should be made to the Oregon Bird Records Committee.

Gr. White-fr. Goose												
Emperor Goose												
Snow Goose												
Ross's Goose												
(Black) Brant												
Cackling Goose												
Canada Goose												
Trumpeter Swan												
Tundra Swan												
Wood Duck												
Gadwall												
*Falcated Duck												
Eurasian Wigeon												
American Wigeon												
*American Black Duck												
Mallard												
Blue-winged Teal												
Cinnamon Teal												
Northern Shoveler												
Northern Pintail												
Green-winged Teal												
Common Teal												
Canvasback												
Redhead												
Ring-necked Duck												
*Tufted Duck												
Greater Scaup												
Lesser Scaup												

*King Eider												
Harlequin Duck												
Surf Scoter												
White-winged Scoter												
Black Scoter												
Long-tailed Duck												
Bufflehead												
Common Goldeneye												
Barrow's Goldeneye												
Hooded Merganser												
Common Merganser												
Red-breasted Merganser												
Ruddy Duck												
Ring-necked Pheasant												
Ruffed Grouse												
Blue Grouse												
Wild Turkey												
Mountain Quail												
California Quail												
Red-throated Loon												
*Arctic Loon												
Pacific Loon												
Common Loon												
Yellow-billed Loon												
Pied-billed Grebe												
Horned Grebe												
Red-necked Grebe												
Eared Grebe												
Western Grebe												
Clark's Grebe												
Laysan Albatross												
Black-footed Albatross												
*Short-tailed Albatross												
Northern Fulmar												
*Murphy's Petrel												
*Mottled Petrel												
*Streaked Shearwater												
Pink-footed Shearwater												
Flesh-footed Shearwater												

Buller's Shearwater												
Sooty Shearwater												
Short-tailed Shearwater												
*Black-vented Shearwater												
Fork-tailed Storm-Petrel												
Leach's Storm-Petrel												
American White Pelican												
Brown Pelican												
Brandt's Cormorant												
Double-cr. Cormorant												
Pelagic Cormorant												
*Magnificent Frigatebird												
American Bittern												
Least Bittern												
Great Blue Heron												
Great Egret												
Snowy Egret												
Cattle Egret												
Green Heron												
Black-cr. Night-Heron												
White-faced Ibis												
Turkey Vulture												
Osprey												
White-tailed Kite												
Bald Eagle												
Northern Harrier												
Sharp-shinned Hawk												
Cooper's Hawk												
Northern Goshawk												
Red-shouldered Hawk												
Swainson's Hawk												
Red-tailed Hawk												
Ferruginous Hawk												
Rough-legged Hawk												
Golden Eagle												
American Kestrel												
Merlin												
Gyrfalcon												
Peregrine Falcon												
Prairie Falcon												
Virginia Rail												
Sora												

American Coot											
Sandhill Crane											
Black-bellied Plover											
American Golden-Plover											
Pacific Golden-Plover											
Snowy Plover											
Semipalmated Plover											
Killdeer											
*Eurasian Dotterel											
Black Oystercatcher											
Black-necked Stilt											
American Avocet											
Greater Yellowlegs											
Lesser Yellowlegs											
Solitary Sandpiper											
Willet											
Wandering Tattler											
Spotted Sandpiper											
Whimbrel											
Long-billed Curlew											
*Hudsonian Godwit											
*Bar-tailed Godwit											
Marbled Godwit											
Ruddy Turnstone											
Black Turnstone											
Surfbird											
Red Knot											
Sanderling											
Semipalmated Sandpiper											
Western Sandpiper											
*Red-necked Stint											
Least Sandpiper											
Baird's Sandpiper											
Pectoral Sandpiper											
Sharp-tailed Sandpiper											
Rock Sandpiper											
Dunlin											
*Curlew Sandpiper											
Stilt Sandpiper											
Buff-breasted Sandpiper											
Ruff											

Short-billed Dowitcher													
Long-billed Dowitcher													
Wilson's Snipe													
Wilson's Phalarope													
Red-necked Phalarope													
Red Phalarope													
South Polar Skua													
Pomarine Jaeger													
Parasitic Jaeger													
Long-tailed Jaeger													
*Laughing Gull													
Franklin's Gull													
Bonaparte's Gull													
Heermann's Gull													
Mew Gull													
Ring-billed Gull													
California Gull													
Herring Gull													
Thayer's Gull													
*Lesser Black-backed Gull													
Western Gull													
Glaucous-winged Gull													
Glaucous Gull													
Sabine's Gull													
Black-legged Kittiwake													
Caspian Tern													
Elegant Tern													
Common Tern													
Arctic Tern													
Forster's Tern													
*Least Tern													
Black Tern													
Common Murre													
*Thick-billed Murre													
Pigeon Guillemot													
Long-billed Murrelet													
Marbled Murrelet													
*Xantus's Murrelet													
Ancient Murrelet													
Cassin's Auklet													
Rhinoceros Auklet													
*Horned Puffin													
Tufted Puffin													

Rock Pigeon													
Band-tailed Pigeon													
*Eurasian Collared-Dove													
*White-winged Dove													
Mourning Dove													
Yellow-billed Cuckoo													
Barn Owl													
Flammulated Owl													
Western Screech-Owl													
Great Horned Owl													
Snowy Owl													
Northern Pygmy-Owl													
Burrowing Owl													
Spotted Owl													
Barred Owl													
Great Gray Owl													
Long-eared Owl													
Short-eared Owl													
Boreal Owl													
Northern Saw-whet Owl													
Common Nighthawk													
Common Poorwill													
Black Swift													
Vaux's Swift													
White-throated Swift													
Black-ch. Hummingbird													
Anna's Hummingbird													
Costa's Hummingbird													
Calliope Hummingbird													
Rufous Hummingbird													
Belted Kingfisher													
Lewis's Woodpecker													
Acorn Woodpecker													
Williamson's Sapsucker													
*Yellow-bellied Sapsucker													
Red-naped Sapsucker													
Red-breasted Sapsucker													
Downy Woodpecker													
Hairy Woodpecker													
White-head. Woodpecker													
Am. Three-toed Woodp.													

Black-back. Woodpecker												
Northern Flicker												
Pileated Woodpecker												
Olive-sided Flycatcher												
Western Wood-Pewee												
Willow Flycatcher												
Least Flycatcher												
Hammond's Flycatcher												
Gray Flycatcher												
Dusky Flycatcher												
Pacific-slope Flycatcher												
Black Phoebe												
Say's Phoebe												
Ash-throated Flycatcher												
*Tropical Kingbird												
*Cassin's Kingbird												
Western Kingbird												
Eastern Kingbird												
Loggerhead Shrike												
Northern Shrike												
Cassin's Vireo												
*Blue-headed Vireo												
Hutton's Vireo												
Warbling Vireo												
Red-eyed Vireo												
Gray Jay												
Steller's Jay												
Blue Jay												
Western Scrub-Jay												
Pinyon Jay												
Clark's Nutcracker												
Black-billed Magpie												
American Crow												
Common Raven												
Horned Lark												
Purple Martin												
Tree Swallow												
Violet-green Swallow												
N. Rough-winged Swallow												
Bank Swallow												
Cliff Swallow												
Barn Swallow												

Black-capped Chickadee												
Mountain Chickadee												
Chestnut-back. Chickadee												
Bushtit												
Red-breasted Nuthatch												
White-breasted Nuthatch												
Pygmy Nuthatch												
Brown Creeper												
Rock Wren												
Canyon Wren												
Bewick's Wren												
House Wren												
Winter Wren												
Marsh Wren												
American Dipper												
Golden-crowned Kinglet												
Ruby-crowned Kinglet												
Blue-gray Gnatcatcher												
Western Bluebird												
Mountain Bluebird												
Townsend's Solitaire												
Veery												
Swainson's Thrush												
Hermit Thrush												
American Robin												
Varied Thrush												
Wrentit												
Gray Catbird												
Northern Mockingbird												
Sage Thrasher												
*Brown Thrasher												
European Starling												
*Eastern Yellow Wagtail												
*White (Bl.-back.) Wagtail												
*Red-throated Pipit												
American Pipit												
Bohemian Waxwing												
Cedar Waxwing												
Tennessee Warbler												
Orange-crowned Warbler												
Nashville Warbler												
*Virginia's Warbler												
*Lucy's Warbler												

Northern Parula												
Yellow Warbler												
Chestnut-sided Warbler												
Magnolia Warbler												
Black-throat. Blue Warbler												
Yellow-rumped Warbler												
Black-throat. Gray Warbler												
*Black-throat. Green Warb.												
Townsend's Warbler												
Hermit Warbler												
Palm Warbler												
Blackpoll Warbler												
Black-and-white Warbler												
American Redstart												
Ovenbird												
Northern Waterthrush												
*Mourning Warbler												
MacGillivray's Warbler												
Common Yellowthroat												
*Hooded Warbler												
Wilson's Warbler												
Yellow-breasted Chat												
Western Tanager												
Green-tailed Towhee												
Spotted Towhee												
California Towhee												
American Tree Sparrow												
Chipping Sparrow												
Clay-colored Sparrow												
Brewer's Sparrow												
Vesper Sparrow												
Lark Sparrow												
Black-throated Sparrow												
Sage Sparrow												
*Lark Bunting												
Savannah Sparrow												
Grasshopper Sparrow												
Fox Sparrow												
Song Sparrow												
Lincoln's Sparrow												
Swamp Sparrow												
White-throated Sparrow												

Species											
Harris's Sparrow											
White-crowned Sparrow											
Golden-crowned Sparrow											
Dark-eyed Junco											
Lapland Longspur											
*Smith's Longspur											
*Chestnut-coll. Longspur											
*Rustic Bunting											
Snow Bunting											
Rose-breasted Grosbeak											
Black-headed Grosbeak											
*Blue Grosbeak											
Lazuli Bunting											
Indigo Bunting											
*Dickcissel											
Bobolink											
Red-winged Blackbird											
Tricolored Blackbird											
Western Meadowlark											
Yellow-headed Blackbird											
Brewer's Blackbird											
*Common Grackle											
*Great-tailed Grackle											
Brown-headed Cowbird											
*Hooded Oriole											
Bullock's Oriole											
*Baltimore Oriole											
*Brambling											
Gray-crowned Rosy-Finch											
Pine Grosbeak											
Purple Finch											
Cassin's Finch											
House Finch											
Red Crossbill											
White-winged Crossbill											
Common Redpoll											
Pine Siskin											
Lesser Goldfinch											
*Lawrence's Goldfinch											
American Goldfinch											
Evening Grosbeak											
House Sparrow											

Index

Numbers in bold type refer to the main species account

Parula, Northern, 36, 46, **295**
Pelican, American White, 72, **203**
Pelican, Brown, 42, **203**
Petrel, Mottled, **201**
Petrel, Murphy's, **201**
Phalarope, Red, 48, 110, **236**
Phalarope, Red-necked, 91, 93, **236**, 237
Phalarope, Wilson's, 57, 72, 76, 91, 93, 224, **236**
Pheasant, Ring-necked, **194**
Phoebe, Black, 36, 54, 108, 116, **268**
Phoebe, Say's, 19, 107, 108, 153, **268**, 330
Pigeon, Band-tailed, 33, 35, 53, 60, 62, 63, 65, 66, 77, 101, 113, 119, 126, 128, 155, 156, **250**
Pigeon, Rock, **250**
Pintail, Northern, 52, 184, **187**
Pipit, American, 51, 85, 144, 146, 152, **292**, 312
Pipit, Red-throated, **292**
Plover, Black-bellied, 82, **217**
Plover, Semipalmated, 91, 146, **219**
Plover, Snowy, 36, 55, 57, **219**
Poorwill, Common, 19, 102, **256**
Puffin, Horned, 50, 51, **249**
Puffin, Tufted, 37, **249**
Pygmy-Owl, Northern, 33, 35, 44, 62, 65, 102, 152, 153, 162, **253**

Quail, California, 153, 154, **195**
Quail, Mountain, 53, 62, 63, 65, 66, 69, 102, 113, 119, 128, 162, **195**, 196

Rail, Virginia, 36, 54, 55, 56, 88, 91, 116, 152, 164, **216**
Raven, Common, 114, 128, 145, **275**
Redhead, 52, 72, 118, 139, **188**
Redpoll, Common, **322**
Redstart, American, 163, 174, **299**
Robin, American, **289**
Rosy-Finch, Gray-crowned, 144,

171, **319**
Ruff, 47, 48, 57, 72, 91, **234**

Sanderling, 42, **229**, 232
Sandpiper, Baird's, 56, 146, **230**
Sandpiper, Buff-breasted, 44, 48, **233**
Sandpiper, Curlew, 40, 57, **233**
Sandpiper, Least, 45, 146, 229, **230**
Sandpiper, Pectoral, 47, 48, **231**
Sandpiper, Rock, 42, **232**
Sandpiper, Semipalmated, 40, 92, **229**
Sandpiper, Sharp-tailed, 47, 72, 110, **231**, 325
Sandpiper, Solitary, 21, 54, 91, 93, 146, 170, **223**
Sandpiper, Spotted, 45, 92, 106, 108, 128, 146, 155, 164, 167, **225**
Sandpiper, Stilt, 48, 56, 57, 72, **233**
Sandpiper, Western, 146, **229**, 232
Sapsucker, Red-breasted, 36, 60, 62, 63, 64, 65, 66, 116, 125, 128, 155, 160, 170, **262**
Sapsucker, Red-naped, 96, 165, **262**
Sapsucker, Williamson's, 148, 167, **261**
Sapsucker, Yellow-bell., 46, **262**
Scaup, Greater, 80, 97, 100, 106, **189**
Scaup, Lesser, 97, 100, 106, 123, 170, **189**
Scoter, Black, 38, **191**
Scoter, Surf, 39, 40, 164, **190**, 191
Scoter, White-winged, 79, **191**
Screech-Owl, Western, 33, 35, 113, 175, **251**, 252
Scrub-Jay, Western, 46, 80, 117, 126, 175, **274**
Shearwater, Black-vented, **202**
Shearwater, Buller's, **201**
Shearwater, Flesh-footed, **201**, 325
Shearwater, Pink-footed, **201**
Shearwater, Short-tailed, **202**
Shearwater, Sooty, 51, **201**, 202